NATURE
PERFECTED

WILLIAM HOWARD ADAMS

PRINCIPAL PHOTOGRAPHY BY
EVERETT SCOTT

NATURE
GARDENS THROUGH HISTORY

PERFECTED

ABBEVILLE PRESS · PUBLISHERS · NEW YORK · LONDON · PARIS

EDITOR: WALTON RAWLS
DESIGNER: NAI CHANG
PRODUCTION SUPERVISOR: HOPE KOTURO
COPY CHIEF: ROBIN JAMES
COPY EDITOR: ELAINE LUTHY
PICTURE COORDINATOR: SARAH KEY

Library of Congress Cataloging-in-Publication Data

Adams, William Howard.
    Nature perfected : gardens through
history / William Howard Adams.
        p.   cm.
    Includes bibliographical references and
index.
    ISBN 0-89659-919-1
    1. Gardens—History. 2. Gardening—
History. 3. Gardens—Design—History.
I. Title.
SB451.A33   1991
712'.09—dc20   91-19327
                                              CIP

Front matter picture credits: page 1, trout
lily, *Calochortus splendens* and *Triteleia laxa,*
collected by David Douglas in the Pacific
Northwest for the Royal Horticultural
Society, *Horticultural Transactions,* London,
1834; pages 2–3, Villa Garzoni in Collodi, Italy (photo: Everett Scott); page 5,
Garden of Love, Chateau de Villandry,
Indre-et-Loire, France (photo: Heather
Angel); page 6, House of Loreius Tiburtinus, Pompeii, Italy (photo: Everett
Scott); page 7, Generalife Gardens, Granada, Spain (photo: Ric Ergenbright);
page 8, bee-balm, *Monarda fistulosa,* Curtis, *The Botanical Magazine,* London, 1791;
pages 8–9, Villa Lante, Bagnaia, Italy
(photo: Felice Frankel); page 9, evening
primrose, *Oenothera caespitosa,* Curtis, *The
Botanical Magazine,* London, 1813; pages
10–11, Barrow Court, Bristol, England
(photo: Everett Scott); page 12, wild
pine, *Tillandsia polystachia,* Catesby; *Natural History of Carolina, Florida and the Bahama Islands,* London, 1731–43; pages 12–
13, pond at Nijo Castle, Kyoto, Japan
(photo: Margaret Hensel/Positive Images); page 13, Turk's cap lily, *Lilium mi-
chauxii,* Curtis, *The Botanical Magazine,*
London, 1822; pages 14–15, roof garden,
Ministry of the Army, Brasilia, Brazil,
designed by Roberto Burle Marx (photo:
Michael Moran).

CONTENTS

Introduction ❖ 17

I. LOOKING FOR EDEN

The Garden in the
Ancient World ❖ 21

Gardens Before
Rome ❖ 23

Temples—The Landscape of
the Gods 29

Egypt ❖ 30

Rome ❖ 36

Town Gardens 39

Trees, Flowers, and Shrubs 42

Imperial Grandeur—
Hadrian's Villa 42

II. THE EARTHLY PARADISE

The Middle Ages ❖ 49

The Islamic Garden ❖ 59

Mughal India ❖ 74

Italy ❖ 89

PERFECTION

France ❖ 113

IV.
THE GENIUS OF
THE PLACE

The English Garden
Before the Revolution ❖ 139

Jacobean and Caroline Gardens,
1603–1649   147

The English Formal Garden   157

The Landscaping of England ❖ 158

The English Landscape Garden
Outside of England ❖ 194

V. GARDENS

The Chinese Garden ❖ 205

The Early Garden 209

The Private Garden 212

The Making of a Chinese
Garden 217

Flowers and Trees 226

OF THE EAST

The Japanese Garden ❖ 231

The Paradise Garden 238

The Tea Garden 244

The Stroll Garden 249

The Modern Japanese
Garden 255

VI.
THE NEW WORLD

Colonial American Gardens ❖ 264

The Changing American
      Landscape ❖ 287

   Aesthetic Reform   288

   Public Parks   294

Victorian Garden Dilemmas ❖ 300

Twentieth-Century Solutions ❖ 302

   The Landscape Architect   302

   Historical Restorations and
      Regional Styles   309

   A New American Style   315

   The Modern Movement   319

Postscript ❖ 329

Notes 341 ❖ Selected Bibliography 344 ❖ Index 347

Introduction

Gardens deal with transformation, mutability, and faith. They fix for only a brief moment nature's flux, but their illusion of order gives us hope. Gardens have been made in every conceivable shape and for equally various reasons. As sources of food, medicine, pleasure, and awe, they have been lofty, refined, universal, ordinary, munificent, and austere. Escape, nostalgia, worldly ambition, and worldly exhaustion have all been excuses throughout the long history of garden-making. These human emotions, often masked in myth, religion, and ritual, not to mention our garden variety psychic needs, give gardening a dimension of interest that goes far beyond plant lists, soil conditions, and the vagaries of the weather.

A civilization without its own garden tradition and garden life would be judged impoverished, flawed, incomplete. Yet documenting and measuring those evanescent achievements over the centuries, where most of the physical evidence has disappeared, has not been easy. Unfortunately the glimpses we get in the paintings, artifacts, photographs, and contemporary descriptions that make up much of our historical knowledge of gardens are secondhand, as are their idealized interpretations. In this century, however, the study of the garden has advanced and deepened through research of these materials, so that our understanding has grown as well.

If people at different times and places have had very different ideas about the way to organize their gardens and to conduct their garden life, it is largely because they have made very different assumptions about the relationship between themselves and nature. The garden has been seen as an allegory of man's own cycle of life and death. The Garden of Eternity is life's reward for Christian and Muslim as well as Buddhist. Gardens can also be a manifestation of our attempt to dominate and control nature for purposes that may be metaphysical or quite worldly. While the manicured gardens of China and Japan represent man's eternal search for a state of spiritual equilibrium in the universe, the very geometry of the gardens of Versailles speaks of the political authority of the king, far removed from Zen tranquility.

Moral imperatives and political agendas aside, gardens and garden-making, no matter what the style, tradition, or rationale, come down to the basic elements of earth, water, air, and, on occasion, fire. The twentieth century's accelerated ability to manipulate these ingredients and to alter the natural environment, bringing ecological devastation to whole continents, only obscures the biological role of these ancient elements. The annual cleansing of the ground by fire still practiced in humble agrarian societies—sometimes called "slash and burn" agriculture—gives the mystical role of fire in the growing cycle a special function that probably surprises the modern urban dweller. He may be puzzled by the reminder in the *Bhagavad Gita* that "even amidst fierce flame the lotus can be planted."

Over thousands of years the respective skills of gardening and agriculture have clearly defined themselves, yet it is important to remember that in the beginning gardening was only one aspect of the production of food. Agriculture has always been a utilitarian, economic means of production. Its routines, discipline, and rhythm require a completely different approach to planting, fertilizing, and harvesting compared to the family garden plot set aside for food and medicine. From all

Nymphaea, 1766–1767, by New Jersey-born nurseryman William Young, an early collector of American plants, many of which were sent to Kew, where a botanic garden was begun as early as 1759. British Museum.

OPPOSITE
A fifteenth-century Adam and Eve in the Garden of Paradise. Pages from a book of hours known as the *Warburg Hours.* Library of Congress.

17

A funeral ceremony in a temple garden. Both earthly and heavenly gardens have figured in the ritual of death throughout recorded history. Copy of a restored wall painting from the Tomb of Min-makht, Thebes, c. 1475 B.C. Metropolitan Museum of Art.

the evidence, the earliest garden craft evolved out of the primitive beginnings of man's grubby attempts to farm, even though our yearnings have conjured up a more romantic, mystical state of origin, including Paradise itself.

From the start, gardens have resulted from a hand-to-hand struggle to impose some kind of order on a turbulent, unpredictable, and often perverse nature. "The first artist," as Camille Paglia has written, may well have been "a tribal priest casting a spell, fixing nature's demonic energy in a moment of perpetual stillness."[1] But if the priest was the first artist, the gardener was surely the second as he asserted his humanity over the landscape in order to harness and redirect nature's unstable energy through his efforts.

At one level, gardening is about striving to find some rational if not ideal accommodation with nature in a rather one-sided match of forces, since nature's own laws are ultimately beyond our control. The natural cycle of life and death can endow a garden with a feeling of melancholy even when it is at its brief moment of triumph. Most gardeners prefer not to dwell on this flaw in nature's character but turn to the simple, underlying human faith common to all gardeners, that the dead seed we put in the ground will in fact spring to life the next season in the mystery of reproduction.

Five thousand years ago, the ancestor of modern corn could not be distinguished from other wild grasses growing in the highlands of Mexico. No one could have imagined that the tiny seeds of this puny weed held the possibility of producing food for millions of people. But through close collaboration with nature, adapting to her laws, the Mayans discovered how to increase the size of the grass by selection and breeding until it reached a mighty stalk of modern corn. In the process, they learned that as much as they depended on this mysteriously altered grain, the plant itself was dependent on them. Because of the construction of its ear, protected by tight husks, corn cannot seed itself. It would be extinct if man did not take a hand, unwrap the cob, and plant the seed each spring. Through this ritual of collaboration it is understandable why corn has entered the theology of the Mayan people. It is also an example of early biological manipulation that would later form the foundation of all of our advanced garden horticulture.

In Japan, the cultivation of rice over thousands of years has helped to shape the countryside into a vast complex of gardens. Rice culture has been embued with a spiritual meaning equal to that of corn in the highlands of Mexico and Central America. Just as the Great Inca turned the first furrow for the planting of corn with a golden plow, so the emperor of Japan executes the primal gesture of the ruler as gardener-cultivator by entering the imperial rice paddy each spring to plant rice, a symbol of the nation's historic dependence on the success of the annual crop.

Aside from the metaphysics of princely horticulture, royal gardens and parks have been established as manifestations of earthly political power in every civilization. Social order emerges with the concentration of power and ceremony in the hands of a ruler. Hierarchy imposed on chaotic, formless nature as a new way of organizing the world was a visible element of the mystique of kings. The theme of the garden as a tool of statecraft runs deep, as we will see, throughout the long history of gardening. Ancient literature takes it for granted. Renaissance rulers, from upstarts in Tuscany to the kings of France, adopted gardening as a link to the Golden Age of Alexander the Great.

Contemporary love of gardening in this urban century is a phenomenon that has spread widely, even though the threads that connect it with its historic roots are lost to all but the specialist. Even the simplest form of gardening is a particular kind of human experience that hints at a long and glorious past, both material and spiritual, but a sense of this continuity seems to elude us.

Gardening, as J. B. Jackson has reminded us, continues to "satisfy the aspirations of everyday existence . . . work that has quality and measure, capable at best of humanizing a small fragment of nature."[2] When gardens with their sticks and stones and leaves of nature do rise above honest craft and are recognized as works of art, they become a part of the continuous process that all art shares. The antecedents that shape our appreciation of gardens include not only the historical past but the common biological heritage of our five senses, which have hardly changed since prehistory. A part of the garden's art is in its ability to stimulate our sight, touch, taste, smell, and hearing. But the use of our sensual apparatus has been greatly impaired in this century because of our isolation in an increasingly hostile, unnatural environment. If nature as we have known it is not hopelessly and absurdly irrelevant and if we are able to return our environment to its once stable condition, then the stimulating proximity of nature may also return the art of the garden to a place of honor. The account of the garden's past that follows is intended to help restore some of its universal significance by encouraging us to recognize the extraordinary diversity of gardening throughout history and its ability to humanize a small but essential fragment of our existence.

A Chamula Indian harvesting corn in Chiapas, much as his ancestors did for centuries.

I. Looking for Eden

THE GARDEN IN THE ANCIENT WORLD

Until the eighteenth century, the long-vanished gardens of the ancient world, like Alexander Pope's Groves of Eden, lived on only in descriptions, poems, and songs. Time, catastrophe, and neglect had obliterated without a trace the gardens Pliny had made so familiar in his letters—only his words had survived to fire the imagination of the Renaissance when the serious art of garden-making was gradually revived near the end of the fifteenth century.

No wonder collectors, connoisseurs, and students of the classics were excited by the startling revelations uncovered from beneath the fields south of Naples where workmen first stumbled onto the remains of Herculaneum while digging a well in 1709. For more than sixteen centuries, the flourishing Roman garden towns of Pompeii and Herculaneum had lain buried under ash, pumice, and volcanic mud. Horace Walpole (1717–1797) was surprised and delighted with engravings of Pompeii's gardens that first were published later in the century, remarking on their sympathetic elegance and "playful waters."

Nature's first ominous signal appeared in a cloud above Vesuvius on the morning of August 24 in A.D. 79. By nightfall hundreds of garden courtyards, potting sheds, and vineyards of the two towns were buried. In terms of documenting the gardens of classical antiquity, nothing has surpassed the archaeological remains of these cities and the remarkable details revealed in the hundreds of wall paintings that were preserved by the tragedy.

Before these discoveries and the advanced skill of modern archaeology, classical garden literature and particularly the letters of Pliny the Younger (c.61–112) were virtually the only sources of information on what a Roman garden looked like. Pliny's descriptions of the walks, arbors, colonnades, and magnificent vistas at his villas had left a lot to the imagination of garden designers beginning in the early Renaissance. What is amazing is how closely these later gardens were able to approximate the feeling and spirit of actual gardens that were not fully excavated and studied until the twentieth century.

The gardens of Pompeii date precisely, of course, to the moment of the volcanic eruption, and Pliny's key letters are of approximately the same era. But the distance between these luxurious villa gardens, with their elaborate trellises, urns, and exotic birds we see in the preserved Pompeian wall paintings, and the earlier rustic gardens admired by Horace's (65–8 B.C.) happy man "far from business cares," working "his ancestral acres with his steers," is enormous even though hardly a hundred years separated the poet's life and the destruction of Pompeii. Horace's Sabine farm was simple, elegiac, close to Emerson's "plain living and high thinking." "Tis pleasant, now to lie beneath some ilex tree," Horace writes of his rural garden. "Meanwhile the rills glide

In the house of Loreius Tiburtinus in Pompeii, a fountain against the rear wall of this columned terrace splashed into the deep channel and formed an artificial river. Decorative sculpture that included a river god lined the edge. Photo: Everett Scott.

beneath their high banks; birds warble in the woods; the fountains splash with their flowing waters, a sound to invite soft slumbers."[1]

Horace's nostalgic sentiments about country life and the small, independent farmer had been explored earlier in the *Eclogues* and *Georgics* of Virgil (70–19 B.C.). Virgil's affectionate view of the pastoral life and his mastery of pastoral poetry set the course of a tradition that would introduce pastoral scenes of shepherds and shepherdesses centuries later into Handel's and Mozart's operas, Spenser's poetry, Shakespeare's plays, and Ben Jonson's masques.

As Roman garden tastes changed with increased wealth and leisure in the first century of the Christian era, gardeners and writers looked back with nostalgia to a more frugal time when men like Virgil and Horace consciously shunned extravagance while they cultivated their rustic plots. The sumptuous gardens of Pompeii, not to mention the showy layouts of imperial grandeur on the Janiculum Hill, did not please many contemporary observers. There was an air of decadence that went against nature and Roman virtue. Pliny the Elder (23/4–79), who died of suffocation while attempting to observe the disaster at Pompeii, railed against seductive garden luxury in his *Natural History* where he recalled with approval an earlier time when the "kings of Rome indeed cultivated their gardens with their own hands" and when "at Rome . . . a garden was in itself a poor man's farm."

The earliest Romans, with their stern cult

of unadorned frugality, viewed pleasure gardens very much like the American Puritans looked upon dancing. The only virtue of a garden was its ability to deliver food to the table and herbs for health's sake. Cato (234–149 B.C.), in his agricultural treatise *De re rustica,* dwells on the moral value of growing cabbage and includes only a brief recommendation that flowers be grown for religious rites. Roman high-mindedness later intruded along the garden path where moral maxims were boldly written out in green boxwood edging. And Roman generals encouraged gardening among the peoples they subdued: "It was always a maxim of policy amongst them to amuse the people they conquered by this means," for gardens were "apt to fill the mind with calmness and tranquility."[2] Gradually, however, those delicate, sensual qualities of gardens—the colors and scents of flowers, the sounds of fountains and birds—became irresistible and were allowed to creep into Roman gardens for their own sake, no doubt through extended contact with the East where Romans had ventured in pursuit of their empire.

GARDENS BEFORE ROME

Centuries before the Romans carried their military ambitions into Asia, the Greeks, who for all of their civilized achievements had not included gardening among the arts, were amazed when they first discovered the great parks of Eastern potentates. It was the exotic magnificence of these royal preserves with their menageries and cultivated plants that caught the Greek imagination. These legendary parks were in no way comparable to a park in the modern sense. The evidence is sketchy in the extreme, but the few fugitive references that have survived suggest a large wooded area or natural forest maintained as a hunting preserve. Tall shade trees were prized, and beneath them were protected shrubbery and perfumed plants. The following lines from an ancient Babylonian epic provide a few details.

The ways are straight and the path is
   wrought fair.
They see the cedar mount, the dwellings
   of gods, the sanctuary of the Irmin.
Her good shadow is full of rejoicing,
It covers the thorn-bush, covers the dark-
   lured sloe
and beneath the cedar the sweet-smelling
   plants.[3]

It is fair to say that this earliest recorded park of history had advanced some by the time of Alexander the Great (356–323 B.C.). Instead of simply a designated natural woodland with little order or calculated intervention, the Greeks found regularly planted trees to admire in the Persian parks. The scale of these open areas was also impressive by Greek standards. Cyrus the Great's (559–529 B.C.) park at Celaenae was reported to be large enough to hold a review of 130,000 troops.

Individual travelers had long fed Western fantasies of oriental garden marvels. Lysander (d. 395 B.C.), the Greek envoy, has left a tantalizing but brief description of the "Paradise Garden" of Cyrus the Younger of Persia (d. 401 B.C.). He was impressed by "the beauty of the trees in it, the accuracy of their spacing, the straitness of the rows, the regularity of the angles, and the multitude of sweet scents." Lysander was also surprised and fascinated to learn that Cyrus had personally planned the vast layout and had actually worked in it. As a Spartan aristocrat, Lysander naturally believed that only war and athletics were appropriate forms of labor for a gentleman. Gardening was infra dig in ancient Greece.

Cyrus was of course carrying on the ancient tradition of Eastern kings reaching back to the earliest rulers of Assyria and Babylonia. As the inheritor of those almost forgotten civilizations, Cyrus's garden-making perpetuated that redeeming Eastern veneration for nature and particularly for trees. Indeed, as the symbol of eternal life, the tree was often represented with a stream flowing out from beneath its roots. For Cyrus the king working in his garden, tree planting was a sacred occu-

Elegant stone benches were placed in land-scaped public spaces as a memorial to citizens of Pompeii. Photo: Everett Scott.

the Persian king is zealously cared for, so that he may find gardens whenever he goes; their name is Paradise, and they are full of all things fair and good that the earth can bring forth. It is here that he spends the greatest part of his time, except when the season forbids."[5] The passage tells us nothing about the king's garden, but it is the first time the appellation "paradise" in a Greek narrative is linked to actual Persian gardens.

In his account of Alexander's conquest of the Persian Empire, Quintus Curtius (1st century A.D.) tells of the "extensive, charming and secluded parks artificially planted" that had so impressed the Greek invaders.[6] The description is all the more tantalizing and frustrating for its lack of physical details. Without a plan or contemporary view of a Persian park we are left with only our imagination. The nearest surviving example of such a park that manages to suggest something of the size and importance of "the secluded parks artificially planted" may be the remarkable twelfth-century royal garden groves of Agedal outside of Marrakesh, Morocco, which are still today maintained in the age-old Eastern tradition by the king of Morocco.

The Eastern myth of luxuriant, extravagant gardens built for the indulgent pleasure of the prince haunted both the Greeks and Romans. When the rituals of ruling—the dispensing of royal favors, the receiving of guests, and the commanding of generals—literally took place in the garden paradise, the sacred resonance and mystique of kingship was intensified and the illusion of social order was confirmed. The extravagance of the royal garden was sanctified by the official grandeur of the setting. The idea that maintaining a garden not only increased the private contentment of the ruler but also improved his ability to govern justly was to pass into princely traditions of the West during the early Renaissance. Following the Italian Renaissance examples of both secular and papal princes, even the most insignificant provincial grandee in remote corners of Europe from Portugal to Sweden and Russia required an appropriate garden

pation as well as a symbolic royal gesture. Reordering nature provided a visible hierarchy in the landscape. The art of gardening was also a routine part of the ruler's education, giving him a link with the body politic. According to the Greek geographer Strabo (64 B.C.–after A.D. 24), all Persian boys received instruction in this humble, classic horticultural art in the evenings after regular classes as a part of their universal education.

In the arid Middle East, trees were scarce and often became prizes of war to be taken and transplanted by the victor. As one Sumerian king boasted, "I carried off from the countries I conquered, trees that none of the kings, my forefathers, have possessed, these trees have I taken and planted them in mine own county, in the parks of Assyria have I planted them."[4]

Xenophon (c. 428–c. 354 B.C.), the Greek historian-soldier, had never seen anything like the luxury of the royal gardens he found during his travels in Asia in 400 B.C. "Everywhere

setting for his palace, country villa, and hunting lodge. The Florentine moralist Matteo Palmieri in 1438 actually discovered and revived the ancient story of Cyrus the gardener-king working in his Persian garden to serve as a lesson for contemporary princes.[7] These Renaissance humanist rulers in a way considered themselves successors to the great princes of antiquity and shared with them their sense of noble duty and mandate to build gardens and parks on the grand scale as an ingredient of effective, visible power.

The literature of gardening and the idealized poetic descriptions of gardens, as much as actual gardens, have fed the imagination of gardeners and garden-makers from the beginning of time. But more often than not, as Christopher Thacker has remarked, these literary gardens teeter "on the edge of fable."[8] Yet the survival of such legendary places throughout ancient literature and in the later scholarship of the Renaissance demonstrates how alluring these vague but stimulating visions of the ideal garden have been to successive generations and civilizations.

Homer's description of the garden of Alcinous in the *Odyssey* is the most celebrated in all classical literature. No matter that it is almost totally devoid of any specific pictorial detail, the passage from the *Odyssey* remains the quintessential image of the garden in antiquity and the earliest, dating in the period of 750–650 B.C.

To left and right, outside, he saw an orchard closed by a pale—four spacious acres planted with trees in bloom or weighted down for picking; pear trees, pomegranates, brilliant apples, luscious figs, and olives ripe and dark. Fruit never failed upon these trees: winter and summertime they bore, for through the year the breathing Westwind ripened all in turn—so one pear came to prime, and then another, and so with apples, figs, and the vine's fruit empurpled in the royal vineyard there. Currants were dried at one end, on a platform bare to the sun, beyond the vintage arbors and vats of vintners trod; while near at hand were new grapes barely formed as the green bloom fell, or half-ripe clusters, faintly coloring. After the vines came rows of vegetables of all kinds that flourish in every season, and though the garden plots and orchard ran channels from one clear fountain, while another gushed through a pipe under the courtyard entrance to serve the house and all who came for water. These were the gifts of heaven to Alcinous.[9]

We share Horace Walpole's disappointment with Homer's words. When they are "divested of harmonious Greek and bewitching poetry," Walpole complained, "we are left with nothing more than a pompous . . . little garden of orchard, vineyard and herbs and . . . enriched . . . with the fairy gift of eternal summer."[10]

The garden of Alcinous was located just outside his palace and was enclosed with walls. Although it was not large, it was distinguished from ordinary gardens by its enchanted, unending springtime, fruit trees that were literally "ever bearing," and a perpetual supply of water. Above all, the garden's everlasting beauty was the sacred gift of the gods to Alcinous, king of the Phoenicians. It was this celestial provenance that made it special. Order over nature was a divine inspiration.

In such a fabled setting, under divine management, the laws of nature had been suspended and the cycle of blooms and fruit proceeded in monotonous, constant production. No flowers, and certainly nothing anticipating the pleasure later Roman artists took in reproducing the beauty of the flowers on the walls of Pompeian houses, intruded on the simple, rustic charms of Alcinous's garden. The poet spares us any reference to the inevitable disappointments and grubby work that goes into gardening. The magic, fairy-tale quality is sustained throughout Homer's account without a weed or wilted seedling in sight.

Since all gardening has its origin in the humble beginnings of agriculture and farm-

In this Mughal miniature, Emperor Bābur is seated in one of the many royal gardens he created in sixteenth-century India. All of the senses are meant to be stimulated, according to the precepts of the Koran, but these garden traditions, adopted by the Mughal emperors, reach back to Persia of 500 B.C.

fountains, and water channels to supply the water for irrigation.

Unlike the other early civilizations of Assyria, Persia, and Egypt, Greece was strangely slow in developing gardens primarily for private pleasure marked by even the rudiments of floriculture. In the archaic Homeric period and later, the images of flowers do not seem to be used to decorate houses or clothes and only occasionally are they represented on household utensils. Given the significance of garden art as a measure of a civilization and an element that no society with claims to the highest advancement would be without, this gap is difficult to explain. Marie-Luise Gothein, that close listener attuned to the most elusive historical clue, was forced to confess that even "in the best period, when the other arts in Greece were rapidly advancing to their highest point of development, we hear nothing of garden culture." [11]

It is possible to conclude that the spirit of a developing democratic society, reflected in the new constitutions, discouraged individual citizens of the Greek state from indulging themselves in activities that smacked of superior, independent, privileged values. Private gardens requiring private property had always connoted personal power, prestige, and extravagance—elitist pretensions that would not have gone down well in a fledgling democratic community. Furthermore the Greeks through their democratic institutions and ideology produced no great and established aristocratic families with the stability of time and money—essential ingredients of most garden traditions—to create hunting park "paradises" and luxurious gardens comparable to those they had long heard of in Persia. These foreign examples of autocracy, perhaps even decadence, were alien to the very nature of Greek democratic, commercial philosophy of social arrangements.

There were also, of course, the incessant demands of military defense on behalf of the state, leaving little time for the private pleasures of its leading citizens, especially in a climate where things grew well enough in

ing, aside from the idealized image, these ancient lines celebrating the garden's production for the table evoke its fundamental source. Only gradually does the garden of utility take on the qualities of both ornament and pleasure. Details of simple order are the first sign of aesthetic concern in Homer's garden and the beginning of our long aesthetic adventures in garden art. We see this primitive search for order in the strict regularity of the layout Homer described, the carefully spaced fruit trees lined up in platoons, the rustic trellises to carry the vines, and particularly in the pools,

season but required more labor and water than could be spared in the hot, dry summer months. Except for a few fertile river valleys, Greece has always been discouragingly short of water. Furthermore, the devastation caused by open sheep husbandry had, even by Homer's time, turned the Greek landscape into a semiarid desert without a natural ground cover and woodland to encourage a flourishing plant environment or economy. No wonder Homer's poetry evoked a protected, walled garden fed by an endless supply of water to nourish the immortal plants and fruit trees. Only Alcinous's vintners would have cause to complain of the drudgery of keeping up with the perpetual grape crop.

If fifth-century Greek democracy did not encourage private gardening, the democratic city-state of Athens can claim the first recorded steps toward civic improvement by creating communal public gardens. In his life of Cimon of Athens (c.510–c.451 B.C.), Plutarch, a contemporary of Pliny, writes that Cimon was "the first to beautify the city with the so-called 'liberal' and elegant resorts by planting the Agora with plane trees and by converting the Academy from a waterless and arid spot into a well-watered grove."[12] Pliny, as a Roman visitor, much later remarked on the poplars, elms, and planes that were still growing to great heights in the Academy's park.

A formal public garden around the temple of Hephaistos in the Agora in Athens, dating from the fifth century B.C., has been uncovered by modern archaeology. Ancient root cavities indicate that shrubs and small trees were aligned with the temple's Doric columns and divided by geometric paths. The temple was built on a rock outcropping, so it was necessary to cut out the bedrock and fill the pits with suitable soil for the planting, a daunting way to make a garden for any purpose, even a sacred one.

Greek gymnasiums were also public gathering places in most Greek cities. Like the Academy, these grounds were also planted out with shade trees. Athens had four large gymnasiums, all set in parks. In other Greek cities, the gymnasium was usually connected to the sacred memorials of heroes. At Syracuse, for example, the magnificent gymnasium with halls, exercise grounds, and gardens was placed at the tomb of Timoleon the Liberator (d. c.337 B.C.), where annual athletic games were staged in the open park-like space.

At the early stage, the Greek city park or garden primarily served some useful communal function—for exercise, for study, and for sacramental purposes connected to temples and shrines. Later, however, in the Platonic dialogues, public gardens inspired by democratic rule are described for the first time as civilized places selected for the sole purpose of walking in the shade for conversation and for resting. The public pleasure garden in the modern sense had emerged at last.

Aside from the legacy of the public garden, Greece's other enduring contribution to garden tradition is the gardens of the Academy and the Lyceum. The "groves of academe," the private garden where Plato (c.428–348/347 B.C.) conducted his famous school, is the primordial academy of antiquity. As a character in one of Aristophanes' plays recalled, the ideal setting for the life of the mind was henceforth to be the garden:

> All fragrant with woodbine and peaceful
>   content and the leaf which the lime-
>   blossoms fling.
> When the plane whispers love to the elm
>   in the grove in the beautiful season of
>   Spring.[13]

This tradition of the academic garden has had a long, continuous history. In modern times it found a strong supporter in Lord Kames (1696–1782), the Scotsman who believed it is "far from an exaggeration that good professors are not more essential to a good college than a spacious garden sweetly ornamented."[14] Thomas Jefferson, who studied Kames's *Elements of Criticism* when he began to plan his University of Virginia, made

The Greek response to the spirit of a natural landscape is repeatedly expressed in the siting of temples and public buildings rather than in conventional gardens. The fifth-century Greek ruins of Segesta, in Sicily, recall Pope's thoughts on the "Genius of the Place" in eighteenth-century England. Photo: Ric Ergenbright.

gardens an essential ingredient of his design, to serve both faculty and students.

When it comes to the strictly domestic Greek gardens of the later Hellenistic period—what they looked like, what kinds of vegetables, flowers, and plants were grown, how they were cultivated—the almost total absence of hard evidence leaves us in the dark. We do know that from the sixth century B.C. onward, Greek religious ceremonies were decked out with flowers, so it is fair to assume that flowers were admired and grown in some private gardens. Both priests and worshipers were crowned with wreaths. Roses, violets, poppies, lilies, crocuses, and hyacinths were known and cultivated both for ceremony and private pleasure. In one of the earliest pieces of Greek literature, a Homeric hymn of the

seventh century B.C., Zeus helps his brother Pluto, lord of the Underworld, to capture Demeter's daughter Persephone by tempting her with a seductive field of blooming narcissus. Persephone's momentary distraction by the flowers allows the terrible god to sweep her up and carry her off in his chariot to his lair. Even though several centuries later Hippocrates (c. 460–c. 377 B.C.) did not seem to be aware of the narcotic and soporific properties of the poppy, in the Homeric hymn Persephone's distraught mother, Demeter, uses it to cushion the shock of her daughter's abduction. The same narcissus was later mentioned in Sophocles' *Oedipus at Colonus* as the flower in the crowns of the Great Goddesses. The gentle centaur Chiron, renowned for his knowledge of the healing powers of herbs, tested the medical property of the cornflower after being hit by an arrow poisoned by the blood of Hydra. The iris is of great antiquity in cultivation and in art, the Minoans in Crete having used it in ceremonies and decoration over four thousand years ago. The iris entered Greek mythology as the messenger of the gods whose duties included leading the souls of dead women to the Elysian Fields. A clump of iris was often used to mark the graves of Greek women.

Modern archaeological evidence of ordinary Greek gardening practices and the private garden leaves a rather austere picture. In the Greek town houses of Olynthus, destroyed in 348 B.C., every courtyard that has been uncovered is solidly paved with stone so that any plant culture that might have existed would have been exclusively in pots.

The traditional Greek pot garden, called the Garden of Adonis, was a ritual spring planting to commemorate the violent death of Aphrodite's beautiful, young Adonis. When he was killed in a boar hunt, Aphrodite made the anemone grow out of his blood. The cult may well have had its dim origin in the East before it was taken up by the women of Athens, who placed an image of the god on their roof terraces to celebrate the arrival of spring. Earth pots were sown with fennel, lettuce, wheat, or barley to grow up quickly, bright and green, then to wither and die in the hot sun. The ritual symbolized the mourning for the young god and nature's own cycle from spring to winter, followed by its seeming death, and then its all too brief reappearance the next season. A number of vase paintings record the ceremony.

There has been the assumption that the Roman use of sculpture and ornament in gardens was somehow following Greek fashion. While a few inscriptions and other literary sources make reference to sculpture and fountains in domestic Greek gardens, archaeologists have turned up no physical evidence of significance.

The open courtyards of houses in Olynthus, and in the even more hospitable garden climate of the Greek town of Himera in Sicily, are uniformly small and democratically apportioned, leaving little space for a decorated garden, unlike the latter and more generous garden courtyards of Pompeii and other Roman cities.

Temples—The Landscape of the Gods

The integration of sacred architecture into the larger natural landscape transcends the man-made garden and passes into metaphysics. At the heart of Greek philosophy regarding the natural environment was the conviction that all architectural intervention—whether temple, stoa, theater, agora, or house—must be in harmony with nature. The natural landscape was sacred. It was literally "the landscape of the gods" and not just that defined portion surrounding the temple or tomb itself. "All Greek sacred architecture explores and praises the character of a god or group of gods in a specific place," Vincent Scully has written. "That place is itself holy and, before the temple was built upon it, embodied the whole of the deity as a recognized natural force." [15]

Within each part of the landscape of Greece—the mountains, hills, valleys, islands, seascape—there existed a *genius loci,* and it was the builder's duty to search out and identify this sacred spirit peculiar to each location. Only after the spirit was divined could the architecture itself be introduced into a holy partnership with the existing features of the topography. As man-made environments, gardens as well as architecture must ultimately have to find a way to fit into the natural world, the ordinary landscape.

The siting of a Greek temple was not the rational, explicit geometric exercise that we associate with Roman, Renaissance, and neoclassical axial planning but rather a much more intuitive, subtle, emotional process with implications we are only now beginning to comprehend. "No Greek building attempted to dominate the landscape," Sir

Farming and gardening were integral to the affairs of a country estate in ancient Egypt. Life was organized around the production of food and wine, as in this copy of a wall painting from the Tomb of Nakht, Thebes, c. 1425 B.C. Metropolitan Museum of Art, Rogers Fund, 1915.

Geoffrey Jellicoe has observed. The Greek genius was to collaborate with it, "as though the elements, wild though they might be yet had some unrecorded harmony," in order to discover an inner balance between man and nature.[16] Whether at Knossos, Mycenae, Delphi, Epidauros, or Athens, the peculiar characteristics of the land, the mixture of open and closed spaces, the contrast of light and darkness—all contributed to the exhilaration of discovery as hidden views were revealed along a calculated but disguised progress leading through the landscape to approach the temple.

EGYPT

When Hadrian went to Egypt as Roman emperor in A.D. 130, the glories of that earlier civilization, its temples, palaces, and, above all, its tombs were just so many abandoned relics strewn along the banks of the Nile. Among spectacular fragments of architecture, colossal sculpture, and ornaments representing a totally new sense of scale and imperial monumentality, Hadrian responded with a natural appetite for Oriental grandeur and theater. His imagination was stirred by these monumental ruins. A number of the tomb frescoes recorded the soul-satisfying pleasures of the deceased pharoah in his earthly garden-paradise, a detailed picture of what he expected in the next world.

The scope of the pharaoh's expectations was not particularly extensive. The ingredients seem commonplace. Shade trees, scented shrubs, and some cool water were the basic requisites of gardens in the heat of Egypt. It was the shade of trees that the god was looking for when he retreated to his garden "in the cool of the day." An inscription on one of the tombs in Thebes sums up in a few words what a garden in the broiling heat of the Nile valley was all about:

> May I wander round my pool each day forever more. May my soul sit on the branches of
> the grave garden I have prepared for myself.
> May I refresh myself each day under my sycamore.[17]

The simple components of an Egyptian garden—water and shade—recited in the petition can be seen in the 3,000-year-old model of a garden placed in the tomb of an Egyptian bureaucrat in 1000 B.C. It may well be the oldest three-dimensional representation of a garden in the world.

Even though it appears to be little more than a child's toy, this model actually represents a fairly advanced development of gardening in Egypt. The walled rectangular space with the pool symmetrically placed in the center is an outdoor extension of the house whose facade closes one end of the garden. Waterspouts extend from the roof and shoot a stream over into the pool where ornamental fish were no doubt kept. The trees are regularly planted in uniform rows, following a garden geometry of the most ancient lineage.

The flooding Nile itself wrested the narrow strip of delta along its banks from the desert when its waters washed over the valley with rich deposits of earth ready for farm crops and

This little model from the Tomb of Meket-Re in Thebes, dating from 1700 B.C., may well be the oldest three-dimensional representation of a garden to survive. Metropolitan Museum of Art, Rogers Fund, supplemented by contribution of Edward S. Harkness.

cane, large trees, and vegetation used in a garden. Plantations of trees could be grown only on highest ground where the flood water did not reach but where water for irrigation could be easily brought.

Over the centuries, through skill and experiment, water from the Nile's flow was carried to more distant parts of the valley floor through an elaborate network of canals, dams, terraces, and sluices. The water was then lifted to higher ground by a well-sweep, a primitive armature mounted on a post with a weight on one end to add leverage to the heavy bucket of water on the opposite end.

It seems likely that the inevitable straight channels for moving water efficiently, not only to gardens but also within the garden from pools and cisterns, gradually imposed the geometric order of design we read about in ancient garden literature. Homer's farm garden of Alcinous, for example, suggests considerable order in its regular division of

A wall painting in the tomb of a royal artisan in Egypt illustrates that culture's arcadian expectations of the afterlife. Date palms have been ornamentally planted with other tree species in the lower panels. Photo: Fred Maroon.

the garden spaces, the rows of vineyards and vegetables united by the water channel that fed the garden plots and orchards. In another Homeric allusion to geometric design, when Odysseus finally returns to his father's palace at Ithaca he identifies himself to Laertes by describing the rows of trees that grew in the garden of his childhood—"I can tell you all the trees you gave me one day on this terrace"— and reminds his father of "the fifty rows of vines that were to be mine."[18]

In Egypt, it is clear, the design of the early gardens grew out of a hydraulic society, which imposed an autocratic, systematic control over the distribution of water, establishing the formal patterns of garden organization, irrigation, and planting. Strict organization seems to have pervaded all levels of Egyptian society. The regimentation of gardening extended down to the evenly spaced and regular rows of plants and trees and is an inevitable pattern wherever the movement of water is paramount.

An Egyptian garden plan has survived in the tomb at Thebes of a high official who served under the New Kingdom pharoah Amenhotep III (1417–1379 B.C.). This gardening bureaucrat—perhaps he was in charge of an all-important irrigation system in his district—surrounded himself in his tomb with souvenirs of happy moments on earth. The wall drawing of his garden was an important decoration, a memory worth taking to the next life. The plan is a stylish and stylized creation but is well understood once we have deciphered the unfamiliar graphic conventions behind the diagram. Partly a ground plan, partly an elevation, but mostly a bird's-eye view, it requires our modern eye to constantly adjust and change as we try to read it.

A thick, protective wall circumscribes the garden and the house. The regular pattern of scallops on top of the wall indicates decorative round tiles. The wall is shaded by trees planted at strict, regular intervals. The entrance gate in the high wall opposite the house is reached from the canal that further contributes to an air of privacy and seclusion. The center of the garden is dominated by eight rows of vines on wooden arbors at either side of the walk running on axis to the house opposite and indicated by an overscale facade with doors and rooms. The upper gardens on raised terraces are symmetrically laid out in avenues of sycamore and palm trees.

The trees are particularly noteworthy. Large trees like these were difficult to grow in the Nile Valley because of the flooding, so inevitably they seem to take on a divine quality in Egyptian literature and ritual. Among the earliest trees recorded in Egyptian documents are the sycamore, or *Ficus sycomoros,* and the "false plane," or *Acer pseudoplatanus.* There seems to be no evidence that the Egyptian garden attempted to recreate or mirror the common landscape. Given its dry, flat, flood-prone condition, it could provide little inspiration.

During the imperialist expansion of the rulers of the New Kingdom, 1559 to 1085 B.C., Egyptian military expeditions into Palestine and Syria brought back all kinds of exotic new trees and plants. In carvings at the temple of Dayr al-Baḥrī of the famous expedition to the Land of Punt commissioned by the daring queen Hatshepsut (r. 1503–1482 B.C.), thirty-one frankincense trees are recorded. According to the queen's boast, they were "for the majesty of this god Amun, Lord of Thebes. Never was seen the like since the beginning. Trees were set up in God's land and set in the ground of Egypt."[19]

Long periods of security combined with rich deposits of soil, a good water supply, cheap labor, and constant sunshine allowed Egyptian gardens like the one depicted at Thebes to flourish. In the wall drawing, we see garden pavilions symmetrically placed near the house where they overlook flower beds and two rectangular pools lined with green grass. Lotuses and ducks decorate the basins. Two other pools placed in opposite directions are on either side of the entrance gate and gatehouse. In the scale, composition, and elegance of this garden, particularly in the thoughtful alternation of different kinds and

The funerary temple of Dayr al-Baḥrī in Egypt was built by Hatshepsut and landscaped with ornamental trees and plants along its terrace. The complex may have been designed by the queen's consort Senmut, c. 1450 B.C. Photo: Fred Maroon.

sizes of trees, it is clear that we are examining a very advanced and sophisticated stage of garden composition where even the architecture has been co-opted by the ordering and unification of nature. The straight line of the Nile cutting through the desert may have first suggested linear order over nature.

For all of its formality and decorative detail, the garden at Thebes, like the Greek garden of Alcinous, was basically a farm garden where fruits, vegetables, and herbs grew side by side with date palms, olives, and vineyards. The dichotomy between pleasure and utility so familiar and so rigid in the later gardens of the West (though this division did not in fact become firmly fixed in modern times, as we will see, until the seventeenth century) had no place in the earliest gardens. But it is obvious that flowers were cultivated and greatly admired in Egypt. That flowers appear in wall paintings, on sculpture, and, most importantly, as decoration for their austere architecture confirms the Egyptian passion. Rulers are shown holding flowers like scepters, priests use flowers in their rituals, and slaves cultivate them along elegant pools and beside terraced canals as shown in wall paintings from palaces and villas at Thebes and Tell el-Amarna.

Temples, religious shrines, and tombs were often landscaped, and avenues of trees lined approaches and entrances, serving as a transition into the architecture where stylized ornamentation repeated plant motifs. The temple of Dayr al-Baḥrī, built by that extraordinary woman Hatshepsut as a memorial to her great accomplishments, achieves a theatrical grandeur unrivaled until the Italian Renaissance two thousand years later. For the pharaoh-gods, rulers of Egypt, the road to the immortal realm of death required a vast otherworldly landscape created to rise in splendor above mere mortal environs. But even though we are filled with awe and speculation when we contemplate this monumental setting of Hatshepsut's tomb, the exclusive Egyptian philosophy of life and death that it symbolizes held little appeal beyond the Nile Valley. As far as colossal Egyptian temple landscapes were concerned, their only influence seems to have been in the twentieth century when Hollywood set-designers were suddenly inspired to recreate them in the film studios. Unlike the labyrinthine approach to Greek temples, expressing a close, mystical understanding of nature through a gradual discovery of the site, Hatshepsut's temple reigns with cold imperial majesty above nature, defying its mortal laws.

Here, for the first time in history, a series of terrace platforms is used to support the shrine on the top level. The ceremonial avenue moves through the center of the three terraces ascending by ramps at the upper level. The terraces themselves are built of stone retaining walls and filled with rich earth from the valley floor to nourish the ornamental trees that were watered by a series of buried pipes. It is in a corridor at the back of the highest terrace garden that Hatshepsut has recorded the expedition to the Land of Punt to bring back the incense trees. The drawings actually show how the trees were carried in containers slung on straps held by four men. A final picture in the series shows the trees fully grown, since they now tower over the cattle below after starting out as saplings no taller than the slaves that carrier them.

Other Egyptian rulers followed the queen's example of royal gardening. Rameses III (1198–1167 B.C.) records his gardening work at his temple at Madīnat-Habu. "I dug a pond before it [the temple] where the ocean of Heaven flows over it, and planted it with trees and green growths as they are in lower Egypt. Gardens of vines, of trees, fruits and flowers are around thy temple, before thy face."[20] Making a gift of a sacred garden to a temple or shrine was an important bequest for kings to make. Rameses had a list of his royal benefactions to the city of Heliopolis drawn up. "I give to thee great gardens," it recites, "with trees and vines in the temple of Atuma, I give to thee lands with olive-trees in the city of On. I have furnished them with gardeners, and many men to make ready oil of Egypt, for kindling the lamps of thy noble temple. I give to thee trees and wood, date-palm incense, and lotus, rushes, grasses, and flowers of every land, to set before thy fair face."[21] The international traffic in exotic trees and flowers from "every land" had a very early and auspicious beginning with royal patronage.

ROME

When Horace wrote his lyric poem celebrating a cool, crystal spring beneath a spreading oak tree, secluded gardens "as a place of inspiration and repose" were still a rather new experience in Roman life. Of course the traditional enclosed garden plot, or *hortus,* made for practical reasons to grow vegetables, herbs, and fruit, had been a part of Italian existence from the early settlements of the Mediterranean back to the beginning of time. Springs and groves were universally dedicated to the gods, and if their sacred powers embraced a particular horticultural function, such as fertility or the cycle of seasons, their temples often included sacred gardens as well. But those ancient Roman virtues of austerity and frugality continued to restrain any natural inclination toward the cultivated elegance of elaborate pleasure gardens until the end of the second century B.C. when Eastern Hellenistic influences and an alarming taste for luxury were reaching all corners of the cultural life of Rome.

The earliest (600–200 B.C.) Roman houses were designed to serve the traditional, complex ritual of the Roman family, which centered on the role and absolute authority of the father. The blank exterior walls of the house enclosed a series of spaces, fixed and arranged

rience and sensibility, of meaning and form.[23]

The villa garden, which had been widely developed in the Hellenic world and particularly in places outside of the Greek mainland itself, was an important legacy that the Romans eagerly appropriated. *Res rustica*—country life—was gradually elevated in elegance and became the ideal existence for the Roman gentleman. Poets celebrated it, painters recorded it, and statesmen considered owning a rural villa their ultimate goal in life. Successive societies, from the Renaissance onward into our own century, have vigorously pursued this same ideal, in forms not so different from the original Roman model.

Originally the country seat or Roman farm was called *hortus* rather than villa. This was a working farm producing important revenues for the urban Roman family who owned it. Cato's *De re rustica* (c.160 B.C.) was in fact a practical agricultural treatise widely read and followed by his fellow gentlemen farmers. Buildings, except to house the workmen and animals, were conventional and unimportant. Cato's dictum, "First plant, then build," summed up the difference between the early rustic Roman farm and the later elaborate, sybaritic country establishments of Pliny and other wealthy Romans two hundred years later, who considered the villa central to elegant rural living.

Even before Cato's treatise the armory of Roman gardening tools and implements had grown. Spades, shovels, hoes, and forks in a variety of shapes designed for different garden tasks were common. Most were iron or ironclad, and their basic forms remain with us today.

When the rich Hellenistic Romans discovered the more refined possibilities of country living and were converted to the belief that it was the only place to cultivate the life of the mind and the life of the senses to the fullest, the Roman villa and its elaborate gardens came into their own. The discovery of a new kind of expansive, personally directed life demanded this new kind of cultivated setting.

The nine books of Pliny the Younger pro-

This large garden of the Villa Poppeae at Oplontis in Italy is enclosed on three sides by a portico supported by columns. The open side looks out to the Bay of Naples. "The whole of the gulf is garnished in part . . . by villas and planted areas," Strabo wrote. "They intervene in unbroken succession [and] present the appearance of a single city." Photo: Everett Scott.

in a formula expressing the traditional family relations they represented.[22] The rectangular family garden was inside the walls of the house and typically to one side rather than in the center, as seen in the later peristyle gardens of Pompeii. These traditional arrangements of ordinary living, and particularly the structure and activities of family life, remained constant for centuries. Later when Roman houses became larger and more elaborate, the atrium, open to the skies, became grander, giving access to the various rooms that opened off of it. With the addition of the peristyle, surrounded by columns, the atrium became the central interior garden space. With the opening up of the world through conquest and wealth, Roman life, its domestic structure, its houses and villas, and its gardens changed. And Greece became the inspiring teacher, initiating the Romans into new, stirring mysteries of expe-

vide us with the fullest picture of high Roman villa life to survive. His letters, and particularly his description of his own villas and gardens, have instructed country gentlemen and would-be country gentlemen from Lorenzo de'Medici to George Washington and Thomas Jefferson, and for as long as the classics were a basic part of a gentleman's education.

When a scholar friend was looking for a quiet place in the country, Pliny explained the essential requirements: "easy access to Rome, good communications, a modest house," and "no more land than will suffice to clear his head and refresh his eyes."[24] In keeping with his academic modesty, Pliny advised, the scholar would need only a single path to stroll around as he became acquainted with his precious vines and fruit trees.

At his own seaside Laurentian Villa near Ostia, Pliny seems to have had the best of all worlds, combining urban comforts with country pleasures, and a seat far grander than the modest retreat he had recommended to his scholar friend. Pliny described his villa as "unpretentious but not without dignity." From his windows and terraces he could look out into the surrounding landscape and the sea below. The open dining room projected just above the shore to catch the "sound of the breakers" as "dying murmurs." In a storm, the room was lightly washed by the spray from spent breakers. On the land side, Pliny could look into a garden "thickly planted with mulberries and fig."[25]

In the summer months Pliny moved to his villa in Tuscany. The very idea that a man could completely change his house and scenery according to the seasons was itself a major shift from the agrarian, fixed, traditional living patterns of the early Republic.

Tuscany provided Pliny and his neighbors with an entirely new and different kind of stage setting for villa life—one of new surroundings, new landscapes, and new gardening problems. "The climate in winter is cold and frosty, and so quite impossible for myrtles and olives," he noted. The house itself was carefully placed in the landscape on the lower slopes of a gently rising hill. Facing south, the rooms "from midday onwards in summer seem to invite the sun into the colonnade. . . ."

In front of the colonnade is a terrace laid out with box hedges clipped into different shapes, from which a bank slopes down, also with figures of animals cut out of box facing each other on either side. On the level below there waves—or I might have said ripples—a bed of acanthus. All round is a path hedged by bushes that are trained and cut into different shapes, and then a drive, oval like a racecourse, inside which are various box figures and clipped dwarf shrubs. The whole garden is enclosed by a dry-stone wall that is hidden from sight by a box hedge planted in tiers.[26]

In contrast to the architectural outlines of the garden, a meadow in the middle distance, "well worth seeing for its natural beauty as the formal garden," served as a transition into the cultivated fields and woods beyond. There is even a suggestion of a "wild garden" in the festoons of ivy on the trees and the laurel mixed in with the box, mingling "its shade with that of the plane trees." The emotional experience in Pliny's garden was further manipulated by strong contrasts of open and closed spaces that also produced changes of intensity of light and shadow: "The right-hand *allée* along the hippodrome is interrupted at its extremity by a hemicycle. . . . It is surrounded and covered by cypresses, which cast a shadow that becomes blacker and denser the further it goes. The *rondpoints* within are very brightly lit."[27]

Of course Pliny's spacious villas also had several inner courtyard gardens, arranged for private contemplation, reading, and relaxation. The courtyard garden had become an important living space in Roman houses throughout the empire wherever enough sun could be coaxed in to warm it. The peristyle screen of columns around the open space underlined the harmony and calm.[28] Pliny enumerates the simple ingredients of his own irresistible courtyard: "Almost opposite the middle of the colonnade is a suite of rooms set slightly back and round a small court shaded by four plane trees. In the center a fountain plays in a marble basin, watering the plane trees round it and the ground beneath them with its light spray."[29]

Dripping, running, gurgling, splashing water was orchestrated like the light and shade throughout Pliny's Tuscan Villa and its gardens. In the corner of one vine-covered arbor, water gushed out of pipes hidden beneath a marble dining seat and then flowed into a basin regulated to remain full but not to overflow, so that dishes shaped like birds and boats could drift by for dinner al fresco. In the sixteenth century, Cardinal Gambara would translate this idea into his own table at the Villa Lante.

Pliny was seventeen when Vesuvius suddenly erupted on the morning of August 24 in A.D. 79. He was staying not far from Pompeii with his uncle, who was in command of the fleet at Misenum in the Bay of Naples, when the first cloud was sighted. Young Pliny's decision to continue his studies rather than to accompany his uncle to inspect the disaster no doubt saved his life, for the elder Pliny was killed in the zone of the eruption.

The ancient tragedy that engulfed Pompeii and Herculaneum preserved beneath the volcanic ash not only the clear outlines of their gardens but the superb wall paintings that so vividly recreate the villa and garden life described in some of Pliny's letters. Pliny's delightful seaside villa some seventeen miles west of Rome made it possible for him "to spend the night there after necessary business is done without having cut short or hurried the day's work," he wrote defensively.[30] Might he well be forgiven if he did occasionally rush official commitments in the city when we see some of the contemporary villas recorded in wall paintings discovered at Pompeii. Like vacation houses of the rich in the twentieth century, these *villae maritimae* were a natural opportunity for all kinds of architectural ex-

periments. From the number of villas that have been discovered, we know the Bay of Naples below Vesuvius was a veritable playground for well-heeled patrons of architecture and gardens. A list of owners of these retreats, with their terraced gardens overlooking the bay, reads like a *Who's Who* of the late Republic. Sulla the Dictator had a villa near Cumae where Cicero also had one of his three villa properties. Julius Caesar, Pompey, Lucullus, the notorious Nero, and Varro the historian also lived in their villas whenever they could escape their official responsibilities in the city. For all of their sophistication and urban comforts—steam baths, sun rooms, and exercise yards—even the most elaborate villas were also self-supporting estates producing crops, vegetables, fruit, and grain. A large enclosure or leporarium could house hare, wild goats, and even deer raised for the table. Ducks, pigeons, and thrushes were also raised in elaborate aviaries. Varro (116–27 B.C.) has left us a detailed description.

Facing the open country is the place in which the aviary stands, shut in on two sides, right and left, by high walls. Between these lies the site of the aviary, shaped in the form of a writing-tablet with a top-piece, the quadrangular port being 48 feet in width and 72 feet in length, while at the rounded top-piece it is 27 feet. Facing this, as if it were a space marked off on the lower margin of the tablet, is an uncovered walk with a *plumula* [facade] extending from the aviary, in the middle of which are cages; and here is the entrance to the courtyard. At the entrance, on the right side and the left, are colonnades in the middle with dwarf trees; while from the top of the wall to the architrave the colonnade is covered with a net of hemp, which also continues from the architrave to the base. These colonnades are filled with all manner of birds.[31]

Just why a number of the wall paintings in the cities of Pompeii and Herculaneum record

Scholars believe this wall painting in the house of M. Lucretius Fronto in Pompeii represents actual villas. Cypress, umbrella pine, and perhaps poplar can be identified. Photo: Stanley Jashemski.

seaside and country villas is not clear. But in these paintings Pliny's own descriptions become vividly real and help to animate the lifeless archaeological remains. In contrast to the inward-looking courtyard garden of the typical Roman town house, the seaside and country villas express a new and dramatic appreciation of natural beauty and of the larger landscape beyond the gardens. Porticoed terraces and windows are placed in ways to take full advantage of the surrounding countryside.

Pliny's description of the pleasure he found in the natural landscape hardly needs an illustration as he sits in his cool arcade looking out at the water.

Here begins a covered arcade nearly as large as a public building. It has windows on both sides, but more facing the sea, as there is one on each alternate bay on the garden side. These all stand open on a fine and windless day, and in stormy weather can safely be opened on the side away from the wind. In front a terrace scented with violets. As the sun beats down, the arcade increases its heat by reflection. . . . Inside the arcade, of course, where there is the least sunshine when the sun is blazing down on its roof, its open windows allow the western breezes to enter and circulate so that the atmosphere is never heavy with stale air.[32]

The more elaborate villa gardens were often decorated with stylized trellis fences and some were painted on walls. Even the urns on pedestals on either side of semicircular *exedrae* were often illusory outlines.

Town Gardens

The unique preservation of Pompeii has provided a vast laboratory for the study of Roman gardens by archaeologists. Wilhelmina Jashemski has been the leading scholar and archaeologist to fully appreciate and explain the role of the urban garden in Roman times. In addition to the excavation of private house

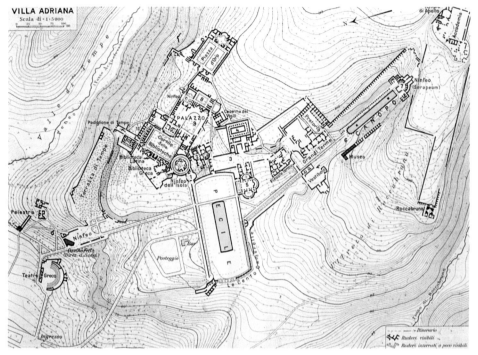

VILLA ADRIANA
Scala di 1:5000

Vettii. The sculpture decoration is finer, and a motif of masks and other theater ornaments is prominent, expressing the owner's interest in the theater. A large rectangular pool with two fountains dominates the center of the garden space.

Even though the peristyle garden is the best-known type of Roman garden, many houses had only small courtyard spaces without columns where plants were grown in pots and vases. The gardens of larger houses reached through a portico extending to the rear of the house. In some cases, the far wall of the courtyard was painted with a trompe l'oeil perspective to give the illusion of even greater size. The garden itself was divided axially by a walk that encouraged the interpenetrations of the house and garden.

Water in fountains, jets, and pools was important both in town gardens and in the

Emperor Hadrian's sprawling garden palace is nestled in the foothills below Tivoli, east of Rome. The extensive use of water is clear in this plan. Photo: Author.

RIGHT
In the center of the House of the Water Jets (Maison aux jets d'eau) in Conímbriga, Portugal, was a water garden with island beds for planting. A series of jets spouted water into the basin from in front of the colonnade. Bureau d'architecture antique du Sud-Ouest, Pau.

gardens, her work has also uncovered public and tomb gardens, gardens attached to restaurants and inns, and even gardens connected to stores and workshops. Gardening and garden life at all levels of society were an integral part of the fabric of Pompeii, something not fully appreciated until the publication of Professor Jashemski's discoveries.

Since the garden played such a basic role in Roman life, it inevitably became a significant element in the evolution of the Roman town house. Of all the Pompeian gardens, the House of the Vettii, first discovered in 1894, is the most famous. Its columned, sun-drenched courtyard is rich in sculpture and fountains. Between the colored, stuccoed columns, a dozen fountain statues on bases sent jets into eight marble basins that stood in the water channels along the edge of the garden. Water for the fountain was fed through a system of lead pipes, while rainwater from the roof was carried in a channel through the garden.

The House of the Golden Cupids is even more elegant and dazzling than that of the

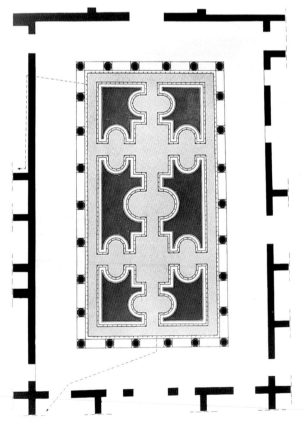

The water basin within the peristyle space of the House of the Water Jets is richly decorated with mosaics. The fountains were restored to working order after the archaeology was completed. Photo: Author.

country villa. One of the most elaborate water gardens, called the Maison aux jets d'eau (c. 300 A.D.), has been uncovered and partially restored at the Roman city of Conímbriga, Portugal. The entire space of this magnificent peristyle garden is taken over by a large and elaborate basin richly ornamented with mosaic tile on the surrounding walks and arcade floors. The basin itself is divided into a symmetrical but intricate pattern of earth-filled islands where flowers and plants hide the heads of more than four hundred jets that shoot their arched streams into the pool. Roberto Burle Marx, who knows these gardens, has adapted the idea in his garden for the Ministry of State in Brasilia.

The gardens of Pompeii were heavily planted with shade trees and shrubs. Pliny mentions that he had four plane trees in one of the smaller courtyards of his Tuscan Villa.

In the more formal and lavish peristyle garden, the pattern of plantings was probably not the low, trimmed hedging that has been extensively used in Pompeii restorations. Horace's reference to "nursing trees amid your varied columns" takes on new meaning through the work of Professor Jashemski and other garden archaeologists who have uncovered asymmetric, irregular plantings. Cultivated flowers were set in beds and borders, but, as we see in the fresco Garden Room of Livia's villa, they seemed to have been deployed with restraint. This does not mean that the Roman garden was without color. Mosaics, painted walls, statuary, and colored marble relieved the green monotony.

tification. Both the archaeologists and the fresco paintings confirm that cypress, bay, oleander, almond, peach, pomegranate, pear, quince, apple, and cherry were the favorite trees. Pliny speaks of citron trees that were imported in pots "with breathing holes for the roots." Lemons, as the wall paintings show, fascinated the Pompeians, and Professor Jashemski has found similar pots with root patterns that have been identified as those of a lemon tree.[33] Pompeii wall paintings also confirm Pliny's references to "various box figures and clipped dwarf shrubs" shaped and trained for the new Roman fashion of topiary.

Flowers were limited in their variety, but paintings record the deep purple germanica, the yellow water iris, the narcissus poeticus, autumn crocus, monkshood, anemone, marigold, amaranth, cornflower, cyclamen, pink, foxglove, gladiolus, jasmine, oleander, and periwinkle, in addition to the many domesticated field flowers first grown by the Greeks.

Imperial Grandeur—Hadrian's Villa

"This vast pile of stone and rubble is about all that is left of the Emperor Hadrian's villa and gardens," Eleanor Clark has written, calling these "tragic heaps of masonry . . . the saddest place in the world, gaunt as an old abandoned graveyard,"[34]

Not all Roman gardens were as small, domestic, and enclosed as those of Pompeii. The emperors of the late Roman Empire dreamed and built on a scale that would have been the envy of Louis XIV at Versailles. Ambitious emperors and members of their court had already set a standard for garden palaces even before Hadrian (A.D. 76–138) appeared on the scene. The ruins are inadequate to reconstruct their general layout with any accuracy so far as their gardens are concerned, but it is clear that these palaces were richly decorated and that garden sculpture was extravagantly displayed. Pliny says little about statuary in the gardens of his own villa, but he does note that Domitius already had enough artwork to dec-

In the enclosed, partially roofed courtyard space of the inner sanctum of a well-appointed town house in Pompeii, the shallow basin was filled by rainwater and by fountains. Photo: Everett Scott.

Trees, Flowers, and Shrubs

Archaeologists have greatly enlarged our knowledge of the use of trees in Pompeian gardens. When impressions of charred roots left in the volcanic ashes are uncovered during excavation, liquid plaster is fed into their cavities to form casts adequate for botanical iden-

orate a large garden on the same day he moved into his new house. The quantity of statuary decoration dug up from Roman gardens during the Renaissance confirms the extent of the fashion.

One wonders when Hadrian found time to supervise and direct the building of his own sprawling villa, since he was constantly moving all over the empire, constructing walls across barbarian Britain, subduing the restless Egyptians along the Nile, while at the same time collecting artworks for his retreat. Although the architecture of the villa itself is Roman, the garden spaces and the sculptured detail are romantically Hellenic in spirit. Hadrian was one of the most cosmopolitan and philhellenic of emperors and he turned particularly to Greek artists when he furnished his villa. It was during Hadrian's reign that cultural cross-fertilization spread infinitely more complex and sophisticated art and building styles throughout the empire. Villa

A garden scene painted on the south wall of the garden of the House of Venus Marina in Pompeii. Photo: Stanley Jashemski.

The largest garden uncovered so far in Pompeii is that of the House of Julia Felix. It is unusually luxuriant, with fluted and carved marble pillars on the left and a vine-covered arbor along the right. The center of the garden is dominated by four large connecting fish ponds crossed by small marble-faced bridges. The garden was first uncovered in 1755–57, then reburied before modern study in 1951–52. Photo: Everett Scott.

gardens in Spain, Portugal, France, and England assumed a new importance. These vital, creative centers began to make their own contribution to the arts, including garden design, in widely separate parts of the dominion. The energy and eclectic vitality of the emperor's villa at Tivoli expresses these new directions that were stirring throughout the Roman world.

The most puzzling thing that strikes a visitor to the Villa Adriana is its unpromising location northeast of Rome. Hadrian could have built his villa anywhere in the known world, but he selected the plain just below the hills of Tivoli at his back. His setting was nothing compared to the breathtaking views of the other contemporary imperial country retreats. Even as a visitor one feels the subtle, brooding quality of the landscape that Clark has so movingly described: "a piece of land chosen by a man worshipped as a god over half the world and to whom elevation must have been insufferable. . . . where the slip of valley, with its suggestion of a moat or a gauze scarf, keeps the hills in spite of everything at their distance and the emperor's inner life inviolate."[35]

In order to reconstruct the villa—and the gardens *are* the house, rather like Sissinghurst where the fragmented architecture is also reunited with trees and plants but on a totally different scale—imagine two things: shimmering water and marble in luxurious profusion, a mélange of great fountains, as at the nearby Villa d'Este, combined with the marble and mirror reflections of the Galerie de Glace at Versailles. The reflecting pool, called the Canopus, with its curving colonnade lined with monumental sculptures of Roman athletes, has an extravagant Hollywood quality to it. Photographs of its restoration teeter on the edge of comparison. Hadrian enjoyed the conceit that the long pool reminded him of the canal of Serapis at Canopus, a sanctuary he had once visited near Alexandria in Egypt. The Greek caryatids across the way, sculpture he had had copied from the Erechtheum in Athens, were another souvenir of his travels.

It takes little imagination to picture Hadrian's guests lounging around the basin on cushions, drinking snow-chilled wine from the vineyards of nearby Frascati, although no contemporary description of such a scene survives.

Because there is no visual, unifying plan such as that of Versailles, where every part is an integral, balanced element of the whole scheme, Hadrian's Villa and gardens, spreading over some 450 acres, are difficult to take in and to grasp. The individual parts of the complex are axially, formally conceived to link the garden space and the architecture. Virtually all of the villa's separate buildings are either open porticoes or closed peristyles. Enormous masses of the architecture are set off against the open spaces. Water in pools, fountains, canals, and cascades becomes the pervasive, unifying element, both visually and psychologically.

Even in the fifteenth century the original outlines and some of the decorations of the ruined folly could still be seen, making a deep impression on early Renaissance scholars of the classics who poked around in the rubble looking for sculptures and mosaic fragments. Pirro Ligorio (1500–1583) claimed in his early survey of the villa that grottoes, mosaics, columns, and sculpture were still plainly visible. No wonder it became a place haunted by the great artist-architects of the Renaissance like Bramante, Sangallo, and Raphael. In 1516, Raphael took Castiglione, the eminent Venetian humanist, and Cardinal Bembo on a guided pilgrimage there at the time he was planning the Villa Madama. Fifty years before, Pius II had recorded his first impressions: "About three miles from Tivoli the Emperor Hadrian built a magnificent villa like a big town. Lofty vaults of great temples still stand. . . . There are also remains of peristyles and large columned porticoes and swimming pools and baths into which part of the [river] Aniene was once turned to cool the summer heat."[36]

During the Renaissance, the villa ruins were repeatedly excavated and pillaged—by Pope Alexander VI at the end of the fifteenth century. Cardinal Alexander Farnese (c.1535), Cardinal Carafa (c.1540), and by Pirro Ligorio between 1550 and 1560 on behalf of the villa's neighbor, Cardinal Ippolito d'Este, who was working on his new gardens up the hill.

Nowhere in the villa can the visitor feel the personality of Hadrian more intensely than in the Maritime Theater. The little "moat-bound shrine," as Eleanor Clark called it, is at the very heart of the complex and was a place where Hadrian could withdraw from the outside, isolating himself in a world within a world. The small pavilion on the island in the middle had yet another inner space, a tiny garden with a fountain. A dining room, library, and a bathroom with stairs leading into the moat completed this miniature hideaway. The water parterre in the Renaissance garden of the Villa Lante and the island in the Boboli gardens in Florence are good examples of how the Renaissance garden-makers imaginatively translated such antique fragments into their own creations.

It is a pity we do not know what flowers and plants Hadrian grew at the villa, but given all of his travels and his trained eye it is easy to assume that there were plenty of exotic botanical delicacies collected and rushed to Rome to add to the color and the perfume of the place. Hadrian also surrounded himself with splendid sculpture, porphyry tubs, and marble urns with marvelous polished surfaces like the shallow cup in the Sala Rotonda of the Vatican. This might well have served as a giant birdbath for some elegant, now-extinct African bird, as Clark has suggested. Hadrian had it made from a single piece of stone in the quarries of Egypt and then somehow carried it to Rome. There were so many sumptuous objects and sculptures buried in the villa ruins that the supply lasted until the end of the eighteenth century. By then it seemed that half the palaces and gardens of Rome were decorated with excavated imperial garden souvenirs.

One of the well-kept secrets of the villa is the vast engineering organization of men and materials it took to build it. Work was probably started not long after the beginning of Hadrian's reign in A.D. 117 and continued to the end of his life in 138. But twenty-one years seem hardly enough time even if one commanded an unlimited work force and unlimited means. When we read that it took five years to build the nearby gardens at the Villa d'Este, that two thousand men dug the canal at Versailles, or that Queen Hatshepsut sent an army to the Land of Punt to bring back thousands of trees for her terraces above the Nile, we cannot help but marvel at the driving energy behind man's gardening obsessions to transform his environment into an artwork.

However removed in time we often feel ourselves when we look at some odd fragment of a vanished civilization in a museum, the connection between the gardens of our modern world and those of the world of Rome, Egypt, and Greece seems even more remote and incomprehensible. Yet flowers and plants that continue to give us pleasure in our gardens link us to the past in an intimate and living form. They are a living piece of history, a link that stimulates all of our senses— and our imagination. To the Greeks and Romans, flowers were a part of nature's mutability, its metamorphoses. Flowers were a part of the very fabric of classical mythology. The rose springs from Venus's blush when Jupiter watches her bathing; the nymph Dauphine turns into a bay tree when Apollo tries to carry her off. Other plants and flowers first grew out of the blood of heroes or appeared miraculously in the tears dropped on the ground by a goddess endowing them with remarkable powers of healing. Roman soldiers planted the Madonna lily near their camps because of its ability to heal battle wounds. Only much later did it become the sign of the Queen of Heaven in the medieval church, with power to cure a much greater range of earthly and spiritual ailments.

Out of the wreckage of the Roman Empire we can piece together some idea of its gardens chiefly with the help of archaeologists. Pliny's letters breathe a little life into the rubble. But the most fragile survivors of Roman gardens—the plants and flowers—are their most enduring link. Through an endless cycle of propagation, cultivation, and survival, the laws of nature have prevailed, enabling us to enjoy the descendants of the same flowers once grown at Herculaneum, at the Tuscan Villa of Pliny, and in Hadrian's retreat at Tivoli.

II. The Earthly Paradise

THE MIDDLE AGES

When we call to mind bucolic scenes of the Middle Ages, we conjure up a picturesque countryside of meadows, vineyards, orchards, and a Disneyland castle on a hill in the distance. But our fantasy of a manicured landscape of tamed, benign nature could not be further from actual conditions for the people living in the castle, working in the fields, and praying in the nearby abbey a thousand years ago. For them, nature was a frightening enemy—a minefield of potential disaster, an adversary they did not care to face. If a knight or his lady happened to look out through one of those high, narrow fortress windows or over the parapet of their castle, it was likely they were scanning the horizon for an approaching invader or a visit by one of nature's unpredictable howling scourges of storms, wild stags, wolves, boars, or even an occasional dragon. Gardens, or what passed for systematic cultivation, had to be protected behind stone walls from the nightmares of nature lurking in the nearby forests and marshes, in untamed rivers, and along the sides of empty roads.

Eventually small, appealing domestic gardens for the well-protected patricians living in castles and towns did reappear as Europe gradually escaped from the wilderness that spread after the collapse of Rome. The gardens may not have been as elegant as the one laid out for Emperor Otto (912–973) and recreated in Dirk Bouts's Flemish painting of 1468, but the emphasis on enclosure and compartmentalization is probably accurate. The very idea of the *hortus conclusus*—the garden secure and protected from a ferocious world—is expressed in those secluded, geometric compositions. The planes of the medieval garden, like an open-air room, were flat and horizontal. Wells served both psychological and practical concerns. Raised plant beds, some as much as two feet above the walks, and an occasional grass bench seem to have been the only relief from the spatial monotony of the tiny plots. And we can be sure that most of these gardens were far more humble and unpretentious than the idealized versions that turn up in the paintings and miniatures of the period. The Christian ascetic ideal called for a self-supporting community where gardens were a necessity.

Gardening was a significant part of the early Christian monastery, serving as a spiritual refuge and an escape from besetting fears and doubts that assailed both the body and soul. The monastery garden's function as a setting for the *vita contemplativa* must have called for a certain simplicity and decorum for meditation even though visual evidence of this is scant. There is an air of uncertainty, however, in some of the views we glimpse in the background of portraits where the religious gardens often appear a little sad and foreboding, haunted with a kind of pathos. No one smiles. The Madonna always seems preoccupied. The

In this detail of a late-fifteenth-century Flemish painting, climbing roses and potted plants are displayed, and on wall brackets specimen plants are being cultivated. The University of Arizona Museum of Art, Gift of Samuel H. Kress Foundation.

tense faces reflect little of pleasure or the kind of enjoyment gardens are supposed to provide. As Nan Fairbrother once remarked, religion had conditioned men to view earthly life "by the light of eternity, but eternity is too dreadful a brilliance for mortal men to live by." [1]

Aside from the meager representation found in a few primitive pictures and the occasional suggestive reference in ecclesiastical manuscripts—lists of herbs and medicinal plants, with fleeting references to a garden set aside for contemplation or study—the evidence of gardening in medieval times is indi-

rect and illusive. Saint Augustine (354–430), the early church father and philosopher who was consecrated bishop of Hippo in Northern Africa in 395, may well have been thinking of the Golden Age of Greece when he founded his religious community. Just as Plato, Epicurus, and Theophrastus had taught their students in their gardens, the saint seemed to be following these ancient predecessors: "I assembled in a garden Valerius had given me," he wrote of the foundation at Hippo, "certain brethren of like intentions with my own, who possessed nothing, even as I possessed nothing, and who followed after me." [2]

The final collapse of the Roman Empire in Europe no doubt brought an effective end to even a vestige of what might pass as garden art in any elevated sense, as described by Pliny the Younger in the first century A.D. Subsistence gardening for food and medicine, of course, continued on a primitive level beneath the notice of contemporary chronicles or artists. Some classical garden manuscripts such as *De re rustica* by Palladius (4th–5th century A.D.) did survive to recount in a kind of gardener's calendar what work needed to be done throughout the year, but garden literature available for common use amounted to very little. Gardening advancement in Europe was pretty much in the hands of practical gardeners until the sixteenth century. Yet it would be fair to say that a rudimentary tradition survived among the ruins of former Roman settlements and in remote corners of the former empire, where the habit and necessity to cultivate plants in some kind of order was still preserved, very much like the primitive gardens we still can see in undeveloped agricultural societies today. It is also true that some 350 species known in Roman times were still available and used in the twelfth century. [3]

When the Roman Empire broke apart, not only were highly advanced horticultural skills and techniques forgotten but even skills in garden-toolmaking and metallurgy were largely lost as well. Iron picks, hoes, and spades widely used throughout the Roman Empire were replaced with crude tools usually made of wood. The digging fork with prongs lined up with the handle, so widely used, especially in Europe, for rough digging and lifting, does not seem to have reappeared until the seventeenth century. Wooden fencing or woven reed panels were sometimes placed around simple checkerboard planting beds, and wooden arbors for vines were common, but nothing as delicate as the trellis fences we see in the garden paintings of Pompeii was to be found. Arbors in the form of open galleries resembling monastery cloisters were often used to enclose the medieval garden. In more elaborate versions these galleries formed a dense tunnel by pleaching or braiding the branches of lime, hornbeam, wych elm, or willow. The new growth would be clipped each spring to hold its architectural form.

By the time we begin to see more advanced gardens in the later Middle Ages, with raised flower beds, espaliered fruit trees, and elaborate parterres, both horticulture and basic gardening technology had progressed dramatically. The iron plant supports illustrated in a manuscript of the *Roman de Renaud de Montauban* dating to about 1475 are an index confirming that gardening technology was moving ahead. Garden tools themselves had evolved into specialized designs to the point where they could be distinguished from heavy agricultural equipment.

As early as 795 A.D. Charlemagne (742–814) had attempted to recover the fragmented tradition of gardening and to reestablish it as a matter of public policy in his regulations drawn up for the administration of towns, the *Capitulare de villis vel curtis emperii*. Although it ultimately met with little success, the Frankish king's decree listed eighty-eight species, primarily herbs and fruit trees, that were ordered to be grown in every town of the empire. Some of these plants had actually been sent to him by his friend the Baghdad caliph Hārūn ar-Rashīd, who also had thoughtfully included an elephant among his diplomatic gifts. It was the beginning, or revival, of plant migration into the West from Turkey and the

Near East that would continue for the next thousand years with rich and wonderful results, transforming the smell, color, texture, and looks of European gardens beyond all recognition.

The famous model plan of the proposed Benedictine Monastery of St. Gall in Switzerland, dating from around 820, is the most complete layout of a monastic complex, which is made up of church, schools, hospitals, living quarters, great houses, farm buildings, and gardens. The famous Rule of St. Benedict, drawn up in the sixth century for the order, provided for gardens within the walls of the community. The simple medicinal herbs and flowers to be grown in the cloister gardens of St. Gall—roses, lilies, sage, and

A modern pleached allée at Old Westbury Gardens on Long Island, New York, suggestive of medieval garden techniques. Photo: Allen Rokach.

Late-fifteenth-century woodcut, possibly by Jacopo di Carlo, showing a monastic garden. Library of Congress, Lessing J. Rosenwald Collection.

rosemary—are clearly marked. The physic garden is placed beside the hospital and has sixteen rectangular beds, each designated for a different plant. The cemetery for the faithful monks is also laid out in regular spaces with fruit trees evenly placed among the graves. The artist who drew the plan was no botanist and simply copied the names form Charlemagne's garden decree, so we find Mediterranean figs, laurels, and pines growing in St. Gall's chilly Swiss setting.

Some of the first monastic gardens were fitted out in abandoned ruins of Roman villas, where the four-square or rectangular enclosure of existing walls no doubt provided a kind of psychological protection from the hostile reminders of human mortality lurking in the terrors of nature. But as John Harvey has pointed out, the idealized cloister garden contained within the main cloisters of the monastery is largely a myth: The less-than-romantic documentary evidence records no more than a well-scythed sward rather than an enclosed, sacred precinct of ornamental flowers and herbs artfully cared for by dedicated monks.[4]

While gardens planted in the wreckage of the Roman Empire were depressingly primitive and remained so for three or four centuries, herbs were cultivated everywhere as cures and potents—a pharmacy by the back door. Even flowers were eaten as medicine. This preoccupation with the healing powers of plants encouraged a growing awareness that nature herself might be coaxed to give up some of her secrets to alleviate or cure the demons she herself had introduced. Gardens became a primitive medical laboratory in the service of health.

The plants in the monastery garden cultivated for medicinal purposes grew in well-kept and defined beds of vegetables, fruits, and herbs. If there was a rose, its blossom might well go into a health salad as easily as a vase, since everything in the garden was edible. Even the thorns of the rosebush had a use. St. Benedict applied them vigorously to his skin in order to exorcise a sinful preoccu-

pation with a vision of beautiful women who tried to intrude on his loftier concentration.

Pietro de' Crescenzi (1230–1305), a retired Bolognese lawyer, wrote his great treatise on agriculture and gardening at the beginning of the fourteenth century. This breathless leap in the narrative over whole centuries to the late medieval period reflects the gap that even modern archaeology has not been able to close in the same way that it has so admirably done for Roman gardens. The fame of Crescenzi's book, *Liber ruralium commodorum* (1305), spread by frequent republication, helped to establish Italy's lead in gardening for the next several hundred years. It remained the unchallenged work on the subject, and illustrated versions of it circulated widely until the sixteenth century. Crescenzi based his treatise on classical manuscripts by writers such as Cato, Varro, Columella, and Palladius, but he also seems to have learned a great deal from the new scientific discoveries reaching Europe from Moorish Sicily.

Crescenzi's most original contribution to the gardens of Europe was to urge the cultivation of a kind of pleasure garden for the upper orders of society. Although his proposals were often vague and general, he insisted on a hierarchy of gardening and believed that the ruler or prince should maintain the largest, most elegant garden in the city and that it should exceed twenty acres in size. Here Crescenzi seems to draw on Eastern inspiration, calling for a grand park reminiscent of those in Persia that had first impressed the army of Alexander. He also recommended exotic trees such as palm, citrus, and cypress, but without regard for their special growing requirements, suggesting that he had copied the names from unrelated sources. Grafting must already have been widespread, for he speaks of the pleasure of "various and wonderful grafting on trees.[5]

We do not know when artificial grafting—in which a shoot of one tree is fastened onto a branch of another—had been revived. Certainly this technique had earlier fascinated the Greeks and Romans. St. Paul in his Epistle to

The numerous illustrated editions of Crescentius have supplied a wonderful record of medieval gardening technique, as here where an orchard is being planted and a vineyard pruned. British Library.

the Romans speaks of "grafting of olives so that the grafts could partake" of the root and fatness of the (wild) olive tree. This biblical reference would surely have been understood by the medieval brethren working in their monastery orchards. It is not certain, however, whether they performed grafts themselves or whether this is one of the many horticultural skills lost after the fall of Rome.

Topiary, or the training of ivy and trees, had also been popular with the Romans. As we have seen, Pliny the Younger spoke of "various box figures and clipped dwarf shrubs" and of walks "enclosed with tonsured evergreens shaped into a variety of forms."[6] But except for trimmed hedges and arbors, the art of topiary had disappeared from Europe in the Dark Ages. By the end of the fifteenth century, however, the technique of sculpting shrubs and bushes was revived in Italy. In Florence, box trees are reported as being shaped into "spheres, ships, porticoes, temples, vases and urns."[7] Renaissance humanists believed they were replicating the topiary sculpture mentioned in familiar Roman literature, but without any visual evidence to guide them.

Throughout garden history, in both sacred

and secular gardens, a fountain, water basin, or wellhead, usually located in the center, was essential garden equipment and this is true of the medieval garden as well, even though the more elaborate models that have survived are quite late. Aside from its necessity, alluded to in St. Jerome's simple advice to "Hoe your ground, plant your cabbage, and water well," water in the middle of a garden flowing out and dividing the space into four parts is our oldest sacred symbol of an ideal paradise layout—older than Genesis or the Koran and extending back into the dimmest reaches of recorded history in Sumer. The image always seems to carry with it recollection of an illusive earthly paradise somehow lost in the

dawn of time. There is an atavism within the four-square form that seems to manifest a recurring nostalgia in both the East and West. Or it may simply be a reflexive perpetuation of the most familiar and ubiquitous garden configuration on earth. So the square garden divided into four parts with a well in the middle may not be loaded with as much ancient metaphysical meaning and symbolism as we would sometimes like to believe.

To speak of the symbolic meaning of water in a garden, and as it is used in an early Christian cloister, may be a platitude, but is nevertheless a profound one. For both the Christian and Muslim, water is above all a symbol of moral and sacred purification. There is hardly

No garden history can resist republishing this well-known painting by the Upper Rhenish Master of the Virgin in the garden. The botanical details of flowers are easily identified as sweet rocket, lily of the valley, rose, lilium, mallow, and flag iris.

a religion in the world that does not use water to evoke life, creation, purity, and rebirth. Norsemen practiced a chilly baptism long before they embraced Christianity, and Hindus continue to wash away their sins every day in the holy river of the Ganges at Benares. Water's sacred power endures simply because all life on this planet depends on it. Our efficient urban water systems deny us the daily affirmation of rediscovering this humbling, cosmic truth. The water sprinkler on the suburban lawn somehow fails to provide much metaphysical insight for modern man. It is not human to treasure the commonplace, at least not in the West. Yet there is hardly a garden in the world, from the most ordinary to the most noble, that does not somehow celebrate the fundamental importance of water. But only where water is scarce or difficult to get, as at Kabul or at Versailles, is it transformed into a major work of art. Who would dream of a water garden in Venice?

Another feature of the medieval garden that had a practical as well as spiritual function was the garden wall. In the medieval castle the garden wall created necessary retreats for privacy—an island in the chaotic, cramped existence of family, friends, servants, dogs, and children—a place where romance itself, if not the Holy Spirit, might be welcomed. Even in the bedrooms, where beds could sometimes accommodate four couples at a time, moments of intimacy were scarce. Constant intrusion was assured, if by nothing more than the prying eyes of a family hawk perched in the corner on its stand. The medieval concept of a garden of Love was not merely a literary conceit.

"It is not the least part of the pleasures of a garden, to walk and refresh yourself alone apart from company that may prove burdensome," one thoughtful garden lover wrote.[8] It is no deep mystery why secluded gardens became a place for lovers to meet as domestic civility and a sense of privacy advanced. The newly discovered emotions of love quickly developed their own ideal characteristics, and this further explains the importance of the

Music, which often figures in the garden life of China and Japan, seemed to have become a conventional pastime in the West by the late medieval period, as in this scene of daily life at the end of the fifteenth century, where the troubadour invariably sings of romantic love. National Gallery of Art, Washington, D.C.

garden's locus. The conditions for romantic love included voluntary choice, a concern for personal values, mutual response, and an absence of compulsion on the part of either party. The more autonomous and independent the choice of the beloved, the higher it stood in the scale of values. In order to encourage all of these ideals, a neutral setting free of confining traditions and associations had to be found, and the idealized garden composed of nature's purest elements seemed the inevitable trysting place.

The lines "I found her in an arbor, sweet, under a bough" could have opened countless medieval songs and sonnets, and invariably the setting for the lover's lament is a garden, the theater of the love scene. The tradition, formula and gestures of the medieval love story and the experience of love were fixed in *The Romance of the Rose* (c.1240) by Guillaume de Lorris (fl. 1235), with its allegorical figures and dreamlike, languid atmosphere. The fountain is always playing in the middle of the walled garden, the water is always crystal clear, birds fly in and out of the flowers, and, of course, the lady is ravishingly beautiful and ageless. The grass is perpetually green and the precisely shaped trees have obviously been imported from the most exotic places. In a word, it is a perfect earthly paradise, an ideal garden existence. While it is doubtful that the fantasies described by the poets and troubadours advanced much understanding of horticulture, the literary garden did inspire artists to give the love garden a visual representation that may have been based on actual models.

Life in these secular gardens of the late Middle Ages seems to have been social if we can judge from the pictorial evidence. Friendship and love as sentiment and ideal have come to occupy an important place in domestic life. For the first time, gardens have been taken over by women—the Virgin Mary, Venus, the goddesses of the ancient world now disguised as the Virgin, and various Christian saints dominate the garden scene. Women are shown tending the flowers while their lords are off fighting, hunting, or searching for the Holy Grail. The chatelaine keeps the key to the garden gate and opens it at the right moment for her lover to enter. If the couple is caught and the damsel is locked up by the irate father, husband, or jealous suitor, she inevitably pines for her true love from a nearby tower, overlooking, of course, the garden where he may yet reappear and rescue her.

The Middle Ages were the Age of Faith, and if a lady longed for her beloved she no doubt would pray that almighty God grant her her heart's desire. Whereupon a falcon would fly into her garden, change into the fairest knight she had ever looked upon in her entire life, and after a few awkward moments, according to the tale, "they were happy together," of course in the garden. If the lady were already married, adultery was a duty: "You are so lovely a knight, so sweet in speech and so courteous, that verily it is my lady's duty to set her love upon yours," according to the troubadour's song. On other occasions, the chatelaine might appear to turn her garden into a smart salon, a drawing room where friends could explore new emotional relationships while being entertained by polite flirtation, music, conversation, and displays of chivalry—minor arts but major steps on the rough, uncertain path to civilization.

The abstract idea of a garden and its trans-lation into spatial reality is a luxury of the imagination as well as the pocketbook. In the harsh, everyday world of the Middle Ages, gardens for members of the knightly orders of society became places to encourage private, even erotic, fantasies such as ladies taming the shy unicorn in their bower, as depicted in the famous unicorn tapestries. These tapestries were made to decorate the stone walls of chilly castle rooms, suggesting a refinement and elegance we seldom associate with medieval life. The costumes of the ladies, the delicate fence, and the flowers contradict our conventional image of a primitive world of uncomfortable furniture, coarse clothing, and bad table manners. The perfecting of private gardens with the luxury of fountains, arbors, benches, and topiary is part of a new sensibility that was greatly encouraged by the growing contact with the East. A number of medieval paintings depicting Bathsheba stepping from an elegant oriental pool confirms the popularity of these imported sensual pleasures.

Whatever the Crusades may have contributed to the advancement of the Christian faith, the life of Europe, and ours, was profoundly altered and enriched by the introduction of all the new luxuries brought back by the Crusaders from the Middle East. Above all, the East taught the West how to orchestrate the human senses in the garden. Exotic fruits, vegetables, flowers, and herbs never seen before suddenly appeared in the kitchens and on dining tables. New colors and perfumes of flowers were introduced. Pools for bathing were built in the garden. The nose was gratified by the exotic smell of jasmine and the rose. Garden pavilions inspired by Eastern models served as secluded places for lovers and appeared for the first time along European garden paths where they would remain for centuries. Climbing plants to enclose the bower—honeysuckle, wild rose, and grape—were planted to grow on the surrounding trellis. The new game of courtly love played out in a garden was a major step both for gardens and civilized living.

The medieval myth of the fabled unicorn held captive in a garden is the subject of this sixteenth-century Franco-Flemish tapestry panel decorated with flowers. Metropolitan Museum of Art, Gift of John D. Rockefeller, Jr., The Cloisters.

THE ISLAMIC GARDEN

The garden tradition of the Muslim world, enormous in its scope and stretching from Asia into parts of Europe and Africa is, along with the mosque, the most ubiquitous art form of Islam. The span of time this tradition represents, paralleling the Middle Ages in Europe, is on a scale with the vast geography of Islam itself. Both literary and archaeological evidence indicate that Islamic gardens existed as early as the first half of the eighth century, following the conquest by followers of Mohammed (c. 570–632) and continuing down to the present time.

By comparison, whatever passed for a gardening tradition in Europe at the beginning of the Islamic epoch in the eighth century was without any particular direction, definition, or widespread support. The instability of the late Roman Empire had contributed to the decline of gardening on any significant scale or its serious study. Even in central Italy, where the creation and cultivation of large pleasure gardens had once been an established prerogative of the ruling classes both in the towns and at their elaborate villas that dotted the countryside, there is little evidence of much gardening vitality of any ornamental quality in the post-Roman era, beyond the humblest sort.

Restless, roaming desert nomads, the Arabs were an unlikely people to have established a garden of any kind, let alone a vital garden tradition strong enough to spread across continents. The dry, arid land, except for a chance oasis or river valley, that they were attracted to was as unpromising as their rootless nomadic character. But as Elizabeth Moynihan has pointed out, the Arab's very lack of any cultural traditions of his own may well have encouraged his genius for absorbing those of the peoples he would eventually conquer.[9] In the late seventh century when the Arab hordes overran the old Persian Empire that centered on the Iranian plateau and dated from the sixth century B.C., an ancient gardening tradition still survived. Cyrus the Great, whose victory over the Medes in 550 B.C. established the first world empire, had built his capital in his native province of Fars and called it Pasargadae. It is astonishing to still be able to see the taut outlines of his gardens and palace, bold, majestic, Cartesian in their rigor, at the foot of the mountain in the fertile plain of the Pulvar River. As with the later Islamic gardens that would eventually appear in places like Northern Africa, Mughal India, and Spain, where the Arab conquest reached, the design of Cyrus's garden at Pasargadae is unified by long watercourses interspersed with basins and pools. It has been estimated that these water channels once stretched for over a thousand meters to feed the trees and shrubs that had been planted in the salt and gravel desert where the annual rainfall never exceeds ten inches.

"The palaces of Cyrus designed as open, crystalline structures with a new, four-sided character, invited inspection from every direction," Dr. David Stronach of the British Institute of Persian Studies has written. "And in keeping with the generous proportions of the site, care was taken to place them in spacious, well-watered grounds. . . . Each inner palace with its stately colonnades and deep shadowed porticoes was first glimpsed amidst a profusion of trees, shrubs and grasses."[10] The open grandeur seems to go with the larger imperial ambitions of power, and the use of the garden pavilion as a viewing platform for the ruler of nature as well as of people would later become an Eastern legacy to the West, following the route of Islam's triumphs. The close relationship and unity between the pavilion and its garden setting, as a number of scholars have pointed out, are, indeed, defining characteristics of the Persian garden. The pavilion was strategically placed as the seat of honor but also in order that the royal party could enjoy the garden's dreamy pleasures of smell, color, and sound from its shelter without

OPPOSITE
This small enclosed garden with fountain and basin within the complex of the Alhambra in Granada, Spain, represents the typical courtyard that appears throughout the Islamic world. Photo: Everett Scott.

needing to explore along the garden walks and terraces. "The Persians don't walk much in Gardens as we do," a French visitor noted in the seventeenth century, "but content themselves with a bare prospect; and breathing the fresh air: For this end, they set themselves down in some part of the Garden, at their first coming into it, and never move from their Seats till they are going out of it."[11]

To the Arab conquerors, armed with little more than a copy of the Koran, an elegant tradition of calligraphy, and, of course, swords, horses, and camels, the conquered gardens of Persia looked like the promised Paradise so vividly described in the words of the Prophet. Indeed, the fountains, the watercourses flowing in channels, the shade trees, and the abundance of green vegetation seemed to have corresponded almost literally to the Prophet's description in the Koran. The very act of making a garden out of the desert carried with it a profound, transcendental message foretelling of God's earthly plans to create gardens—plans which the faithful were prepared to execute wherever they went. Not only was making a garden an act of faith on the part of the Arabs, it was a way to suppress the age-old oriental fear and antipathy to nature's hostility, a hostility expressed on every side by the dry, trackless desert, the stinging winds, the relentless sun, and, most of all, the pervasive uncertainty of finding a permanent supply of water. This anxiety produced by everyday existence underlines the appeal of the words of the Koran and its creed, promising an everlasting garden paradise in the next world. The universal life-symbol represented by the garden takes on a new meaning in the Persian and later in the Islamic world where nature's lack of generosity is an everyday fact of life and death. Nature's reassuring color of living green used on the roof tiles, green banners, and green mosaics in mosque courtyards became a sign of Islam.

By the end of the ninth century, Arabian expansion of empire stretched eastward to Egypt, Tunisia, Morocco, and all across Northern Africa, Sicily, and into southern Spain. The unexpected swiftness of the invaders was without precedent, and the conquest brought terror and confusion to crumbling Europe. The terms of surrender under the Conquest were just as uncompromising as those of the invaders' Christian adversaries. The conquered had to approach the conquerors for mercy and accommodation, and they could do so only by serving Allah as the conquerors served him by reading the Koran. They had no choice but to learn Arabic, the sacred and consummate language of the Prophet himself. The words of the Koran, expressly speaking of Heavenly Paradise as a central tenet of faith, reinforced the importance of gardens in both earthly and celestial manifestations wherever the new religion was established by the book. The Prophet's words describing the pleasures of Paradise taken from the Koran were used to decorate the walls of mosque courtyards throughout Islam.

In this detail of a miniature from a Mughal manuscript showing Emperor Bābur supervise the layout of the Bagh-i-Wafa (Garden of Fidelity), the architect is shown holding his grid plan for laying out the garden for the emperor's inspection. Victoria and Albert Museum, Crown copyright.

Gardens in the Islamic tradition first appeared in North Africa in the ninth century at Tunis, where sultans established enormous pleasure gardens that also produced fruit for the marketplace. This type of vast orchard garden was called an *aguedal* and was laid out in large geometrical squares divided by irrigation channels and was usually quite flat so that the water could flow easily. It was the luxuriant scale, the lavish use of water, and an occasional pavilion that gave the garden its unique aesthetic appeal. One of the oldest *aguedal* gardens, dating from the twelfth century and heavily restored in the nineteenth, still flourishes under the care of the king of Morocco on the outskirts of Marrakesh. Dominated by a rectangular basin nearly one kilometer around, its setting dramatically incorporates the snow-capped Atlas Mountains seen from a distance of sixty miles. The water for the garden is taken from melting snow on the mountains, feeding the river and irrigation ditches with an unending supply across the intervening desert waste. The shimmering basin served by the irrigation system gives welcome visual relief to the expanse, and was also used occasionally for boating parties.

The second type of garden introduced into Africa and Spain was the familiar enclosed Islamic courtyard. The high walls enclosing the Islamic garden created the mystique of an absolutely private world, an artificial paradise where all of the voluptuous, staggering pleasures of the senses could be enjoyed to the fullest, as the Koran had also promised the faithful in eternity. It is this image of the Islamic courtyard evoked by paintings and Western fantasies that distinguishes Muslim gardens everywhere in the world. Mohammed may have been competing with followers of Zoroaster when he offered to send all gardeners to heaven automatically. The Prophet had further upped the ante in the Koran with enticing visions of "green pastures . . . fountains of gushing water . . . fruits, palm trees and pomegranates . . . and maidens good and comely in cool pavilions . . . reclining on green cushions."[12] However

Small garden fountain in the Generalife gardens in Granada. Photo: Lynne Meyer

An Oriental persimmon in the Alhambra. Photo: Charles Marden Fitch.

suggestive these words may be, it is difficult to relate them specifically to an actual garden layout.

As far as flowers, vegetables, and fruit trees were concerned, within the walled Islamic garden all were mixed—kitchen garden, flower garden, herbs, and orchard—planted together in colorful confusion without any apparent class distinctions or hierarchy. And there certainly were no dull, well-shaven grass lawns to maintain. The structure of the Islamic garden was never covered up with ill-considered horticultural displays, as in our contemporary preoccupation with the cultivation of individual plants at the expense of the garden's underlying form. Straight lines and right angles made for a clear, crisp framework, giving a sense of horticultural order. The shape of the courtyard garden itself was resolutely geometric, like a series of outdoor

OPPOSITE
The eleventh-century
palace gardens of Madi-
nat al-Zahra, outside
Córdoba, represent the
most important archaeo-
logical testimony in
documenting the early
Arab gardens of Spain.
Two of the large gardens
are identical in scale and
plan but on different
levels. Both are quadri-
partite in form. The
upper garden has an
enormous pool to reflect
the palace pavilion.
Photo: Everett Scott.

rooms, and, indeed, the balance and unity between the architecture and the garden, seen in
the line of trees extending the interior arches
of a nearby pavilion out into the garden, bring
the two arts into a harmony we rarely encounter in the twentieth century. Walking in
Spanish or Moroccan gardens, enjoying their
interlocking complexity with the architecture, we are reminded of the peristyle
courtyard of a house in Pompeii, and the inspiration for these Moorish garden spaces
may well reach back even further than the beginning of the Islamic Empire. When the
Moors arrived in Spain, some of the old Roman aqueducts and irrigation systems were
actually still in operation, and vestiges of ancient villa gardens may also have survived to
impress the invaders.

Given the clamor and dirt of Eastern cities
and the ever-present reminder of nature's lack
of hospitality in the desert, the preoccupation
with order in the garden space is not surprising. The symmetry of Islamic gardens also
represents transcendent purity and perfection
compared to mankind's and nature's predictable imperfection, if one may take one of the
grander interpretations of garden making.

The very idea of God-imposed, cosmic order subduing a turbulent, ill-kept world is
best communicated in abstract symbols, so
the Islamic artist and architect had little diffi-
culty in expressing a belief in geometric designs in every kind of medium, from
buildings and gardens to carpets and ceramic
tiles.

The squares, circles, and octagons we see in
the gardens could be there for good theologi-
cal reasons: the square represents the earthly
order of things, the circle indicates God's
celestial perfection of eternity, and the oc-
tagon—the circle squared—signifies our
earthly struggle to achieve everlasting unity
with God's higher plans. The four-square garden, or *chahar bagh*, signifying the four quarters of the universe with the four rivers of life
intersecting at the garden's center, was based
on a design far older than Islam or even the
Persian Empire. In its primitive form, water

channels or walks divided a flat, rectangular
space into four quarters. The Book of Genesis
describes its idealized pattern: "And a river
went out of Eden to water the garden: and
from thence it was parted and became into
four heads." In the Islamic garden the open
watercourses and pools, the sheets of water
pouring over stone tips imposed a formal order and unity on nature that was at once both
practical and symbolic, as it visibly carried the
garden's life-blood to each tree and plant with
exquisite, aesthetic efficiency.

With the driven, nomadic energy of Islam,
it is remarkable how firmly the essential elements and characteristics of the Islamic garden were rooted and could be transplanted
over a vast territory—and even transplanted
by Islamic converts such as the Mughals in India and the Moors in North Africa and Spain.

When Abd ar-Rahmān (731–788), a surviving member of the Umayyad dynasty of Islam, fled Damascus in the middle of the
eighth century, he finally settled in Andalusia
on the Spanish peninsula where he was
crowned emir of Córdoba. One of his first
acts was to create a garden in the new country.
It is impossible to reconstruct the palace garden of the emir in detail, but the number of
workmen—ten thousand by some accounts—
and the forty years it took to build it are
statistics oriental in their extravagance, over-
shadowing anything that would be done in
the rest of Europe in the next four or five hundred years.[13] There were, according to contemporary accounts, canals, fountains, and
terraces heavily planted with luxuriant plants.
Recalling gardens he had known in Damascus, the emir brought pomegranates, jasmine,
roses, and other plants from India, Syria, and
Turkestan to his palace at Córdoba. After introducing the beloved palm tree from its native Syria to share his exile he wrote a
nostalgic poem to it.

O lovely Palm, a stranger thou
like me in a foreign land,
here in the West dost languish now,
far from thy native strand.[14]

It was not the first time or the last that nostalgia added an informing element to the design of gardens. Nostalgia in any culture is, after all, a concomitant of change. The homesick Persian wife of a Moorish ruler in Spain was cheered up by her husband when he ordered cherry trees planted on a nearby hillside so that the white blossoms in the spring would recall the snow on Persian mountains.

By the tenth century, chroniclers report the existence of thousands of private gardens in and around Córdoba. Muslim laws governing the use of water were enacted. Baths, aqueducts, and irrigation channels were built. Córdoba was becoming a major center for botanic studies, and advanced gardening treatises were written there and followed closely. While most of these urban gardens were no doubt utilitarian, evidence of their exact configuration is vague. Most were probably a small, rectangular enclosed space divided by a watercourse channel on the main axis with secondary axes of water or walks crossing at right angles. Unlike Persian and Mughal gardens, these contained no large water pools. Parallel to the watercourse, rows of fruit trees were planted, and occasionally a pavilion might cover a fountain in the middle.

Existing evidence for the accurate reconstruction of an authentic Hispano-Arab garden of Andalusia, as James Dickie has pointed out in his essay on the Islamic garden in Spain, "is tenous in the extreme."[15] The restored gardens of the Alcázar in Seville and the Alhambra at Granada are post-Reconquest. In the case of the Alhambra, the garden we actually see can be no earlier than post–Spanish Civil War. The box edging, ubiquitous ivy, and long perspectives in the style of Le Nôtre's Versailles are in fact diametrically opposed to the Muslim sensibility with its emphasis on the intimate and the private.[16]

These famous Spanish gardens are at once so familiar to us as representing authentic surviving Arabic gardens that it is almost impossible to cut through the centuries of changes and destruction, followed by countless restorations and reconstructions, to determine their original, essential character beyond the basic outlines established by the surrounding architecture.

With the fall of Córdoba and Seville in the middle of the thirteenth century, the Christian kings continued to maintain and build their gardens in the Moorish tradition. The bloody disputes of religion did not prevent Peter the Cruel (1334–1369), for example, from holding on to his talented Islamic gardeners when he rebuilt the Alcázar in Seville. The beautiful city of Granada became the last Moorish foothold in Europe, where Islam held on until the Reconquest was completed in 1492.

In spite of all their countless alterations, the Alhambra and the Generalife, dating from the thirteenth and fourteenth centuries, remain the only gardens in Europe that have survived with any Islamic character. Even more than the alterations, the unusual site itself adds a further distortion of the conven-

An ornamental orange typical of southern Spain. Photo: Charles Marden Fitch.

A courtyard pool in the Alhambra in Granada. Photo: Lynne Meyer.

tional image. Because the gardens of Granada are set on steep hillsides with open views out over the city and from different levels of perspective, the impressions they make are quite at odds with the more traditional Islamic garden layout, although the pervasive presence of water and the intimacy within the spaces does convey more than a hint of their earlier genealogy.

The Court of the Long Pond, or Patio de la Acequia, is the focal point of the Generalife's garden complex. The original level of the Arab parterres are now covered over with two or three feet of earth and have been restored with plants completely alien to the original scheme. The long canal in the quadripartite garden, however, still continues to proclaim in its form, the ancient genealogy.[17]

The Alhambra was first built as a royal residence by Mohammed ben Al-Ahmar in the mid-thirteenth century. Since it was also a for-

tress, the gardens were enclosed and hidden well within the high walls. The famous Patio de los Arrayanes, or Court of the Myrtles, built by Yusuf I in the mid-fourteenth century is a splendidly proportioned, sunlit space dominated by the long, dark pool of water in the middle. Only the anachronism of the clipped myrtle hedges strikes a discordant note in an otherwise perfect Islamic courtyard.

The floor of the equally celebrated Patio de los Leones, begun in 1377 by Mohammed V, has also been raised over the centuries so that the contrasting level between the parterres and the walkway are not as great as they once were or should be in a classic Islamic garden. This elevation of paths and walks is of particular importance to the Islamic garden, allowing the flowers, shrubs, and even trees to form a colorful carpet within the sunken spaces below the walks. Of all the Islamic garden courtyards in Spain, the Court of the Lions carries the strongest suggestion of a Christian cloister; even though its historic origins are Persian, a part of this impression is the result of later alterations. A marble fountain with its lion supports, dating from the eleventh century, rests in the center of the water channels, evoking both Christian and Islamic interpretations of the designs.

Nothing in the modern plantings of the restored gardens of Moorish Spain suggests the luxuriant variety of flowers and plants familiar to Islamic gardeners in the thirteenth and fourteenth centuries; all those nuances of color, texture, and season so important to a garden's imagery cannot be re-created. In matters of botanical research, we know from surviving documents, the Islamic world was far in advance of anything happening in Europe at the time. A Spanish Muslim of the eleventh century, Al Himyari, in his "Novelties in Description of the Spring," lists twenty of the commonest flowers from Muslim Europe, but the list compiled by John Harvey from other Arab catalogs, identifying flowers and plants that made both the color and smell of Islamic gardens in Spain the envy of the rest of the world, numbered nearly two hundred species that were under cultivation by the beginning of the twelfth century.[18]

Medieval Europe's early encounters with the Islamic gardens must have been puzzlingly familiar and at the same time strange and exotic. The high, enclosing wall so characteristic of the medieval castle gardens and the cloister of the monastery had its counterpart in the courtyards of Spain, Sicily, and in the Byzantine gardens of the Near East. The role of water in the fountain or well placed in the center of the garden and the space divided with channels or walks fit into the garden symbolism of both the Bible and the Koran, although the Koran is far more explicit in its appeal to the senses. Beneath these familiar garden elements lurked the mutual distrust and fear of nature shared by both Christians and Muslims. On the transcendental issue of the perils of nature, the two religions were united.

Where the Arabs were far more advanced over their European contemporaries was in the science and technology of gardening. The Arabs were nothing if not great technicians when it came to the mechanics of irrigation and the manipulation of water, for both practical purposes and for pleasure. The ubiquitous Islamic fountain basin and jet inspired extravagant descriptions by European visitors. The sensual play of water and the lush plants and flowers it produced through careful irrigation heightened the whole erotic character of Eastern gardens in ways unimagined by foreigners traveling from Northern Europe. Appropriately using secondhand descriptions of a twelfth-century Arab villa that once existed between Palermo and Monreale, in Islamic Sicily, Boccaccio (1313–1375) in 1342 trans-

Easily the most famous Arab garden to survive in Europe, the so-called Court of the Lions in the Alhambra is surrounded by a palace built to beautify the garden and not, as some have said, to serve as a Christian cloister. The fountain dates from the eleventh century. Photo: Author.

The Alhambra lions. Photo: Charles Marden Fitch.

OVERLEAF
Hundreds of private Moorish gardens made the old Arab city of Granada, seen below the walls of the Alhambra, one of the first garden cities of Europe in the eleventh and twelfth centuries. Urban life has spawned gardens throughout history. Photo: Ric Ergenbright.

Decorative tilework in the Alhambra in Granada. Photo: Jonas Lehrman.

A view of the Generalife
gardens in Granada.
Photo: Ric Ergenbright.

formed the villa into a setting for his great ro-mance, *L'Amorosa Visione*. "There was a splendid garden with all possible combina-tions of trees, and ever-flowing waters, and bushes of laurel and myrtle. From entrance to exit there ran a long colonnade with many vaulted pavilions for the king to take his plea-sure in. One of these is still to be seen. In the middle of the garden is a large fish-pond, built of freestone, and beside it a lofty castle of the king."[19] This description fits almost precisely the sultan's great garden with its ruined palace outside of Marrakesh in Morocco, where the tops of orange trees can still be seen growing

in a green carpet below the level of the stone walks dividing the garden.

In 1426 when the young Italian architect Leon Battista Alberti (1404–1472) visited Sicily, he saw in the ruined gardens of the Pal-azzo La Zisa (completed 1154–89), outside of Palermo, a small garden pavilion and Islamic pool that impressed him very much. Alberti also was impressed by the orange and lemon groves that surrounded the pool—exotic fruit that were in fact first imported into Europe by the Arabs. The Sicilian pleasure gardens and parks had been modeled on the oriental para-dise garden, and Alberti noted in particular

Even though the original thirteenth-century Arab garden was discovered beneath five centuries of debris, the present Generalife gardens in Granada, the Court of the Long Pond, Patio de la Acequia, is a modern surface planted with flowers unknown to the Moors. Photo: Jonas Lehrman.

The Patio de los Arrayanes, Court of the Myrtles, in the Alhambra, a nineteenth-century view by Isidore Taylor. Postcard.

the water and ornamental fountains, displays that had earlier charmed Count Robert II of Artois when he saw them on his return from the Crusades in 1270. When Artois returned to France, according to the historian Marguerite Charageat, he attempted to incorporate some of the Islamic water tricks and automata into his garden, the park of Hesdin. Enclosed in 1295, this fantastic garden briefly became a legend in Europe before it vanished without a trace. The series of water engines built at the pleasance at Hesdin may owe something to the Arabic *Book of Mechanical Devices* (1206) by Ibn al-Razzaz al-Jazari. The assumption is that the Arabic manuscript had been translated at the Castilian Spanish court and then had passed to France where French craftsmen built mechanical owls, surprise water jets, and other garden toys. Recent scholarship has argued that Northern European technology could have done the work at Hesdin without help from the infidel.[20]

The intellectual and cultural conquest the Persians had achieved over their Arab invaders was significant in the field of the sciences, for the Arabs were not a particularly cultivated race. Inspired and educated by their Persian advisors, translators working on early Greek texts were set up as an academy in the eighth century by Hārūn ar-Rashīd. The Arab translation of the Greek classic *De materia medica* of Dioscorides (c.40–c.90), for example, became the botanical bible throughout Islam and eventually reached European courts through

The vast garden reservoir of the Royal Park in Marrakesh. Photo: Author.

An interior courtyard at the Alhambra. Photo: Author.

Peacock Water Fountain, 1354, illustrated in the *Book of Mechanical Devices* by Ibn al-Razzaz al-Jazari. Museum of Fine Arts, Boston, Harvey E. Wetzel Fund.

combined with Byzantine examples seen by travelers and Crusaders, gradually penetrated northern Italy, where botanical research and plant cultivation had been far behind the Moorish and Islamic world. In 1333, the city of Venice gave official support to the laying out of a physic garden. Twenty-five years later an even more medicinal garden was established in the university town of Padua under the emperor Charles IV. Private herb gardens were beginning to be widely cultivated, and Petrarch laid out an herb garden, closely following classical texts, in 1348 before fleeing the plague in Parma that killed his beloved Laura. It was the same plague that Boccaccio's fugitives in the *Decameron* had fled from in Florence, escaping to the healthy air of a country villa. There the refugees enjoyed the villa garden:

> . . . around the edges and through the middle long arbors covered with vines . . . joined the other flowers in bloom to give off an exquisite scent. Roses both white and red and jasmine, clad the walks to keep off the sun. There is no need to mention the kinds of plants and their elegant arrangement, since all that will grow in our climate was there. . . . In the midst . . . was a meadow plot of green grass, powdered with a thousand flowers, set round with orange and cedar trees. . . . In the centre . . . from a fountain of white marble, exquisitely carved, a jet of water gushed . . . falling with a most delightful sound. . . .[22]

MUGHAL INDIA

The Mongols like the Arabs were nomads when they suddenly emerged from east of the Altai Mountains as a force to be reckoned with in the thirteenth century. Without traditions of religion, art, science, or anything that would pass for racial history to constitute a recognizable past, these Mongol invaders

Islamic scholars. At Montpellier, Arab physicians founded a medical school with a botanical garden in 1221, establishing a center for botanical research that later inspired Christians to follow the Muslim model. Moorish rulers had in fact maintained even earlier scientific botanical gardens at Seville and Toledo. "The comparative study of plants," as John Harvey in his exemplary work on the medieval garden has pointed out, "and the systematic introduction of exotic species with experiments in their cultivation," first began in Moorish gardens in Southern Europe.[21] By the thirteenth century, Ibn al-Baytār of Malaga, the leading botanist of his time, managed to include some fourteen thousand kinds of plants in his monumental *Pharmacopoeia*. Much of his research and identification was based on ancient Greek sources and plant lists.

The garden influence of Moorish Spain,

were little more than a drifting horde organized into a fighting machine that would ultimately overrun large parts of Central Asia. These were the ancestors of the great Mughal emperors of India who in the sixteenth and seventeenth centuries created some of the most magnificent gardens to be seen on earth.

When the raiding parties of Genghis Khan (c. 1162–1227) rode out of the east and reached Central Asia in what is now Afghanistan and Iran in 1218, systematic destruction of wells and irrigation was a part of their finely tuned devastation. The invaders' policy of vandalism reduced entire cities to archaeological ruins and the countryside to desert. Yet hardly more than a century or so later, their descendants, who had converted to Islam, had begun to absorb the superior learning and aristocratic culture of the Persians whom they had conquered. In a breathtaking rise to ascendancy, the successive waves of nomadic Mongol tribes began to establish vast royal encampments with open spaces for ritual and ceremony in imitation of their Persian enemies. Ralph Pinder-Wilson's recreation of the Garden of the Golden Horde, begun in 1302 near Tabriz in northwest Iran, gives us a fair picture of such a camp.

Preparation for festivities had begun three years previously by a large team of skilled craftsmen and engineers. A square area had been enclosed by a wall "in order to provide a pleasant and agreeable meadow for the sojourn of the emperor." Tanks and cisterns were installed to feed rivers and streams [watercourses], avenues were planted round the edge with willows to provide a passage for the populace who had to be confined to the periphery of the walled enclosure, the central area being reserved for the Golden Pavilion and the towers, booths and lofty buildings. This type of garden was evidently developed by the Mongols for a purpose peculiar to their own traditions and usages. The assumption of royal power required a garden setting for the nomadic encampment. . . . [23]

By the time that Timur (Tamerlane, 1336–1405) had established his capital at Samarkand (now in the USSR), there were beginnings of a fourfold (*chahar bagh*) garden encampment resembling garden forms of royal Mughal gardens that would later appear in India beginning with Humayun's tomb in Delhi in 1562. Some idea of royal camplife in a Timurid garden is captured in an early biography of Timur's son Shah Rokh who died in 1447.

In the royal garden were erected tents which had 80 to 100 poles, scarlet pavilions, and tents made of silk. In these tents were thrones of gold and silver, encircled by garlands of rubies and pearls. From the carpets issued vapors of amber, whilst the Durbar tent was perfumed with the soothing odor of musk. . . . Singers sang the melodious tunes, the songs formerly heard at the Court of the Sassanians. Skilled musicians touching deftly the lute and lyre ravished the reason of the listeners. The diversions were prolonged for many days without interruption. [24]

It would be the princely descendants of this fierce, restless race, now beginning to civilize themselves in a splendid Timurid garden, who would in the next century establish the glittering Mughal dynasty in India. The Golden Age of Mughal gardens (1526–1700), which began just as the Renaissance was reaching its highest moment in Italy, represents the work of six Imperial Mughal gardener-rulers.

The recurrent theme of an extravagant garden life as both symbolic and actual manifestations of power raises fascinating issues of social and cultural history that have been largely ignored. The ancient Greeks had first been astonished by the royal gardens and hunting parks they had seen in Asia Minor and in Persia itself. Alexander's invasion had opened all of Asia as far as India in one blow, and the marvels of high garden culture created by oriental princes immediately impressed him. The romantic Greek hero lost no time in

Brilliantly sited on Lake Dal outside Srinagar in Kashmir, Nishat Bagh dates from the first quarter of the seventeenth century. The series of terraces and the long water axis manage to bring the mountains down into the garden. The open, magnificent views, as in other gardens of the reign of Emperor Shāh Jahān, are dramatic, even though Nishat Bagh is not a royal garden. Photo: Lynne Meyer.

following the oriental model by conducting his court and military business in a theatrical outdoor setting recalling the ancient Persian *pairidaēza,* receiving his generals on a golden throne while they sat on silver stools surrounded by luxuriant plants and flowers. Later, Greek rulers would experiment with imported palm trees in Greece. Improved grains were brought from the Middle East, and in Egypt a Hellenic satrap commanded that quantities of fir trees, like the ones he had seen in Persia, be planted in his park because of the conifer's striking appearance in a desert setting.

Why have gardens in different societies and times been given a political role? For the intrepid oriental ruler always on the move, es-

tablished garden-camps scattered throughout his kingdom made convenient places for his vast traveling retinue to stop and rest. Court business could be conducted in an impressive outdoor setting and with plenty of military trappings in evidence as symbols of power to awe the populace. The enormous scale of Eastern parks, which served to establish territorial control, was also a fitting backdrop for assembling and reviewing entire armies in an impressive, organized fashion.

The great royal progresses that European rulers perfected in the sixteenth and seventeenth centuries were devised for the same purposes: as political propaganda to enhance the royal image symbolically over an extended kingdom. The progress was a traveling show that could be easily transported among the awed populace. Later, when the dramatic state entry into a city or province became too elaborate to be moved physically through narrow streets, it seemed inevitable that the whole performance could be better organized in a park or large outdoor public space. The professional designers, stage managers, hydraulic engineers, musicians, choreographers, and fireworks specialists could use the space to rehearse and mount their court spectacles. The legendary fetes in the garden and park of seventeenth-century Versailles can trace their origins to ancient oriental models, described first by the Greeks, which were adapted by the Romans and later by the papal court of the early Italian Renaissance.

A royal garden also served other purposes of the ruler. Through the exercise of royal power over resources and labor, the prince could create an idealized world of nature in which he would appear larger than life to the ordinary citizen. The very act of controlling and transforming nature into a perfect work of art—moving water, transporting trees, making a desert bloom—were all acts that carried an element of the miraculous and supernatural. The making of a royal garden as a kind of oasis carried with it a visible sign of divine connections and support. Within his garden the king could also display universally understood symbols of religion that further reinforced his own sacred being and reminded visitors of his divine genealogy. As James Wescoat has written, it was a "place where births were celebrated, wars were planned, and justice was meted out." [25] For Islamic potentates to build a garden paradise according to the command of the Koran and then to be able to exercise the earthly power of governing from it was the best of all possible worlds—where "the righteous . . . shall dwell in peace together amidst gardens and fountains, arrayed in rich silks," declared Mohammed's creed. Allah himself had provided all the materials of the garden: "vineyards and cornfields and groves of palm, the single and the clustered. Their fruits are nourished by the same water: yet we give each a different taste. Surely in this there are signs for me of understanding." [26]

The king's success in producing a magnificent, productive garden out of desert wasteland was living proof that he was acting as God's earthly representative and under his instructions. The curative plants and flowers he grew for medicinal purposes in his garden provided an obvious link between medical science and God's generosity and thoughtfulness in such mysterious details of his earthly kingdom.

There is yet one other connection between the garden and royal power, especially in the Orient. This has to do with control and manipulation of water in an arid landscape where power over this essential element—to hold it, to move it, to dispense it, or to withhold it—literally meant power over life itself. The hydraulic societies—Babylonia, Ancient Syria, Egypt, Persia—that perfected the technology of irrigation understood water's naked power over everyone dependent on it. The official bureaucracy that managed the irrigation ditches, water gates, reservoirs, and canals was the means of controlling vast hordes of people spread over an equally vast territory. Thus stark political power was covert in sparkling ornamental garden pools, fountains, and cascades—an aspect of the garden as a

Another terrace, one of twelve, at Nishat Bagh in Srinagar. This central canal, laid out c. 1620, is the main feature of the garden and parallels similar axes in Italian Renaissance gardens. Photo: Ric Ergenbright.

gesture of power that has remained carefully disguised down through the centuries. It remained for the revolutionary, nature-obsessed eighteenth century of the Enlightenment to begin to lift the veil on this well-kept secret expressed in hydraulic energy.

Ẓahīr-ud-Dīn Moḥammed Bābur (1483–1530) understood all about garden power when he swept into India to establish his new political centers at Delhi, Agra, and Lahore beginning in 1526. A descendant of Genghis Khan as well as Timur, Bābur was a poet and musician with the native instincts of a naturalist, all appropriate qualities for a good gardener. He also had an instinct for building and design and a taste for practical engineering, inspiring him to build new gardens or restore

Emperor Bābur's grandson Akbar commissioned a memoir of Bābur, illustrating in it the emperor's Bagh-i-Wafa, or Garden of Fidelity, near Kabul. This miniature presents an idealized image, but its emphasis on water may be more than poetically accurate. British Library.

OPPOSITE, ABOVE
The garden palace of Fatehpur Sikri is a series of buildings and paved spaces of striking red sandstone built by Akbar to honor the Sufi saint Salim Chisti in 1570. It remained the court's headquarters for a short fifteen years. Photo: Lynne Meyer.

OPPOSITE, BELOW
The white marble throne platform pavilion at Shalamar Bagh in Lahore, Pakistan, is in one of the best preserved gardens built by Shāh Jahān, in 1642. The plantings around the basins were of orange, apricot, peach, plum, and quince, along with many aromatic herbs and flowers. Photo: Lynne Meyer.

old ones wherever he went. He used his gardens for three simple activities: rest stops, landscape observations, and drinking parties.

"I laid out the Fourfold-gardens known as the Bagh-i-Wafa [Garden of Fidelity] on a rising ground, facing south and having the Surkhrud between it and Fort Adinapu," he recalled in his memoirs.

There orange, citrons and pomegranates grow in abundance. . . . I had plantains brought and planted there; they did very well. The year before I had sugar cane planted there; they did very well. The gar-

den lies high, has running-water close at hand, and a mild winter climate. In the middle of it, a one-mill stream flows constantly past the little hill, on which are four garden plots. In the South-West part of it there is a reservoir 10 by 10, round which are orange trees and a few pomegranates, the whole encircled by a trefoil-meadow. This is the best part of the garden, a most beautiful sight when the oranges take color. Truly that garden is admirably situated.[27]

Fifteen years later Bābur revisited the Garden of Fidelity to see "its pomegranate-trees yellowed to autumn splendor, their fruit full red; fruit on the orange-tree green and glad. . . ."[28]

Bābur was surprised to find that the Hindus seemed to have lost both their taste and skills for gardening. He was particularly struck by the lack of irrigation. "It always appears to me," he wrote, "that one of the chief defects of Hindustan is the want of artificial water-courses. I had intended, wherever I might fix my residence, to construct water-wheels, to produce an artificial stream, and to lay out an elegant and regularly planned pleasure-ground."[29]

He then went on to describe the steps he took to lay out the garden. Water delivered from a nearby river or lifted from a well was the key element. "First of all I began to sink the large well. . . . I next fell to work on the piece of ground on which are the Ambli [Indian tamarind trees] and the octagonal tank."[30] Building tanks or pools was the next priority. "We were annoyed with three things in Hindustan: one was its heat, another its strong winds, the third its dust." Baths, he concluded, "were the means of removing all three inconveniences." Bābur was pleased with the results of his work of having created gardens of "considerable regularity" out of the Hindus' shabby lack of order, finally planting "roses and narcissus regularly and in beds corresponding to each other."

It was left to Bābur's grandson Akbar

(1542–1605) to consolidate the Mughal Empire in India. Akbar continued the tradition of garden-builder, and his reconciliation of the Hindu rulers with the Mughal ascendancy produced a Mughal-Rajput style of architecture and garden design that completely superseded the old Persian style. In garden architecture and in the ornamental details using Hindu craftsmen, this collaboration was to be a major contribution to Mughal garden art in India. Akbar's son Jahāngīr (1569–1627) and grandson Shāh Jahān (1592–1666), both of whom inherited his dreams of power and wealth, continued the dynasty's passion for landscape design, gardening, and architecture. It was Shāh Jahān who completed the palaces in Delhi, Agra, and the Taj Mahal, all before Louis XIV as a young man would begin the major work on his father's old lodge and grounds in the family hunting preserve of Versailles outside Paris.

The geometric form of Mughal gardens symbolizes a divine unity and order between man and nature. Both are creations of God. The abstract, intellectual language of mathematics is reflected in God's formal design. Geometry, symmetry, form, proportion, and even surfaces are all united in the search for God's order of the universe. Whatever the sum of the constituent parts of the garden layout, the fundamental system of measure itself, using the finger, palm, foot, and cubit, is based on man. Spaces are defined and relate to the human body and human scale. It is this ancient formula inherited from Persia and Islam that prevailed and was further perfected under the direction of the Mughal princes. Speaking of the original site of the Garden of Fidelity near Kabul, Bābur in a revealing comment writes how he had found the natural winding stream running through the old garden: "Formerly its course was zig-zagged and irregular; I had it made straight and orderly; so the place became very beautiful." [31]

It is obvious when looking at the Mughal gardens in Kashmir or along the banks of the Jumna River that the controlled, predictable geometry was not meant to ignore or chal-

running streams and fountains beyond count. Whatever the eye reaches there are verdure and running water."[32] Unlike much of India where a stable supply of water required elaborate irrigation systems and other hydraulic technology, the Vale of Kashmir challenged gardeners to find new ways to exploit the aesthetic possibilities of water. Reservoirs, pools, waterfalls, canals, and fountains were used to the fullest. Later, an entire Lake is incorporated into the brilliant island garden of Amber at Jaipur.

For Mughal garden designers, the conquest of the Vale of Kashmir by Emperor Akbar was a major turning point. The emperor's journey itself was an epic worthy of the search for paradise, for the valley was entirely surrounded by mountains and reached by an 11,000-foot-high pass. When the emperor's entourage finally arrived, half of the fifty thousand troops and horses that made up the royal assembly were left at the mountain pass in order not to strain the valley's beautiful meadows and water supply. It was a gesture of environmental restraint and sensibility that appeals to our late twentieth-century concerns.

The name Shalamar Bagh, or Abode of Love, was given to three great Mughal gardens in Lahore, Delhi, and Kashmir on Lake Dal. The most celebrated is, of course, Shalamar on Lake Dal. First laid out by Emperor Jahāngīr in 1620 and enlarged by his son Shāh Jahān, Shalamar Bagh is a masterpiece of scale, proportion, and refinement.

The garden is connected to Lake Dal by a canal, and it is in a silently gliding boat like those used on the Lagoon of Venice that one should first enter Shalamar through its canal. Visitors entering the garden in the seventeenth century reached the presence of the emperor in the Hall of Public Audience, seated on a black throne set over a waterfall. This large pavilion is positioned on the long axial canal that divides the rectangular garden down the middle. Other small pavilions are positioned along the canal.

Beyond the Audience Pavilion the garden is

Garden pool at Achabal in Kashmir, near Srinagar, where an upper reservoir provides enough pressure to power fountains all through the garden. Photo: Ric Ergenbright.

lenge the larger, natural landscape. The subtle placing of platforms, the use of terraces, the positioning of pavilions to take advantage of sweeping views, and the long, open water channels were employed to take advantage of the surrounding environment beyond the garden itself.

The great Mughal gardens were built primarily either as settings for princely tombs or for pleasure and entertainment. It was for pleasure that the Mughal emperors built their gardens in the Vale of Kashmir where there was plenty of water, the ground was fertile, and the Himalayas protected the valley from the monsoons. Emperor Jahāngīr, with his practical gardener's eye, summed up its virtues: "Kashmir is a garden of eternal spring or an iron fort to a palace of kings—a delightful flowerbed and a heart-expanding heritage for dervishes. Its pleasant meads and enchanting cascades are beyond all description. There are

divided into two parts: one for the emperor's private use and, beyond, the *zenana* or ladies' garden. Each is square and approximately the same size. In the ladies' garden there is a stone cascade with rows of small niches where lamps could be placed to reflect through the thin sheets of falling water. The causeways of the cascade were built to allow the water to pour freely through them, creating an illusion of great depth although the water is actually quite shallow. Tall chenars and poplars shaded the open, grassy spaces, and it was here that members of the court could watch theatrical spectacles of music and dancing. As Susan Jel-

The great water basin at Shalamar Bagh, Lahore, Pakistan, with its white marble fountains around the edge and the pavilion to one side, evokes life in a fantasy garden called "Shalamar." Photo: Ric Ergenbright.

Another view of the water basin at Shalamar gardens. Photo: Ric Ergenbright.

licoe has remarked, even in the dry season of summer it requires "no great feat of imagination . . . to understand the emotions that inspired the inscription on [one of] the pavilions" at Shalamar: "If there is a paradise on the face of the earth, it is here, it is here, it is here."[33] These lines were apparently a favorite couplet from the Persian and also appear inscribed on the wall of the Hall of Private Audience at the Taj Mahal.

The garden of Shalamar Bagh at Lahore, now in Pakistan, has been extensively restored after major damage during the eighteenth century. It follows the traditional Mughal garden pattern, but its size and the extravagant use of water, particularly fountain jets in the reservoir, give it a splendidly noble quality. The walks and pavilions were once entirely covered with marble and agate, giving the garden the feeling of great luxury and elegance. Orange, apricot, peach, plum, quince, and other fruits were used in the rich plantings. The present buildings now stripped of much of their decoration and restored with brick and plaster give little hint of the original splendor of the place.

Mughal tomb gardens seem to have descended originally from ancient Mongol or Hindu traditions and mythology. Although Persian gardens did serve as burial places, so that the deceased symbolically entered into Paradise and at the same time could continue to enjoy his earthly garden, during the lifetime of the emperor or patron the unused tomb-pavilion served as a pleasure house where festivals and banquets were staged. When the pavilion ultimately became a tomb, the surrounding gardens and terraced platforms were opened to the public who wished to pay homage to the deceased. On the anniversary of the death of Mumtaz Mahal, Shāh Jahān's wife, and before her tomb, the Taj Mahal, was completed, an elaborate assembly "of public feeding and general dispersal of alms for the rest and repose, and the tranquility, gladness and exhilaration, of the Lady of ladies of the world and the Chief of all womankind in Paradise" was staged in the grounds and "courtyard" of the unfinished tomb.[34] Although not all pilgrimages were so festive, it is reported that when Jahāngīr visited his father's tomb and garden, royal ladies whirled in erotic dance formations around the mausoleum while holy men recited verses from the Koran, "singing and dancing and practicing ecstasies."[35]

The plan of Mughal tomb gardens, like the pleasure garden, followed the four-part *chahar bagh* pattern, with the tomb-pavilion usually placed in the center where the axial walks or channels intersected. Channels and pools radiated out in harmony with the architecture.

The Taj Mahal (built 1632–54) departs from this classic arrangement, and the tomb is placed at one end of the central axis so that it can be easily seen from the Jumna River below. Shāh Jahān designed the Taj Mahal, and the record is explicit: "For the majority of the buildings he himself draws the plans."[36] He, of course, worked with professional architects and engineers. It is astonishing that the emperor's team, under his supervision, completed the work in six years. The placing of the marble mausoleum to one side near the river, rather than at the center, follows the Islamic chronological diagram of the gardens of paradise on the Day of Resurrection. The garden plan thus becomes an allegory of the presumed celestial model. Persian couplets at the gateway into the garden read:

> These are the gardens of Eden,
> enter them to live forever!

The water channels, pools, and fountains are essential to the magic of the Taj. Indeed, the creative use of water throughout the history of Mughal gardens is the one animating element that saves their relentless geometry and bare expanses from sinking into a boring monotony, especially when there are no ladies whirling in ecstatic dance formations. This fascination with water and the pleasure of manipulating it seem to have been bred into the first Mughal emperors, as Bābur illustrates:

> One of the great defects of Hindustan being its lack of running waters, it kept coming to my mind that waters should be made to flow by means of wheels erected wherever I might settle down, also that grounds should be laid out in an orderly and symmetrical way. With this object in view, we crossed the Jun-water to look at a garden-grounds a few days after entering Agra. Those grounds were so bad and unattractive that we traversed them with a hundred disgusts and repulsions. So ugly and displeasing were they, that the idea of making a *Chahar bagh* in them passed my

Floral bouquets in mosaic on the walls of a Mughal garden pavilion. Photo: Author.

The architecture of the Taj Mahal in Agra, India, is so dominant that the garden complex is secondary even though it is larger than the area of St. Peter's in Rome. The romantic myth of a tomb in memory of a lost loved one has also obscured the historical significance of the grounds in Islamic garden art. W. E. Begley has at last clarified matters in his study *Taj Mahal, The Illumined Tomb*. Photo: Heather Angel.

Taj Mahal plan. The grand simplicity of the Taj Mahal garden makes it a classic of Mughal landscape design. The entrance pavilion (A) is directly opposite the white marble mausoleum (B) on its terrace. To the left and right are a mosque (C) and meetinghouse (D). In the center the raised tank (E) with its channels in four main directions divides the whole into the typical *chahar bagh,* recreating the ideal plan of Paradise. Jonas Lehrman, *Earthly Paradise.*

0 5 10 20   50   100m

mind, but needs must! As there was no land near Agra, that same ground was taken in hand a few days later.[37]

Water for the pools and fountains of the Taj, when it was built two hundred years later, posed certain engineering problems that were solved by lifting water in a system of buckets and storage tanks built on ascending levels. Since symmetry and scale must prevail down to such details as the height of the individual jets of the fountains of the Taj, an ingenious system was installed to equalize the water pressure and control the flow.

Aside from a powerful sense of composition and structure, the Mughal garden did contain a number of varieties of trees and flowers. These included exotics such as the poplar from Italy and the Oriental plane and chenar imported from Asia Minor.

The Earthly Paradise of literature has many botanical problems, including identification and nomenclature. Poetry and scripture do not lend themselves to scientific precision, and scholars of the Islamic and Mughal garden have had to be content with rather vague if elegant sources when it comes to identifying plant material. More often than not the garden described is mythological rather than an actual place, giving the enumerated trees and flowers a stereotyped quality.

It would be inaccurate and unfair to put into a footnote the great post-Mughal garden in New Delhi designed in 1917 by Edwin Lutyens (1869–1944) for the Viceregal Palace. The Viceregal garden brings the Mughal garden tradition into the twentieth century. Lutyens had studied the fourfold garden designs in Agra and Delhi, and those at Lahore and Kashmir before taking on the commission for the Viceregal Complex when the seat of government was transferred from Calcutta to Delhi. Earlier he had worked to revive an interest in water gardening in Great Britain.

Lutyens's garden uses water brilliantly at New Delhi to give theatrical unity to the Viceregal garden. The Rajpath, or ceremonial approach, is flanked by reflective canals lined with Ashoka trees. Circular fountains of sixteen-tiered lotus leaves fashioned from overlapping tiers of sandstone discs hold water jets that shoot up twelve feet above the sandstone petals. A 200-foot-square green island raised above the surrounding plane, as is the entire garden, made a perfect place to celebrate the sovereign's birthday and to hold other great receptions of state. Once again the subtle but effective display of political power

Emperor Humayun's tomb and garden, completed in 1573 by Humayun's senior begum, is the earliest Mughal garden to survive with little change. During the emperor's lifetime, it served as a setting for great entertainments and, like other royal tomb gardens, was the scene of lavish fetes on anniversaries. Water was supplied for the fountain by a reservoir built atop a false gateway in the north wall. Photo: Lynne Meyer.

is celebrated in a garden, an ancient tradition of the East that still functioned well into the twentieth century in New Delhi. "The formal palace edifice and its geometric garden, juxtaposed against the untamed Delhi Ridge, was meant," as Robert Irving has pointed out, "to be a telling affirmation of power and of the passionate British resolve to bring order to India—tangible proof, to use poet John Davidson's words, of the 'ruthless obligation . . . to be despotic for the world's behoof.' "[38] Cascades, grotto tanks, stairs, pergolas, and pools completed Lutyens's splendid scheme for the "world's behoof."

III. Labors in Perfection

ITALY

"Yesterday I came to my Villa of Careggi," Cosimo de' Medici (1389–1464) wrote to a young protégé in 1462, "not to cultivate my fields but my soul."[1] The banker's invitation to Marsilio Ficino (1443–1499) to visit him at Careggi included a reminder to bring his Orphean lyre and a copy of Plato. Clearly Cosimo's old castellated farmhouse, where he had camped every summer to oversee the farm work, was no longer regarded as simply a fortified dwelling, yet its rural, domestic quality, alive with country concerns, was a sympathetic setting for reading ancient literature. In many ways the Roman villa lived on in the medieval Tuscan farmhouse. The spirit of the place may still have been one of plain living, but there was also a new, elevated atmosphere of high thinking as well, which Cosimo wanted to share with Marsilio.

Cosimo's villa and garden had become a place for contemplation where the old humanist, nearing the end of his life, could sit on the new double loggia he had added and look out over the garden and the Tuscan countryside beyond. The small garden itself reflected the changing times as much as did the activities of the seigneur, whom we can imagine taking his ease on the loggia, reading Horace, listening to music on the lyre, or recalling earlier affairs of the heart in the Garden of Love. Among the flowers that grew at Careggi were a number that had been brought back during the Crusades. The splash of fountains added

more than a touch of Islam to the rustic farm and made a perfect background for the potted orange and lemon trees imported from Sicily or North Africa. Most of the garden was planted with bay, cypress, myrtle, box, and pomegranate, all with classical pedigrees out of Pliny's encyclopedia *Historia naturalis*.

Over the years Cosimo had consciously worked to model his life at the villa on Plato's Academy, a place where well-read friends could gather in his garden to pursue their study of ancient literature, learning, and history. When Cosimo died there in the summer of 1464, Careggi had become the intellectual center of the humanist movement of the early Renaissance.

At the heart of humanist ideals in fifteenth-century Italy was the hope of recapturing and reviving the spirit of the classical world, a rational world "of beauty allied to knowledge and the perfection of the human personality," in Georgina Masson's words.[2] Cosimo and his friends desired "nothing so much as to know the best road to happiness," and the road invariably led to a villa garden where one could read Plato in the cool shade. Ancient writers and poets impressed the Florentines with their love of nature and the garden, an ideal setting to discuss philosophy and to listen to music. With no more than scattered hints and references in Pliny, Cato, Varro, and Virgil, these Italian humanists constructed a concept of a garden they believed was Roman in design,

The gushing cascade of Garzoni's water staircase disappears in the bosquet behind the statue of Fame seen with raised trumpet. Photo: Heather Angel.

ornament, and simplicity. Most early Renaissance gardens, however, were modest, private affairs inspired more by vernacular garden traditions than by any fantasies of Rome. As Bartolomeo Pagello of Vicenza wrote in the middle of the century, he did not want his villa and garden to be as opulent as Pliny's, although he confessed a fondness for "apples, pears and pomegranates, damascene plums and generous vines; many plane trees near the house, clipped box and beautiful bays; and a fountain more clear than crystal, dedicated to the muses like the Castilian Spring at the foot of Parnassus." [3]

In this vibrant age of stimulating new literature, new ideas, and new art, gardens became the place to cultivate the art of love. Even though the association of the pleasures of love with the charms of a bucolic landscape goes back to the *Iliad* and the Song of Solomon, neither romantic love or garden-making for pleasure had fared well in the ascetic moralism of early Christian virtues. Both activities were reprehensible temptations along the torturous path to righteousness, if ever they were considered by the seriously faithful.

With the revival of interest in classical poets, the humanist could find in the late Latin poet Claudian (c. 370–c. 404) a legacy of romantic imagery—of bowers, fountains, groves, and sylvan landscapes—to open up the eye and fantasy of painters and poets who suddenly discovered the garden's erotic possibilities to tempt the senses. Who could resist Claudian's secluded shrine to Venus: "The enclosed land is bright with flowers, though the only gardener is Zephyr; no bird may enter its peaceful groves until the goddess herself approves the quality of its singing. Those which please her are admitted, the others leave. The very leaves on the trees live only for love and every tree comes to know the power of love."[4]

In the early part of the thirteenth century, provincial troubadours wandering around southern France had first begun to sing of courtly love in a modern garden—a secret place for anxious lovers, heady with luxuriant flowers, shade trees, fountains, and well-trained birds that Venus would have approved of. Sorrow as well as love is mixed in Petrarch's (1304–1374) landscapes "warmed by the sun or watered by the sea; and hidden in the midst of a shadowy hill with fragrances so sweet and streams so clear. . . ."[5] The allegorical tale of Provence, *The Romance of the Rose,* composed by Guillaume de Lorris around 1240, was widely read in Italian circles, and its imagery had affected Boccaccio. Members of the idle house party in his *Decameron* sing, dance, dally, and picnic by garden fountains while reading "lines from the Romans" in the afternoon. "Whoever truly perceives must become sad, and his heart embittered on leaving that gracious place. There beauty, nobility

and worth, charming words, the very model of virtue, and the highest happiness dwell with love; there a desire impelling man to his salvation, there so much of good and of delight as many could ever have; there fulfilled are worldly dreams, and their sweetness is seen, and felt."[6]

A rather surreal picture of garden life in fifteenth-century Italy is portrayed in a curious allegorical romance written about 1499 by Francis Colonna, *Hypnerotomachia poliphili,* or as the English version mislabeled it, *Love's Struggle in a Dream.* What the book really is about is Colonna's fantastic theories of architecture, and gardens in particular. In his descriptions and in the illustrations there are all manner of garden ornaments, garden views, and even designs for parterres. Classical motifs are used with refreshing bravura, unrestrained by any depth of serious understanding of the vocabulary of classical architecture. It is likely that Colonna's allegory is based on actual gardens existing in his day and is more instructive in historical details

The woodcuts of the French edition (1486) of Pietro de Crescenzi's international garden tome, *The Patrician Garden,* are justly famed for their strong composition but only hint at the realities of medieval Italian gardening routines. The tree to the left of the house has a seat of wattle to protect its base from animals. Library of Congress, Lessing J. Rosenwald Collection.

than its imaginative woodcuts might first convey.

The other garden book the early Italian Renaissance knew well was Pietro de' Crescenzi's *Liber ruralium commodorum,* which as we saw in Chapter 2 was particularly effective in advancing the notion that pleasure gardens had a special role to play in the life of the rich and powerful. Dedicated to Charles II of Anjou, king of Naples and Sicily, the work eventually reached France, England, and Germany in a number of translated editions, giving it widespread influence.

By the end of the fifteenth century the reputation of the Italian garden carried a sensual impact of extraordinary potency. With the colors of its flowers, the perfumed scents, the sounds of birds and fountains, and enlivened with flirtation and feasting, it evoked the heavenly Paradise promised in the Koran more strongly than did the Christian gardens of the cloister and abbey. "As part of its ability to play with the human senses," Eugenio Battisti has written, "the Renaissance garden is an intriguing conceptual system."

> The garden is a place of pleasure, the *locus amoenus,* filled with joy, but it resounds in love, laments of poets; it is a refuge for private meditation; it is a place for feasts, entertainment for friends, a place according to Boccaccio, of sexual and intellectual freedom, a setting for philosophical discussions, and a restorative for both the body and the soul. It is a measured and well-ordered model of the universe, an experiment in immortality, a never-ending apparition of spring. It assumes the function of a sculpture gallery, a *pinacotheca,* a horticultural encyclopedia *in vivo,* a center of botanical and medical research, and a theater for fantastic imitation. . . . Finally it is a perpetual source of moral instruction.[7]

Unlike the ruins of Roman architecture littering the Italian countryside, which invited Renaissance scholars and architects to attempt

to reconstruct their original appearance, vestiges of the classical garden had utterly disappeared. This meant that the new garden was based entirely on antique literary fragments rather than any physical evidence. While architects adhered to mathematical discipline, proportion, and harmonic simplicity in their art, the possibilities of an ordered landscape left enormous scope for the garden-maker's historical imagination. Nothing remotely resembling the romantic building fragments available to architects like Filippo Brunelleschi (1377–1446), who carefully studied the ruins of Rome, existed for the quattrocento garden designer or patron. "First of all, through the study and diligence of Filippo Brunelleschi," wrote the architect-historian Giorgio Vasari (1511–1574) in his *Life,* "architecture, rediscovered the proportions and measurements of the antique, applying themes in round columns, flattened pilasters or rusticated projections" and then translated them into "correct architectural projections."[8] Using the same mathematical formulas and a few literary hints, Renaissance gardeners had to flesh out their gardens with a few pieces of antique sculpture and a vernacular horticultural tradition to give the garden verisimilitude.

Not only have most of these early humanist gardens themselves disappeared, but in the desolate urban landscape of the late twentieth century it seems impossible even to recapture or recreate the mood of such an environment in our mind's eye. Our own contemporary alienation from nature is so overwhelming that the enchantment conveyed by the descriptions of the period are quite literally unbelievable.

While men of Cosimo de' Medici's day understood and coped with the unhealthy urban conditions of cities much as the earlier Romans had, they understood that the center of their business and community life was primarily in the city. Their country life in villas and gardens was a temporary but necessary relief that made it possible to function in the city. Florentine humanists were quick to find precedents in classical literature where similar

Roman preoccupations grew out of familiar urban tensions. The resolution of those tensions utilized the same rural elements of farming, husbandry, and plant cultivation that had continued in its primitive way for millennia without much change due to the vagaries of empire.

By the beginning of the sixteenth century the Tuscan countryside and the rich farmland of the Veneto were scattered with comfortable rural retreats in easy reach of the nearby urban centers of Florence, Siena, Milan, and Venice. These villas were not simply privileged refuges from the confusions of the city, though; they were first of all linked directly to the management of productive, seasonal agricultural centers. Only later did they harden into centers of pomp and ceremony as a background of luxury quite alien to the rural life around them and in which they had their historic roots. As Cataneo wrote in his contemporary treatise on architecture: "It is customary in many provinces but more than any other in Tuscany, as at Rome, Siena, Florence, Lucca, and many other places for the merchants as well as various lords and gentlemen to seek relaxation at their estates or villas, a location of particular salubrity, beauty and charm than all others so as to take the air during spring, autumn, and sometimes in summer."[9]

When Lorenzo de' Medici (1449–1492) decided to build his villa at Poggio a Caiano (c.1480), it was partly to be able to supervise the cheese- and wine-making of the estate and partly to enjoy the open, intoxicating Tuscan countryside, an easy ride north of Florence. Giuliano da Sangallo (1445–1516) was his architect, and in his siting of the villa he could survey not only the garden terraces and vineyards but also the larger landscape. Sangallo no doubt was following Leon Battisti Alber-

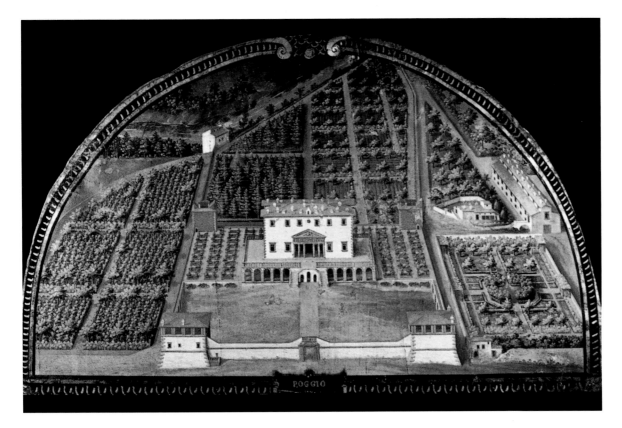

In this famous lunette in the Museo Topografico, Florence, Lorenzo de' Medici's villa of Poggio a Caiano appears to be surrounded on three sides by gardens or vineyards. The rectangular walled space at the lower right is exclusively ornamental and can be viewed from the upper terraces and principal rooms of the villa.

ti's recommendations in his treatise *De re aedificatoria* (1452). Alberti's formula was to place the country house in accordance with nature's laws of light, air, and temperature in order to enjoy the inherent pleasures in all of nature's works. Throughout his book, Alberti quoted "the ancients," who were in fact the source for many of his dicta. The villa, he wrote, should be placed on a hill for both the views "that overlook the city, the owner's land, the sea or a great plain and familiar hills and mountains. . . . In the foreground there should be the delicacy of garden."[10] All this recalls Pliny's Laurentian Villa and particularly the carefully integrated relationships between architecture, the garden, and the site. Many of Alberti's recommendations on garden design, while aspiring to the latest humanist quattrocento ideals, are probably closer in detail to the world of ancient Rome than those of his contemporary gardening friends in Tuscany. Yet the villa life of Lorenzo de' Medici, Michele Verino, and other villa owners was not that far removed from first- or second-century Rome in its everyday routines. Here is Verino's account of his daily schedule in the country villa at Lecore in the late 1400s.

> I rise early, go for a walk in my long dressing gown in a little garden, where, recreated by the fresh breeze in the morning I retire to my little study, glance through some poetry, study the precepts of Quintilian, read not without amazement the orations of Cicero. I take pleasure in the letters of Pliny. . . . After lunch I sleep a little . . . and after I sleep I enjoy myself at checkers, or at the royal board. Near the villa is quite a big vineyard with many fruits, in the middle of which runs a river of freshest water. The quantity of little fish is most great, the hedges thick and the nightingales, day and night languish with the song of ancient offenses. In this place I read a little something and then with my lute sing improvised and sometimes prepared verses. When the sun declines, I exercise with the ball. In like manner I spend

the summer, as long as the spread of the diseases in the city does not stop.[11]

Aeneas Silvius Piccolomini (1405–1464), who became Pope Pius II in 1458, was a friend of Alberti and shared the architect's interest in classical archaeology. He was also among the first antiquarians to inspect the remains of Hadrian's Villa at Tivoli. After he was elected pope, Pius decided to rebuild his village birthplace, Corsignano, as a model town, renaming it Pienza· in honor of his family. The Piccolomini Palace's splendid triple loggia, looking out over a small garden and the breathtaking Val d'Orica beyond, still manages to capture the feeling of discovery the early Renaissance expressed in its appreciation of beautiful, natural settings, as Europe gradually moved out from behind thick battlements and fortified houses. The garden is hardly more than a small, elegant, outdoor room, an extension of the lower loggia, but its intimate scale seems right in contrast to the expansive landscape framed through the openings on axis with the garden walks. These views spaced along the outside wall work very much like a series of landscape paintings hung at regular intervals.

At about the time Lorenzo de' Medici and the Piccolomini pope were building their retreats, Alfonso II (1448–1494), then Duke of Calabria, began his pleasure villa Poggio Reale on the edge of Naples, completing it in time for the festivities of his daughter's wedding in the summer of 1489. Ten years before, Alfonso had defeated Lorenzo in battle, and the Florentine was forced to travel to Naples to negotiate a truce. The two men became friends, and in the best tradition of the humanists, Alfonso's former enemy was asked to serve as his artistic advisor on the villa and gardens. Lorenzo introduced his architect, Sangallo, to Alfonso, and he participated in the design of the Neapolitan villa.

Among Italian villas of the fifteenth century, Poggio Reale was built purely for the entertainment and pleasure of a prince and his

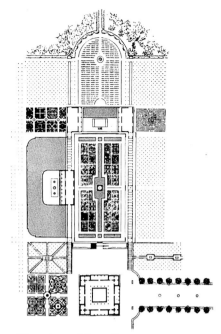

The plan of the villa Poggio Reale near Naples, summer residence of Alfonso, Crown Prince of Naples, which was created exclusively for court entertainments. Its open setting above the Bay of Naples made a deep impression on French visitors. Studio di ricostruzione di Anna Calcagno.

OPPOSITE
The triple loggia of the Palazzo Piccolomini in Pienza, Tuscany, looks out over the small garden and into the Val d'Orica with humanist appreciation. It celebrates the deep love of landscape of the humanist Piccolomini pope, Pius II, who received ambassadors in his garden at the Vatican and even held a consistory in the open air. Photo: Everett Scott.

This late-sixteenth-century fresco in the Villa Chiericat at Pozzoserrato shows a villa garden that may not be completely idealized in its classical symmetry. Photo: Author.

Bird's-eye-view engraving of the influential Belvedere Court at the Vatican, designed by Bramante after 1503. Photo: Author.

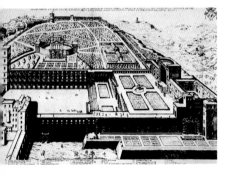

nation broke new ground in its exploration of the theatrical possibilities of the views and topography. When Charles VIII (1470–1498) first saw the villa in 1495, the French king's own dark, fortified castles of Amboise and Blois must suddenly have seemed quite primitive by comparison. He immediately wrote his brother-in-law to report his envy and astonishment. Charles's encounter, and the skilled Italian gardeners and artisans the king took back north to the Loire, would give French landscape design a significant link with Italian precedent.

The most revolutionary step in landscape architecture of the Italian Renaissance was taken by Donato Bramante (1444–1514) when he designed the monumental Belvedere Court at the Vatican commissioned in 1503 by Pope Julius II. Bramante landscaped with drama in mind and followed theatrical design principles. The new court, which linked the existing palace of the Vatican with the old Villa Belvedere on the hill above, measured three hundred by one hundred meters. The sloping ground was divided into three parts, with the palace and villa at opposite ends of the vast, rectangular space. Pageants and spectacles were presented in the arena space at the lowest level. The middle terrace provided a viewing platform overlooking the arena. The upper area was laid out as a formal garden, climaxed by a semicircular niche on an axis with the papal apartments in the palace at the opposite end of the courtyard. This upper terrace garden, decorated with newly discovered antique sculpture, also served as a sculpture museum. In their study on *Taste and the Antique,* Francis Haskell and Nicholas Penny have vividly recreated the Belvedere's sculpture garden in their description.

As he entered the court, the sixteenth century visitor would have seen first the rows of orange trees symmetrically placed on the paving stones which covered the enclosed space. Opposite him was a loggia, at one end of which was a fountain to water the oranges, and, outside the court itself

court, and this links it with later royal pleasances. The two Trianons at Versailles and the Amalienburg at the Nymphenburg Palace at Munich are among its most famous descendants. Poggio Reale was an idealized structure and garden built for no particular function other than its own splendor. Placed above the Bay of Naples on the hillside, its terraced gardens commanded both views of the sea below and Vesuvius behind it. Drawing on inspiration from classical sources, Alfonso's imagi-

The ruins of the Roman emperor Hadrian's villa garden were still imposing in the early decades of the Renaissance, especially as a source for antique sculpture to decorate newly laid out gardens. Photo: Everett Scott.

but well visible from it, there towered above this loggia the tall mulberries and cypress which grew in an informal garden behind. . . . In the center of the court were two huge reclining marble figures of the *Tiber* and the *Nile,* each mounted on a fountain—and still more fountains were placed elsewhere. It was in this cool, fresh and orange-scented atmosphere that the visitor was able to see the great sculptures that were placed in elaborately painted and decorated niches (*Cappelette*) at four corners of the court and in the center of each enclosing wall; around and set into these walls, level with the upper part of the niches, were thirteen antique masks.[12]

So in addition to the international acclaim and influence of Bramante's bold outdoor theatre, was the far-reaching impact of his equally revolutionary dramatic use of antique sculpture in a garden setting. Among the works in the garden collection were the *Apollo,* the *Laocoön, Commodus as Hercules,* the *Hercules and Antaeus,* the *Cleopatra,* the *Venus Felix,* and the *Tiber.* This collection of classical antiquities placed in the garden among orange trees and fountains became an aesthetic yardstick of the arts for more than three hundred years throughout Europe. Among the arts was, of course, gardening, now calling for the recreation of an idealized, classical landscape populated with appropriate gods and goddesses. The Belvedere's sculpture collection would be an important source for the garden pantheon.

Bramante was no doubt stimulated by Hadrian's Villa and other ancient ruins in and around Rome where fragments of classical sculpture were beginning to turn up. The scale of some of the pieces uncovered, as well as the sheer quantity of marble ensembles, de-

The great fountain basin at Villa d'Este was in fact the first artificial cascade in a European garden. Through engravings and travel accounts, the Villa d'Este became the most influential Italian garden of the age. Photo: Felice Frankel.

manded outdoor garden installations even without archaeological evidence that suggested an antique precedent for garden sculpture. After François I (1494–1597) imported quantities of original pieces and copies to Fontainebleau, other ambitious potentates were fast to follow his lead. Courts throughout Europe ordered cartloads of replicas of Roman sculpture to decorate their palaces, villas, and gardens until the fashion finally subsided in the middle of the nineteenth century. Before it was finished, Venus, Apollo, and other deities were even cast in industrial iron.

While the present condition of the Villa d'Este, with its romantic, overgrown slopes and decaying stone ornaments, scarcely suggests its original sixteenth-century grandeur, its continuing influence over the centuries can hardly be overestimated. Begun in 1550 by Cardinal Ippolito II d'Este (1509–1572) on the edge of the hill town of Tivoli overlooking the

Campagna, it was immediately on everybody's itinerary as a four-star tourist attraction. The spectacular water displays in the fountains and cascades and a sensational hydraulically operated organ were internationally famous. Two centuries later when the gardens had succumbed to nature and were overgrown and decrepit, French artists like Fragonard and Hubert Robert haunted its romantically shadowed avenues.

The cardinal's palace was at the summit of the steep hill, and from its terraces Claudian views stretched away in the golden mist to the dim outline of Rome itself floating in the distance. "The whole complex of its landscape," Goethe wrote to friends in 1787 on his second Roman visit, "with its details, its views, its waterfalls, is one of the experiences which permanently enrich one's life."[13] The original site of Villa d'Este was irregular and must have been quite unpromising before its elaborate transformation. A strong, central axis runs through several levels, imposing a firm unity before reaching the dramatic Fountain of the Dragons below the central terrace. The fountain is encircled by two curving staircases whose balustrades support a narrow stream of water channeled into the handrail.

Like the nearby villa of Hadrian, water in every conceivable manifestation is a primary element of the d'Este garden. And as Eleanor Clark has observed, this elaborate use of water helps us to get some notion of its extravagant deployment earlier by Imperial Rome.

A long curving staircase in the garden of the Villa d'Este has two streams running down its side walls, falling through a succession of cockleshell basins to disap-

This elegant marble basin now on the upper terrace of Villa d'Este was removed from the garden ruins of the nearby villa of Roman emperor Hadrian. Photo: Everett Scott.

pear at the bottom in a pair of those funny, tortured heads typical of fountains of the time—the only use ever found in Italy for the tragic muse. The delight of it is beyond design; you have dreamed exactly that, or should have: to walk in stateliness down garden stairs whose banisters were running water.[14]

The secret to the Villa d'Este's endless water supply was an aqueduct from Monte Sant' Angelo and a conduit that diverted the water of the River Aniene. The waterworks were completed by 1565 and were capable of delivering an astounding twelve hundred liters a minute to the garden's fountains. The manipulation of falling, gurgling, splashing, dripping, plopping water to produce all kinds of sounds made the garden a veritable aquatic orchestra. But the visual displays of fountains, cascades, and streams throwing off mists in the sunlight are also unforgettable. According to Montaigne's journal entry of April 3, 1581, one group of fountains made a "thick and continuous rain . . . falls into the pond, and in the air, and all around the place a rainbow so natural and distinct that in no way falls short of what we see in the sky."[15]

LEFT
A fountain originally at Hadrian's Villa, now at Villa d'Este. Photo: Everett Scott.

Now a ruin, the Villa Madama was built in Rome between 1516 and 1520 from designs by Raphael, Antonio Sangallo the Younger, and Giulio Romano. The spectacular siting and monumentality of the structure had an important influence on later Roman villas and gardens. Photo: Everett Scott.

The ruins of Hadrian's Villa nearby provided the cardinal with a convenient source of antique sculpture to decorate his garden in an elaborate iconographical program laid out by architect Pirro Ligorio. Since most of the sculpture is now missing, the best guide to the decorative program is David Coffin's excellent reconstruction in *The Villa d'Este at Tivoli.*[16]

A half-century before Cardinal d'Este began his country estate at Tivoli, Cardinal Giulio de' Medici (afterward Pope Clement VII) had commissioned the first great Renaissance villa on the outskirts of Rome, the Villa Madama (built 1516–20). The Roman grandeur evoked by Raphael (1483–1520) and Antonio Sangallo the Younger (1483–1546) for the Medici cardinal was inspired by a close but imaginative reading of Pliny's letters describing his own seaside retreat. Although the complex was never completed and was burned in the sack of Rome in 1527, its brilliant handling of large-scale integration of architecture and site ranks with the Belvedere courtyard. Raphael followed Vitruvius, the first-century B.C. authority on classical architecture, and Alberti in carefully choosing the hillside for the views but also to catch the pre-

vailing winds and the direction of the sunlight both for the rooms and for the garden. Raphael adopted the Roman concept of relating the architecture to the gardens in a series of open courts and loggias. Provision for both summer and winter quarters within the villa and the incorporation of a hippodrome and an open amphitheater carved into the hillside were also directly inspired by classical texts. As at Hadrian's Villa there were many fountains but none more poetic than the one placed in a secluded woodland some distance from the formal terraces. "It was surrounded by a wood," Vasari recalls, ". . . and was made to fall with fine artifice over rough stones and stalactites dripping and gushing so that it really appeared to be natural. . . . It is impossible to imagine the grace of that wild fountain."[17]

Given the growing power (and vanity) of the papacy, not all Renaissance villas and their gardens served Alberti's rural ideal of a "retreat near the town where a man is at liberty to do just what he pleases." The Villa Madama and other Roman villas that followed in the sixteenth century were clearly intended as a backdrop for the higher rituals of state in the middle of the metropolis, requiring the utmost theatricality and grandeur.

Already by the fifteenth century, the whole ritual of the ceremonial entry into Rome by foreign rulers, special embassies, and foreign representatives had evolved into its own art form of pomp and civic display. When a guest of honor neared the Holy City, he would send word ahead to announce his approach so that the state receptions and ceremonies would be ready when he arrived at the gates. Just outside the city itself the entourage would stop and spend the night, rehearsing the magnificently staged ceremonial entry and parade for the following day.

Most visitors approached from the north by the Porta del Popolo or by one of the gates nearer the Vatican. The Villa Madama served for a time as the official stopover for the first stage of entry, but in 1551 Pope Julius III began construction of the Villa Giulia as an official guest house. Vasari was the architect in charge, and he was assisted by Giacomo da Vignola (1507–1573) in working out the elaborate water system for the gardens and fountains.

The design of the Villa Giulia is organized by what appears to be a strong, driving central axis. But for visitors who try to follow it from the entrance through the great courtyard once decorated with a porphyry basin taken from the Baths of Titus, there are a series of surprises and hidden digressions. After reaching the Nymphaeum, one is forced to proceed down to its lowest level before finding hidden stairs that lead up to a terrace, there to discover a private, enclosed *giardino segreto* as the final reward of the exploration. The various stages reached in the progression through the Villa Giulia's gardens feel almost like stations of a ritual initiation into some mysterious cult or fraternity. The music of Mozart's *Magic Flute* seems quite appropriate in the place, the loggia of the nymphaeum serving as a perfect setting for the aria of the Queen of the Night. When Pope Julius died in 1555, sixty boatloads of sculpture were removed from the villa and floated down the Tiber to join the

The giardino segreto of the Villa Giulia in Rome. Photo: Everett Scott.

Vatican's collection of antiquities.

It is interesting to consider why the medieval secret garden survived into the radically different garden complex of the Renaissance. We find *giardini segreti* not only in the Villa Giulia and the Villa Medici at Fiesole but at Caprarola, the Villa Lante, and on a much enlarged scale at the Villa Gamberaia dating from the eighteenth century. It is easy to see the importance of these relatively small garden rooms, accessible but secluded from the big, public, and often overwhelming spaces that are quite desolate when not filled with milling, costumed courtiers. In its early medieval form, the *hortus conclusus* could be secular or ecclesiastical and inevitably contained a fountain, rose parterres, arbors, and turf seats along the walls, at least in surviving prints and paintings. In the Renaissance the secret garden had lost its religious symbolism associated with the Virgin Mary and functioned chiefly for private pleasure and intimate entertainments.

Just as the intricate spatial organization of the Villa Giulia relieved the otherwise static form of the Renaissance garden, the Villa Lante also brilliantly orchestrated the axial

LEFT
The nymphaeum of the Villa Giulia in Rome. Photo: Everett Scott.

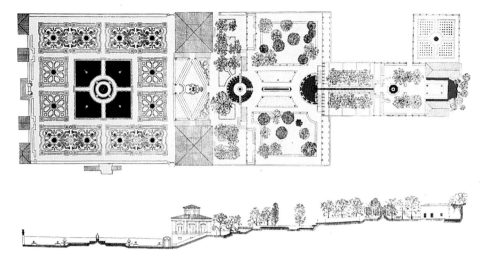

Plan and elevation of the Villa Lante in Bagnaia. The two villa buildings to the right of the elaborate twelve parterres at the left are completely integrated into the composition. Francesco Fariello, *Architettura dei Giardini*.

layout for maximum effect. The Italian terrain, especially around Florence and Rome itself, with its steep hills, narrow valleys, and sweeping campagna also inspired Renaissance designers to use descending terraces, stairs, and moving water to animate rather predictable garden spaces.

The Villa Lante at Bagnaia, not far from Viterbo, was begun in 1566 as a summer retreat for Cardinal Gambara, who was related to the Farnese family. Vignola's two villa pavilions placed side by side on the lowest level of the space are transformed by the scale and development of the garden into two great garden decorations complementing the overall design. The two buildings also allow the central axis, composed of water, to descend between them from the thick, mysterious woods at the top of the hill as a kind of formal ablution.

Symmetry is found here for the first time to be a garden's dominant theme, anticipating the gardens of Versailles by a hundred years. Beginning with the fountain called the "Deluge" at the top of the hill, the central axis of water flows down the water staircase then into more fountains and basins before making its final plunge into the grand water parterre at the foot of the slope. Intended to cool the cardinal's wine, a small stream of water is diverted into a narrow six-inch channel cut into

the top of a long marble table set on the garden's axial alignment at the middle terrace. It is only one more civilizing touch of garden life in one of the most supremely civilized creations in the world. The cardinal may well have gotten the irresistible idea from Pliny's description of a similar table where the dinner dishes floated by on a miniature canal in front of his elegant guests.

In contrast to the highly organized, formal part of the Lante garden, a romantic, irregular woodland or hunting park with long, diagonal avenues was laid out on the rough hillside beyond the walks of the formal part of the garden space. Fountains were scattered through these woods, allowing the poetry of the Renaissance garden to actually penetrate and make contact with the natural wilderness.

Throughout the evolution of the Italian garden in the fifteenth and sixteenth centuries, garden-makers seemed to be responding to the complex and changing demands of an essentially urban society. The Medici in Florence were reacting as much to the unhealthy atmosphere of the city when they built their country villas and gardens as they were recalling with metaphysical nostalgia a vanished Golden Age. The Villa Madama and the Villa Giulia created an artificial, ideal world to entertain and impress visiting potentates before they were confronted with the narrow, rough, and less-than-ideal streets of urban Rome. Although on a different scale, the Villa Lante itself fits into and is linked to the larger urban setting of the adjacent town of Bagnaia, where the villa's water system ultimately feeds the town's fountains. As a pleasance, Lante was also a rural park for a busy cardinal who spent most of his time at papal court in Rome.

The villa architecture and gardens of the Veneto in the sixteenth century followed much the same basic pattern of self-contained country retreats removed from the tumult of the city. The Palladian villas that so impressed the English visitors often had large, well-organized gardens closely integrated with the proportions and lines of the architecture. The restrained, balanced symmetry of these gar-

The cascade of the Villa Lante, from the top. Photo: Everett Scott.

Water from the cascade at Villa Lante flows through this stone table to cool wine for banquets before continuing its course through the garden and into the village of Bagnaia outside the villa gates. Photo: Everett Scott.

The Boboli Gardens in Florence is the most famous of all the gardens of the Medici family, which extended its garden-making into France through the French Medici queens Catherine at the Tuileries and Marie at the Luxembourg Palace. La Grotta Grande is the most fantastic surviving grotto of the period. Photo: Author.

den compositions confirms the universal appeal they enjoyed. Their open, serene spaces bathed in sunlight seem calculated to challenge the memory of dark streets and cramped passages of Venice not far away.

Fountains and water displays in the Italian garden can be traced to Islam and the Byzantine Empire. Beginning in the Middle Ages, European travelers ventured into Islamic centers in southern Spain, North Africa, and even into the caliphate courts of Baghdad. Some adventurers reached Samarkand, Bokhara, and western parts of India. By the fifteenth century, accounts of exotic Islamic gardens and their fountains were widely circulated in Italy.

One of the first fountain designs to be appropriated from the East has been identified in Filarete's *Tratatto d'architettura,* written in the 1460s. In it the author describes a fantastic fountain in the form of a bronze tree inspired by a similar automation that actually had existed at the Byzantine court in Constantinople.

In the middle he wanted there to be a fountain, part of marble and part of bronze,

alongside the oaks. In it would be kept the oak with the eagle above. This was [to be] the shaft in the center of the fountain. It was of bronze, made like an oak with the starlings arranged in such a manner that they poured water from their mouths. The eagle's nest was like a vase. In the middle of it there was the figure of the eagle with its water supply and arranged in such a way that water issued from the vases and the branches.[18]

An elegant bronze and gilt descendant of this tree-fountain appeared briefly in the bosquet de Marais at Versailles in 1676 when it was commissioned by the king's mistress Madame de Montespan.

The play of light on water, in fountain jets, sprays, cascades, runnels, or on the still, mirrored surface of a pool is the very stuff of illusion. Moving water, as Dame Sylvia Crowe has pointed out, is the only element in a garden besides birds, people, and an occasional breeze to give it animation, to bring it alive. The exuberant spirit of the Italian response to water's possibilities in every imaginable form is an important legacy from the Italian Renaissance. To the same extent that earlier reports of water tricks in Constantinople had stirred the Italian imagination and curiosity, the voluptuous pleasure of manipulated water in Italian gardens had enthralled the rest of Europe by the end of the sixteenth century. Italian hydraulic engines were in demand all over Northern Europe.

With the discoveries of Galileo, Kepler, and Newton, powerful intellectual and scientific changes rocked the very foundation of religious and philosophical beliefs in the sixteenth century and affected all the arts, landscape art included. Out of the finite, predictable, ordered world dominated by Renaissance ratio and proportion, the Baroque Age ushered in the uncertainties of the infinite. Contrived spatial distortions in architecture and garden were inevitable. "The expression of the finite is factual," Geoffrey and Susan Jellicoe have written, but "that of the infinite can only be imaginative. The mind and not the eye takes charge, and it was on the creation of the imaginative space and movement that Baroque Art depended."[19] Following the revolutionary changes in church and theater design that exploited the advanced theories of perspective, landscape art in Italy embraced these dynamic new sources of creative energy to transform outdoor spaces. In the architecture of the new town plans, "the parts were in constant and imaginative movement symbolized by curve chasing curve." Garden layouts also suddenly expressed an uneasy "awareness that man was now only a part of a swirling complex that embraced rocks and water as well as the heavens."[20]

The urge to escape the old, predictable geometry was breathtaking, as princely gardens were given over to an unfolding drama of artificial boulders, grottoes, secret fountains, and towering giants. Entire courtyards, as in the Boboli Gardens in Florence, could be turned into an artificial sea where fantastic boats, sea monsters, and barges were propelled in an aquatic choreography. Ambiguity, tension, and fear were the new emotions expected in the grotto at the Boboli Gardens, in Vincino Orsini's (c.1513–1584) fantastic park at Bomarzo with its colossal monsters, or in front of the sumptuous water contortions at the Villa Aldobrandini and Villa Garzoni.

The grotto, although the form has its origins in antiquity, is a quintessential Baroque garden element evoking a number of the expected emotions fashionable at the time. Even at the height of the Renaissance Leonardo da Vinci (1452–1519), recalling the inspiration for the use of the grotto in a painting, had written that "after having remained at the entry [of a grotto] some time, two contrary

The Crooked House at the Villa Orsini was deliberately built to read on the outside as slipping down the hill while the interior planes remained level. Photo: Everett Scott.

Gardens with mosaic paving at the rear of the Casino Villino at the Palazzo Farnese in Caprarola. Photo: Everett Scott.

emotions arose in me, fear and desire—fear of the threatening dark grotto, desire to see whether there were any marvelous thing within it."[21] As Baroque sensibilities developed, garden designers could not resist introducing the same powerful emotions into the landscape.

At the Villa Aldobrandini, begun in 1598 at Frascati, a semicircular nymphaeum theater wall cut into the hillside is composed of a series of niches and grotto rooms filled with water devices. In the middle stands Atlas holding the world on his back. The water that finally gushes down and around the weary god actually begins in an artificial, rustic grotto near the top of the hill, flowing over a water staircase and rising again around a pair of spiraling columns before continuing its fantastic journey to the fountain at the lowest level. The *grand salon* of the villa is centered on axis with the water theater so that guests could comfortably enjoy the display from the second-story loggia.

At Aldobrandini the transition from the early Renaissance type of garden to that of the Baroque can be observed as the formal order of the space near the house recedes into theatrical contrasts of light, shade, and contorted shapes and finally merges into the arcadian woods on the surrounding hillsides. By the last quarter of the seventeenth century, natural growth of the vegetation and the onset of decay caused by neglect were beginning to submerge these Italian gardens—Aldobrandini, Lante, and the Villa d'Este among them—into romantic, picturesque landscapes that would make a deep and lasting impression on French and English travelers and artists. Even though these gardens were only fifty or a hundred years old, a romantic patina had already spread over their terraces, fountains, and avenues, recreating an antique atmosphere that seemed to bring alive the world of Virgil and Pliny. The Italian landscape recorded by Claude and Poussin and later by Robert, Fragonard, and other artists conveyed an image of what everyone thought the classical countryside and garden must have once appeared.

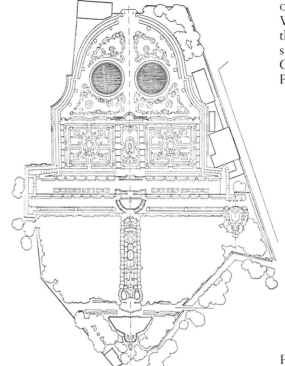

Plan of the Villa Garzoni. Francesco Fariello, *Architettura dei Giardini*.

Pierre Nolhac in his study of French painters in Italy describes the mysterious quality that only age can give.

What increases the charm of the Roman gardens is that venerable impression of the hand of time. Created during the centuries of opulence, with a disposition according to the regular forms of art, the change of fortune and other natural causes have caused their upkeep to be neglected, and nature in part has resumed her rituals. Her conquests over art and the intermingling of their effects produces the most picturesque scenes. This negligence, this antiquity, and this impetuous vegetation compose the most wonderful pictures.[22]

The recovery and conscious pursuit of the pastoral life as idealized in a garden setting is one of the abiding themes of the Italian Ren-

Plan of the Villa Aldo-brandini. Francesco Fariello, *Architettura dei Giardini*.

aissance from the pastoral retreats of the early Medicis down to nature's nostalgic mutations in the great Roman gardens that so entranced northern painters in the seventeenth and eighteenth centuries. As the actual life of the nobility became increasingly complex, the romantic appeal of the idyllic life of the shepherd's rustic freedom to discourse, read poetry, make music and love became irresistible to the jaded grandees of Rome, Venice, Florence, and Paris. This dreamworld of the shepherd's life was one of the strongest motives of the Middle Ages, and its appeal was so pervasive and powerful that it continued in art, literature, and in gardens all over post-Renaissance Europe. The pastoral life was an ideal existence constructed out of classical mythology and inevitably located in an arcadian or, as later generations would inevitably assume, an Italian landscape. However modified by new ideas and new imagery, this theme of the innocent, simple life confronting the realities of less-than-perfect existence extends into the twentieth century. Even Le Corbusier succumbed to the nostalgic contemplation of an antique arcadia where his twentieth-century suburban villas outside of Paris would achieve a reconciliation with nature, an impossible truce. "Grass will border the roads," he rhapsodized, "nothing will be disturbed—neither the trees, the flowers, nor the flocks and herds."[23] This nostalgic literary image of the garden first inspired by the Renaissance is among Italy's enduring garden legacies that still maintains its enchantment and vitality.

Unlike Villa Garzoni, Villa Aldobrandini has been placed at the foot of the exedra and water staircase, which are to be enjoyed, as it were, from the position of the orchestra pit in an opera house. Photo: Everett Scott.

FRANCE

Natural landscape transformed into a work of art is a prodigious vision that has never been surpassed outside of France. Miniature dreamworlds of meticulous perfection—holding in balance a field of forces of art and nature shaped into islands of order—French gardens, even the earliest documented, displayed a meticulous, sober system of ancient gardening skills and traditions. The French garden, like the French cuisine and code of manners, equals the exalted, rarefied standards of civilization once held by the Chinese.

By 1400 when the Louvre was first established as the original royal residence, the Ile de France, centered on Paris and the valley of the Seine, became the heart of French civilization. The scenery of this comparatively flat basin with its abundance of water and endless hardwood forests could not have been in greater contrast to the exuberant landscape of Italy discovered by the French armies at the end of the century.

Unlike the landscape of Italy, with its sharp hills and narrow river valleys intensely cultivated in irregular patterns of olive and vine plantations and punctuated with ilex and cypress around farm buildings and villages, the French countryside was utterly predictable. In France, villages developed in clusters of more or less ordered buildings and streets separated from the heavy forest by a belt of uneventful meadows and croplands, an oasis of open space in the continuum of surrounding woods.

That brooding, dark, continuum of the French forest instilled an abiding suspicion of nature's reliability, an uneasiness that was not shared in the more hospitable, pantheistic environment of the Mediterranean world of the Greeks, Romans, and the later Italians. The Gothic specters we sometimes see in Northern paintings, with only an occasional hint of an Earthly Paradise, are the very spirit of the irrational domains of nature, of the suffocating threat of organic life and overwhelming vegetation. No wonder the French garden would finally emerge as an absolute and total conquest over time, space, and organic nature itself. To venture into the forest was to run the risk of losing one's soul. To reduce the forest to an ordered, tidy ideal world was salvation here on earth.

It is hard to say precisely when the idea of a garden as simply a small, structured area confined behind the castle and cloister walls finally emerged in the post-Roman world from its stereotype. But it is clear from the poetry, allegorical tales, and particularly *The Romance of the Rose* that something was stirring in southern France in the twelfth century before spreading to receptive humanist scholars in Italy. In songs, poetry, and ritual, there was an awakened interest in bucolic surroundings, plants, and animals that promised a new reconciliation between man and nature. Romantic love itself became a literary theme, acted out in pastoral bliss, of the French troubadours. Suddenly the courtier in search of his true love is introduced into the civilizing environment of a garden. Gradually he will extend his romantic musings into the meadows and the inviting countryside beyond. In the garden, the courtier discovers that life has taken on a heightened sensitivity to nature's beauty and its refining atmosphere. Erotic, pastoral songs based on ancient sources are sung in celebration of the new experience. Classical writers like Ovid (43 B.C.–A.D. 17) had acclaimed the sensual pleasures of nature, and one of the consequences of the rediscovery of these authors was that their poetic descriptions of the garden idylls began to add new psychological and emotional dimensions to the contemporary garden of France and Italy.

Although the Italians and the French drew upon the same classical documents at the same time, the Italians were far more advanced in their sense of a garden's possibilities than anything that passed for garden art in France in

The Basin of Apollo in the gardens of Versailles. Photo: Robert Polidori.

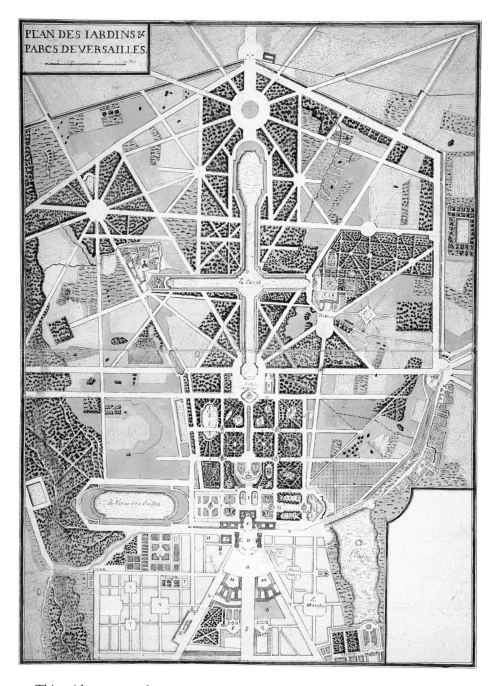

PLAN DES IARDINS &
PARCS DE VERSAILLES.

This mid-seventeenth century plan reveals how the formal layout was integrated into open meadows and farmland. Collection of Walter Chatham.

sculpture, and open terraces to take advantage of distant views, were indeed "an earthly paradise," Charles wrote back to his brother-in-law Pierre de Bourbon.

The oriental luxury of Poggio Reale's gardens, with spacious terraces, baths, marble fountains, and an open-air theatre, could only have reminded the king of the inadequacy of his own dank, constricted courtyards hidden within the walls of the fortress-château of Amboise. To Charles, the very idea that artists and craftsmen could create such a fanciful version of Paradise here and now on this earth must have seemed irresistible.

When it became necessary for Charles and his troops to suddenly abandon Naples in July of 1495, the retreating army carried with it enormous quantities of Italian art—"countless marvels" in the words of one chronicler—including tapestries, paintings, and sculpture to enliven their austere castles and manor houses. But from the standpoint of the future of French gardens, the imagination of artisans who followed the king north—Fra Giocondo, Pacello da Mercogliano, Guido Mazzoni, and Domenico da Cortona—was far more important. Some fifty years later, engravings of the greatest of the early French Renaissance gardens, in Jacques Androuet du Cerceau's (c.1515/20–c.1584) magnificent *Les Plus excellents Bâtiments de France* (1576–79), illustrated the French translations of the Italian garden vocabulary.

These opening decades of the sixteenth century coincided with early stages in the evolution of France into a modern state. Elegant and often grandiose in concept, the borrowed Italian finery of France's gardens only partially concealed the old medieval French habits worn underneath. It was rare if the château itself was new from the ground up. More often than not a remodeled feudal establishment had thriftily incorporated old towers, walls, and even moats into the new complex. These early French gardens lack the openness and generosity that the less inhibited Italian gardens already displayed.

Even as the French nobility took on the

the fourteenth century. As late as 1495, when Charles VIII invaded the kingdom of Naples, he was startled by the sumptuous new pleasure villas and gardens built by his enemy Alfonso II. Alfonso's villa gardens, with their spectacular hydraulic systems, fountains,

humanistic trappings of the Renaissance and began to move confidently beyond the protection of fortified castle walls, absorbing pastoral sentiments, gestures, and bucolic imagery, the conservative structure, values, and rituals of life remained those of the hunter-soldier. French aristocrats who created gardens as a sign of status and class were invariably trained as soldiers, beginning with the king. In fact, every king of France from Charles VIII down to Louis XV (1710–1774) not only considered himself the first gardener of the realm but actually carried out major constructions to advance garden art. It is no surprise that environments of unadulterated

The evidence of elaborate Italian parterres in this mid-sixteenth-century French painting leaves no doubt of the influence of Italy on French garden design at an early stage. Musée des Beaux-Arts, Lille.

Palm trees have been brought out onto the terrace at Versailles from the great orangery visible in the background to the left. Photo: Steven Still.

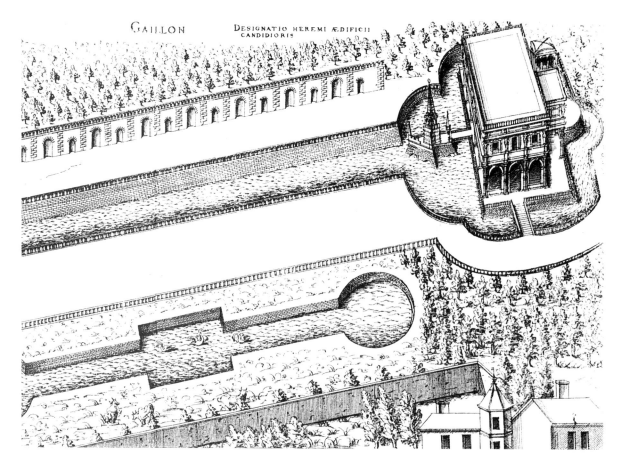

One of the most famous French gardens of the early Renaissance, Gaillon, Eure, was created by Cardinal Georges d'Amboise, who had traveled widely in Italy. It is a complete ruin today and a fit subject for archaeology. The rock hermitage and canal seen here were built after 1550. Du Cerceau, *Le Premier Volume des plus excellents Bastiments de France*.

symmetry in the garden would become the ultimate expression of absolute monarchy.

The monumental scale of the classic French garden that would eventually extend, in a few cases, over hundreds of acres was from the beginning preeminently masculine, as was its order, rationality, and boldness. Its design, whether by patron or architect, or a collaboration of the two, was exclusively by men who had some training in military discipline and in military engineering. The traditional French hunting park in the forest surrounding the château, with its long radial avenues extending deep into the wilderness to facilitate movements of the hunting parties, was laid out with great military efficiency and insight. In the middle of the seventeenth century when the garden at Versailles was extended beyond Louis XIII's old hunting lodge by his son, the

original, axial avenues of the hunting park were easily assimilated by the young king's gardener, André Le Nôtre (1613–1700), into his grandiose garden scheme. Jacques de Boyceau (1580–1633) served Henri IV as a military officer long before he took charge of the royal gardens and wrote his *Traité du jardinage selon les raisons de la nature et de l'art* (1638).

In the hands of ambitious gardener-kings like François I, the magnitude of moving earth in order to create terraces, ramps, canals, and roadways required all kinds of military technology and engineering skills. When the military resources were not being employed to build and repair fortifications, men and material were diverted to the king's garden construction at Fontainebleau, Saint-Germain-en-Laye, or the Tuileries. Later in the seventeenth century, Versailles could easily monopolize any available military support to continue the king's megalomania, and the minister Colbert (1619–1683) wisely encouraged the building passion of young King Louis XIV (1643–1715) as a less costly alternative to military adventures.

Charles VIII lived for only three years after his return from Naples, but his sudden death in 1498 did not halt the work he had started at Amboise. His successor, Louis XII (1462–1515), continued to build and improve the royal châteaux and their gardens throughout his reign of seventeen years. Even though Italian garden art was imperfectly understood by the French, the gardens at Amboise and Blois did manage to move beyond the cramped castle walls into the landscape beyond.

In the du Cerceau engravings we can see how the old defensive ramparts and water moats were employed to take advantage of the views that formerly had been hidden behind fortress walls. No country, as almost everyone has observed, has realized the philosophical implications of formal water more readily than France. The small castle reflected in flooded moats or nearby lakes leads up to the

A view of the terraces at Versailles. Photo: Everett Scott.

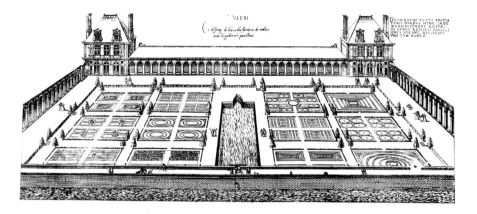

perfection of the great canal gardens in the seventeenth century. Probably the finest example of an early water garden was the exquisite little château of Dampierre near Boissy-sur-Seine, built around 1550. The château, with its large courtyard garden, was surrounded by an ornamental moat overlooking an open lake with a view into the surrounding country. Artificial lakes and flooded moats at Chantilly and Fontainebleau were also used as a similar device to open up the inward-looking, enclosed medieval garden, much as

the ha-ha, or sunken fence (also a French military invention), was used to transform the English garden in the eighteenth century.

At the Château de Vallery the new garden, built around 1550, was ingeniously detached from the antiquated château nearby, an imaginative step to escape existing constrictions. A handsome gallery running across the terrace connecting two pavilions allowed the viewer to establish a coherent relationship between the garden and the surrounding landscape by looking out over the lake. Water from an upper garden flowed through the ornamental basin dividing the formal parterres before joining the lake below.

The *jardins de plaisir* of France in the first half of the sixteenth century reflected the growing obsession with all things Italian, and the center for Italian fashion in France was, of course, the court of François I, who claimed Rome as his ideal model. In painting, sculpture, music, dance, literature, architecture, and garden settings the court at Fontainebleau was enthralled with the luxurious, theatrical Italian style.

François's enthusiasm for the antique world permeated every aspect of French culture and led to a second Italian invasion of artists. Even Leonardo da Vinci could not resist the king's invitation, only to die at Amboise two years after he arrived in France. Equally important were the new architectural books and engravings illustrating *"la bonne manière italienne."* The published works of Vitruvius, Alberti, and Sebastiano Serlio (1475–1554) introduced an entirely new vocabulary of architectural theory to French architects based on classical sources. By the sixteenth century the well-known gardens under royal or court patronage are generally associated with major architects such as Philibert de l'Orme (c. 1510–1570), who designed the Château d'Anet, and Salomon de Brosse (1571–1626), who is identified with the Château Montceaux and the Luxembourg Palace. The Luxembourg gardens of Marie de Médicis, queen of France, had been inspired by the Boboli Gardens in Florence.

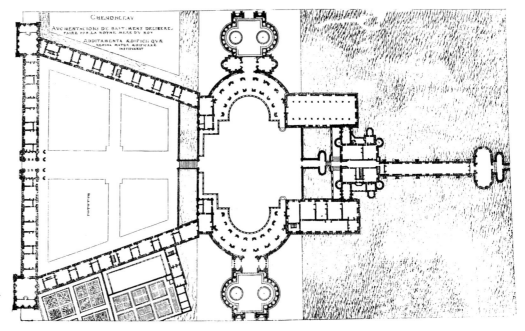

To speak of this sudden enthusiasm for all things Italian is not to say that French borrowings included the mature Italian architecture and garden design principles carried out in such masterpieces as Raphael's Villa Madama or Vignola's Villa Lante. The châteaux along the Loire—Blois, Amboise, Chenonceaux—the list is very short at the beginning of the sixteenth century—were not the work of Italians in any sense, despite their occasional Italian decorations. French architecture beyond the vernacular was at once original, conservative, and composite, a mixture of enduring building traditions that looked as much to the north and to the Flemish as it looked south over the Alps.

When François recruited Italian artists to Fontainebleau in the 1520s, they were set to work on the walls and foundations of a ruinous medieval castle, a mediocre, isolated complex with little to recommend it. Disappointed in his dream of becoming the Holy Roman Emperor, François no doubt plunged himself into this work to forget his *"melancholie."* Fontainebleau's setting, on an artificial lake and surrounded by the requisite moat,

The plan of Chenonceaux. Du Cerceau, *Le Premier Volume des plus excellents Bastiments de France.*

OPPOSITE, ABOVE
The gallery of Château de Vallery has the quality of a medieval cloister in this engraving. Du Cerceau, *Le Premier Volume des plus excellents Bastiments de France.*

OPPOSITE, BELOW
The massive terrace of Chenonceaux, Indre-et-Loire, was laid out between 1551 and 1555 for Diane de Poitiers. The restored gardens are a nineteenth-century interpretation of *parterre de broderie.* Photo: Everett Scott.

could not have been more removed from contemporary Italian models. As a result, the garden that emerged in the later part of the century, except for decorative elements of stone work and sculpture, was purely a French ensemble.

What gave Fontainebleau its special vitality was the racy, idiosyncratic blending of mythology, legend, and history into the decorative program, celebrating a parvenue Valois monarchy. Ovid's poetry had recently become the new religion, and his art of love was usually celebrated in a garden. So the decoration of Fontainebleau was rich with Ovidian images of the erotic life of gods and goddesses. Ovid's themes were made for garden settings. There was Daphne fleeing through woods that she was literally about to join as a laurel tree in order to escape the embraces of Apollo; Pomona, the wood-nymph goddess of gardens; Persephone, snatched from her native meadows of Sicily by Pluto, god of the Underworld, returning each year in the spring for an earthly vacation; and Neptune, presiding over virtually every garden basin—the *Metamorphoses* was a gold mine of repertoire garden myths for sculpture decorations.

One of the functions of the Renaissance garden was to stimulate and lure the mind of the visitor into the legends of history and to remind him, through allegorical references to the Golden Age, of the Olympian fame and high connections enjoyed by the garden's creator. Antique deities, nymphs, and satyrs in bronze and marble quickly moved into the avenues, glades, and along the waterways of Fontainebleau, establishing a perpetual lease on French garden soil. That these classical deities would continue to inhabit damp royal gardens down to the end of the eighteenth century says a lot for the surprisingly congenial asylum they had found so far removed from their warm, native Mediterranean climate.

By the 1520s Pope Julius II's collection of antique sculpture in the Belvedere garden had set the fashion, and François commissioned his Italian sculptor Primaticcio to bring back from Rome—along with a marble *Ulysses* by Michelangelo—casts of Roman sculpture in the Vatican collection for his gardens.

The art of Fontainebleau was meant to define and magnify the image of the king as a living hero, using an antique vocabulary. "The aim is clear," Henri Zerner has written. "It was only fitting to celebrate the glory of the king, the beauty of the women, the valour of the heroes of the day, to ornament the life of the court" and its immediate world.[24] It was also a formula for a royal garden decoration that would continue to serve French kings over the next 250 years. Achilles, Hercules, Venus, Apollo, Diana, their relatives, friends, and extended families carried their mythological message into every royal park and garden, declaring their right and privilege to be there through the most ancient and august genealogies.

For all of the fascination with classical mythology, French gardens were not immune to the scientific discoveries of the sixteenth century, including the growing fascination with the laws of optics and perspective. Jean Martin's translation of Serlio's treatise on the architecture of the theater, published in Paris in 1545, emphasized the importance of perspective in architectural design, and his techniques were quickly picked up by French architects and garden designers. Olivier de Serres's (1539–1619) practical guide for laying out garden designs in his *Théâtre d'agriculture et mesnage des champs* (1600) ingeniously noted that rows of trees and plants must have greater space between them, "*par la raison de perspective,*" if they were to be seen from a distance rather than at close range.

Following the Italian gift of turning gardens into an illusionary realm of theater for great court spectacles and pageantry, the court at Fontainebleau experimented with its own version of garden theater. The château's main courtyard opening onto the lake was extended into the water by a rectangular platform stage designed for just such events. Fanciful ships and barges were built to carry actors and musicians around the lake as part of the fabulous

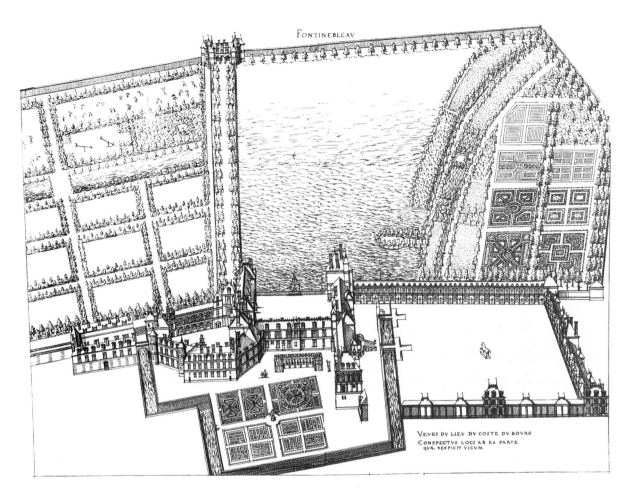

FONTINEBLEAV

VEVES DV LIEV DV COSTE DV BOVRG
CONSPECTVS LOCI AB EA PARTE
QVÆ RESPICIT VICVM

The main lines of the gardens and castle of Fontainebleau, Seine-et-Marne, were first established between 1528 and 1547 by François I. The garden was redesigned by André Le Nôtre in 1645 with a *parterre de broderie,* before he began his celebrated commission at Vaux-le-Vicomte. The use of large water basins and artificial lakes here and in other French gardens of the period is without precedent in Italian gardens. De Cerceau, *Le Deuxieme Volume des plus excellents Bastiments de France.*

tableaux. Two hundred years later royal French garden fetes would reach their climax at Versailles, where Louis XIV staged his magnificent *Plaisirs de l'Île Enchantée* in 1664 with orchestra, ballet, and Italian fireworks. The production extended over three exhausting days. The outdoor fete had added another element to the garden's political propaganda services on behalf of the monarchy.

Shortly after his accession to the French throne in 1547, Henri II (1519–1559) appointed Philibert de l'Orme, who had studied architecture in Italy, to take charge of the royal buildings and gardens. Unlike the fragmented court life of Italy where change and experiment were the rule, the centralization of power in the person of the king's architect had grown steadily, and de l'Orme's appointment

would have a concentrated and far-reaching impact on the royal domains. If the king himself showed little dynastic interest in building or gardening, both his wife and his mistress more than made up for his lazy indifference. One of de l'Orme's first commissions was to create for the king's powerful mistress, Diane de Poitiers, *Les Paradis d'Anet* (1546–52). Even though de l'Orme had seen both classical ruins and the best Italian gardens during his travels, Anet maintained a distinctly inward, medieval feeling about it, with its galleried walls surrounding the level courtyards.

The château was intended to serve as a glamorous hunting box for the king and court, so Diane de Poitiers was naturally transformed into a fashion-plate goddess of the chase in honor of her mythical namesake.

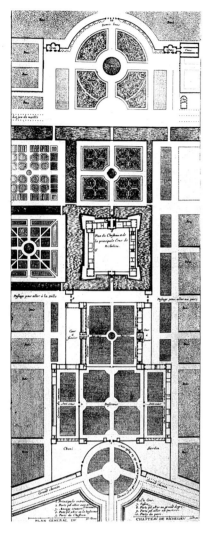

Daniel Marot's plan for Richelieu. *Jardin Français Crées a La Renaissance.*

The classical Diane with her bow, her deer, groves, and crescent moon were reproduced in sculpture and decoration throughout the château. No one who was invited to Anet could question the powerful role of the king's mature charmer, twenty years his senior.

In order to fully appreciate the essentially conservative quality of Anet's garden, for all of its allure, one has only to compare it with the progressive development of contemporary gardens in Italy where dramatic, unexpected perspectives combined with a confident manipulation of water, foliage, and earth at Vignola's Caprarola and Villa Lante, and at Pirro Ligorio's Villa d'Este, were pointing garden architecture in other more imaginative directions.

The leading architects of the Italian Renaissance assumed that the art of landscape design was an inevitable extension of their architecture into the surrounding space. This primary role of the architect was not lost on sixteenth-century French architectural students who studied in Rome. But the more adventuresome French architects were handicapped by their clients' parsimonious attachments to outmoded castles and keeps with limited visual possibilities. The dramatic difference between French and Italian terrain was also a significant factor. The relatively flat topography of the Ile de France and the Loire Valley encouraged expansive, horizontal gardens rolled out like a carpet that would have been inconceivable in Italy. The French seemed hypnotized with the point in the distance where the horizon touched the sky.

The château and garden of Montceaux begun by Henri II's Italian queen is in marked contrast to her rival's cloistered hunting box at Anet. Catherine de Médicis (1519–1589) had spent the early years of her marriage in the confines of the Château of Amboise, a prison compared to the Medici family palace in Florence. Montceaux was to be her answer to narrow, conservative French taste. The long, central axis of the garden of Montceaux runs along and parallel to a low hill to take advantage of the views. A forecourt and the plat-

form for the château take up half the site, while two monumental parterres are placed on successive terrace levels below the château. Even from the existing ruins of the château, one can still experience something of the Italianate drama of the confident axial line running through the descending terraces below, leading the eye with a fine Italian guide out toward the rolling countryside to the horizon. It is a significant step toward Le Nôtre's great central avenue running to the horizon at Versailles a hundred years later.

The latter part of the sixteenth century produced three major garden designs at Charleval, Verneuil-sur-Oise, and Saint-Germain-en-Laye (1599–1610). But except for monumental terrace walls at Saint-Germain, nothing of these gardens survives. The plans for both Verneuil and Charleval (neither of which was actually built) emphasize the dominating axial scheme of Roman Renaissance gardens, and there are a number of similarities between Verneuil's plan and that of the Villa d'Este. Bramante's Belvedere courtyard and the Villa Lante with their inspired handling of different hillside levels are also obvious Italian antecedents.

With an eye and imagination already anticipating André Le Nôtre at the beginning of the seventeenth century, the garden laid out for Cardinal Richelieu and his adjoining new town, which also bears his name, is an important if often overlooked link in the evolution of the French garden. Since Le Nôtre's brilliance so completely dominates the history of the French garden in the seventeenth century, it is necessary to underline the broader tradition that he grew out of.

The Château de Richelieu, begun in 1626 along with its garden and town, was the work of the cardinal's favorite architect, Jacques Lemercier (1583–1654). The scale of the park, whose skeleton outlines still can be followed outside the town of Richelieu, is astounding, anticipating by thirty years the development of Versailles. As a young designer-apprentice, Le Nôtre may have worked for Lemercier at Richelieu.

The flat, monotonous water-logged topography at Richelieu is no more promising than that of Versailles. The commanding scale is everything, and Lemercier understood this when he planned the three straight roads leading to the château and converging at acute angles in the pattern of the traditional *patte d'oie*, or goose foot, of French hunting forests, and centered on a great circle three hundred feet in diameter. After passing through a series of courtyards, one reached the château, standing anachronistically on a moated platform, by a bridge. On the other side, another small bridge led to yet another moated parterre that looked into a large, slightly tilted hemicycle embankment that terminated the main axis.

Two canals formed from a small existing river run at cross axis with the central avenue to extend the longer perspectives on either side of the château. The diversion of a natural stream or river to form ornamental canals would become major garden features at Chantilly and Vaux. Richelieu clearly expressed the design system of the *"jardin de l'intelligence,"* a rationally controlled space intended to enhance the abstract, circumscribed representation of the cosmos.

What had taken place at Richelieu and would occur in overwhelming dimensions later at Versailles was the subordination of architecture and nature to a total hallucinatory statement of power. This concept of the completely ordered assembly of parts into a coherent whole would continue to inspire town planning well into the twentieth century. Imposing rules of order on the environment as rigid as those of the military, the classic French garden summed up the absolute monarchy of the Sun King. Versailles—the town, palace, and garden—was the ultimate, visible symbol of a united nation ruled by one man. For those trapped in its grid, the symbol assumed reality.

Between André Le Nôtre's birth in 1613 at his father's house on the edge of the king's garden of the Tuileries and his death in 1700, the classic French garden takes on its decisive form. The dynamic shape that the garden

took under Le Nôtre's direction and through the patronage of Louis XIV (1643–1715) was the result of a long tradition. Gradually the work of the garden designer had been elevated into that of a major art form capable of serving the highest policies of state and sharing acclaim with architecture, painting, and sculpture.

The original garden of Louis XIII's old hunting lodge was so modest that it was ignored by most contemporary travelers and topographical artists. It could not in any way be compared to Vaux-le-Vicomte (1656–1661), begun twenty-five years later for Louis XIV's *surintendant des finances,* Nicolas Fouquet (1615–1680). Fouquet was a man of extraordinary talent with a deep interest in the arts. Charles de Sercy, in his dedication to

Although restored by Henri Duchene, the nineteenth-century landscape architect, Vaux-le-Vicomte, Seine-et-Marne, represents the most authentic and arresting masterwork of Le Nôtre. Photo: Everett Scott.

Claude Mollet's *Théâtre des plans et jardinages* (1652), paid tribute to the "superbs jardins de Vaux-le-Vicomte" six years before Le Nôtre actually joined Charles Le Brun (1619–1690) and Louis Le Vau (1612–1670) to work on the château pleasance, so Fouquet no doubt had a major role in Vaux's basic design.

One of the essential things to grasp at Vaux, Versailles, or any of the classic French gardens (and this is true in sixteenth- and seventeenth-century Italy as well) is that they were not the creation of a single artist's vision or execution. These productions were very much like the ensemble collaborative of contemporary Baroque opera or ballet, requiring the skill of all manner of artisans and craftsmen working together. The same kind of organization and management was required for Baroque garden-making. The work at Vaux was a stupendous enterprise, anticipating the even greater undertaking later at Versailles. Vaux also required a minister of finance if not the king himself to pay for such an imperial project. When the work was rushed to completion in 1661, the informing genius of Fouquet, Le Nôtre, and that of their colleagues had created nothing less than one of the world's garden masterpieces.

Le Vau's château, placed at one end of the central axis and reached though a relatively short forecourt, surprisingly does not determine or dominate the garden beyond. Rather it has become an integral part of a grand composition. The garden itself manipulates the Baroque illusion of unity between sky and ground, achieved by the reflection of water and by the relentless main avenue leading the eye into infinity. As the visitor explores the avenue, sculpture and fountains manage to give the overwhelming space a human scale, rhythm, and punctuation. Le Nôtre had a brilliant grasp of the science of optics and used his theatrical skill at Vaux to create all manner of illusionist perspectives. Above all there is a heroic dignity in the terraces, steps, cascades, and canals that is larger than life, giving the visitor a feeling of having entered into the Parnassian landscape of the gods. Not even Ver-

sailles manages to evoke such a feeling of mythical grandeur. Versailles propaganda is too heavy-handed, the distances exhausting, and the air too "aristocratic and demoralizing" in Proust's words. "One is not even troubled by remorse that the lives of so many workmen should have served only to refine and increase, not so much the joys of another age, as the melancholy of ours."[25]

The fairy-tale story of the great fete staged by the proud Fouquet to celebrate the completion of Vaux, an extravagant event that led to his arrest and imprisonment by the young king, with Colbert's conniving, has entered the lore of garden history. Lully composed the music for the ballet commissioned for the occasion. Molière's pastoral masque *Florimen,* with a cast of elegant courtiers disguised as rustic shepherds and shepherdesses, was performed. La Fontaine composed a panegyric poem in honor of his host and patron. The real significance of these two extravagant evenings, however, was to underline the power the French garden had assumed as a political

The Grand Cascade of Vaux-le-Vicomte is placed at a right angle to the central axis overlooking the great canal but is below eye level and does not reveal itself until one reaches it. Fish for the table and for sale were raised in the basin of the cascade. Photo by Everett Scott.

OPPOSITE
Louis Le Vau's château, Vaux-le-Vicomte, rises above Le Nôtre's garden. Subtle shifts in elevation and secondary cross axes orchestrate the balanced composition. Photo: Everett Scott.

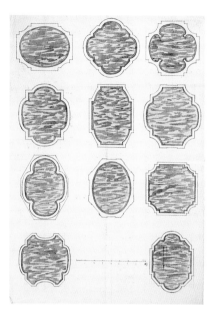

These anonymous plans of water basin shapes indicate the range of patterns used in the designing of classical garden basins. National Museum, Stockholm.

Water for the extensive fountain system of Versailles was stored in the large tanks shown in this detail of a c. 1669 painting by Pierre Patel. It was released by gravity, but if all the large fountains were playing the water supply could be quickly exhausted. These tanks still exist, but a new opera house was constructed in the space at the left end facing the garden. Musée de Versailles.

statement. It is no wonder the king felt threatened by this arrogant display by his servant. Three months after the minister's arrest, his orange trees, appropriated by the king, began to arrive at the greenhouses of Versailles. It was an age-old prerogative of a royal victor to claim the trees of the vanquished, dating back to ancient Syria.

The triumphant achievement of Vaux also challenged Louis to do something about his father's dilapidated hunting lodge at Versailles, where over the next thirty years, his palace, town, and garden would reach a magnificence that would astonish the entire world. By the time he died in 1715, the Sun King had expanded the original gardens of 250 acres to more than 4,000; the *Grand Parc*, reserved for royal hunts, would eventually embrace nearly 15,000 acres of forest enclosed with a stone wall twenty-six miles long.

For all of its cultural, political, and historical importance, Versailles's garden is in the end simply too grandiose and falls apart in sprawl, unable to achieve the integrated perfection of Vaux-le-Vicomte or even the eccentric order of Chantilly. The principles of composition that are followed at Vaux are also followed at Versailles, but the results—that moment of completion when the design should come together in eye and imagination—always seem to elude us.

In 1668 the king approved Le Vau's plan for new additions to the palace, an enormous "*Enveloppe*" to house the court and government. It was no longer to serve as a royal amusement park, and architects, gardeners, sculptors, and above all water engineers now set about transforming Versailles into the seat of a mighty empire.

Once again, military technology in fortifications, in earth-moving, and above all in hydraulic engineering was called upon by the king and his designers. The constant expansion of the gardens ultimately required fourteen hundred fountains to relieve the numbing monotony of the space. Not even the army was able to solve the chronic water crisis. One mad plan, costing thousands of lives in the ef-

fort, involved nothing less than bringing the River Eure itself to the palace, until it was discovered that the river was too far below the level of the palace gardens to use a conventional gravity system. Finally in 1684, the *Machine de Marly,* with its Rube Goldberg system of fourteen gigantic waterwheels, buckets, and 221 pumps, lifted water from the Seine to reservoirs 162 meters above the river where it flowed in canal ditches to the palace's tanks five miles away.

As if exhausted by the endless building at Versailles, where the imperial demands to build had taken on a life of their own, the king in 1679 chanced upon a dramatic, narrow declivity in woods opening onto the valley of the Seine some five miles from Versailles. The hills, forming an elongated horseshoe, could not have been less promising terrain for a French garden, though Italian designers would have found the Marly hillside ideal. Gardens of the Villas Lante and Aldobrandini had been deliberately placed in similar rugged slopes, where water could be creatively used and deployed by gravity. By the time Louis decided on the plan for his new hermitage, engravings of Italian gardens were widely circulated in France, and many of them had been visited on the grand tour of Italy.

The king's little pavilion-château of Marly was placed on a platform at the foot of the steep north end of the valley. Twelve smaller pavilions were arranged in rows on either arm of the terraces running toward the river. The center was dominated by the Pièce des Nappes and other smaller water basins. The hills on either side of the elaborate, architectural terracing were heavily wooded, serving as a dramatic contrast to the refined, elegant walls of hedge, arbors, and topiary trees and shrubs. Marly's intense ordering of nature into perfect man-made forms marks the last architectonic phase of the French formal garden. Diderot rightly appraised Marly's special character as "the contrast between the delicacy of art in the bowers and bosquets and the rudeness of nature in the dense bank of trees which overhangs them and forms the background. This

One of the four famous *Chevaux de Marly,* which stood on the terrace of Louis XIV's retreat at Marly. After the Revolution, Marly fell to ruin, and the statues made their way to the Champs-Elysées. Photo: Everett Scott.

The Pagoda of Chanteloup, Indre-et-Loire, was designed by Louis-Denis Le Comus between 1775 and 1778. The great classic vistas ranging from the pagoda still control the composition one hundred years after Le Nôtre's Golden Age. Photo: François Halard.

Fountain in the gardens of Het Loo near Apeldorn in the Netherlands. Photo: Everett Scott.

continual transition from nature to art and from art to nature produces a truly enchanting effect."[26] Even the cascade terraces of the water basins were subtly sculptured to animate the water with controlled, man-made patterns as it flowed over them.

Because Marly was designed to serve as a retreat for the king, away from the stifling etiquette of Versailles, privacy was of the utmost importance, so at the foot of the park near the river end, a high bank and wall were thrown up above the *abreuvoir,* or watering tank for the horses, which skillfully shielded the privileged few who had been invited to join the king.

Scholars have long puzzled over the respective roles of Le Nôtre, the king's architect Jules Hardouin-Mansart (1645–1708), and the king himself in the final design of Marly. The highly architectural quality of the terracing, the water basins, and the cascade suggests that the architect played the decisive part in the final scheme. Rather than a stage for large outdoor court productions, the garden of Marly and its elaborate water displays, sculpture, and bosquets were all the entertainment required by a fading and aging court.

André Le Nôtre's incomparable achievements as a garden designer and his long professional life in the service of the most powerful ruler of Europe made him and his creations the quintessential symbol of the age. As the inscription on his tomb in the church of St. Roch reads, his accomplishments were "so outstanding in the art of gardening that he can be regarded as having invented their principal beauties and carried all others to their utmost perfection. . . . Not only did France profit from his industry but all the princes of Europe sought his pupils. He had no comparable rival."

Even with its own vaunted garden tradi-

Daniel Marot, a French Huguenot artist, fled to the Netherlands in 1685, becoming designer to William III. His sumptuous gardens for Het Loo combine both Renaissance and Baroque influences in a uniquely Dutch creation and were laid out between 1686 and 1695. Splendidly restored in 1984, Het Loo is the most lavish of all Dutch gardens. Photo: Everett Scott.

tion, Italy followed the irresistible French fashion when Louis XIV's great-grandson Charles III, king of Naples, commissioned Luigi Vanvitelli (1700–1773) to build the formal gardens of Caserta in 1752. Inspired indirectly by Versailles, Caserta's immediate model was the Spanish summer palace of La Granja near Madrid where Charles had grown up. La Granja had been built by the Spanish Bourbon king Philip V—Louis XIV's grandson and Charles's father—and while its overall design lacked the cohesive central axis of the traditional French garden, the cascade easily rivaled the Rivière at Marly.

As the French formal style became more international in its influence, it was inevitable that hybrid variations would evolve to reflect regional garden traditions and different topography. At Het Loo (built 1686–95), in The

Netherlands, Daniel Marot (1661–1752), the Huguenot artist, adopted a Baroque interpretation for the Le Nôtre style, using heavy ornamentation and elaborate sculpted parterres that seemed to suit Marot's Dutch clients, William and Mary of Orange.

Almost contemporary with Het Loo is the garden of Drottningholm laid out between 1680 and 1700 in Stockholm for the dowager queen Hedvig Eleonora of Sweden by the Francophile architect Nicodemus Tessin the Younger (1654–1728). Tessin, who had traveled and studied in France, had assembled a remarkable collection of French architectural drawings and designs and actually once submitted projects to Louis XIV for a pavilion in the garden at Versailles. It is possible that Le Nôtre reviewed his plans for Drottningholm.

The formal, architectural gardens of the

English Renaissance continued to evolve with their own special character, drawing inspiration from many sources, but it was not until after 1689, when the French influence was translated by the new Dutch rulers William and Mary at Hampton Court, that conspicuous Le Nôtrean elements were introduced on a large scale. In most of the post–Le Nôtre gardens, there is a distinct rigidity and lack of understanding of the deeper possibilities of the formal style. Hampton Court, like Drottningholm and Het Loo, is no exception. The vocabulary of *parterres de broderie, tapis de gazon,* and *rondelles* may be endlessly elaborated, but Le Nôtre's creative genius has been lost in the repetition. Hampton Court's plan does include a large, semicircular parterre of fountains and a requisite *patte d'oie* of long radiating avenues of double rows of trees that link the palace and the garden.

Since Russia had no royal gardening tradition of its own, it was natural for Peter the Great (1672–1725) to turn to France and to Versailles for a model. He had traveled to Paris in 1709 and had been deeply impressed with the Sun King's grandeur even in its fading twilight. When the imperial palace of Peterhof was built in 1715, French garden designers and gardeners were summoned to St. Petersburg. The site near what is now Leningrad could not have been more different from the French prototype Peter had seen at Versailles. But the plateau some forty feet above the Baltic Sea did make it possible to construct dramatic terraces and ostentatious water effects, including a long canal or water *allée* that unites the garden with the sea beyond.

One of Peter's imported designers was Alexandre-Jean-Baptiste Le Blond (1679–1719), a pupil of Le Nôtre. Le Blond's designs were published by Antoine-Joseph Dezallier d'Argenville (1680–1765) in *La Théorie et la pratique du jardinage.* Appearing first in 1709 and translated into English by John James in 1712, Dezallier d'Argenville's work became the standard international text on the French grand style. It ranks as one of the most influential garden books ever published. A copy of the James translation was among the first volumes in the garden library of the young Thomas Jefferson in Virginia.

The Baroque concept of town planning based on Le Nôtre's ideas and his garden models was to brilliantly serve the military engineer Major Pierre L'Enfant (1754–1825) when he was commissioned to lay out the new city of Washington. Le Nôtre's radiating avenues became the civic lines of republican order strong enough to subdue and hold back the wilderness spread out along the banks of the Potomac River at the end of the eighteenth century.

The geometric, architectural pattern of the French garden conceived to control and dominate nature made horticulture quite secondary. The technical control of water allowing buildings and gardens to be placed on high ground was far more important than the introduction of new plant material. The dramatic illusions that Le Nôtre introduced into his vast works at Vaux, Versailles, and Chantilly through the manipulation of perspective simply overwhelmed any horticultural preoccupations except as subordinate decoration. In the level, horizontal spaces of the earlier French Renaissance gardens that du Cerceau illustrates at Blois, Gaillon, Vallery, and Anet, intricately designed flower beds or parterres are sketched in. With the technology of water still primitive and sculpture difficult to come by, these geometric, medieval floral patterns were one of the few ways to give variety and to relieve the monotony of the gardens' compulsive, predictable order.

By the middle of the sixteenth century, designs for garden compartments of intricately arranged plant materials were sufficiently advanced to be included in Charles Estienne's (1504–1564) *L'Agriculture et maison rustique,* first published in Latin in 1554. These designs were intended as models for both flower and kitchen gardens, and in fact Estienne recommended that they be laid out side by side, separated only by walks. By far the best example of sixteenth-century planting can be seen in the reconstructed garden of Villandry

OPPOSITE
In 1716 Peter the Great brought Alexandre-Jean-Baptiste Le Blond, a pupil of Le Nôtre, to Russia, where he took charge of planning the gardens and park for the king's summer palace, Peterhof, on the Bay of Finland near what is now Leningrad. On the death of Le Blond in 1719, Niccolo Michetti continued the Baroque designs of fountains, cascades, and pavilions. The dramatic cascades flow into the canal below the gilded figure of Samson and then into the sea beyond. Photo: Lynne Meyer.

OVERLEAF
The gardens of Château de Villandry, Indre-et-Loire, below the restored twelfth-century château, were actually created between 1906 and 1924, based on careful study of the sixteenth-century plans drawn by Du Cerceau. The great Jardin Potager is divided into nine large squares. Photo: Sonja Bullaty/Angelo Lomeo.

Ornamental cabbage grown at Château de Villandry. The château's layout is the finest example of a sixteenth-century French garden, but original in that its designs were based on historical research rather than on restoration. Photo: Heather Angel.

OPPOSITE
Dr. Joachim Carvallo, who created the garden at Villandry, established the strictly ordered walks and beds for vegetables to great effect. The small trees planted at the ends of the beds represent a detail of precise historical accuracy. Photo: Heather Angel.

near Tour. Olivier de Serres illustrated several garden designs in his great folio work *Le Théâtre d'agriculture et mesnage des champs.* De Serres had taken these designs from various royal gardens laid out by Claude Mollet.

In his own book, *Théâtre des plans et jardinages,* Mollet claimed that he actually introduced the "embroidered" patterns of floral designs into French gardens in order to break up the pervasive geometry. The Mollet family perfected the use of boxwood to outline flowing, intricate configurations against a background of colored earth and stones. In 1638, Jacques de Boyceau collected his own designs together in a folio. Boyceau realized that the fundamental flaw in the formal garden design

was its tedious order and insisted on the introduction of visual variety in the parterres, bosquets, and *salles de verdure.* It was an idea that Le Nôtre later exploited so successfully in his own great creations.

No surviving French garden in the twentieth century can adequately convey the complexity and refinement of these parterre plantings. Because of their labor-intensive requirements and a lack of understanding of their subtle horticultural composition, the parterres of Versailles and other great public gardens have been allowed to deteriorate into horticultural caricatures of their former grandeur.

The royal gardens did in fact provide spectacular displays to impress the court and please the king. Flowers were used for their color and smell, to be regularly replaced as they faded. The quality of flowers on the scale required for the large *parterres de fleur* was a great luxury and demanded an army of trained gardeners working in the nurseries and greenhouses to supply the gardens on a daily basis. At Versailles the most elaborate flower displays gradually became centered at the Grand Trianon. When we recall that Saint-Simon reported that the court was obliged to retreat indoors when the tuberoses were in bloom at the Trianon, we realize the importance of scent in the French garden. Jean-Baptiste La Quintinie (1626–1688), in his *Instruction pour les jardins fruitiers et potagers,* lists over thirty scented plants that he recommended for the parterre.

Both Louis XIV and his gardener André Le Nôtre were targets of Saint-Simon's censorious words, *"ce plaisir superbe de forcer la nature"*—"this proud pleasure in compelling nature."[27] And while Le Nôtre studied painting as well as the basic skills of architecture—mathematics, perspective, construction techniques—it is important to remember that he was by family heritage and tradition a gardener's gardener who adopted the gardener's tools for his coat of arms. Both his father Jean (d. 1655) and his grandfather Pierre (active c.1570–c.1610) served as royal gardeners. Catherine de Médicis appointed Pierre in 1572 as one of the chief gardeners of the Tuileries, where he was put in charge of one of the great parterres.

The Mollet family represented another important gardening dynasty whose influence, before the ascendancy of André Le Nôtre, was even greater primarily because of the publication of works on garden design by both André and Claude Mollet. This uniquely French tradition of practical yet sophisticated gardening under the patronage of demanding royal patrons, combined with a native intellectual and theoretical bias, was to give the classic French garden its unrivaled international strength for nearly three centuries. The widespread circulation of engraved views of French gardens by Israel Silvestre, Jean Le Pautre, and others in the seventeenth century also helped to spread the style, much as photography contributed to the modern movement in the twentieth century.

OPPOSITE
Intricate boxwood parterre at Villandry.
Photo: Sonja Bullaty/ Angelo Lomeo.

IV. The Genius of the Place

THE ENGLISH GARDEN BEFORE THE REVOLUTION

In 1770 when Horace Walpole looked back over the history of the English garden he was depressed with what he saw. The majority of the gardens he had visited or knew from Johannes Kip's (1653–1722) engravings he found tiresome in their "returning uniformity." At Lady Orford's estate at Piddletown, Walpole was numbed by an enclosure divided into an enfilade of thirteen square spaces that could only be reached through a series of gates. He predicted that, "though these and such preposterous inconveniences had prevailed from age to age," the moment had finally arrived in England to establish a new garden tradition that was distinctly English and one that would be "at once more grand and more natural." [1]

In fact the English garden revolution had already arrived when Walpole wrote his *History of Modern Taste in Gardening* (1771). By the end of the century, the full development of an open, asymmetrical garden design based on new concepts of natural beauty championed by Walpole and others had virtually swept the old gardens of geometry into oblivion. The widespread use of the word "revolution" when speaking of the rapid and progressive change in the gardens of England, beginning with the age of Shaftesbury, Addison, and Pope in the late seventeenth and early eighteenth centuries, obscures an involved story.

The image of the rolling, arcadian English eighteenth-century park, with its negligent clumps of trees in contrast to the tight geometry of the Elizabethan and Tudor knot garden, is so strong in our minds that it is difficult to grasp the more complex historical forces and ideas that have shaped the English landscape. This alluring, romantic English countryside so familiar to us through books, paintings, and movies—and as we actually know part of it today—is almost entirely the man-made product of the last 1500 years. Much of the basic outlines of the rural landscape are, for the most part, no more than 250 years old. [2]

Prior to the period we speak of, around the time of the Norman Conquest, rural England lived on a narrow fringe of marginal existence between a grinding hard life and outright starvation. Vast forests dominated the topography, with thin settlement clustered in small villages scattered rather sparsely around the edges. The countryside itself was cleared for open-field farming only to the point that it could just barely support the inhabitants on a subsistence basis. By 1550, near the beginning of the reign of Elizabeth I, there were still only two-and-a-half or three million people scattered throughout the whole country. On the other hand sheep numbered eight or ten million—three sheep for every man, woman, and child, as Oliver Rackham noted in *The History of the Countryside*.

Even after a thousand years of active settlement, there were still far too few people to populate the whole landscape, too few to work the rich mineral resources, and too few to develop any large industry. Houses were built of stone and wood on a fairly modest scale, and the widespread use of brick for grand manor houses would be delayed until the seventeenth century.

At the beginning of the sixteenth century, the towns were small and insignificant fea-

The reconstructed Knot Garden of Hampton Court, near London, where Queen Elizabeth enjoyed walking. Photo: Steven Still.

tures in the landscape, and most were nothing more than neat, self-contained villages. Great stands of impenetrable timber would have been the most memorable feature of the landscape to strike a visitor. When we read that one man in Durham alone claimed to have felled more than thirty thousand giant oaks in a lifetime (and similar destruction was going on all over the country for fuel, for building, and particularly for the navy), we get some idea of the immense forests that were lost during this period. Even fairly good-sized towns appeared to be submerged in trees. The provincial town of Norwich was described as "either a City in an Orchard, or an Orchard in a City, so equally are Houses and Trees blended in it."[3]

Few people growing up in the sixteenth century lived beyond easy walking distance of nearby woodland and heaths. This wilderness was simply taken for granted, which is confirmed by the fact that there are not many English descriptions of wild, natural, woodland scenery of forests, moors, and wild places. The fashion for picturesque views and "scenery" was still in the future, and the few travelers who mentioned the "wilderness" did so only in terms of fear and distaste. Such unoccupied and inhospitable country was unproductive and was believed to be dangerous for anyone who wandered into its unnatural, threatening embrace.

The conventional English attitude toward the wilderness is summed up in the following passage from Daniel Defoe describing his feelings as he traveled in the early eighteenth century through the Bagshot Heath in Surrey, now a densely populated bedroom suburb of London.

Here is a vast tract of land, some of it within seventeen or eighteen miles of the capital city; which is not only poor, but even quite sterile, given up to barrenness, horrid and frightful to look on, not only good for little, but good for nothing; much of it a sandy desert, and one may frequently be put in mind here of Arabia Deserta, where the winds raise the sands, so as to overwhelm whole caravans of travellers, cattle and people together; for in passing this heath in a windy day, I was so far in danger of smothering with the clouds of sand, which were raised by the storm, that I could neither keep it out of my mouth, nose or eyes; and when the wind was over, the sand appeared spread over the adjacent fields of the forest some miles distant, so that it ruins the very soil. This sand indeed is checked by the heath, or heather, which grows in it, and which is the common product of barren land, even in the very Highlands of Scotland; but the ground is otherwise so poor and barren, that the product of it feeds no creatures, but some very small sheep . . . nor are there any villages, worth mentioning, and but few houses or people for many miles far and wide; this desert lyes extended so much, that some say, there is not less than a hundred thousand acres of this barren land that lies altogether, reaching out every way in three counties of Surrey, Hampshire and Berkshire. . . .[4]

The image of forest and the wilderness like the one in Defoe's vivid description has always been unsettling to the Northern European, very much as the desert has terrified the Is-

lamic world. Whatever the power of the imagined demons in such places might have been, even as late as the Enlightenment, they symbolized an old uneasiness about certain characteristics of nature as it pressed relentlessly against the ordered world of farms, gardens, and villages.

Beginning as early as the middle of the fifteenth century and continuing well into the seventeenth, the English open-field system of medieval agriculture gradually gave way and disappeared under a number of economic and political pressures. By the sixteenth century counties like Kent, Essex, and Devon had been transformed into enclosed, cultivated farmland. Enclosure proceeded over wide areas, spurred on by acquisitive Tudor and Stuart squires and lords. Small freeholders who had traditionally farmed the open fields were either bought out or removed by private parliamentary acts of enclosure. After the Glorious Revolution in 1660, open-field parishes all over England were swallowed up by wholesale agrarian policies of ownership and farming without any opposition. Nothing like this transformation of countryside fueled

A view of the Dutch Garden at Hampton Court, which was first acquired as a royal palace by Henry VIII. The glory of the gardens, however, was the inspiration of William and Mary, who remade them after Christopher Wren rebuilt the east front of the palace beginning in 1689. Daniel Marot and Henry Wise, among others, worked on the new design. Photo: Pamela Harper.

A twentieth-century border at Hampton Court. Lobelia Crystal Palace, geranium, century cardinale, verbena, and aobelita perfection pander to the English love of colorful flowers. Photo: Steven Still.

by a fundamental change in agricultural practices had occurred anywhere on the Continent. Estates in France for both farming and hunting were granted by royal patent and had often been in the same family for centuries. But the family rarely lived on the land. Because of the central organization of the French government and the military, the nobility did not establish and pass on to their descendants the kind of deep-seated love and mystique of country life that shaped the values of the English nobility and squirearchy. This gradual taming and molding of the larger landscape with its peculiarly English devotion to nature and to the rhythms of rural living is an important, even decisive, element in the landscape gardening movement of the eighteenth century.

But before we can gather the threads that lead us to one of the central events in garden history in the eighteenth century, it is impor-

tant to understand that English gardens, before they took a decisive turn toward the newly discovered "natural" style, were originally something else entirely. There was more to them than just "leaping fences" as Walpole put it in his Whig account of the English garden revolution.

Although W. G. Hoskins in his study of the English countryside has provided us with a splendid, sweeping view of the early vernacular landscape, the rudimentary state of garden history has yet to produce a comparable picture of the English garden in the same medieval period. We think we know more than we actually do because of our familiarity with the stereotyped medieval garden illustrations drawn from *The Romance of the Rose* and other continental sources. Yet as that careful historian Miles Hadfield has pointed out, we have almost no documentary evidence and no picture to prove that English gardens in the late fifteenth century have much to do with the Flemish or Burgundian models used in those well-known miniatures. "Before Tudor times," Hadfield has warned, "we search in vain among British sources for anything comparable." From the scanty evidence that has survived, he concludes that except for "purposeful" vegetable gardens and orchards, "gardening as an art and the aesthetic appreciation of flowers scarcely existed until the fifteenth or early sixteenth centuries."[5] Certainly the earliest known English treatise on gardening, the manuscript *The Feate of Gardening,* written around 1440 by "Mayster Ion Gardener," supports the impression that most gardening was for a utilitarian purpose. Written in verse, the treatise is so thoroughly practical that it could be easily followed today. What is also valuable in the manuscript is the extensive list of plants cultivated in England at that time.

There is no mistaking that the writer was an experienced gardener, noting such details as that pears should be grafted onto hawthorn. Ninety-seven plants are listed, sixty-one of which are native while twenty-six have been identified as foreign. Only ten are not adequately described to determine their origin. He lists flowers that are still identified with the old-fashioned English cottage garden—cowslip, daffodil, foxglove, hollyhock, honeysuckle, lavender, Madonna lily, lupine, periwinkle, hepatica, primrose, rose, and scabiosa. Descendants of these same flowers were to be brought back into the mainstream of English gardens by Gertrude Jekyll in the twentieth century.

Plant lists, as valuable as they are, give us little with which to construct a three-dimensional image of either the freeholder's patch or the abbot's *giardino segreto.* John Harvey's careful works on medieval gardens have gone further in challenging Hadfield's restrained conclusion. English records are full of brief, unadorned references to gardens attached to monastic precincts, churches, and chapels. Alicia Amherst has noted, for example, that Henry VI in his will left a chapel garden to the church at Eton College: "The space between the wall of the church and the wall of the cloister shall conteyne trees and flowers, for the service of the same church," and be surrounded by a "good high wall with towers convenient thereto."[6] Yet the figure of "Jentyl Gardener" in Lincoln Cathedral with his iron-shod wooden spade brings us closer to an actual garden of the fourteenth century than a hundred legal references from wills and inventories of the period.

Nothing remotely resembling the early humanist gardens of contemporary Renaissance Italy that attempted to recreate the gardens of classical antiquity existed in England. Nor did the English have the benefit of even a verbal glimpse of Pliny's villas in Tuscany and Laurentum to animate the transformation from the simple geometry of the medieval garden into the garden splendors of the High Renaissance. Secondhand interpretations of classical garden art by way of France and the Low Countries may have impressed the occasional English visitor, but not enough to spark serious change in the traditional English garden. Even more rare would have been a copy of Colonna's *Hypnerotomachia poliphili,* which was not translated into English until 1592. The fine illustrations in Colonna's romance, with their classical allusions in garden settings, did, however, ultimately reach an eager and receptive audience during the late Elizabethan and early Jacobean periods. The book's fantasy vision of the antique world—a dreamland of classical ruins, pyramids, antique trophies, fountains, pools, arbors, and topiary work—would ultimately affect English garden styles as it had earlier affected those of Italy and France.

Even a cursory comparison between sixteenth-century Italy, a civilization that had produced the Villas Madama, Giulia, Lante, and d'Este, and an England that had barely ventured beyond the castle keep and manor yard dramatizes the distance that separated the two cultures. "Civil strife is not conducive to the arts of either building or gardening," and as Roy Strong has pointed out in his study of

Dutch artist Leonard Knyff (1650–1721) painted this view of Hampton Court Palace. Marot's parterres are clearly shown spread out before Wren's new palace front. The original avenues were laid out by Charles II with the help of André Mollet. Royal Library, Windsor Castle.

the English Renaissance garden, "it is only with the establishment of the Tudor pax after the Battle of Bosworth in 1485 that their arts begin again." [7]

The development of the English country house with its gardens and parks does not seriously get under way until the first decades of the sixteenth century and after the accession of the eighteen-year-old Henry VIII (1491–1547) in 1509. Suddenly, astonishing palaces on a royal scale were built, and ostentatious

country houses resembling palaces began to spring up to dominate their surroundings with their gardens. By the time of Elizabeth I (1533–1603) the country house catalog included Longleat (built 1550–80), Montacute (1580–1601), Burghley (1577–87), and the Countess of Shrewsbury's Hardwick begun in 1576.

From the standpoint of the cultivated landscape, the parks that encircled these new rural palaces were eventually to play an important

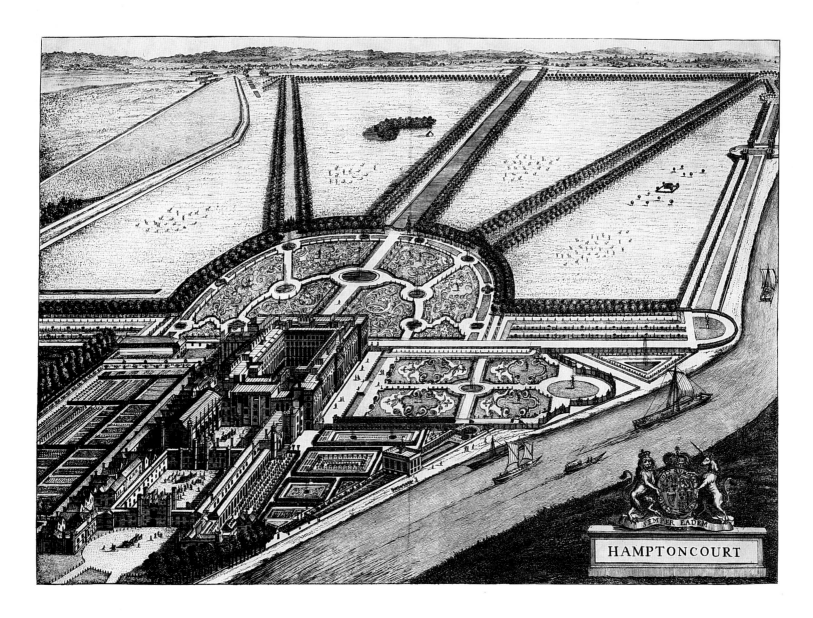

HAMPTONCOURT

role in the development of English garden aesthetics. Originally the English "park" was nothing more than a large, enclosed, wooded tract maintained primarily for hunting deer. Arthur Rackham has estimated that some 2 percent of the land of England was emparked in the heyday of parks in the eighteenth century, enough to give an impression of well-cared-for woodland over large, strategic areas of the countryside. Anyone who could afford a park could have one, and, as Rackham has pointed out, large preserves for the production of venison, wood, and timber became an important status symbol.[8] Many of the surviving great parks that were transformed and landscaped by Capability Brown and others in the second half of the eighteenth century actually had a long history and originated centuries before. Blenheim Palace's Woodstock Park where Brown worked was actually fenced in and separated from the surrounding forest by the Anglo-Saxon King Alfred before the year 1000. In the eighteenth century old, unused parks were expanded and new ones created until whole sections of countryside were absorbed into these vast preserves converted into "laid-out" landscapes.

During the first years of his reign, the young Henry VIII energetically played the warrior-prince, consolidating Tudor power at home and abroad. Borrowing from the French court where the politics of spectacle had been perfected, he staged fetes, tilts, tourneys, and masquerades to rival if not challenge the splendor of François I and Fontainebleau.

With Henry's dissolution of the monasteries in 1536, the crown suddenly had far more money for extravagant building than ever before. The king's new role, in defiance of the Universal Church and the rest of Christendom, as God's exalted representative on earth required new ceremonial settings worthy of his triumphant reign. After Cardinal Wolsey had turned his palace of Hampton Court over to the king in 1525, the building and gardens underwent a major expansion and remodeling. Henry's gardens at Hampton Court became a perfect backyard for the conspicuous display by a parvenu dynasty of Tudor heraldry. The dragons, greyhounds, lions, horses, and antelopes that were brilliantly painted and gilded or shaped from topiary left no doubt that the king's gardens were intended to establish and celebrate his dynasty's legitimate claims to the throne. The royal gardens carried the message loud and clear.

Henry was familiar with the gardens of the French kings, beginning with those of the Château of Blois laid out for Louis XII between 1500 and 1510 by the Italian Pacello de Mercogliano (d. 1534) and the later work carried out by François at Fontainebleau with the help of Italian architects, painters, and gardeners. But perhaps the most famous garden was that of Gaillon built by Georges Cardinal d'Amboise. Du Cerceau's engraving shows a layout of magnificent scale centered on an elegant pavilion and surrounded by square parterres laid out in elaborate geometric patterns.

James Gibbs (1682–1754), who worked at Stowe, redesigned the garden and park at Hartwell House, Buckinghamshire (shown here in a 1738 painting by Balthasar Nebot), where he explored new relationships between the classical and romantic. Buckinghamshire County Museum, Aylesbury.

Sir Roy Strong has called Wollaton Hall, Nottinghamshire, a unique example of an Elizabethan house and garden conceived as a single architectural unit. The house was built in the 1580s. Had it survived into the eighteenth century, Lancelot Brown would surely have swept it away. Yale Center for British Art, Paul Mellon Collection.

In many ways Hampton Court's use of galleries and arbors in the gardens resembles Blois and Gaillon more than Fontainebleau. But the extravagant display of heraldry that turned the garden into a vehicle for blatant royal propaganda was distinctly English, although not without French precedent. In the ancient Persian tradition, the pleasure garden is seen to relate to the king and to the court as an outward sign of regal magnificence. It is a tradition that Henry quickly adopted and expanded with the remodeling of other royal palaces at Whitehall and at Nonsuch. These gardens like the architecture were designed and built by the Office of Works under the king's surveyor, also following French court precedent.

Even though everyone speaks knowingly of "the Elizabethan garden," just as we speak of the "cloister garden," there is in fact little surviving evidence of these gardens created between 1550 and 1600 to tell us what they actually looked like. Whatever existed was quite removed from consistent garden fashion. For a half-century after England turned Protestant in 1558, the country was virtually isolated from the rest of Europe, in particular from the creative, energizing influence of Italy during the critical period of its golden age of garden-making. It was during this period that the Italian Renaissance concept of the garden as an extension of the architecture came into its own. This meant, in terms of the garden, that architectural principles of harmony and proportion, expressed in geometry, were extended into a man-made landscape. The rational, inexorable results were to sustain the basic principles of garden design throughout most of Europe for the next three hundred years. By the end of Elizabeth's reign, gardens laid out over the previous fifty years, like Theobalds, Kenilworth, and even the remodeled Nonsuch, were out of date and isolated from the European mainstream of Renaissance aesthetic formulas.

Even though the English Renaissance garden developed in ways that reflected its own national and cultural history, separating it in fundamental ways from the gardens of Europe, England's garden ideology more or less followed Renaissance principles of the pleasure garden. First of all, the bounty and beauty of a garden expressed man's ability to tame and control nature. Second, and this theme is consistent throughout the European Renaissance, a garden was a visible and important attribute of its owner's standing in the social and political pecking order. Closely related to the garden's function as a sign of social and political status was the use of the garden for entertainment and the ceremonial purposes of court life. Finally the garden was a place to systematically collect and study the variety and complexity of God's creation in nature by gathering rare plants and trees from the newly discovered corners of the earth. As the British Empire grew, England's gardens dramatically expanded in order to contain the new horticultural wonders that could easily thrive in the temperate English soil and climate.

Jacobean and Caroline Gardens, 1603–1649

The peace and stability introduced by the reign of James I, with the court's open, imaginative patronizing of the arts, had, of course, an important impact on English garden design. For the first time in fifty years the country was opened to new aesthetic and horticultural influences from the Continent. Anne of Denmark and Henry, Prince of Wales, both patronized Salomon de Caus (c. 1576–1626), who laid out the gardens at Somerset House and at the palaces of Richmond and Greenwich. A French Huguenot engineer, de Caus had traveled and studied in Italy before arriving at the English court in 1610, bringing new continental ideas with him. Trained in mathematics, he was fascinated with perspective, writing a treatise on the subject in 1612 while working for the young English prince. In 1613, James I's daughter Elizabeth married Frederick V, the elector Palatine, and de Caus followed her to Heidelberg where he became the engineer for the elector's gardens there. Without question his most important contribution to garden art was the publication of *Les Raisons des forces mouvantes* in 1615, laying out the principles of hydraulics. The work became the foundation for the elaborate garden water systems of the seventeenth century that were to become so popular throughout Northern Europe.

De Caus brought to English garden planning a solid background in Renaissance engineering studies and a firsthand study of the latest continental garden fashions. All this enabled him to pioneer the architectural alignment of house and garden and the use of perspective in garden planning. He and his

brother (or nephew) Isaac, who followed him to England, also pursued the family preoccupation with the technology of fountains, grottoes, and automata.

The garden of Wilton begun by Isaac de Caus in 1632 for the fourth earl of Pembroke, Philip Herbert (1584–1650), is a landmark in English garden history. Not only do we know more about it than any other garden of the period before the civil war, but it represents the most complex, sophisticated pleasure garden of seventeenth-century England. Nothing like it had been seen in the country before. Wilton's transformation of the medieval *hortus conclusus* into a major expression of Renaissance garden art was no doubt the result of de Caus's collaboration with Inigo Jones (1573–

An aerial view of the garden at Wilton, designed by Inigo Jones, looking toward the classical grotto built into the raised terraces. Isaac de Caus, *Le Jardin de Wilton*.

1652). In its confident, generous, aristocratic interpretations of Italian garden design principles, Wilton House and its garden is the perfect symbol of those halcyon years between 1629 and 1640 called the King's Peace, when Charles I ruled without benefit of Parliament. The earl of Pembroke had already established himself as a patron of gardening at Moor Park, Hertfordshire, a garden Sir William Temple (1628–1699) called "the perfectest figure of a garden I ever saw." Temple's famous description of a classic Jacobean garden in his 1685 essay *Upon the Gardens of Epicurus* may well be based on Pembroke's first garden at Moor Park.

It was no doubt the theater designer and painter Inigo Jones, who had traveled and studied Palladian architecture firsthand in the Veneto, who laid down Wilton's coherent, formal plan organized on the broad avenue

extending through the garden from the house. Jones was preeminently a man of the theater, and his study of Italian theater design and architecture inspired him to use the latest garden designs in his stage and masque productions for the Caroline court. The drawing for a garden backdrop in *The Shepherd's Paradise* in 1633, with its steps, terraces, and fountains set in geometric beds, represents the garden ideal just then coming into vogue in Europe.

Before entering the garden at Wilton the visitor could first admire it from the windows of the *piano nobile* of the house. Later, after strolling down the middle walk reaching to the grotto, another overview could be obtained on the far side from the balustraded terrace stretching the entire width of the space. The grotto was the climax of Wilton's waterworks designed by de Caus. In his grotto, rusticated on the exterior, sea monsters, gods and goddesses, and mechanical birds delighted visitors. De Caus had actually described in detail the mechanics "To counterfeit the voice of small birds by means of Water and

Air" in his book *Waterworks*. Water stored in reservoirs on the roof of the grotto, fed by gravity, operated the mechanical theater hidden in the dark rooms below.

The first of the garden's three cross divisions, as the visitor descended by steps, was an elaborate display of *parterre de broderie* in the latest French style. The arabesque scrolls and band volutes are similar to designs published by André Mollet. Mollet had been summoned to England in the 1630s, according to his preface in *Le Jardin de plaisir* (1651), to introduce French garden art to the English court, but precisely where he worked is unclear. His chief patron was Henrietta Maria, wife of Charles I, and his first royal commission was for the garden at St. James's Palace. Later, in 1642, Mollet redesigned the gardens of Wimbledon House for the queen.

The midsection of Wilton, called the "wilderness," is remarkable for the designer's disdain (expressed by the symmetrical plan) for the free spirit of the River Nadder as it follows its irregular channel diagonally across the rectangular garden and through the geometry. The heavy plantation of trees and landscape on either side may have been intended to hide the river's intrusion, although French garden designers of the period would quickly have manipulated the watercourse into well-defined canals and formal basins.

Beyond the wilderness was a large oval circus in front of the grotto dominated by a cast of the Borghese *Gladiator* by Hubert Le Sueur, "the most famous Statue of all that antiquity hath left." The oval walks around the statue were planted with cherry trees in a pattern that recalls the work of André Mollet's father Claude. The large arbors on either side of the wilderness have both Italian and French precedents. All these French touches must have pleased Queen Henrietta Maria, who had come from France to marry Charles I in 1625.

Before he was executed, Charles visited his friend Pembroke at Wilton every summer, and he would stroll in the gardens surrounded by the cultural expression of his political ideals. The garden at Wilton was indeed the king's Arcadia. Pembroke, who inherited Wilton when his brother died, was a great friend of the king's, and it well may have been the king who suggested that he remodel the south front of the house and build the garden.

Wilton's garden could easily have served as a setting for one of Ben Jonson's masques, which Pembroke loved. It could also have reminded him of the chivalric scenes in Honoré d'Urfé's *L'Astrée* (1620) and Saulnier du Verdier's *Romant des Romans,* both popular French romances that were translated and dedicated to the earl. Fifty years later, following the restoration of Charles II, de Caus's *Le Jardin de Wilton* and his treatise on waterworks spread the fame of Wilton not only in England but internationally. As John Woolridge, in his *Systema Horti-Cultura,* wrote of the grotto in 1688, eulogizing the work of de Caus: "The most famous in this kind that this Kingdom affords, is that *Wiltonian Grotto* near unto *Salisbury,* on which no cost was spared to make it complete, and wherein you may view, or might have lately so done, the best of water-works. . . ."[9]

English garden art in the seventeenth century had little impact on the Continent, but the Hortus Palatinus in Heidelberg, commissioned by James I's daughter when she moved with her husband to Germany in 1613, is a notable exception. In fact, it was far more in the international Renaissance style, a hybrid affair laid out on the slopes of the hills above the Neckar River valley. Elizabeth invited her former drawing teacher, Salomon de Caus, to design and construct the garden over five narrow terraces. Each terrace was divided in the Renaissance fashion by hedges and pergolas. One terrace placed at a right angle to the rest of the garden provided a breathtaking view of the river valley below. All of the Renaissance vocabulary of mazes, gazebos, statuary, and tubs of trees decorated the garden. Waterworks, grottoes, and animated figures were also deployed along the walks, retaining walls, and connecting stairs. In many ways the German garden must have resembled the garden of Richmond Palace, also designed by de

A topiary bird at Levens
Hall. Photo: Derek Fell.

Caus for Henry, Prince of Wales. No visual evidence of Richmond survives, but we are tantalized by the fragments of the garden of Hatfield begun by de Caus in 1607 for Robert Cecil (1563–1612), the king's first minister. The Renaissance garden of Hatfield comes vividly alive in the description left by a visiting Frenchman, Monsieur de Sorbière.

It stands very advantageously, from which you have Prospect of nothing but Woods and Meadows, Hills and Dales, which are very agreeable Objects that present themselves to us at all Sorts of Distances: Our Nobility . . . would have made Use of the Waters here, for some Excellent Uses and Inventions; and more especially of a small River, which as it were forms the Compartments of a large Parterre, and rises and secretly loses itself in an Hundred Places, and whose Banks are all Lined or Boarded [presumably the Island and Dell]. . . . When you come through the Chief Avenue to the Park Side, and when the Gates of the lower Courts are open, there are Walks present themselves to your View, that reach to the further end of the

Park, and make you loose your sight. . . . We dined in a Hall that looked into a Greenplot with Two Fountains in it [Chaundler's and de Caus's], and having Espaliers on the Sides, but a Balister before it, upon which are Flower-Pots and Statues: From this Parterre there is a way down by Two Pair of Stairs, of about Twelve or Fifteen Steps to another, and from the Second to the Third [this seems to be a muddled account of terrace and upper and lower garden]: From this Terrace you have a Prospect of the great Water Parterre I have spoken of [the Island and Dell]. . . . I ought not to forget the vineyard, nor the several small buildings on the side of it, some of which serve for a Retreat to several sorts of Birds, which are very tame. There are also Arbours or Summer-Houses, like Turkish Chiosks, upon some of the Eminences, which have a Gallery round, and are erected in the most Beautiful Places [e.g., standing in the Dell], in order to the Enjoying of the Diversified Prospects of this Charming Country: You have also in those Places, where the River enters into and comes out of the Parterre, open Sort of

Boxes, with Seats round, where you may see a vast Number of Fish pass to and fro in the water, which is exceeding clear; and they seem to come in Shoals to enjoy all the Pleasures of the Place; and quitting their own Element by jumping sometimes out of the Water, this they do as it were to observe all the things I have describ'd to you.[10]

Hatfield's walled Italianate terrace system falling away from the house continued to set a garden style to the end of the seventeenth century. Old Elizabethan and Jacobean manor houses, usually perched on a hill, were given fashionable new face-lifts to reflect the newly discovered but imperfectly understood continental garden designs, especially with terraces that were already being replaced.

Restored box maze in the sunken knot garden beside Old Palace, Hatfield House, Hertfordshire. Photo: Heather Angel.

While Robert Cecil promoted the concept of the Renaissance pleasure garden in the grand manner at Hatfield, John Tradescant (c. 1570–1638) represented the horticultural dimensions of Cecil's complex undertaking, where hydraulic engineering was of equal if not more importance than the horticulture. The first of a long line of dedicated professional plant collectors, that "circle of curious gardeners," Tradescant was described by John Parkinson (1567–1650) as a "painful industrious searcher and lover of all nature's varieties."[11] English botanical studies were not fifty years old when Tradescant first came into the orbit of the powerful Lord Cecil at Hatfield. Tradescant's financial interest in the Virginia trade brought in many North American plants. Later the plantsman traveled in Russia and even made two dangerous excursions along the coast of Algeria. England's close ties to Holland provided him with another important source of imports, plants the Dutch were bringing in from the Middle and Far East.

Within the decade that the first botanical gardens were laid out in Pisa (1543) and in Padua (1545), England got under way with the publication of *The Names of Herbes in Greek, Latin, English, Dutch and French with the Common Names That Herbaries and Apothecaries Use* (1548). This provincial collection of names had been "gathered" by William Turner, who studied medicine and traveled widely on the Continent to France, Germany, Italy, and Switzerland where botanical studies were far more advanced. His book is often cited by scholars as evidence of the date when many foreign plants, described for the first time, actually entered England, but this is obviously misleading. Many plants were already well established in Britain before their names first appeared in print.

In the sixteenth century exotic plants, shrubs, and trees were beginning to pour into Europe as the West continued to expand its empire around the world, bringing about a revolution in food, flowers, and the looks of the landscape. Between 1500 and 1700 the arrival of foreign imports in Britain included

many novelties that are often now considered native. It is this tradition of quickly and successfully absorbing not only plants but gardening practices from abroad that continues to give the British garden its cosmopolitan quality.

Botanical gardens had already spread from Italy to such cities as Leiden, Leipzig, and Heidelberg, when England's first plant collection for systematic study was assembled at Oxford in 1621. Books also began to play an important part in England in the early seventeenth century with the appearance of John Gerard's (1545–1612) great *Herball* in 1597 and John Parkinson's *Paradisi in sole Paradisus terrestris* in 1629. Parkinson is far more accurate in his description of nearly one thousand plants then cultivated in Britain, and he seems to have had a greater appreciation for the decorative value of plants than earlier writers, providing some eight hundred illustrations in his catalog. Between Parkinson's birth in 1567 and his death in 1650, the great Elizabethan-Jacobean period in the study and practice of gardening of all kinds had advanced in remarkable ways. It was a solid foundation on which the English garden would continue to build over the next three hundred years.

Following the Restoration in 1660, the Golden Age of Jacobean and Caroline gardens under the cosmopolitan patronage of an enlightened court would be looked upon as the ideal framework for the future of the English garden. But when William Temple described from memory in 1685 his vision of an ideal garden, recalling Moor Park in Hertforshire laid out fifty years earlier, he was also documenting nostalgia for a garden setting that had already irrevocably disappeared in England.

The perfectest Figure of a Garden I ever saw, either at Home or Abroad, was that of Moor-Park in Hertfordshire, when I knew it about thirty Years ago. It was made by the Countess of Bedford, esteemed among the greatest Wits of her Time, and celebrated by doctor Donne; and with very great Care, excellent Contrivance, and much Cost; but greater Sums may be thrown away without Effect or Honour, if there want Sense in Proportion to Money, or if Nature be not followed; which I take to be the great Rule in this, and perhaps in every Thing else, as far as the Conduct not only of our Lives, but our Governments. And whether the greatest of Mortal Men should attempt the forcing of Nature may best be judged, by observing how seldom God Almighty does it Himself, by so few, true, and undisputed Miracles, as we see or hear of the World. For my own part, I know not three wiser Precepts for the Conduct either of Princes or Private Men, than "*Servari Modum, Fineque tueri, Naturamque sequi.*"

Because I take the Garden I have named to have been in all Kinds the most beautiful and perfect, at least in the Figure and Disposition, that I have ever seen, I will describe it for a Model to those that meet with such a Situation, and are above the Regards of common Expence. It lies on the Side of a Hill, (upon which the House stands) but not very steep. The Length of the House, where the best Rooms and of most Use or Pleasure are lies upon the Breadth of the Garden, the Great Parlour opens into the Middle of a Terras Gravel-Walk that lies even with it, and which may be, as I remember, about three hundred Paces long, and broad in Proportion; the Border set with Standard Laurels, and at large Distances, which have the Beauty of Orange-Trees out of Flower and Fruit: From this Walk are Three Descents by many Stone Steps, in the Middle and at each End, into a very large Parterre. This is divided into Quarters by Gravel-Walks, and adorned with Two Fountains and Eight Statues in the several Quarters; at the End of the Terras-Walk are Two Summer-Houses, and the Sides of the Parterre are ranged with two large Cloisters, open to the Garden, upon Arches of Stone, and ending with two other Summer-Houses

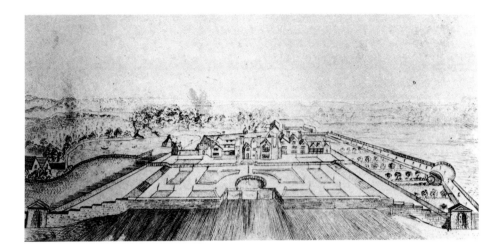

Wotton House, Surrey, sketched by John Evelyn in 1653. One of the first genuine Italianate garden layouts in England, according to John Harris, even though the house itself is vernacular Tudor. Collection: Trustees of the Will of the late J.H.C. Evelyn.

even with the Cloisters, which are paved with Stone, and designed for Walks of Shade, there being none other in the whole Parterre. Over these two Cloisters are two Terrasses covered with Lead, and fenced with Balusters; and the passage into these Airy Walks is out of the two Summer-Houses, at the End of the first Terras-Walk. The Cloister facing the South is covered with Vines, and would have been proper for an Orange-House, and the other for Myrtles, or other more common Greens; and had, I doubt not, been cast for that Purpose, if this Piece of Gardening had been then in as much Vogue as it is now.

From the Middle of the Parterre is a Descent by many Steps flying on each Side of a Grotto that lies between them (covered with Lead, and Flat) into the lower Garden, which is all Fruit-Trees ranged about the several Quarters of a Wilderness which is very Shady; the Walks here are all Green, the Grotto embellish'd with Figures of Shell-Rock-work, Fountains, and Waterworks. If the Hill had not ended with the lower Garden, and the Wall were not bounded by a common Way that goes through the Park, they might have added a Third Quarter of all Greens; but this Want is supplied by a Garden on the other Side the House, which is all of that Sort, very

The outline of the gardens of Montacute House, Somerset, has survived with little change from the sixteenth century. The balustraded walls with stone lanterns and finials form the forecourt of the house. However, the twentieth-century borders are designed in the style of Gertrude Jekyll, and other later elements distort the picture of an Elizabethan garden. Photo: Everett Scott.

Wild, Shady, and adorned with rough Rock-work and Fountains.

This was Moor-Park, when I was acquainted with it, and the sweetest Place, I think, that I have seen in my Life, either before or since, at Home or Abroad; what it is now I can give little Account, having passed through several Hands that have made great Changes in Gardens as well as Houses; but the Remembrance of what it was is too pleasant ever to forget, and therefore I do not believe to have mistaken the Figure of it, which may serve for a Pattern to the best Gardens of our Manner, and that are most proper for our Country and Climate.

What I have said, of the best Forms of Gardens, is meant only of such as are in some Sort regular; for there may be other Forms wholly irregular, that may, for aught I know, have more Beauty than any of the others; but they must owe it to some extraordinary Dispositions of Nature in the Seat, or some great Race of Fancy or Judgment in the Contrivance, which may reduce many disagreeing Parts into some Figure, which shall yet upon the whole, be very agreeable.[12]

Temple, in the same essay, was the first to point out—later to be followed by Shaftesbury, Addison, and Pope—that the abstract French notion of idealized nature had nothing to do with the ordinary, everyday variety that actually surrounds us. In the era of Le Nôtre and to a large extent in that of Temple, "nature" was somehow equated with reason and the ideal of universal order. Nature might well be present in the formal garden, but as Pope says in his *Essay on Criticism,* it is disguised as "nature methodized," or as Dryden wrote, "nature corrected and amended." Temple's suggestion that "wholly irregular" forms could have more beauty is followed by a reference to the Chinese scorn of "proportions, symmetries or uniformities," after which he praises their unorthodox approach to gardens, utterly unknown in the West: "Their greatest reach of imagination is employed in contriving Figures, where the Beauties shall be great, and strike the Eye, but without any order or disposition of parts that shall be commonly or easily observed."[13] Temple then claims that the Chinese word for their freer, informal taste in garden layout is "sharawadgi." Aside from the word's exotic, un-Chinese look, garden historians have ever since identified "sharawadgi" and the passage describing it as the first prophetic words predicting the dramatic new direction the English Picturesque or landscape style would take over the next fifty or sixty years. Temple's suggestions were not, one hastens to add, taken up during his lifetime, and it is only in retrospect that so much importance has been placed on his words by scholars, particularly in the twentieth century.

The English Formal Garden

As late as the 1760s, Horace Walpole could not understand why the English had not "stumbled on to the principle of modern gardening" three centuries earlier, in places like the embowered retreat of Henry II's Woodstock Park where the king had romantically imprisoned the beautiful Rosemond, his mistress, in a bower labyrinth. Having once discovered the delights of paradise in such an unlikely place as Woodstock, Walpole found it incomprehensible that "we should have persisted in retaining its reverse, symmetrical and unnatural gardens."[14]

Certainly international garden fashions dominated by the axial thrust, in common with the rest of Europe and strongly influenced by France, continued to spread throughout England in the last quarter of the seventeenth century. André Mollet, whose *Le Jardin de plaisir* was the modern textbook for design, had been made royal gardener at St. James's in 1661. In 1662 and again in 1668, Charles II tried to lure André Le Nôtre across the Channel to be his garden advisor.

Leading practitioners of the new formal style such as George London (d. 1714) had traveled and studied in France. John Evelyn (1620–1705), who had also admired firsthand the major royal gardens of the Tuileries, Luxembourg, Saint Cloud, Versailles, and Cardinal Richelieu's famous gardens at Rueil, was along with Stephen Switzer (1682–1745) one of London's admirers. The gardens London laid out in partnership with Henry Wise (1653–1738) at Longleat, later destroyed by Capability Brown when he landscaped the park in 1757, give a fair idea of the English interpretation of the formal garden tradition. With the accession of the Dutchman William III, London was made royal gardener and took over the responsibilities at Hampton

Court and Kensington Palace. Radiating avenues had in the Restoration period become the rage, and in these long drives lined with lime trees, grandees like the duke of Beaufort at Badminton took command over nature as firmly as their French or Dutch contemporaries.

Not far away from Badminton, Lord Bathhurst's Cirencester Park (built c. 1714) rivals its ducal neighbor in scale, measuring eight kilometers long and some five kilometers at its widest point. The park at Cirencester is without question the best (and largely surviving) example of Stephen Switzer's "Rural and Extensive Gardening."

Switzer worked with Lord Bathhurst at Cirencester about the time that the first volume of his magnum opus, *Ichnographia rustica,* was published in 1715. Switzer's theory that the whole estate should become part of the landscape design was an important step toward Walpole's "modern principles." Great axial lines like those that still exist at Cirences-

Badminton House, Gloucestershire, by Antonio Canaletto. An idealized lawn sets off the magnificent palace of Badminton, giving it a stage-set quality. Collection of the Duke of Beaufort. Photo: Bridgeman/Art Resource, New York.

ter—Switzer's "boldest strokes"—could efficiently organize a vast estate in the grand manner, and as he wrote, "all the adjacent country [should] be laid open to view." When Lord Bathurst invited Alexander Pope to inspect the work at Cirencester, the poet thought it was lacking in contrast and variety, an aesthetic principle then widely believed by writers and artists to be critical. His lordship, Pope observed to a friend, "should have raised two or three mounts because his situation is all a plain, and nothing can please without variety." Walls that had provided the English with their much needed privacy and "by which the eye is as if it were imprisoned and the feet fettered in the midst of the extensive charms of nature" must come down, the poet concluded. "All the adjacent country [should] be laid open to view."[15]

THE LANDSCAPING OF ENGLAND

In 1711, four years before the first volume of Switzer's major work appeared, Joseph Addison (1672–1719) had launched his famous attack on the garden as a formal geometric extension of architecture in the pages of *The Spectator,* No. 34. Both in his arguments appearing in *The Tatler* and *The Spectator* and in his romantic fantasy *Leonora,* Addison was a leading advocate of a more relaxed approach to garden design that would imitate "the rough careless Strokes of Nature." Laying the groundwork for the English garden revolution later in the century, he argued that nature and reason must go hand in hand and that works of nature were "more delightful than artificial show." His writings have become basic documents of the ideology of the English landscape school.[16] For Addison and his followers, the ideal garden was one that aspired to an ideal state of nature in its freedom and openness. But his ideology went even further when he insisted that, just as the English temperament had rejected the absolutism of

French political theory, England's gardens and its landscape should be cleared of the artificial, contrived order imposed upon nature by the autocratic Le Nôtre and his followers. Every good Whig landowner in the free and open possession of his estate had a duty to celebrate the land as the visible manifestation of his political base. "To view your estate," as John Dixon Hunt explained, "in a Prospect which is well laid out, and diversified with Fields and Meadows; Woods and Rivers . . . is to realize palpably the idea of your citizenship and its place in traditions which go back to the Romans."[17]

Alexander Pope (1688–1744) was to become both the virtuoso spokesman and practitioner of the new school. But Pope's and Addison's writings may well have their genealogy in a new garden literature that had first appeared nearly a century earlier with *Elements of Architecture* (1624) by Sir Henry Wotton (1568–1639), one of the first writers to celebrate a garden's irregularity. "I must note a certain contrariety between building and *gardening,*" he wrote after observing Italian gardens on steep, irregular hillsides. "For as Fabrigues should be *regular,* so Gardens should be *irregular,* or at least cast into a wilde *Regularitie.* . . . The Beholder descending many steps, was afterwards conveyed again by several mountings and valings, to various entertainment of his sent and sight: which I shall not need to describe (for that were poetical) let me only note this, that every one of these diversities, was as if he had been magically transported into a new Garden."[18] Agreeing with Wotton, his contemporary Francis Bacon (1561–1626), in his famous essay *Of Gardens,* urged diversity and variety, particularly in a garden's horticultural profusion and richness.

Every writer on the genesis of the English landscape garden since the eighteenth century, when Walpole compared lines from John Milton's *Paradise Lost* to the gardens of Stourhead and Hagley Park, has linked the English garden revolution to Milton. Earlier Stephen Switzer also had credited the poet with inspiring his grand garden schemes, exclaiming "How noble and majestic that inimitable Description of Paradise by Mr. Milton."[19]

When both national poetry and politics are introduced into the debate on what was the most rational, modern, and appealing approach to the laying out and ornamenting of a garden or park, the subject and the underlying philosophy are bound to become more complicated. What was happening, in fact, during the first decades of the eighteenth century was the working out of a doctrine among poets, knowledgeable garden amateurs, and the garden "professionals" like Charles Bridgeman (d. 1738) and Stephen Switzer who advanced a stylized simplicity and a simplified landscape grandeur to correspond to the gardens described in classical literature. It was, as a number of scholars have concluded, more of a poetic concept than a visual one, at least in the beginning.[20] With the rise and popularity of classical architecture based on Renaissance notions of antiquity, the English Augustans, no doubt encouraged by paintings of the Roman campagna by Claude and other landscape painters, began to imagine an affinity between the Italian countryside, which was in fact classical ground, and their own undulating fields, woods, and natural turf.

Beginning with the seventeenth century, Italy had become the chief focus of English travelers making the Grand Tour. Italian gardens and their villas were an important part of the itinerary. The very complexity of the Italian garden experience, which included sculpture galleries, theaters, living botanical encyclopedias, and modern reconstructions of the classical *hortus,* was incomparably appealing to the astonished northern tourist. Travelers like Evelyn, Addison, William Kent, and Joseph Spence assembled in their notes and diaries anthologies of gardens and architecture in their imagined relationship to their classical past. Great Renaissance gardens such as those of the Villa d'Este and the Farnese Palace on the Palatine Hill in Rome represented "a creative confusion of old and new," and this conjunction of antique souvenirs with new

building based on classical principles was to have a major impact on English garden taste.

One must also visualize the gradual transformation of the entire English countryside by enclosure throughout the seventeenth and eighteenth centuries. The movement was accelerated by the economic value of animals grazing on a vast scale. The large, walled agricultural estate became a fixture in the landscape. At the same time a concerted effort to replant and increase the depleted woodlands marked the beginning of wholesale rural improvement. There is no question that agricultural enclosure and reforestation affected the simultaneous laying out of ideal eighteenth-century landscape parks that gradually imposed themselves on the entire countryside right up to the foundation of the Georgian manor house itself.[21] From the standpoint of the great Whig landowners who were the most ambitious proponents of the garden revolution, the idea that one could profitably improve the estate and woods while creating a humanistic landscape that reflected both ancient tradition and the new scientific advances in agricultural management had a powerful, irresistible appeal. "Lord Bathurst, Lord Cobham of Stowe and Lord Carlisle can be shown to have been men of high principles," wrote the late Christopher Hussey of three landowners he believed were sincerely convinced of their duty to improve their piece of the world for posterity.[22] The sublime park of Lord Carlisle (1670–1738) at Castle Howard can still evoke, in Horace Walpole's words, "the grandest scenes of rural magnificence." "Nobody had told me," Walpole wrote to a friend, "that I should at one view see a palace, a town, a fortified city, temples on high places, woods worthy of being each a metropolis of the Druids, the noblest lawn in the world fenced by half the horizon, and a mausoleum that would tempt one to be buried alive. . . ."[23] There is no reason to doubt Carlisle's daughter's poem declaring that her father had been moved by classical description to create an Elysium, an ideal world in Yorkshire.

Castle Howard, the great palace in Yorkshire, is perfectly scaled to the grandeur of its setting. Photo: Fred Maroon.

Building the proper Points of view adorn
Of Grecian, Roman and Egyptian form
Interspersed with Woods and verdant
   Plains
Such as possess'd of old th' Arcadian
   Swains.[24]

Not only do the majestic, sweeping views confirm the inspiration of the poetry of Virgil, but the composition, scale, and the antique buildings in the park at Castle Howard explicitly recall the landscape paintings of Claude, leading us through successive visions of a lost Golden Age.

Castle Howard did not derive, as did Lord Cobham's Stowe, from an evolution of garden design through stages of change, but rather from an original new approach that incorporated the entire visible landscape of the Howard estate into a heroic panorama. Even though Sir John Vanbrugh (1664–1726) was commissioned by Lord Carlisle to design the house, followed later by Nicholas Hawksmoor (1661–1736) who worked on other structures, there is little question that Carlisle himself was the "directing mind" behind the splendid conception.[25] Unlike Stowe, its contemporary, whose parks became a changing display for the work of talented landscape designers like Bridgeman and Kent, no such celebrated names appear on the work contracts of Castle Howard. And unlike Stowe, where there was a constant, almost restless fiddling and changing of the plan or plans over the years, Castle Howard represents a consistent, controlled development that allowed the dramatic scenery to unfold as a complete conception based on a strong master plan, or at least on the idea of a strong personality in charge of its execution.

In the tradition of the good Whig landowner, virtually all Lord Carlisle's buildings, and, of course, the family mausoleum, were intended to serve some practical or symbolic function and not become the landscape ornaments and sham "eye-catchers" that were beginning to appear in much lesser settings. Hawksmoor's noble mausoleum is the scenic

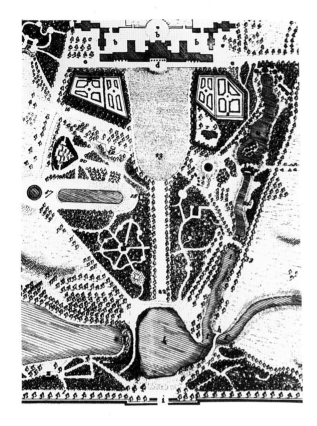

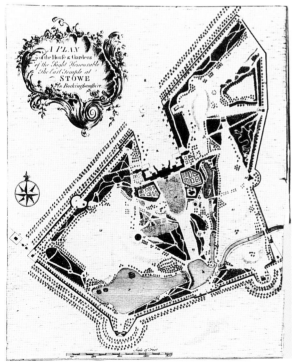

climax of the whole composition.

The great Whig estate at Stowe in Buckinghamshire was more celebrated and visited in the eighteenth century than the remote Castle Howard in Yorkshire. Because of Stowe's well-publicized inclusion in guides to the English garden that began to be published in the early eighteenth century and because of its association with important, avant-garde garden designers of the period, it remains one of the most influential landscapes in English garden history. Lord Carlisle's architect Vanbrugh designed a new house, almost contemporary with Castle Howard, at Stowe for Sir Richard Temple (1634–1697). In 1715, the architect, along with Charles Bridgeman, was commissioned to create an appropriate landscape setting. The changes, expansions, and adaptations to the latest landscape styles and theory over the next fifty or sixty years made Stowe a veritable laboratory for eighteenth-century landscape design.

The main lines of Stowe's grounds were settled by 1719 and are seen in the remarkable bird's-eye view by Charles Bridgeman. Alexander Pope's astonishment and pleasure when he first saw it—"a place to wonder at," he declared—is easy enough to understand after looking at Bridgeman's drawing made about the time of the poet's visit. As the residence of Viscount Cobham, the leading figure in the Whig establishment, Stowe embodied in its scenery the perfected aesthetic of the Whig concept of Ideal Nature. The garden of over four hundred acres, and the park into which it merged, was in many ways to be as influential in the eighteenth century as Versailles's formal grandeur had been in the seventeenth.

Even though the long, radiating avenues, the monumental octagonal pool, and the classical temples seem far removed from the natural landscape called for by Pope and other literary gardeners, Bridgeman's brilliant deployment of the ha-ha to separate the lawns from the working meadows and fields opened up the countryside in a dramatic, revolutionary way that was to alter the course of the English garden. This hidden barrier that pre-

OPPOSITE
The Palladian Bridge at
Stowe. Photo: Everett
Scott.

The Temple of Ancient
Virtue at Stowe. Photo:
Everett Scott.

Drawing attributed to George Lambert of the new ha-ha and lake at Claremont. Huntington Art Gallery.

RIGHT
Drawing of a temple scene that John Dixon Hunt suggests may be at Chiswick. Devonshire Collection, held at Chatsworth.

OPPOSITE, TOP
A satyr, one of the many statues at Rousham, Oxfordshire. Photo: Heather Angel.

OPPOSITE, BOTTOM
Serpentine rill running through a cold bath in the wood at Rousham. The narrow channel seems Islamic even in the snow. Photo: Heather Angel.

served uninterrupted vistas was derived from a French military bastion or trench. It first appeared in the English garden at Levens (c. 1695) where it was apparently introduced by a French gardener. For the Whig grandee the ha-ha created the illusion that the surrounding idealized grounds were boundless and led to the horizon, while it allowed his profitable agricultural operations of prize cattle and sheep to continue without actually intruding on the more cultivated environs around the house. The entire visual landscape, both private and public, was suddenly conceived in movement and in three dimensions. The "genius of the place," in Pope's words, was secretly held hostage by the hidden ditch and intensified by "sweet concealment's magic art." [26]

What has been called the pictorial phase of Stowe began in the 1730s when William Kent (1685–1748) laid out the little valley called Elysian Fields. Lord Cobham retired to Stowe in 1733 after resigning from Walpole's ministry, and a major assault on Bridgeman's original stiffness was launched with the cutting down of long avenues of trees, the thinning of groves, and the redesigning of lakes and pools along irregular, natural lines. Garden buildings and temples were removed or relocated

in order to harmonize with the new, open compositions of the idealized picture settings.

William Kent's "notion of gardening viz., to lay them out, and work without either level or line," as Sir Thomas Robinson wrote in 1734, has been credited as a major contribution to the landscape garden. Kent was trained as a stage and interior designer and had traveled with Lord Burlington (1695–1753) in Italy before returning to work on Chiswick House and other properties connected with Burlington's circle. Both Burlington and Kent had been impressed with the theatrical quality of Italian gardens where classical mythology and history were imaginatively drawn upon. Kent's design for a hillside at Chatsworth, where the replica of the Sybil's temple at Tivoli is shown at the top with cascades recalling those at the Villa Aldobrandini flanked by two classical pavilions, reflects an inspired English translation of Italian garden ideas. Horace Walpole, with some Whig exaggeration, cred-

ited Kent with having single-handedly invented the new garden style, and his praise was both elegant and penetrating. Kent was "born with a genius to strike out a great system from the twilight of imperfect essays," Walpole wrote in his often quoted encomium. "He leaped the fence, and saw that all nature was a garden." [27] It is good Whig garden history, even if a bit overstated.

More than at Stowe, Kent's park at Rousham, laid out for General James Dormer in 1738, continues to express Kent's brilliant pictorial manipulation. It embodies many of the original poetic and visual ideas that Kent used to transform nature. Both Addison's advice to throw a whole estate "into a kind of garden" and Pope's invitation to call in the surrounding countryside were followed at Rousham. But as Mavis Batey has pointed out, Kent understood the new dynamics and above all the exhilarating possibility of movement in the landscape offered by the revolutionary abandonment of "line and level" when laying out a garden. Walking in the park at Rousham reminds one of a passage in Thomas Whately's *Observation on Modern Gardening* (1770) where Whately recalls being "enchanted by the perpetual shifting scenes; the quick transitions; the total changes. . . . The illuminated recesses, the fleeting shadows and the gleams of light glaring on the side, or trembling on the stream and the loneliness and stillness of the place all crowding together on the mind almost realize the ideas which naturally present themselves in the region of romance and fancy." [28]

In all of Kent's garden work, the art of the landscape painter, aimed at creating idealized nature, is expressed in three dimensions. Horace Walpole captures this important quality of his technique.

The great principles on which he worked were perspective, and light and shade. . . . Where the view was less fortunate, or so much exposed as to be beheld at once, he blotted out some part by thick shades, to divide it into variety, or to make the richest

Seven-arched portico built into a hillside at Rousham, called Praeneste in memory of the Roman town south of Rome. Photo: Everett Scott.

scene more enchanting by reserving it to a farther advance of the spectator's step . . . something allowing the rudest waste to add its foil to the richest theatre, he realized the compositions of the greatest masters in painting. Where objects were wanting to animate his horizon, his taste as an architect could mediate termination. His build-ings, his seats, his temples, were more the works of his pencil than of his compasses.[29]

"All gardening is landscape painting," Alexander Pope declared, and no matter how often the quote has been misapplied or misunderstood since, it does sum up the pictorial quality of the best designs of the period.[30]

Pope was a leading influence on the direction of English garden design in the eighteenth century. Through his poetry, through his friendship with other garden enthusiasts, and through his connection with Kent, Pope's role was pervasive.

Even though Pope never visited Italy, he was immersed in the classical accounts of its literary landscape "much frequented by the ancient Romans who had their villas."[31] So, as with all of his contemporaries seriously interested in improving their gardens, Pope owed a debt to ancient models described in classical literature. The poet had translated Homer's famous description of the gardens of Alcinous and approvingly quoted William Temple's

Old garden and dovecote at Rousham. Photo: Everett Scott.

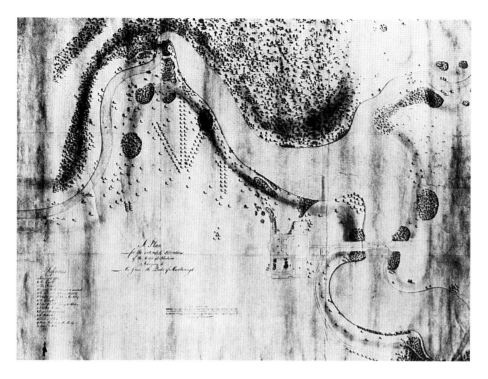

of Kent's plans for the Palladian Bridge, the Temple of Venus, and the Grotto. There is no doubt that Kent's method of working encouraged Brown also to absorb some of Kent's design theories and his approach to large-scale composition. Before long, Stowe's genial young gardener was supplying schemes for remodeling the grounds of several influential Whig friends of Lord Cobham. By the early 1750s and for the next thirty years, the bluff, practical, confident Brown was without any serious rival in the business. The indefatigable garden chronicler Horace Walpole saw a new Brown garden at Warwick Castle and was very impressed: "The view pleased me more than I can express. The river Avon tumbles down a cascade at the foot of it. It is well laid out by one Brown who has set up on a few ideas of Kent and Mr. Southcote." [33] The list of Brown's clients during England's great estate-building prosperity in the second half of the century allowed him to leave an indelible imprint on the man-made landscape of the country. His reply to an invitation from an Irish squire to work in Ireland, that he was not

A plan by Lancelot Brown for improving the grounds at Blenheim Palace, c. 1765. The damming of the small river Glyme to form two lakes, in keeping with the monumental scale of Vanbrugh's palace and bridge, was Brown's masterpiece. This drawing is one of the few documents relating to his work at Blenheim in the 1760s. Dorothy Strand, *Capability Brown*.

RIGHT
Alexander Pope in his grotto. Devonshire Collection, held at Chatsworth.

conclusion that it contains "all the justest Rules and Provisions which can go towards composing the best gardens." [32] Homer's account was conveniently vague enough to allow Pope to recreate it mostly out of his dreams and visions, something the poet often enjoyed doing in his grotto at Twickenham. Pope's realization that the new style could be adapted and adjusted to rather modest proportions, in contrast to the vast grandeur of a Cirencester or Stowe, was not only appropriate to the period, but such restraint was in sympathy with the classical spirit of Horace and other Latin writers who championed the Roman virtue of frugal, simple rural pleasures.

Lancelot, or "Capability," Brown (1716–1783) began his professional career working in the kitchen garden for Lord Cobham at Stowe in 1741, seven years before William Kent died. Although there is no evidence that Brown carried out any specific design at Stowe, he may have been asked to collaborate on some

quite finished yet with England, was only a slight exaggeration. During Brown's lifetime he worked on or improved as many as 150 estates, from the remodeling of the old-fashioned parks at Blenheim and Chatsworth to Lord Sheffield's poetic grounds of Sheffield Park in Sussex. Elizabeth Montague remarked that he was not only an "agreeable pleasant companion but a genius in his profession . . . a great poet." Brown's success confirms that he was both. The poetic, dreamlike quality of Brown's work evoked around the

Lancelot Brown and Humphry Repton, as well as nineteenth- and twentieth-century landscape architects, all worked at Sheffield Park in Sussex. The rich collection of mature trees and shrubs makes it a veritable Paradise Garden out of mythology. Photo: Everett Scott.

lakes below the house at Sheffield Park still endorses Mrs. Montague's perceptive observation.

Quite often Brown had to sweep away the existing, formal gardens left from an earlier age, some of which had matured for a hundred years. But he carried out his plans with ruthless self-confidence and with no hint of remorse. By the end of the century, through the destructions of Brown, Humphry Repton, and their imitators, the English Renaissance garden had been obliterated as if by a phalanx of bulldozers passing through the countryside. The success of the landscape style left hardly a single example of the old formal garden intact. The bird's-eye views of country houses illustrated in Kip's *Britannia illustrata* (1707), with their ordered avenues, terraces, bosquets, quincunxes, etoiles, cascades, fountains, grottoes, and statues, are a sad record of the wholesale loss. Even though the buildings of Longleat, Chatsworth, Wilton, Hampton Court, Woburn, and Hatfield survive, their gardens, expressing the English version of Renaissance ideals and integral to their initial conception, have totally vanished, largely because of Brown's timely ability to create a sympathetic background for the way people in his own age wanted to be seen, reconciled with untouched nature.

The ultimate secret of Brown's achievements, despite the select and limited range of his design vocabulary, was that he had a complete grasp of the physical, visual landscape counterpart to his patrons' idealism, their politics, and their concept of beauty. That concept was best summed up by William Hogarth in *The Analysis of Beauty* (1753), published about the time that Brown announced his career as landscape "improver." "Most people," Hogarth explained, "must have observed the sort of sense they have had of being swiftly drawn in an easy coach on a smooth turf, with gradual accents and declivities. This will give a better idea of beauty than almost anything else." Or in Dr. Johnson's paraphrase, happiness is the recollection of "being swiftly drawn in a chaise over undulating turf in the company of a beautiful and witty woman."[34] As for the expense, which at Brown's park of several hundred acres was considerable, it "was only suited to the opulence of a free country," Walpole boasted, "where emulation reigns among many independent particulars."[35] The landscape paintings of Brown's contemporary Richard Wilson have perhaps captured the visual qualities of texture, color, and contrast of a Brownian park with greater fidelity than any other contemporary document.

William Kent's Vale of Venus pool at Rousham. Water from this pool could be used to activate a waterfall below the dam. Photo: Everett Scott.

OPPOSITE
A series of small lakes leads back to Sheffield House. Photo: Everett Scott.

The new fashion was not without its critics, who felt that the predictable Brown landscape lacked any real vitality or visual excitement. Richard Payne Knight (1750–1824), in *The Landscape* (1794), made it clear that he was speaking of Brown's "desolating hand":

> Oft when I've seen some lonely mansion
>   stand
> Fresh from the improvers desolating hand.
> Midst shaven lawns that far around it
>   creep
> In one eternal undulating sweep;
> . . . .
> Hence, hence! thou haggard fiend,
>   however call'd,
> Thin meager genius of the bare and bald.
> Thy spade and mattock here at length lay
>   down,
> And follow to the tomb thy fav'rite
>   Brown:
> Thy fav'rite Brown whose innovating
>   hand
> First dealt thy curses o'er thy fertile land.[36]

An element basic to Brown's designs, along with the encircling, wooded belt and a water piece disguised as a river, was the use of ubiquitous round clumps of trees casually positioned. William Kent had first introduced groups of trees or groves at Holkham Hall, but Brown put Kent's clumps to maximum use in his parks, or as Price called them, "the middle distance garden." Brown wrote no books, and his straightforward principles seemed to be devoid of any complicated aesthetic philosophy. All that was required, he declared, was a "perfect knowledge of the Country and the objects in it whether natural or artificial and infinite delicacy in the planting etc., so much Beauty depending on the size of the trees and the colors of their leaves to produce the effect of light and shade." If such a simple formula was followed, then the English garden would be "exactly fit for the owner, the Poet and the Painter."[37]

In a 1797 guidebook to Burghley House, written thirty years after Brown had wiped out the old formal gardens of an earlier age, we can savor the proud approval given by his clients and by most of his contemporaries.

> It was the genius of the late Lancelot Brown; which brooding over the shapeless mass, educed out of a seeming wilderness, all the order and delicious harmony which now prevail. Like the great captain of the Israelites, he led forth his troops of sturdy plants into a seemingly barren land; where he displayed strange magic, and surprised them with miracle after miracle. Though the beauties with which we are struck, are more peculiarly the rural beauties of Mr. Brown, than those of Dame Nature, she seems to wear them with so simple and unaffected a grace, that it is not even the man of taste who can, at a superficial glance, discover the distance.[38]

After the removal of garden walls and hedges and in the imperceptible merging of the park with the larger landscape, the distant groves, fields, and meadows, "the ecology of human consciousness" took another extraordinary turn.[39] Suddenly there appeared a new faith, almost a religion, that nature, instead of being an uncomfortable presence, if not an active threat, was itself a kind of wild garden to be enjoyed and contemplated. Rousseau, Goethe, and Schiller embraced the new romantic, transcendental values represented by nature's visible order, even when it was improved by the seemingly subtle assistance of a Brown or Repton.

Water, an important element in all of the great gardens of the world, exerted an immense fascination on English gardeners throughout the eighteenth century. Brown had an instinctive understanding of its qualities. In Batty Langley's book *New Principles of Gardening* (1728), a treatise Brown was familiar with, Langley's model garden, designed in "a more grand and rural manner," was awash in pools, fountains, canals, and cascades. Kent expressed imaginative homage to Langley's principles in his water garden at Rousham

with its fifty-foot fountains shooting up below the lake and cascade in the Vale of Venus.

When in the Garden's Entrance you
    provide
The Waters, there united, to divide:
First, in the center a large fountain make;
Which from a narrow pipe its rise may
    take,
and to air have waves by which, tis fed,
Remit Agen. . . . [40]

Brown thought Kent's delightful Italianate creations old-fashioned, a "disgusting display of art" that should be carefully disguised by nature. Nothing seemed to give him greater satisfaction than to take an old, formal basin or pool and transform it into a "natural" lake. At Blenheim he dammed the insignificant little River Glyme to form two large lakes into an idealized river whose new appearance, scale, and majesty finally matched the Roman grandeur of Vanbrugh's palace and bridge. Brown also built a wonderful cascade "au natural" to allow the Glyme to resume its modest proportions as it proceeded on its way out of the park. At Chatsworth, aside from replacing the countless, geometrical parterres with smooth lawns near the house, Brown leveled the ground in order to make a view of the river, which he had dammed and widened. His work at Chatsworth has been regularly deplored by succeeding generations of Devonshires, who have quarreled with the assessment of Palladian designer James Paine (1716–1789) that Brown's work was a masterful complement to his own bridge and "contributed towards making it, perhaps, one of the *noblest* places in *Europe*." [41]

In many ways, Brown asserted his mastery over nature just as firmly and confidently as Le Nôtre had done in the seventeenth century, as Brown's improvements spread across all of England. Where French designers employed geometric forms, and the spouting water of the fountains jetted against gravity through the workings of complex man-made machinery, Brown chose to conceal his *forces de la nature,* giving them a natural disguise. But hidden beneath the transformed slope at Chatsworth and the remade rivers there, at Blenheim and a number of other parks, Brown's command over nature was just as autocratic as that of French garden designers. The "naturalness" of Brown's work required just as much ingenuity and effort and as much designer's art.

In 1754 when Henry Hoare (1705–1785) created the large lake in the valley of the River Stour below and out of sight of his Palladian house, the garden at Stourhead became an unusual exception to the classical ideal of the relationship between architecture and the landscape, separated but not completely isolated from each other. For the first time, water became the dominating, organizing focus for the entire garden. Even before the work on Stourhead's garden was completed, Joseph Warton wrote that it represented "exquisite scenes . . . of practical poetry!" [42]

Around the "closed circuit" of the lake's bank, the water reflected the Claudian woods and splendid garden architecture carefully positioned along its shore. As Walpole noted, this exquisite piece of landscape poetry was primarily the work of the sophisticated, well-traveled owner, Henry Hoare, an amateur who proceeded without any professional direction. He had had "the good sense," his grandson wrote, "not to call in the assistance of a landscape gardener." [43]

The Grotto with its circular, domed chamber contains springs and a cascade beneath a sleeping nymph. Nearby the River God recalls the *Tiber* in Salvator Rosa's painting of the *Dream of Aeneas.* While Walpole thought most grottoes "splendid improprieties," he called Stourhead's "judiciously indeed most fortunately placed. . . ." [44] The Pantheon, a domed rotunda, dominates the scene, a recreation of a Claude painting that is greatly enriched with ornamental trees on the hillside actually planted in the nineteenth and twentieth centuries. The pictorial evocation of the painter's framed vision of the classical world at Stourhead ranks with the poetic views at

OPPOSITE
A view of the lake at Stourhead from Stourton Village. Photo: Heather Angel.

Palladian and Indian styles in an exotic hybrid influenced both the house and garden of Sezincote, Gloucestershire, which dates from the early nineteenth century. Repton contributed to the design of the grounds. Photo: Everett Scott.

Castle Howard and at Stowe. It is a painterly approach to the creation of idealized nature in marked contrast to Brown's contemporary "place-making" parks.

Brown had a number of imitators and followers, but it was not until Humphry Repton (1752–1818) turned to landscape gardening that a talented successor established himself. He was the last of the great designers who dominated the English landscape movement from 1720 to 1820, when vast acreages of the uncultivated English countryside were transformed into parks and gardens.

Neither Kent nor Brown published his theories, nor did many of their working drawings survive. In Repton's case, however, his writings and the famous Red Books he specially prepared for individual clients were instrumental in establishing his fame. In 1794, six years after his belated decision to take up the practice, Repton prepared a list of the "Sources of Pleasure in Landscape Garden-

OVERLEAF
A Hindu temple above the pool at Sezincote. Photo: Everett Scott.

A bronze snake from the Garden of Eden spouts water into a pool at Sezincote. Photo: Everett Scott.

Humphry Repton's Trade Card, engraved after a design by Repton. 1788. Private collection, British Architectural Library. Photo: Norfolk County Library.

ing," sources that he had studied and identified in the Brownian landscape. They were congruity, utility, order, symmetry, picturesque effect, intricacy, simplicity, variety, novelty, contrast, continuity, association, grandeur, appropriation, animation, and the seasons. Of these, "variety" became his favorite word and for him replaced the eighteenth-century "nature." The application of the label to garden design was not new, and, as we have seen, variety had been a widely praised quality at the end of the seventeenth century. Repton had possibly become familiar with earlier references in his reading and may have been familiar with Henry Peacham's *The Compleat Gentleman* (1622) where the importance of "variety" in the landscape and garden was first mentioned.

Since "variety" evaded any precise defini-

tion and rules, it served Repton's purpose to avoid the hard and fast formulae that were beginning to be applied by Brown's followers without much talent or imagination. What Repton sought to do, and in fact did beautifully in his celebrated Red Books, was to visually dramatize the vague character of "appropriateness" and "variety" through illustrations. Luxuriously produced in delicate watercolors and with an overlay that when lifted revealed the Reptonian Transformation, these book were often bound in red morocco for presentation. The Red Books not only became his trademark, they also established the work of the professional landscape designer on a plane that had never been seen before or since.

Repton had read the gardener-poet William Mason (1725–1792) and the garden observer

Thomas Whately in preparing for his career. He was also familiar with the French *physiocrat* Louis-René Girardin (1735–1808) who believed that a "virtuous citizen" overcome by humanity's suffering could regain his sensibilities and equilibrium through the "admiration of picturesque moral landscapes which delight the mind."[45] Girardin had in fact attempted to regain high moral ground in his park at Ermenonville, his own picturesque *jardin anglais* north of Paris begun in the 1760s.

In his *Essay on Landscape* (translated 1783), the Marquis de Girardin described the method he used in laying out the park at Ermenonville, a problem that perplexed most French gardeners who were trained to begin their geometric plans with the line and ruler. It is not a minor problem: How does a gardener actually lay out a landscape garden that has to be planned in the three dimensions of an open landscape? The marquis's procedure is interesting to follow and was in many respects similar to Repton's technique.

First you began with a rough sketch of the proposed landscape. Next an assistant places rods in the ground according to signals from the designer to indicate graduations of perspective, contour of ground, and the outline of paths, plantations, and riverbanks. If water is an element, a white cloth is spread out on the ground to suggest the effect and to determine the location.

All this was, of course, a radical departure from the illustrated steps set out in John James's translation of Dezallier d'Argenville's *La Théorie et la practique du jardinage*. James gives very detailed directions for "the manner of ruling out a general plan" of geometric patterns and then transferring the designs with the aid of string and stakes to the usually flat ground itself. The line and rule was so deeply ingrained in French garden training that designers had great problems with the laying out of *jardins anglais* when they first became fashionable. The Scots gardener Thomas Blaikie (1758–1838), who had been commissioned to introduce the new English garden style in and around Paris, astonished the French gardeners at Bagatelle when he laid out an irregular scheme without benefit of "line or tois," relying instead on trial and error.

Even though Repton employed sketches and watercolors to work out his plans (and to impress his clients), he did understand the fundamental difference between the perspective drawing and its actual translation onto the site. Marie-Louise Gothein identified Repton's most important contribution to garden art when she wrote that

he was the first man to free himself from the exaggerated idea of a similarity between painting and landscape gardening. He laid his finger on the difference between them, caused by the constant alteration in

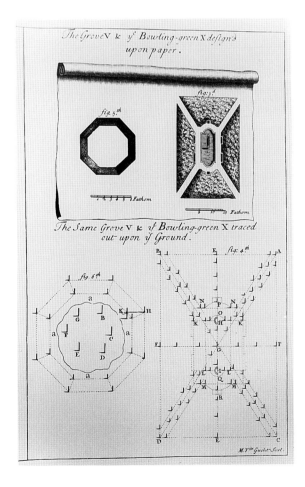

Plan and directions for laying out a bowling-green, from Dezallier d'Argenville's influential *Theory and Practice of Gardening.*

The Rosary at Ashridge, Hertfordshire, designed by Humphry Repton in 1813. Drawings Collection, British Architectural Library. Photo: Norfolk County Library.

the spectator's point of view, and the changes of light in the garden. To his mind what is much more to the point is concord between the architect and the gardener, for a house is presupposed for every garden. . . .[46]

Repton was inexhaustible in his study of the essential character of a given landscape from every angle in order to accommodate his improvements to a particular place. For Repton, the "character" of a place was comprehensive and included that of the house itself as well as the client's personality and even his station in life. "The landscape in its present state is not unpleasant," Repton wrote in his *Red Book for Rode* in 1790, ". . . but it is much more consistent with a view from a cottage or farm-

house than the portico of a gentleman's seat."

As the eighteenth century came to a close, the old landed gentry that had provided the foundation of Brown's and Repton's practice was giving away to a new breed of clients produced by war and industry without traditional roots in country life. Repton's "Picturesque" controversy with Richard Payne Knight and Uvedale Price, who had considered his lavishly improved estates "foolish vanity," faded in the face of new social and political issues presented by the Industrial Revolution. By the end of Repton's life, the unprecedented visual and social threat to the landscape brought on by unbridled manufacturing and industrial development had little to do with a park designed to reflect the taste and intentions of a benevolent, classically educated Whig squire or lord.

Lancelot Brown's meadows had swept across the hills right up to the foundation and portico of the usually (new or remodeled) classical manor house, banishing flower beds and ornamental plantings. But Repton, in another characteristic departure from Brown's formula, reinstated the terrace near the house, which was often enriched with flower beds and small specialized flower gardens for roses, for example, or imported exotics from the wilds of America.

To satisfy his clients Repton could hardly have done otherwise, since an avalanche of new and exotic plants and flowers were beginning to pour into Britain from the empire, demanding to be accommodated and naturalized in the English garden. When George III's mother died in 1772, the king bought Kew House where she had lived, west of London, and united it with Richmond Lodge to form a royal botanical garden. Joseph Banks (1743–1820) was named the king's horticultural advisor in 1771. The following year Francis Masson (1741–1806) sailed to South America to gather plants for the new royal gardens. It was the first of a succession of great plant expeditions to be sponsored by Kew. The British had taken the lead in gardening just as they had taken command of trade, manufacturing, and world exploration. The king's example in sponsoring the gardens at Kew added to the already burgeoning interest in horticulture and botany. Horticultural societies, beginning with the Horticultural Society of London in 1804, brought plant enthusiasts together. Gardening was rapidly becoming a major popular art form, and these new associations resulted in an unprecedented exchange of new knowledge and plants, an exchange that had decades earlier been limited to a few rich land and garden enthusiasts. The three hundred varieties of hyacinth George Johnson could record in 1829, compared to only fifty varieties Parkinson had recorded two hundred years earlier, is a fair index of what was happening. What had happened to the hyacinth could be multiplied hundreds of times with other botanical explosions of discovery and development. For the first time scientific and technical advances fueled by exploration were profoundly changing the look of the English garden. Any contributions by the garden-maker and designer were secondary and in response to these new influences.

W. T. Stern has organized the main geographic sources of plant material that revolutionized the gardens of Europe and has given dates according to their most important periods of influence.

Near East, 1560–1630
Canada and Virginia, 1620–1686
    (mainly herbaceous plants)
Cape of Good Hope, 1687–1772
North America trees and shrubs, 1687–1772
Australia, 1772–1882
Japan and North America, 1820–1900
    (mainly glass-house and hardy plants)
West China, 1900–1930
Hybrids bred in Europe, 1930 onwards.[47]

This is not to imply that Britain was alone in the promotion of horticultural exploration or that it was by any means the first, even though the country's welcoming temperate climate did give the country a distinct advantage. Following the founding of the botanical gardens at Pisa (1543), Padua (1545), and Florence (1550), others had quickly followed on the Continent. The Jardin Royal des Plantes Médicinales, or Jardin du Roi, connected to the Faculty of Medicine in Paris, had been started by Louis XIII in 1626. Plant-collecting expeditions sponsored by the French government were dispatched around the world to enlarge these important scientific collections. By the time of the American Revolution, the Jardin Royal was preeminent, and international garden enthusiasts like Thomas Jefferson corresponded regularly with its director André Thouin, exchanging scientific information, plants, and seeds.

The contribution of Carl Linnaeus (1707–

Carl Linnaeus's botanical garden in Uppsala, Sweden. Photo: Everett Scott.

1778), with his introduction of a consistent, international system of botanical nomenclature, was an important and lasting structure for organizing these new scientific discoveries. Aside from introducing his convenient system, Linnaeus understood that the theory and practice of horticulture required knowledge of plant geography and ecology. He wrote several works on the need to study the limits of heat and soil conditions, recommending that botanical gardens with a controlled greenhouse climate be used to carry out such studies. His botanical garden at Uppsala, Sweden, was a model botanical study center, and students came there to study from Norway, Denmark, Finland, Germany, Switzerland, Russia, Britain, and America.[48]

For professional garden designers and amateurs, the deluge of new plants, coupled with the steady shrinking in size of domestic gardens, posed major problems. All these new plants, and particularly exotic flowers, had to be somehow accommodated. But the character of the flower garden in its color, texture, and scale, as Repton had pointed out in his *Observations* of 1803, was "totally different from the rest of the scenery," and its success depended as much on art as on nature. The introduction of art, he wrote, must "beautifully harmonize with that profusion of flowers and curious plants which distinguish the flower garden from the natural landscape."[49]

Sadly, both in Repton's late flower gardens, often antiquarian in inspiration, and in the garden designs advocated by John Claudius Loudon (1783–1843), the results favored a self-conscious display of horticultural expertise over any sound or discernible aesthetic principles. Many of the new generation of gardeners and their patrons of the early nineteenth century, with backgrounds almost exclusively in practical horticulture and botany, were aware of the shortcomings and defects in their personal taste and knowledge. Inevitably the development of cheap, inexpensive printing methods resulted in a veritable explosion of popular garden books and periodicals written to serve the enthusiastic new audience. Garden journalism had arrived.

One of the leading figures in the garden journalism revolution was John Loudon. He started four periodicals during his lifetime, and his *Encyclopedia of Gardening,* first published in 1822, went through nine editions before his death in 1843. It was through his role as "the most distinguished gardening author of the age," in Andrew Jackson Downing's words, rather than through his garden designs that Loudon gained historical significance. As leading spokesman for the democratization of gardening, it is fitting that he called his first article "Hints for Laying Out the Ground in Public Squares." In an eclectic age formed by the rising middle class and its diverse background, it was a mass gardening audience that Loudon was determined to serve through his magazines. And it is important to appreciate the international composition of his audience. Loudon was read both in Paris and in villages along the Hudson River. In 1827 Thomas Blaikie, still living and gardening in Paris, wrote Loudon: "I received with pleasure your valuable works, *The Gardener's Magazine.* Which is well-known here, and read by M. Soulange Bodin, M. Cels, M. Boursault and other eminent cultivators and amateurs."[50] It was also well known and widely read in Andrew Jackson's democratic America spreading up the Hudson Valley, later championed in the gardens of his namesake.

Loudon's *Encyclopedia of Gardening* was the first book to treat the subject of gardening

A decorative water garden, part of Linnaeus's botanical garden in Uppsala. Photo: Everett Scott.

comprehensively from the historical, technical, aesthetic, and horticultural points of view. Before beginning the *Encyclopedia* Loudon had traveled widely in Europe and had seen many of the great gardens. These firsthand investigations qualified his enthusiasm for the conspicuous fashion for the informal and irregular as opposed to the older style of formal layout. "To say that landscape gardening is an improvement on geometric gardening," he wrote, "is a similar misapplication of language, as to say that a lawn is an improvement of a cornfield because it is substituted in its place. It is absurd, therefore to despise the ancient style, because it has not the same beauties as the modern, to which it never aspired. It has beauties of a different kind, equally per-

Bee-balm. Curtis, *The Botanical Magazine,* London, 1791.

White/purplish-red prim-roses. Curtis, *The Botanical Magazine,* London, 1813.

fect in their kind as those of the modern style."[51]

Even before Loudon's *Encyclopedia* was published, there had been a growing interest in antiquarian garden designs and in revival styles. Eclectic historical styles in garden design followed similar developments in nineteenth-century architecture. Repton's Elizabethan garden at Beaudesert, which was to complement the "pristine character" of the Tudor mansion, is an interesting early attempt at garden restoration, a subject whose nineteenth-century origins have not yet received sufficient attention and study.

Among the early Victorians, where there was already a "prevalence of bad taste that accompanies wealth suddenly acquired," the revival garden style encouraged all manner of aesthetic disasters. Italianate terraces, French parterres with colored stones, Swiss bridges, Chinese pavilions, German cowsheds, and all manner of other appalling eccentricities sprang up to litter parvenu suburban estates. Suburban yards were crammed with exciting new imported plants, along with an amazing assortment of varieties produced by aggressive commercial plant breeders. Skilled "quick-change" artist-gardeners executed "bedding out" schemes in bizarre, lavish patterns that could be ordered by mail. The debris of tender, gaudy flowers was to be quickly swept away as soon as the flowers faded in order to be replaced by even more flamboyant and extravagant confections grown in the essential prefabricated greenhouse.

The invention by Nathaniel Bagshaw Ward (1791–1868) of the Wardian case, a sealed glass container providing a protected environment for the transportation of delicate living plants and flowers, had suddenly increased the introduction of new exotics into England from China, South Africa, India, and the South Pacific. Head gardeners were expected to display their tender or half-hardy and brightly colored newcomers in the owner's garden to best advantage. By the 1840s an elaborate bedding system had evolved, allowing gardens to be changed annually or oftener and making the gardener with his well-stocked greenhouse as important as the architect or landscape designer. Exotic planting by the 1850s and '60s had completely replaced the eighteenth century's goals of replicating nature.

Ornamental shrubs and trees often with bizarre shapes and colors—anything that "weeped" was an immediate success—suggested further sentimental possibilities that appealed to the corrupted Victorian eye. If the ornamental effect was not sufficiently exotic through the natural process, the grafting together of different species might produce the right results. The same overloaded eclecticism that ruled in the decoration of the parlor and drawing room had been extended into the garden through the advance of horticultural and scientific techniques.

When William Robinson (1838–1935), a querulous Irish gardener's boy, arrived on the scene in the 1860s, he seemed to be alone in his lament that "the art of garden design is yet in a very barbarous state.[52] Trained as a gardener at the Irish National Botanical Garden, Robinson first worked under the head gardener of a high Victorian estate in Northern Ireland. Fed up with bedding-out tender hot-house plants in the estates's ugly garden, legend has it that Robinson set off a quarrel with his boss. The story ends with Robinson throwing open the windows of the greenhouse and turning off the furnace as he departed from what he considered a center of "the Dark Ages of flower gardening." The marshaling of platoons of garish flowers into military rows had turned gardeners into drill sergeants. Their job was simply to carry the architectural lines of the building into the landscape in a mechanical exercise of deadening monotony.

The Wild Garden (1870) was a distillation of Robinson's philosophy of plant cultivation, a lifelong mission to challenge the contrived gardening practices that so outraged him at every turn. Some readers were puzzled by what seemed a lack of specific directions, its annoying "indefinableness." Robinson replied that he was not laying down a pat formula but rather had written the book "to encourage the gardener to put some beautiful life in his garden grass, shrubberies and half waste places, leaving it to each gardener's individual imagination and ability to create his own private, personal wilderness,"[53] To the late twentieth century with its growing interest in ecology and the natural environment, Robinson's landscape philosophy has a special appeal. In his meadows covered with massive drifts of bluebells and daffodils, a clematis hidden in an old fencerow, a Virginia creeper thrown over a dead tree, Robinson's gardening aesthetic could well be summed up in Pope's words:

In all let Nature never be forgot
But treat the goddess like a modest fair.
Nor overdress, nor leave her wholly bare.[54]

Robinson was no doubt more sympathetic to the poetry of William Wordsworth, a poet much closer to his own gardening philosophy. He had also tramped through Wordsworth's Lake Country on long nature hikes and studied the romantic beauty of the landscape.

When Wordsworth moved into the old farm-house Rydal Mount, he set out from the start not to remake the garden but to make sure that, in his words, "the invisible hand of art should everywhere work in the spirit of nature. . . . A garden should be informal and should harmonize with the countryside around and should consist of lawns and trees carefully planted so as not to obscure the views."[55]

To banish garden designs that were "opposed to every law of nature's own arrangement of living things" was Robinson's passionate, reforming goal when he began a magazine, *The Garden,* in 1871. His writings and his garden popularized the "wild garden," a style that had a close affinity with the old vernacular English cottage garden. Its renewed appreciation was very much in the spirit of John Ruskin and William Morris's Arts and Crafts movement. Before long, Robinson had attracted considerable attention and a following that included the young Gertrude Jekyll (1843–1932). Her own naturalistic gardens, following Robinson's ideas and advice, were to carry the reforming spirit of her mentor well into the twentieth century. Since by definition a garden is man-made, "cultivated not wild," Robinson's and Jekyll's label "wild garden" may seem self-contradictory. But as Jekyll wrote and her critics did not miss, a wild garden had to be "well planned" if it was to succeed.

In the works of Robinson and Jekyll the Victorian garden had been directed back to the beginning of garden-making when the first plants to be cultivated were wild species, often selected for their medicinal value. Francis Bacon, in his essay "Of Gardens" (1625), had hinted that even his own geometric garden might harbor a miniature "heath or desert." Bacon's "heath" consisted of a series of molehills, each covered with a different wild plant along with thyme, violet, and primrose. So the spirit of reform advanced by Robinson's *The Garden* could claim respectable English origins that dated back to the seventeenth century. Pope and Addison both claimed that they longed for a "well-planned" wilderness in their gardens. Addison liked to surprise a visitor to his garden with "flowers that he might have met with under a common hedge, in a field or a meadow." Pope quoted Martial's *Epigrams* on the beauty of a Roman Villa where he savored "the true rustic, the un-trimmed farm" over "plantations of fancy clipped boxwood."[56] Classical garden literature from antiquity contained many hints and praise of what might be called a "wild garden." Pliny the Younger wrote that his villa in Tuscany "owes as many beauties to nature, as all I have been describing within [the walled garden] does to art. . . . in the midst of the elegant regularity you are surprised with an imitation of negligent beauties of rural nature."[57] Capability Brown's landscape school of gardening was far too civilized, smooth, and controlled to admit much true "wilderness," even with classical credentials, not to mention Baconian molehills as a decorative ornament.

Payne Knight and Uvedale Price's attack on Humphry Repton in the "Picturesque" controversy did advocate a much more relaxed appropriation of nature's unpredictable ways into the garden and landscape composition. But it was the impetus of Robinson and his followers who revived the earlier notions and gave them form. Robinson had his share of skeptical critics, so he was careful to spell out exactly what he meant in *The Wild Garden:*

What it does mean is best explained by the winter aconite flowering under a grove of naked trees in February; by the Snowflake, tall and numberous in meadows by the Thames side; by the blue Lupine dyeing an islet with its purple in a Scotch river; and the blue apennine anemone staining an English wood blue before the coming of our blue bells. Multiply these instances a thousand fold, given by many types of plants, from countries colder than ours, and one may get a just idea of the "wild garden."[58]

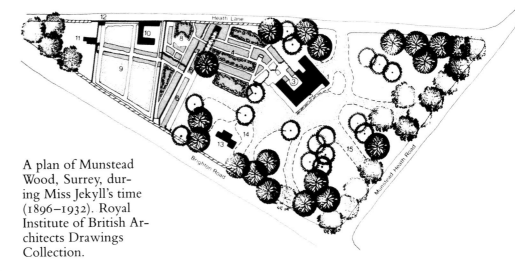

A plan of Munstead Wood, Surrey, during Miss Jekyll's time (1896–1932). Royal Institute of British Architects Drawings Collection.

At Gravetye Manor, bought by Robinson in 1885, he surrounded his old Elizabethan manor house with a wild garden. English native wildflowers were naturalized in the adjoining meadows flanked by great Sussex oaks festooned with all kinds of romantic climbing vines. Around a string of lakes he mingled cultivated exotic plants in with wild loosestrife.

The unity in Robinson's design embraced not only the composition, which he had deftly worked out, but also the lakes, terraces, and woodlands; he had brought about a cohesion that was subtly informed by design, no matter how carefully it was hidden in the contrived entanglements, colors, and illusions of a natural wilderness. Plant conservation and the threat of the disappearance of many wildflowers from the countryside did not play a part in the thinking of the earliest advocates of the wild garden. But in retrospect—considering the ravages of industrial society, the sprawl of cities, and the widespread irreparable damage that would result from the economic and social upheavals of the nineteenth and twentieth centuries—Robinson and Jekyll's gardening philosophy can be seen as squarely in the forefront of the environmental conservation movement.

OPPOSITE, TOP
The pergola at Hestercombe, Somerset. This recently restored garden of 1906–8 was the first important collaboration between Gertrude Jekyll and Edwin Lutyens, which began in 1899. Photo: Heather Angel.

OPPOSITE, BOTTOM
The east border in the Jekyll walled garden beside Lindisfarne Castle, with orange alstroemeria, *Stachys lanata,* harebells, and thrift self-seeded in paths. Photo: Heather Angel.

Sissinghurst Castle Garden, Kent, where roses, lupines, lilies, *Gillenia trifoliata,* and *Stachys byzantina* surround the sixteenth-century gatehouse. Photo: Pamela Harper.

The rose garden at Sissinghurst, which displays *Rosa Henri Martin*, *Filipendula purpurea*, and *Mimulus lewisii* in abundance. Photo: Pamela Harper.

Clematis and perl d'azur predominate in this section of the gardens at Sissinghurst. Photo: Pamela Harper.

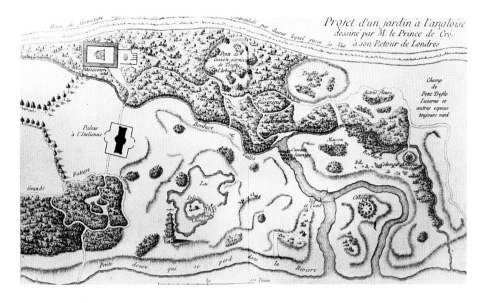

Projet d'un jardin à l'angloise dessiné par M. le Prince de Crôye à son Retour de Londres

The plan of a *jardin anglais* attributed to the Prince of Crôye. A French version of an English garden somehow lacked the loose improvisation of the original in plan or execution, although there was improvement in the nineteenth century. Le Rouge, *Nouveaux jardins.*

THE ENGLISH LANDSCAPE GARDEN OUTSIDE OF ENGLAND

In 1771 Horace Walpole was in France, and he was appalled by attempts to create what the French called a *jardin anglais.*

English gardening gains ground here prodigiously. . . . There is a Monsieur Boutin, who has tacked a piece of what he calls an English garden to a set of stone terraces, with steps of turf. There are three or four very high hills, almost as high as, and exactly in the shape of, a tansy pudding. You squeeze between these and a river, that is conducted at obtuse angles in a stone channel, and supplied by a pump, and when walnuts come in, I suppose it will be navigable. In a corner enclosed by a chalk wall are the samples I mentioned, there is a strip of grass, another of corn, and a third *en friche,* exactly in the order of beds in a nursery. They have translated Mr. Whately's book, and the Lord knows what barbarism is going to be laid at our door. The new Anglomanie will literally be mad English.[59]

The informal or loosely irregular garden was just beginning to attract converts in France and on the Continent when Walpole wrote, but within a decade it had made major inroads. In fashionable centers like Paris there was a growing boredom with the old geometry, even though formality never completely disappeared. Variations on the classic French garden were still being carried out elsewhere, but in rather dry, academic fashion, as at the vast Esterházy estate called Süttör in Hungary, begun in 1764. It was still the proper garden setting for the older, conservative aristocracy of Europe.

Walpole's contempt for what he construed as uninformed French efforts would only have been exacerbated by the attempts of fashionable squires in Germany or Poland, who were receiving their direction second- and third-hand mostly from French garden treatises. Claude-Henri Watelet (1718–1786), who promoted the *ferme ornée* in his *Essai sur les jardins* (1774), was dismissed by Walpole as "absurd," superficial, with "no idea of situation."

Walpole's theme in his letters and in his *History* is that the French did not have a feeling for the natural topography and did not study it adequately in order to let it "call forth the genius of place" to determine and direct the design. Where the works of Brown and Repton had often been carried out with the intimate collaboration of a squire or lord who was an enthusiastic garden amateur, the French aristocracy did not share the same traditions, sympathies, and understanding of rural life. The land was rarely a combination of a family seat and an agricultural investment like the English estate. It never had the benefit of generations of husbandry. And as Fletcher Steele remarked, a Frenchman "is never infatuated with nature. . . . Nature belongs to him and his domination should be in all propriety—evident."[60] It was a crucial flaw and one the French never quite overcame, even though the *jardin anglais* in small examples at Versailles, Chantilly, Rambouillet, and Malmaison or in large, ornamented estates dotted with buildings in exotic styles, as at the Désert de Retz, Bagatelle, Ermenonville, and Méréville, became the rage. In 1787 Arthur Young (1741–1820), the English agriculturalist, visited Marie Antoinette's new English garden at the Petit Trianon and was not impressed. "There is more of Sir William Chambers here than of Mr. Brown—more effort than nature—and more expense than taste. It is not easy to conceive anything that art can introduce in a garden that is not here," he observed with contempt. "Woods, rocks, lawns, lakes, rivers, islands, cascades, grottos, walks, temples, and even villages" had been crowded into some one hundred acres. Domination of nature was assured, no matter what the label or guidebook claimed.[61]

As in England, the movement away from the formal garden tradition in France also had its roots in literature. But where interest in the English garden of the eighteenth century reflected new economic and political forces and centered on agriculture as a keystone in national life, the French saw the countryside as more of a place to retreat, particularly during a period of political and economic decline and uncertainty. The garden, as Jacques-François Blondel (1705–1774) wrote in *Cours d'architecture* (1753), should be a place "to walk and a retreat for philosophical meditation." But for Blondel the architect's gardens were something to be created and intellectually systematized rather than composed as in England, and where more often than not the landowner himself directed the actual work with little or no professional assistance. It was a role the English squire and nobleman was peculiarly fitted for through his daily contact with the landscape. When he was not supervising his agricultural operation, he was on horseback riding to the hounds over the same farmland, another important experience that the French did not share in the same way. The smaller *jardin anglais,* or *jardin anglo-chinois* as it was sometimes called, was usually an extension to or made-over part of old formal gardens. As a result the French interpretation perpetuated many of the transitional, fussy, Rococo elements of earlier garden fashions. But places

like the estate of Marquis de Girardin, consisting of some nine hundred hectares, were on a scale with English counterparts. The landscaped estate of Ermenonville, begun in 1776, is one of the earliest French gardens in the new style. Girardin's object was to compose a series of "pictures." From the château the view framed a brilliant, sunlit Italian landscape à la Claude Lorrain, with a lake beyond where on an island ringed with poplars stood the tomb of the marquis's friend the philosopher and novelist Jean-Jacques Rousseau (1712–1778).

Rousseau, who had disapproved of highly organized society and its corrupting effects, had described in his novel *La Nouvelle Héloïse*

The Temple de la Philosophie at Ermenonville, Oise, France, recalls the ruins of the Roman temple at Tivoli. A similar temple ruin was also built at Méréville, south of Paris. Photo: Everett Scott.

The Isle of Poplars at
Ermenonville, where
Jean-Jacques Rousseau's
original Roman-style
tomb stands. Photo:
Everett Scott.

ger (1744–1818). It was a project carried out very much on the scale of a great French park of the seventeenth century. The gigantic dimensions of Laborde's visionary premises reflected a similar taste for the grandiloquent statements in architecture one sees in Piranesi's engravings and in the building projects of Boullée and Ledoux. "The cult of the colossal" had been foreshadowed in Edmund Burke's definition of the Sublime and the Beautiful, rejecting the Rococo conception of architecture and garden as a sequence of well-bred, intimate, informal environments. The park of Méréville, with its dramatic cascade and greatly "enhanced" river flowing through the middle of it, expressed neoclassical ideals of mastering nature's powerful forms and appropriating nature as if with a magnifying glass to further enlarge it to enormous, idealized proportions. Once again, and in a tradition that reaches back to the early Italian Renaissance, the elements of theater and opera are employed at Méréville to exploit nature's emotional possibilities in a garden composition.

In order to give some scenic balance and scale to the overwhelming presence of nature and to control the theatrical perspectives, Laborde commissioned Hubert Robert and Bélanger to compose the different pictures. Several of Robert's paintings of the tableaux at Méréville have survived. No English artist of comparable ability was even asked to arrange similar "scenes" in an English picturesque setting. In many ways, employing in this particular role an important painter trained in Italy has a special French quality to it. There is a kind of *tour de force* aesthetic orchestration in Robert's creations out of nature that is as artificial and as thoroughly dominating as that of André Le Nôtre at Vaux-le-Vicomte one hundred years earlier. In a strange way, Robert's monumental romantic grotto at Versailles looks quite at home.

In spite of patronizing English complaints about French gardens, French garden-makers at Ermenonville, Méréville, and the Désert de Retz were able to "create anew by the hand of

Ile de Peupliers, Ermenonville, from the guidebook written by the Marquis de Girardin (1735–1808), who created the park and acted as Rousseau's host for the last two months of the philosopher's life. Girardin's treatise on the relationship between farming and picturesque beauty was translated into English in 1783.

(1761) a wild garden, the "Elysée," created by the heroine Julie. The writer had lived briefly in a hut in the park at Ermenonville as a guest of Girardin and had died there. The marquis built the tomb on the island and surrounded it with tall Lombardy poplars. To be able to incorporate the actual tomb of such a celebrated advocate of romantic, unspoiled nature was the ultimate garden ornament–memorial of the eighteenth century. Long after Rousseau's remains were removed from this "Island of Poplars," the site remained a moving, poetic souvenir that attracted kindred souls who came to pay homage.

Twenty years after the work had begun at Ermenonville, the Paris banker J.-J. Laborde laid out Méréville in the wooded valley of the Juine south of Paris between 1784 and 1794, with the assistance of François-Joseph Bélan-

The Pyramid at Désert de Retz, Chambourcy, with an icehouse beneath it, may also have been slated as a mausoleum for its builder, M. de Monville. Photo: Everett Scott.

Temple ruins at Désert de Retz served as a backdrop for small picnics in the park. Photo: Everett Scott.

taste an ideal setting, protected by natural ramparts and mountains, a new Golden Age, intended by nature as the last asylum of peace and liberty," declared Girardin.[62]

The Désert de Retz (begun 1774), while much more modest in scale than Laborde's or Girardin's park, was almost contemporary and just as famous. Thomas Jefferson was quite taken with the Désert when he visited it in 1786. He was particularly fascinated with the five-story Column House that stands in the middle of walks winding through the Désert's collection of rare specimen trees. Sixteen other pavilions and garden structures were scattered around the rugged, naturally picturesque piece of woods next to the walls of Louis XIV's old royal domain of Marly.

Although François Racine de Monville (1734–1797), who owned the Désert, was assisted in the beginning by an obscure architect, it is uncertain exactly whose hand was involved in the ultimate realization of the garden of the Désert. De Monville was an accomplished man and no doubt took a major role. He was, like the duc de Chartres and several other French garden enthusiasts of the time, a prominent member of the Freemasons, and it is possible that Masonic ritual and symbolism entered into the garden's design. Rousseau had earlier proposed the natural wilderness or desert isle unmarred by civilization as the place for man to begin his regeneration, so de Monville's intricate, mysterious garden might have been used for the initiatory ritual of Freemasonry redemption. If so, this would also explain the rather ceremonial circuit that connects the various garden structures.

The visitor entered the Désert through a contrived pile of rocks arranged to look like the mouth of a cave or grotto. On the garden side of the entrance, torch-bearing satyrs in lead stood guard on either side of the theatrical entrance. A drive wound down the natural slope, past a stone pyramid that served as an icehouse and may have been intended ultimately to serve as Baron de Monville's mausoleum. The center of the garden's composition was an eighty-foot fragment of a

The famous Column House at Désert de Retz, photographed during its recent restoration. A drawing of the original building is seen at right. Photo: Everett Scott.

An engraving of the entrance to Désert de Retz from the Forest of Marly shows the entry to be in the form of a grotto with guardian satyrs holding torches. Le Rouge, *Nouveaux jardins.*

monumental broken column of the Tuscan order. Inside its fluted exterior was concealed an elegant house of five floors. The prince de Ligne (1735–1814), himself an outstanding amateur gardener, remarked that it looked like a part of a colossal temple, which like the Tower of Babel had suddenly called down upon itself the wrath of God.

The use of the circular form of the Column House was, in fact, a brilliant solution to the vexing problem of uniting architecture with a sinuous, irregular landscape composition and eliminating all of the shapes and geometric angles of the old, formal gardens. The winding walks encircle and converge on the column without any forced transition through the conventional architectural garden setting, as at nearby Bagatelle or the Petit Trianon where the formal lines of the pavilions sharply confront the surrounding parks.

From the upper floors of the Column House, de Monville could see a temple of Pan, an outdoor theatre in a dell below the house, an obelisk, and an elegant *tente tatar* made of painted tin. The Désert's tent has disappeared, but two similar tents still stand on the hill

overlooking the English parks built by Gustaf III at his country retreat of Haga, outside Stockholm.

The Désert's Maison Chinoise was one of the most elaborate chinoiserie pavilions to be built in the eighteenth century, even though the fad for things Chinese was rather late in reaching France. The inspiration had come from William Chambers (1723–1796), who had led the way in promoting charmingly bogus designs for pavilions, gates, bridges, and garden benches. Chambers had his own good-humored, decidedly imaginary ideas both for architecture and for "Chinese" gardens. He called then "a piece of nonsense of my own." At about the time he had been engaged to lay out the grounds of the botanical gardens at Kew for Princess Augusta, Chambers published his *Designs of Chinese Buildings* (1757). His cluttered plans for Kew included a Chinese temple, an aviary, menagerie, orangery, mosque, Palladian bridge, twenty classical pavilions, and a ten-story pagoda that still stands.

In 1772, with Capability Brown at the height of his influence, Chambers published his celebrated *Dissertation on Oriental Gardening* to protest the bare, shaved expanse of the Brownian park. Beneath Chambers's argument was a reasonable plea for a garden of variety, texture, and color, laid out to stir curiosity and to invoke a sensation of surprise, alarm, and delight.

> The Chinese . . . avoid all sudden transitions both with regard to dimension and color. They build up gradually from the smallest flowers in front through a row of medium height, to the taller ones in the back. In the same style, color is graded from white through primrose and yellow and so forth . . . to the deepest blues, and most brilliant crimsons and scarlets. They frequently blend several roots together, whose leaves and flowers unite and compose one rich harmonious mass . . . and the same method they use with flowering shrubs, blending white, red and variegated

L'île Adam, an elegant late-eighteenth-century Chinese folie near Paris, restored by Olivier Choppin de Janury. Photo: Everett Scott.

A royal park in the English style was designed about 1785 by F. M. Piper for King Gustaf III at Haga, near Stockholm, Sweden. The copper-clad tent, similar to one that once stood at the Désert de Retz, housed the corps de gard and was designed by the French architect Louis Deprez. Photo: Everett Scott.

roses together; purple and white lilacs; yellow and white jasmine; azaleas of various sorts; and as many others as they can with propriety unite. . . . [63]

That the Chinese were actually composing their gardens in the way Chambers imaginatively describes is highly questionable, but the introduction of an exotic, distant land gave his argument a certain romantic appeal. Paintings of Chinese gardens of the seventeenth and eighteenth centuries do not confirm it, nor do any of the contemporary Western descriptions coincide with what Edward Hyams has called

Chambers's visionary projection of poetic English gardens that would not actually appear for another hundred years or more—when William Robinson would advance the wild garden that would in turn inspire the dreamlike twentieth-century gardens at Bodnant, Dartington, and Mount Usher. Chambers's comments on colorful Chinese flower beds also served to generate interest in reintroducing flowers into the proper English garden, flowers that seemed to have been banished to the cottage yard during the years of Brown's ascendancy.

Although Repton had been quite willing to

introduce shrubs and flowers near the house for ornament and pleasure—his beds of American plants, "the ancient garden," and the modern terrace-walks—his ornamental garden, "following different characteristics of taste," could not be further from Chinese garden traditions.

In his *Observations* of 1803, Repton praised the new flower garden at Nuneham (c.1771), a house outside Oxford, as a precedent and prototype. Nuneham was the creation of the second earl of Harcourt, a close friend of the writer and poet William Mason, who worked with him. In a letter dated 1771 Mason is credited with directing its laying out with "poet's feeling and painter's eye."[64]

Repton felt that flower gardens should be hidden from general view and that their decorations should be as much art as nature: "The flower garden at Nuneham, without being formal, is highly enriched, but not too much crowded with seats, temples, statues, vases or other ornaments, which, being works of art, beautifully harmonize with that profusion of flowers and curious plants which distinguish the flower garden from the natural landscape. . . ."[65]

Mason, who had been responsible for this mélange, advocated the principles of informal flower gardening in Book 4 of his poem *The English Garden.* While it is not much of a practical garden manual, Mason does make an eloquent plea for the flowers that had been missing from the large monotone landscapes of preceding generations. Even though Mason claimed no inspiration for his English garden from the Chinese, he and they did at least agree that the true principles of gardening had to be first established by the poets and painters.

Even though Mason's principles and his works at Nuneham were closely akin to Chambers's ornamented garden at Kew, the poet launched a broadside attack on Chambers's *Dissertation on Oriental Gardening* when it appeared. Politics were behind the assault since Chambers was a conspicuous representative of the Tory court opposed by Mason.

Yet in Mason's work at Nuneham and in Chambers's own praise of his imaginary Chinese flower garden, they anticipated by nearly fifty years the Gardenesque movement led by Loudon and his magazines.

Even though the English had perfected their own artificially irregular landscape gardens long before Chinese influence could have played a significant part in the development, there was, as Osvald Sirén points out in *The Gardens of China,* a similarity in attitudes toward nature and other parallels in methods of composition. Both the English and the Chinese garden, "considered as a special kind of landscape gardening, may with more reason than most other types of parks or gardens be characterized as a work of the creative imagination, or in other words as something corresponding to the demands that must be made upon a work of art."[66]

As for Chinese garden architecture in England, in France, or in other parts of the Continent, where the fashion rapidly spread from Potsdam to Stockholm and St. Petersburg, these buildings were simply pleasant little Western follies gotten up with bits and pieces of ornament and trim to give a superficial oriental appearance.

By the end of the eighteenth century the demand for exotic decoration in gardens and parks seemed to be inexhaustible. Inspiration from Turkey, Egypt, Greece, and India as well as the Far East was sought out by garden designers, architects, and impresarios who had been invited in to add a few theatrical set pieces of amusement and visual relief. The summer residence of the Palatine court at Schwetzingen got a new English garden in 1776 when other follies were added, including an enormous Turkish mosque. By the time various electors had finished, the garden of Schwetzingen resembled nothing so much as a large amusement park for German aristocrats. Some of the inspiration for both garden and architecture might have been lifted from the pages of *Détails de nouveaux jardins à la mode* published by Georges-Louis Le Rouge, a French engineer and geographer. German

The little stage-set village created for Marie Antoinette in the park at Versailles has a distinctly "English" air, but the composition may also have been inspired by Flemish genre paintings. Photo: Everett Scott.

garden plans were included among Le Rouge's engravings, and the book was widely consulted since it represented a kind of catalog of the latest garden designs, imagined and real.

No doubt one of the things that contributed to the mania for exotic, foreign garden buildings was the growing interest in exotic horticultural collections from all over the world, and particularly from the Far East. More than a few of the distinctive colors in the twentieth-century English garden came from the botanical storehouse of China, which contains one of the richest arrays of flora in the world. Although the direct importation of plants did not get under way on the mainland until the Treaty of Nanjing in 1841, with this opening, British merchants, traders, and botanical explorers gained easy access to the Chinese treasure trove. A century earlier the French Society of Jesus had sent out a missionary who also happened to be a trained botanist. Father Pierre d'Incarville lived mostly in Peking from 1740 to 1756, and through his efforts the seeds of many plants that were new to the West first arrived. Some of these seeds reached Philip Miller at the Chelsea Physic Garden in London via the Jardin du Roi in Paris. D'Incarville's best-known introduction is the invasive tree of heaven, or *Ailanthus*.

The natural, irregular, asymmetrical garden was England's gift to the eighteenth century. It expressed the dynamic energy and intellectual drive of the Enlightenment. Like the Enlightenment it was international and cosmopolitan, carrying with it more than a hint of subversive politics. In America, the open, free, "wildly picturesque and richly productive" countryside was seen as particularly receptive to the new mode. The conservative geometry of what Andrew Jackson Downing called "the ancient style" gradually gave way. After the American Revolution, it was seen in many quarters as a symbol of old, bankrupt, European society that smacked of autocracy and hierarchy. It was not a style that would prevail in the United States where, as Downing declared, "the rights of man are held to be equal." Like the English common law and the English language, the English garden was a legacy that could be easily Americanized.

V. Gardens of the East

THE CHINESE GARDEN

After a series of practical instructions, *Yuan Ye* (Yüan Yeh) or *Garden Tempering* (1634), the famous Chinese treatise on gardening by Ji Cheng, concludes on an existential note: "There are no definite rules for the planning of gardens." If an Italian, French, or even an English gardener steeped in his native pragmatism had read *Yuan Ye* when it first was published, he would have instantly dismissed the book as nonsense. For the French at least, gardening was nothing if not a set of fundamental rules reflecting their skepticism toward the ways of unfettered nature. In 1632, when Louis XIII bought the hunting estate outside of Paris called Versailles, a garden laid out by precise, geometric rules was firmly in place, and its underlying principles, all agreed, were unchallenged and seemingly unchallengeable. The relentless logic extending from the architecture of the little hunting lodge would remain the fundamental foundation for all of the subsequent and sweeping enlargements of Versailles over the next fifty years. The long, straight avenues reaching to infinity, the perfect symmetry of the parterres, the predictable balance of the composition were a visible manifestation of God's pact with the king and the destiny of the state expressed by the formula of the architecture. Yet before the century was out and before the twilight of the Sun King had cast a shadow over André Le Nôtre's gardens, rumors of the radical, hardly conceivable gardens of China were circulating throughout Europe. These accounts, brought back by travelers and Jesuit missionaries, appeared without warning and without relating to anything in previous Western gardening experience that would provide an understandable translation of such fundamentally opposite principles of garden-making.

At least a hint of *le goût chinois* had in fact touched a corner of the park at Versailles in the winter of 1670–71 when Louis XIV decided to build a little pavilion for his ambitious concubine, Mme. de Montespan. By the following spring the Trianon de Porcelaine à la Chinoise was completed as the first of a long line of little garden pleasances that would soon appear all over Europe. It was reported in the *Mercure galant* in 1673, only two years after the Trianon was finished, that both courtiers and bourgeoisie were already busy attempting to convert their suddenly unfashionable garden huts in frantic imitation of the king. But the enchanting little retreat designed by the court architect Louis Le Vau and supposedly inspired by a pagoda at Nanjing was in fact a glittering Rococo extravaganza of blue and white Delft tile walls and gilded roof. Furthermore it was firmly anchored in Le Nôtre's classic garden formula, which he had employed. Aside from the garden's geometry, the flamboyant displays of flowers in beds that were often changed daily could not have been further from the spirit of a Chinese garden or gardening philosophy and practice. In fact the conservative French preferred to let the English make the first experiments with Eastern influence to break with established garden tradition some fifty years later.

The most remarkable thing about Sir William Temple's long meditation, *Upon the Gardens of Epicurus,* written in 1685, was his

suggestion that the exotic Chinese models should be taken seriously.

Among us, the beauty of Buildings and planting is placed chiefly in some Proportions, Symmetries or Uniformities; our walks and our trees ranged so as they answer one another, and at exact Distances. The Chinese scorn this way of planting. . . . Their greatest reach of imagination is employed in contriving Figures where the Beauties shall be great, and strike the Eye, but without any order or disposition of part, that shall be commonly or easily observ'd. . . . And though we have hardly any Notion of this sort of Beauty, yet they have a particular Word to express it; and where they find it hit their Eye at first sight, they say the *Sharawadgi* is fine. . . .

Even though Temple's famous word "Sharawadgi" was thought at the time to be his own invention, it probably derives from the Chinese *sa-lo-kwai-chi,* meaning "the quality of being impressive or surprising through carelessness or unorderly grace."[1] Temple's intro-

duction of the term did not noticeably advance English understanding of Chinese design principles or lead to efforts to achieve similar results in English gardens, but it did arouse interest in discovering the original meaning in Chinese and this in turn has provided a ray of insight into the oldest garden tradition in the world.

For the West the Chinese and Japanese garden traditions have been the most complex to fully grasp and to translate into Western terms and experience. More than any other garden traditions, they seem to establish a relationship between man and nature, a reconciliation that has been extremely difficult for Westerners to comprehend. Osvald Sirén declared in his landmark *Gardens of China* that the Chinese garden is "characterized as a work of creative imagination," a work of art that demands the same order of conception, the same expression of artistic ideas in execution, and ultimately the same trained faculty on the part of the viewer as any other creative production.[2] His point is indisputable and reminds us of the concentrated dedication that is required to fully decipher the Chinese art of gardening. A similar concentration is required to separate the superficial connections between the Chinese and Japanese garden traditions.

Sirén frankly admits, as did the writer in *Yuan Ye,* that "much of what is most essential in the Chinese garden eludes formal analysis," since the results are "due less to the layout and the formal arrangement than to what vibrates through and around the various elements of composition, enhancing their power to bring out the rhythm of Nature."[3] His words are a challenging introduction to a highly poetic and imaginative subject.

What is identified as the rhythm of Nature and its manifold forces (or even the negative power of their absence, as the Chinese recognize) is, of course, at the heart of much of Chinese philosophy. So, some rudimentary understanding of the underlying philosophies are essential at the outset.

Both the art of gardening and that of land-scape painting drew their inspiration from rather romantic readings of Dao (Tao) and the Daoist philosophies. According to Daoism, man was placed in the most intimate connection with all aspects of nature, spiritually and materially. Gardens, therefore, were intended above all to advance and to heighten their owners' communion with the natural world and to bring them ultimately into contact with the creative forces of the universe, forces they should then introduce and express in their lives and works. The root meaning of *Dao* has been translated as the "totality of all things"—past and future—in its constant and dynamic state of transformation.[4] If a follower was able to give himself up to the changing currents of nature he could become one with those forces that produced them in celebration of an unalterable cosmic plan. The rational was as one with the irrational. Such a strong belief in a sense of unity with nature as a benign wilderness, as a source of awe, magic, and sustenance, no doubt inspired the Chinese desire to attempt to recreate its poetic wonders both in the garden and in landscape paintings. It should be said that both garden and painting were works of the imagination and were never intended to be an attempt to present nature in any literal way.

The cycle of nature and of the seasons, of life and of death was given added meaning by Daoism.

> Since death and life . . . attend upon one another why should I account either an evil? Life is accounted beautiful because it is spirit-like and wonderful. Death is accounted hateful because it is foetid and putrid. But the foetid and putrid, returning, is transformed again into the spirit-like and wonderful; and in the universe there is one *Ch'i* [breath] and therefore the sages prized that unity.[5]

To become one with the ebb and flow of the natural order of things was and is a source of great creative power for the garden designer in any tradition.

Daoism itself, like the garden treatise *Yuan Ye,* was without rules beyond those intuitive powers inspired by the conditions of a particular place or setting. Everything is suggested by aphorism and contradiction, or in Maggie Keswick's words, "to gain, you must yield; to grasp, let go; to win, lose." [6]

Within all of this introspective philosophy was the belief in and reliance on human intuition. In following his intuition, a man made his garden become an expression of his character, "a haven of inner strength." No wonder the late Fletcher Steele summed up the Chinese garden as "the sanctuary of the introvert." [7]

The intuitive, subjective, contradictory approach to practical gardening can be found in an eleventh-century manuscript, when Kuo Hsi (fl. 1060–1075) wrote out some characteristically Daoist advice on landscape composition: "Too much emphasis on slopes and banks makes the work crude; too much emphasis on calm and quiet is trite; too much emphasis on humanity makes the work commonplace; too much emphasis on houses and arbors makes it confused; too much emphasis on stones makes it bony; while too much emphasis on soil makes it fleshy." [8]

This recommendation to strike a kind of balance between the polar coordinates represented in ordinary garden characteristics exemplifies the Chinese preoccupation with what might be called the continuum of possibilities of a garden. It also appears to be an exercise in harmonizing the qualities of yin and yang, those two essential cosmic forces that underlie all creation and animate the Chinese universe. Garden features like "mountains," rough and masculine (yang), are balanced with soft, reflective water (yin). The orchestration of high places leads to low ground, open spaces suddenly close, shade becomes sunny, and a wide passage turns narrow in the garden's composition. This spirit of yin and yang is the magic to be discovered there. Or using the metaphor of the swinging pendulum, the darkness of night is already beginning when the sun reaches its zenith, or winter is present in the summer solstice. With the constantly renewing rhythms of nature in a garden, this ebb and flow, the metaphysical possibilities of the duality of yin and yang are infinite.

The Early Garden

The underlying and dramatic topography of China—great mountains, misty river valleys, lakes, and waterfalls—has inspired Chinese poets, landscape painters, and garden-makers

The fantastic Lu-shan mountains in South China were also among those that furnished inspiration for introducing hills and rocks into Chinese landscape gardens. This painting is a subjective representation of the cliffs and falls of Lu-shan as painted in the twelfth century by Chiang Shen, after Fan K'uan. National Palace Museum, Taipei.

Li River near Yangshuo, Guangxi Province. Photo: Charles Marden Fitch.

for countless centuries. The vast, square track of country bounded on the north by the Gobi and Mongolian deserts and on the west by snow-covered mountains is broken up in sharp mountain ranges, fertile valleys, and a network of rivers. The monsoon blows in from the sea in the summer, making the native forests of the south luxuriant and prolific. Crisscrossed by alluvial plains, the southern part of China is just within the tropic zone, so the number and variety of plants and trees exceed those of any other country in the world. The very geniality and variety of China's environment, particularly in the south, stimulated very early a friendly, comfortable dialog between man and the natural landscape that was to be the basis of all Chinese thought and philosophy. Unlike the Christian West, China assumed no divine Creator separate from and dominant over his creation.

Royal gardens reaching back into the mythic past are mentioned in poems from the Zhou (Chou) dynasty (c.1027–256 B.C.). In the Qin (Ch'in) dynasty (221–206 B.C.), great hunting parks with collections of rare animals and plants became a powerful symbol of imperial power under the emperor Shi Huang Di, who had first unified the Chinese states. Animals and plants for his park were gifts of tribute from his conquered provinces. Even after an emperor had relinquished his throne in retirement, a garden was still an important symbol of his position: "Every emperor and ruler must, upon returning from his official duties and audience, have a garden in which to stroll, to look around and find rest in his heart," declared one court memorialist.[9] The Han emperors (206 B.C.–A.D. 220) that followed Shi Huang Di continued the tradition of a garden as a symbol of power. Described in the great prose poems of the Han dynasty, these Chinese parks take on the quality of the royal Persian parks that so startled and impressed Alexander during his eastern campaign. According to Han bards, the imperial parks were created as a portrait of the empire in miniature. It is the first recorded suggestion that a man-made landscape might in fact represent in its richness and variety a microcosm symbolizing the known universe.[10]

Recreating a miniature universe inspired the emperors to stock their parks with all kinds of curious and exotic animals and birds. Rare fowl of every kind from all over the empire

were particularly prized and acquired at great cost as living garden ornaments. It is recorded that in 716 the Tang emperor Xüan Zung (Hsüan Tsung; r. 712–756) sent court eunuchs into the region of the Chang Jiang (Yangtze) River,

> . . . to take Pond Herons and Tufted Ducks desiring to place them in his park. Wherever these agents were there was vexation and trouble. . . . "they capture birds and waterfowl in their nets to supply frivolities for garden and pond. From far beyond the river and mountain passes, these are transferred under escort by water and land and fed with millet and meat so that watchers by road and highway cannot but take it that Your Enthroned Eminence esteems birds while despising men!" [11]

Another, and peculiarly Chinese, theme in these earliest but vaguely documented gardens was the legendary search for immortality. It is not clear just when and how this mythological exploration was somehow transformed into the recreation of an idealized natural landscape, but the ancient legends of immortality did give Chinese gardens an otherworldly dimension that has compounded their complexity for Westerners. The mythological Immortals—enchanted demigods of Chinese lore—divided their time between mountaintop palaces and islands located somewhere in what was called the Eastern Seas. They commuted between their retreats on the backs of storks, and if mortals attempted to approach their islands they would simply dissolve into the mist. It is the memory of these magical island dwellings that was to later inspire the miniature "mountains" built of rock piles and the strange, freestanding, ubiquitous stones in gardens throughout China.

From the earliest visual evidence of Chinese gardens, even in those modest philosopher's huts set down beneath a towering mountain in a bamboo grove, it is clear that man has achieved an armistice with nature's domain.

A Yuan Dynasty (1279–1368) hanging scroll, *Spring Dawn over the Elixir Terrace,* by Lu Kuang. Metropolitan Museum of Art, Edward Elliott Family Collection.

The very intensity of the interpenetration of man and nature, the aesthetic awareness of the significance in every tree, rock, leaf, and blossom seems to heighten not only man's connection with nature but also his implicit dominance over it. Having once identified and appropriated a hillside, a piece of mossy turf, or a mountain stream, it appears that man never has to do anything more about it except occasionally to reassure himself of his secure place in the universe.

The lonely philosopher living deep among the mountains or woods, or in communion with the mythical immortal islands that vanish and miraculously reappear, is a recurring image in Chinese art and in landscape design. "In your fancy you enter a painting," a philosopher told his pupils. Because artists and gardeners saw themselves in spirit akin to all physical objects, analogy and symbolism were used even in nature, as well as with the brush, to convey their message. As the ideal Chinese garden slowly evolves, the intuitive world of spirit endows the trees, rocks, and water with a special mood and occasion. Above all, stillness is essential, for gardens are places for expiatory meditation, private conversation, and poetry reading, all activities of the highest human expression.

The Private Garden

While emperors were recreating miniature "mountains and islands" of the Immortals, so that those who were endowed with the secrets of eternal life could live under the patronage of the ruler in the imperial gardens, lesser subjects were beginning to indulge in private pleasure gardens of their own. The development of these early private gardens followed closely the same lines as Chinese painting. Both in paintings and in the poetic descriptions of gardens, one of the main themes was the introspective character of Daoism expressed in the motif of a rustic solitary pavilion, or hermit's hut, under shady trees on a mountain terrace where one could live in complete harmony with nature, an idea that appealed both to painters and garden-makers. The poet Hsieh Ling-yin (early 5th century) evokes the refined, romantic atmosphere of such idealized places in his revery called "Tree Planting in a Garden in the South."

I have banished all worldly care from my garden; it is a clean and open spot. I chose the place in the lee of the mountains to the north; the windows open towards the hills in the south. I have dammed up the stream and built a pond. I have planted stock roses in front of the round window, but beyond them appear the hills. . . . [12]

About the time that the poet was building his intimate little garden with its roses, and no doubt some chrysanthemums, landscape painting itself was beginning to emerge as an independent branch of art. And it is clear that even at this early date the art of gardening and the art of painting were inseparably connected in composition.

Both the lyrical descriptions of the poets and the equally lyrical paintings illustrate variations on the theme of the sequestered, primeval hut with little plantations of fruit trees, flowers, and bamboo either on a hillside or near a lake. More often the philosopher-gardener is alone and in meditation. On a rare social occasion, he may be seen with a single friend who has joined him for a philosophical conversation or a private chuckle. Much of the space is empty, and the restraint is underlined by a pervasive patience approaching a resignation we can scarcely comprehend— a patience "enduring from generation to generation," Fletcher Steele remarked, "contentedly watching a lone plum tree grow from youth to maturity and from strength to age." [13] From the earliest Daoist gardener who chose a perfectly aged and gnarled pine tree to contemplate from the doorway of a thatched pavilion, restraint, patience, silence, and the zeal to retard and control nature has been the Chinese ideal. When the garden treatise declares that there are no rules for making a

Garden rocks, flowering trees, bamboo, and miniature plants, with a white heron and two noble ladies. Part of a painting from the sixteenth century called *Early Spring in a Palace Garden*.

garden, these intuitive, native qualities seem to have insured faultless results with the simplest of elements and effort. "Since my youth," the poet Po Chü-i (772–846) wrote, "I have lived in varying circumstances, sometimes in a hut, sometimes in an elegant dwelling, but wherever I have lived, even if it were only for some days, I have built a terrace, piled up stones, and excavated a pond, for my passion for mountains and waters was irresistible."[14]

The pile of stones was to represent, of course, the potent, awesome presence of the "magic" mountains, symbols of immortality. Chinese painters had also been captivated by rock conformations. It is as the enchanted

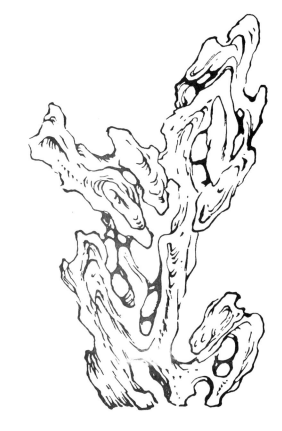

In China, ancient stones, such as this one from Lake Tai, serve the same decorative function as sculpture in European gardens. *Su Yüan Shih P'u.*

Plan of the Imperial Park of Ch'ang Ch-un Yüan. Francesco Fariello, *Architettura dei Giardini.*

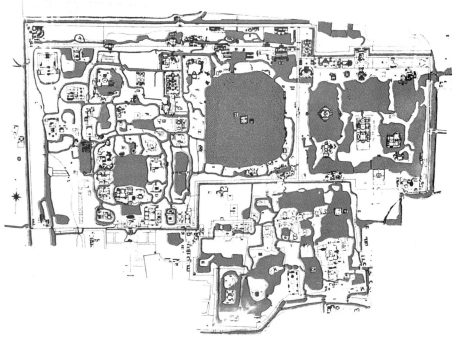

habitat of the Immortals, rather than as an attempt to recreate nature in miniature, that the "mountain-rocks" became an important theme in Chinese garden art.

Beyond the symbolism of the legends of the Immortals, a manifestation of primitive stone-worship seems to dominate private Chinese gardens. Heavy, grotesque, monochromatic rocks are as pervasive in the Chinese garden as boxwood is in a Virginia garden in Williamsburg. Strangely shaped boulders from early times were in fact believed to have special power and were worshiped as local gods. In their dense, sinister, sculptured shapes, it was believed, the stones condensed the forces of irrationality in nature. By appropriating them for the garden, the gardener was in a subtle way demonstrating his control over nature's unruly powers. As artificial mountains, a pile of rocks took on even more peculiarly Chinese meaning, which Chang-lun, a minister of agriculture, describes:

> He built up a mountain called Ching-yang as if it were a work of Nature, with piled-up peaks and multiple ranges rising in steep succession, with deep ravines and caverns and gullies tortuously linked. So lofty were the forests, so gigantic the trees that sun and moon could not penetrate their shadowed obscurity; so luxuriant were the vines and creepers in their festooning as to control the passage of wind and mist. Here the [Daoist] adepts, the lovers of mountains and wilderness, might have roamed until they quite forgot to return to their heaven. . . . [15]

Not every garden "mountain" was made of the most rustic, rough boulders that could be found and moved. Xüan Zung (Hsüan Tsung) built a microcosmic island-mountain of dazzling lapis lazuli. A splendid piece of garden decoration, it was placed in a pool where the girls from his seraglio paddled around in skiffs made of lacquered sandalwood. The shimmering pile of blue gemstone marks a high point in extravagant, aristocratic garden decoration.

This extraordinary reverence for rocks and stones in the Chinese garden is balanced by an equally prominent role for water. The significance of water in the Daoist philosophy of nature was profound. Rivers, visible or hidden, represented the life arteries of the earth, while the mountains were thought to represent its skeleton. The living organism of the planet itself was built up of the same elements as those that make up man, and it is the ultimate challenge of the artist whether he is a gardener or painter to "exploit the different elements," in Sirén's words, "and in this way invest his creation with an expression of life."[16] Water, as an essential part of the artist's expression of universal life, was therefore important in the composition of the Chinese garden.

Daoist philosophers had long contemplated the character of water and used the metaphor of its properties in their early writing. "Nothing under heaven is softer or more yielding than water," the authors of *Tao Te Ching* observed, "but when it attacks things hard and resistant there is not one of them that can prevail."[17] The force of water, of course, had eroded and shaped the fantastic rocks used in gardens and these may well have served as subtle reminders of water's irresistible power to transmute the harder material.

Song dynasty (960–1279) landscape painting is so close to the work of Song garden designers that observations on either of the two art forms are often interchangeable. Landscape painting itself was called "mountain-water painting," referring also to the two essential elements of the Chinese garden. Instructions for the handling of water in paintings provide an insight on the use of water in garden compositions as well.

> In drawing water, if the peaceful, the raging, the whirling, the dashing and the overflowing are all portrayed; if the river is shown leading out towards a far expanse; then the representation of water is varied, and is abundant and satisfying in itself.

If water does not flow forward then it is dead. Water is a living thing; hence its aspects may be deep and serene, gentle and smooth; it may be vast and ocean-like, winding and circling. It may spout like a fountain, shooting and splashing; it may come from a place rich in springs and may flow afar. It may form waterfalls rising up against the sky or dashing down to deep earth; it may delight the fisherman making the trees and grass joyful; it may be charming in the company of mists and clouds or gleam radiantly, reflecting the sunlight of the valley. Such are the living aspects of water. . . . With mountains, water becomes charming; with arbors and terraces, bright and pleasing; with fishing and angling free and spacious.[18]

With such a painterly analysis of water as a part of the garden designer's aesthetic equip-

A decorative lotus cartouche set into a tile surface at Yu Hua Yuan, the Imperial Palace Garden in Beijing. Photo: Charles Marden Fitch.

A garden at the Summer Palace in Beijing. Photo: Charles Marden Fitch.

ment, there seemed to be no limit to the themes and variations that could be extrapolated from it. In artificial streams, lakes, and pools, calm and mirroring the vegetation or rushing from a waterfall in a pulsating cascade, water became, in the hands of the Chinese garden designer, a life-giving ingredient in every sense of the term. One treatise advised the designer to carefully conceal the ends of the waterways so that they appear to be a flowing river, much as Lancelot Brown often did in eighteenth-century English parks. If water was not available for a stream or pond, then dry stones could be laid out to evoke a running brook. An empty pond was supposed to stimulate the viewer's imagination into conjuring up a reflecting mirror or water. For all of the designers' poetry, it is in these flights of pure fantasy that a Westerner is apt to be left in a state of confused disbelief recalling the tale of the emperor's new clothes. Nothing in Western values and philosophy can bridge by analogy the cultural gaps represented in a Chinese river composed of flat, dry stones.

The great imperial parks often employed water extravagantly for dramatic effect. Large lakes, ponds, and canals were deployed by the Ming emperor Yong-lo (r. 1402–1424) in Beijing to suggest the yin-yang harmony of opposites in the tension between the geometrical grid pattern and the curving streams that intersect it. While the forms of the man-made lakes and the natural stream of the garden are completely different from the landforms, they somehow complement and complete each other. The juxtaposition of mountains and water in the Chinese landscape is an even more explicit expression of yin and yang.

Dynastic splendor and extravagance have been the hallmark of royal gardens in every civilization. Chinese history is strewn with tales of rising and falling dynasties leaving in their wake rumors and reports of lost gardens and parks rivaling anything built later in the West. At the beginning of the Sui dynasty (581–618) to celebrate the glorious splendor of the restoration of imperial unity, the future emperor Yang Di (r. 605–618), then viceroy in south China, built sixteen palaces strung out like so many pearls along a chain of lakes and waterways. Guests were carried to these parks on elaborate barges. One account claims that a million people were employed on the construction and that half of them died in the process. Although fountains were not used in traditional Chinese gardens, the imperial gardens of the last emperor of the Yuan dynasty (1279–1368) incorporated water jets, tiger and dragon robots, and even mechanical boats.

The Making of a Chinese Garden

In her note on the making of a Chinese garden, in *The Oxford Companion to Gardens,* Maggie Keswick points out that skill and imagination on the part of the garden-maker are only the initial requirements. He also requires a knowledge of *feng shui,* the art of discovering the powerful, hidden cosmic currents that affect a site, as well as a tradition that prepares visitors for the "suspension of disbelief." Quoting the modern historian Chuin Tung she adds, "The question of reality will not bother the visitor as long as he ceases to be in the *garden* and begins to live in the *painting.*"[19]

As everyone who has written even twenty-five words on the subject has pointed out, the Chinese garden unfolds along winding paths very much like a scroll painting unwinding from right to left. Even though there is a homogeneous composition, the isolated scenes or sections succeed one another as the visitor, relaxing his grip on his "disbelief," strolls past the lakes, mountains, over bridges, along walls, and through doorways. In small spaces, doorways and gates are particularly important elements of design. They further divide the space to create mystery and surprise. The shape of the door or opening is quite often fanciful and symbolic—a circle, perhaps, used as a sign of heaven.

Paths provide the third dimension to the garden design and are also an important, dis-

The Imperial Palace Garden in Beijing. Photo: Charles Marden Fitch.

crete decorative element of the garden layout, often in mosaic or brick patterns. Sometimes pebbles set to create pictures in relief are used as visual accents. Since one of the earliest meanings of the word *Dao* is "road," "path," or "way," the garden path itself takes on a higher allegorical implication beyond its obvious, prosaic function of simply leading you through the garden's scenes without getting your feet wet. As the *Yuan Ye* author casually advises, "Plan the walks and footpaths. Yield to the enchantment of the flowers and the willows. Make a setting of stones round the pond; then pack down the earth around them hard. The soil that has been dry may be used to throw up a 'mountain ridge,' which, whether high or low, will produce a good effect."[20]

Yuan Ye is vague and contradictory, but its chapter titles and some of its terse, aphoristic language do evoke a poetic image of a garden. The following summary of some of the book's sections may help illustrate the subjective approach to oriental garden designs.[21]

DISCOURSE ON GARDENS

Following the charming introduction, which speaks of the orchids and irises planted along the stream, the author recommends first of all to lay out garden paths for "three kinds of friends." Apparently this classification of garden paths according to friendship was first defined in the *Analects* of Confucius (551–479 B.C.). But what is of the utmost importance to the garden-maker at the outset is to remember that his garden should be made to last a thousand years.

THE SELECTION OF SITE

Selecting the site for a garden that might be some distance from the house was, of course, crucial and assumed some understanding of *feng shui* principles. "The garden may be given the form of a square or a circle; it may be irregular and surprising; it may be surrounded with a curving wall or be dispersed like a great cloud." And as for uneven topography,

"where the ground rises one may build terraces and pavilions; in the depressions one may excavate ponds and lakes." "Borrowed prospects" from beyond the garden's precincts are important whether it is a distant mountain peak or the blossoming plum tree in one's neighbor's garden. If the buds are just opening, "one may bid them welcome as the ambassadors of continual spring." Dramatic, sweeping views and panoramas in these "appropriations," and in the Chinese garden generally, were not desirable. What was to be expressed in these small vignettes of the larger landscape was the deep Chinese reverence for the "vital spirit" or "cosmic breath" that runs, according to *feng shui* principles, through the topography of the earth as mysterious forces or currents, both physical and psychological. To do this was far more complex than identifying the "genius of the place" and required the services of a special practitioner to analyze a garden site before the garden itself was designed. Unlike the Occident where gardens developed behind walls out of an uneasy, threatening sense of the wilderness, Chinese garden-makers from the earliest times seem to have been free of any such paranoia. Walls, in fact, were built to preserve and hold the good spirit inside the garden. The Chinese belief in the therapeutic value of direct contact with nature, both spiritually and intellectually, may be one reason why lawns are considered meaningless. There is, as the writer puts it, nothing in a shaved, green sward to "refresh the heart."

AMONG THE TREES IN THE MOUNTAINS

This section simply celebrates the wonders of spring, how to enjoy to the fullest "nature at liberty, how to listen for the melancholy sound of water while watching the cranes dance." Reality and disbelief at this point in *Yuan Ye,* as well as in the garden, have evaporated into the mist.

IN THE CITY

"One should preferably not plan a garden in

the city," the writer advises, but if it is necessary, and even if the neighborhood is vulgar, a wall can shut out the assault on one's sensibility.

In fact, city gardening, or more accurately garden cities, are as old as China. Most of the aristocratic towns in China were a rich mosaic of countless private gardens and plantations. Just as the early Medicis drew their impulse to build country villas from the filth and anxieties of Florence as much as from antique models, Chinese garden designers also responded to city pressures and conceived their retreats as a complement to the city, but not too far removed from urban society and urban stimulation. The guiding principle was to create the feeling of isolation and separation from the city's commotions. "If one can seek out remoteness within a noisy place," the author of *Yuan Ye* concludes, "why should he abandon a nearby site in his desire for distance." It is always these appealing, practical solutions that help to mitigate the abstract, metaphysical tone of Chinese garden philosophy.

Marco Polo, who was in China from 1275 to 1292, thought that urban and landscape design, in common with all the arts, seemed to have reached their zenith in the city of Kin-sai (present-day Hangzhou), perfectly sited along the Qian Tang Jiang (Ch'ien-t'ang Chiang) estuary. Tidal waters flushed the town's canals while a protected, artificial lake fed with fresh water from the mountains gave the city a tranquil water landscape. Marco Polo's vivid description captures the urban magic of the "noble and magnificent city."

At the end of the three days you reach the noble and magnificent city of Kin-sai, a name that signifies "the celestial city," and which it merits from its preeminence to all others in the world, in point of grandeur and beauty, as well as from its abundant delights, which might lead an inhabitant to imagine himself in paradise. This city was frequently visited by Marco Polo, who carefully and diligently observed and inquired into every circumstance respecting

it. . . . According to common estimation, this city is an hundred miles in circuit. Its streets and canals are extensive, and there are squares, or market-places, which, being necessarily proportioned in size to the prodigious concourse of people by whom they are frequented, are exceedingly spacious. It is situated between a lake of fresh and very clear water on the one side, and a river of great magnitude on the other, the waters of which, by a number of canals, large and small, are made to run through every quarter of the city, carrying with them all the filth into the river, and ultimately to the sea. This, whilst it contributes much to the purity of the air, furnishes a communication by water, in addition to that by land, to all parts of the town; the canals and the streets being of sufficient width to allow of boats on the one, and carriages in the other, conveniently passing. . . ."[22]

The placing of buildings in absolute harmony with their natural surroundings is one of the great arts of the East, but the treatise *Yuan Ye* reveals no secrets, saying simply that the architecture should "be placed so as to harmonize with the natural formation of the ground." The evidence of how deft this skill became is documented throughout the history of Chinese landscape paintings as well as in the gardens themselves. There is, we can be sure, a great deal more to it than the bald direction to erect the "pavilion where the view opens and plant flowers that smile in the face of the spring breeze."

The genius of establishing an organic, almost biological connection between nature and a man-made structure is not merely the inevitable outgrowth of an aesthetic system. Its roots reach much deeper into the Chinese psyche and the philosophy of nature that has been cultivated from time immemorial. Perhaps the ancient admonition, "To be in harmony with and not in rebellion against the fundamental laws of the universe," is the first step toward discovering the way of Dao and

serves as a profound summary of a fundamental principle underlying the relationship between Chinese architecture and nature. The deceptive appearance of buildings and rooflines nestled in among trees and shrubbery, with their spontaneous air of unconscious guile, captures the essence of the Daoist aphorism.

Chinese gardens are invariably divided into a series of complex spaces. This allows the man-made landscape to easily accommodate and absorb the architecture. Spaces that are not broken up and divided by buildings, terraces, galleries, walls, and latticework would be inconceivable. It is between, around, and behind these elements that the garden is unified. The interpenetration of indoor and outdoor spaces manages to dissolve the distinction between "indoor" and "outdoor."

Because of its warm climate and abundant water supply, the ancient, prosperous city of Suzhou (Suchow) is the most celebrated garden city in China. A few restored or reconstructed town gardens in the city are still able to convey the magic of its early gardens. A comparison of the reconstructed garden of Cang Lang Ting (Ts'ang Lang T'ing) with a view engraved on stone in 1044 reveals how well the modern model captures the essentials of its prototype.

Shen Fu, a romantic, failed poet from Suzhou, wrote a brief memoir, appropriately called *Six Chapters of a Floating Life,* in which he described a summer living with his wife in a garden pavilion in Suzhou: "Beyond the eaves of the pavilion an old tree raised its gnarled trunk; its branches throwing a dense shade across the window, dyeing our faces green. . . . hot summer days together, doing nothing but reading, discussing the classics, enjoying the moonlight or idly admiring the flowers. . . . In all the world, we thought, no life could be happier than this."[23] To be an impoverished writer living in an elegant, albeit borrowed, garden without any visible responsibilities or support was the essence of the civilized romantic life, with a tradition that reaches back to the philosopher's thatched hut

Wang Shi Yuan, the Master of the Fishing Nets Garden, in Suzhou. Photo: Charles Marden Fitch.

of the Tang period (618–907), a thousand years earlier than *A Floating Life*. The poet Po Chü-i describes his retreat located at a safe distance from any urban disturbances: "It had only two rooms and four windows; the walls were clay without any white facing, the steps were of stone. . . . Before the hut extended an open court covering about 100 square feet . . . along this grew pines and other conifers. . . . There was also a spring, and a tea plantation, inviting to the pleasure of tea drinking."[24]

Even in private city gardens, water could be lavishly used, as in the Zhuo Zheng Yuan (Cho-cheng Yüan), or "Garden of the Humble Politician," still preserved in Suzhou. More than half of the space is given over to labyrinthine pools and small lakes. While the architecture of Zhuo Zheng Yuan is regular and geometric and is set out in a rectangular plan, the playful irregularity of the garden somehow liberates the formal lines of the houses, courtyards, and pavilion. This calculated freedom in the handling of the garden is one of the fundamental principles of Chinese garden art.

In 1782, the French missionary Frère Cibot tried to sum up the way nature and the natural surroundings were orchestrated in Chinese gardens to absorb the rigid angles and straight

LEFT
A corner of the Master of the Fishing Nets Garden, featuring a stone balustrade, a fantastic rock formation, and a glimpse of a moon gate. Photo: Charles Marden Fitch.

OVERLEAF
Potted landscape garden and azaleas in Zhou Zheng Yuan, the Garden of the Humble Politician, in Suzhou. Photo: Heather Angel.

PAGE 223
Window with blue glass in the Garden of the Humble Politician, Suzhou. Photo: Heather Angel.

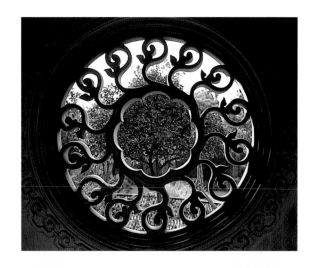

Circular window at Ou Yuan, the Garden of Couples' Retreat, Suzhou. Photo: Heather Angel.

Latticed window at Wang Shi Yuan, the Master of the Fishing Nets Garden, in Suzhou. Photo: Heather Angel.

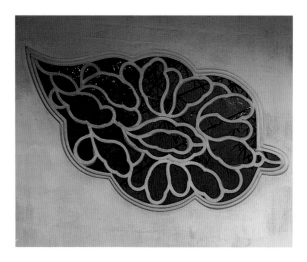

Leaf window at Cang Lang Ting, Pavilion of the Dark Blue Waves, in Suzhou. Photo: Heather Angel.

lines of the architecture in a romantic embrace of greenery. It is the sensuous curves of the garden that refine and subdue the uncompromising rectangular sheds that make up the complex.

> Everything that is ruled and symmetrical is alien to free nature. There one never finds trees growing in lines to form avenues, flowers brought together in beds, water enclosed in ponds or in regular canals. It is the realization of these facts that forms the basis on which the composition of the Chinese gardens is planned. Their hills and slopes are generally completely covered with different kinds of trees, sometimes planted in the woods, sometimes scattered and isolated as in the field. The shades of their green, the luxuriance of the foliage, the form of the crown, the thickness and the height of their trunks are the factors that decide whether they shall be placed on the north or the south side, on the top of the slopes of the hills or in the valleys between them. This distribution must be made with true taste.[25]

It is a description that Humphry Repton would have been pleased to have written.

The heavy plantations of trees and shrubs ingenuously arranged to absorb the stiff, alien lines of the buildings create much of the enchantment and beauty of Chinese gardens even when they are relatively small, and in city compounds. "The bamboos are tall and the trees luxuriant, the willows dense and the flowers brilliant," the author of *Yuan Ye* declared. "Even if the spot does not cover more than five mou . . . one may nevertheless . . . feel happy in solitude. . . . As long as the body still lives in this world one should not look around with [critical] eyes. One can, true, create something that will last for a thousand years, but one cannot know who will be living in a hundred years. It is sufficient to create a spot for pleasure and ease, which envelopes the dwelling with harmonious stillness."[26]

A stand of bamboo seen through casement doors, at Cang Lang Ting in Suzhou. Photo: Heather Angel.

A moon gate frames water-worn rocks at Yi Yuan, the Garden of Ease, in Suzhou. Photo: Heather Angel.

Flowers and Trees

"Chinese sentiment," Fletcher Steele remarked with both humor and truth, "seems to regard opulent vegetation much as fastidious people . . . feel about the Fat Lady in the circus."[27] Steele's reference to "vegetation" was, of course, limited to flowers and blooming shrubs, since thick, opulent plantations of trees have been used in Chinese gardens for centuries. Furthermore, there is a horticultural paradox here that a gardener in England would find incomprehensible: that the botanically richest and most diverse country in the world has always been diffident and restrained in the cultivation of flowers in the garden. Western gardens simply overflow with species of rhododendron, rosa rugosa, azalea, lilac, camellia, lily, giant clematis, tree peony, and primula that first appeared in China. Ernest Wilson (1876–1930), one of the great plant collectors at the beginning of the twentieth century, alone introduced into England more than a thousand plants from the wilds of

China. Earlier in the nineteenth century, Robert Fortune (1813–1880) carried out celebrated field trips in China for the Royal Horticultural Society. In the twenty years following the 1842 Nanjing treaty, Fortune established a program for the systematic search for rare and unknown flora. He was in turn followed by the remarkable Charles Maries (1851–1902) and then the intrepid Wilson.

What is astonishing in all of this adventure and scientific effort is the fact that the Chinese themselves were and are unmoved by their obvious horticultural wealth. Chinese horticulturists remained totally indifferent to the varieties of plants and trees being discovered by these Western explorers. They simply continued to cultivate and develop the same plants that had always been grown in Chinese gardens. Why this extraordinary conservatism in the face of such natural bounty?

Part of the answer is no doubt buried in China's inherent conservatism, perfected over centuries of isolation. If a garden was to be built to last a thousand years, then constant horticultural invention and experiment would seem totally inappropriate and irrelevant to such a perspective. "Gardens, to the Chinese, represent life in all completeness," and not just a fleeting moment of passing fulfillment provided by a changing parade of untested and unproven plants of dubious genealogy and value. First of all, plants in Chinese gardens "must be studied and their habits and tempers known," Fletcher Steele has perceptively pointed out. "They must live and flower with virtue and die suitably. For the death of a flower is watched with intent, poetic philosophy."[28] So the constant introduction of new and "alien" plants, whose character is unknown, into the rarefied, spiritual world of the garden would be alarming to a traditional Chinese gardener.

There has always been, of course, a wide range of flowers and plants cultivated in the microcosmic universe of the Chinese garden, a universe that embraces nature in its totality and not just its springtime of colorful blossoms. There are specific pleasures to be enjoyed and savored in every season of the year: "In spring there are the flowers in Brocade Valley; in summer the mist that rises over Stone-gate Stream; in autumn the moon over Wildcat Gorge, and in winter the snow on Lu Peak. Cloudy or clear, bright or dim, dusk or dawn, subtle or obvious, there are a thousand changes, ten-thousand shapes, such as cannot be recorded."[29] Or more succinctly: "The spring water fills four lakes; the summer clouds form numerous strange-shaped peaks; the autumn moon raises shafts of light; on the winter ridge a lone pine sparkles."[30] In this model of perfection within the enclosed space of a garden, the vegetation itself is not even referred to as a measure of the changes of the seasons—something that could not be imagined in a Western garden. In the Western garden tradition the cataloging of *locus amoenus* delights in the ideal garden landscape and is restricted almost exclusively to the flower-bedecked springtime and summer seasons. The Earthly Paradise in distinctively Western terms, as Andrew Plaks has pointed out, is the moment when imperfection striving for ideal perfection according to divine law reaches its highest point in color, form, scent, and abundance. It is a concept of nature and the universe that the classic Chinese gardener could not comprehend. In practical, down-to-earth Chinese terms, each flower has its own life, meaning, virtue, and beauty that is admired throughout its cycle from birth to death. So in the Ming period Yüan Chung-lang mentions how his family would move their beds outdoors when a remarkable tree was about to bloom in order to be "able to observe how the flowers developed from childhood to maturity and faded and died. Others planted masses of flowers in their gardens in order to study all the variants. . . . Some could deduce the size of the flowers from the smell of the leaves, others could judge from roots what color the flowers had. These people were real flower lovers and cherished a deep feeling for flowers."[31]

Flower motifs appear in Chinese art and each conveys a specific meaning, unlike in the

A spectacular Lake Tai rock set amidst camellias at the Lingering Garden in Suzhou. Photo: Heather Angel.

West where flowers in paintings are more often used for purely aesthetic purposes. Chinese poets also play with the same floral vocabulary, so it is not surprising that gardeners have followed the other arts and employ the same varieties. The existence of this universal vocabulary no doubt also played a role in inhibiting the introduction of new plants that had no meaning within it.

Flowering trees such as the blossoming plum tree were prized and cultivated for their blooms rather than their fruit. Hua-kuang, a painter, wrote a treatise on "Kuang" plum blossoms extolling the beauty of their life cycle. "The flowers weep dew or fill calyxes with mist as if they grieved and lamented. . . . They are the harbingers of the first beginnings of spring. . . . The buds form real necklaces. . . . Then come the bees and the butterflies and after them the wind that tears the blossoms from their stems. In this way their life cycle is accomplished . . . and until they fade they express their love in a glorious way."[32] The painter's pleasure in the life of the plum blossom is absolutely interchangeable with the gardener's pleasure in the same rhythms of growth and death. To underline the relationship between the art of painting and the art of the garden, illustrated artist-handbooks were written on the composition of paintings of tree peonies, bamboo, hibiscus, persimmons, cherries, plums, chrysanthemums, roses, and lotuses. The woodcuts in these manuals of typical garden motifs were represented with the greatest accuracy and double as botanical illustrations.

Bamboo, the symbol of lasting friendship and longevity, is without question the single most important plant in the Chinese garden. More than a hundred different species of bamboo were distinguished as early as the Song period. It was often combined with the plum and the pine, the latter a tree that symbolizes hardiness and strength of character. The green bamboo provided contrast against the harmony of gnarled pine branches and picturesque garden rocks, which was no doubt part of the appeal of its use.

A little garden with flowering tree peonies beside a stone. Woodcut after a drawing, probably by Ch'en Hungshou (1509–1657), for "The Story of the Western Pavilion."

The orchid and chrysanthemum have been among the most popular of the flowering plants in Chinese gardens, each expressing its own particular meaning. "Beside the wattled fence," the *Yuan Ye* recommends, "one plants chrysanthemums. . . . One should plough up the mountain slope and plant it with plum trees, so that it may be compared with Yu Kung's gardens in former times. Flowers are planted where they may enhance the views."[33]

In any summary of revered flowers in Chinese gardens, the lotus, sacred flower of Buddhism, must also occupy a central place. As well as being the seat of Buddha, it is the flower of Paradise, and the symbol of noble endeavor and spiritual purity. Since the lotus was also sacred in Daoist philosophy and for the Confucianists as a model for the "superior man," it was symbolically loaded with a resonance beyond any other single Chinese flower.

If the Chinese were not particularly interested in the indigenous plants discovered by foreigners in the eighteenth and nineteenth centuries, exotic plants were admired in earlier times. During the receptive atmosphere of the Han and Tang dynasties, new plants from both within and without the country reached the imperial capital where they were cultivated in the emperor's gardens. But even during this period of relatively open botanical commerce, the number of new plants introduced into China and cultivated was limited.

THE JAPANESE GARDEN

Unlike the desert prophets of the Old Testament who denatured the natural world of its special divinities in order to establish a transcendent, orthodox godhead, the Japanese have always accepted nature's pantheon of mysteries and sacred deities. For them, nature is not something that must be transcended by man or used to serve a higher, abstract purpose. If the great gardens of the West represent ambition achieved over a subdued nature, the Japanese garden is the consummate reconciliation. Yet to the Westerner trying to grasp the underlying aesthetics and values that inform the garden art of Japan, the word "spiritual" both summarizes and obscures the ancient, impenetrable cultural framework that makes up these unique works of art. The sublime, intuitive use of simple things like plants, rocks, water, and gravel elevates the architecture and landscape at a place such as Katsura Imperial Villa, in the words of Walter Gropius, "onto a high spiritual plane."[34] The viewer can find himself literally off balance in the rarified experience as he contemplates the seemingly ordinary stones of no value placed in the rectangular sandbox of the famously austere Ryoan-ji. When it comes to trying to figure out the means a designer employed over a period of years finally to achieve a masterpiece, comprehensive, precise understanding eludes us.

An undisturbed pantheism existed in Japan even before there was a move to adopt the guidelines of Chinese civilization, including the art of gardening, beginning in the seventh century. From the viewpoint of the ancient cult of Shinto, "any remarkable phenomenon," in the words of Sir John Pilcher, "from a splendid tree to a striking rock, from a waterfall to a cliff can be an object of worship and have its divinity."[35] The worship of the intimate beauty of nature found in the very topography and landscape of the islands of Japan is at the heart of the national cult. From the earliest times, nature, for the Japanese people, represented an all-encompassing, preeminent force that had to be accommodated by a peaceful detente. Where the medieval European saw malignant spirits in every forest and mountain waste demanding to be exorcised or subdued, the contemporary followers of Shinto seem to have felt an instinctive reverence for every stone, tree, plant, and animal. For the primitive Japanese, the sun, moon, sea, earth, mountains, wells, and springs were imbued with a spiritual quality worthy of veneration and worship. The quotidian landscape itself had become a conscious ground for religious worship. The objects of Japanese piety could be seen wherever a Shinto shrine was placed to house the native Shinto gods.

In its first appearance in Japanese literature, the word *niwa,* or garden, is used to indicate a piece of ground purified for the worship of the gods. While it is not possible to reconstruct precisely this sanctified prehistoric space, it may well have resembled the austere sacred precinct that still survives at the Manakata Shrine in Fukuoka Prefecture. The empty, graveled space at the Shrine of Ise, awaiting the structures that are renewed every twenty years, also deepens one's understanding of the spiritually freighted word *niwa.*

Within every such courtyard was the stamp of its locality, a sacred, communal memorial to "the genius of the place"—marking a grove, a sacred tree, a view or piece of scenery on a hilltop, beside a river bank, or on a lake. This awareness, this spiritual congress with things, distilled and refined over the centuries, has given the Japanese garden an intensity of emotional detail difficult to explicate or even to describe in terms of Western garden art and gardening experience. The same daring, mysterious, untranslatable sensitivity is present whether we see it in a painted Japanese screen where a forest is suggested by only a few treetops that intrude into the lower part of otherwise blank, gold panels, or in a Kyoto garden where a single miniature palm is surrounded

The compound of the Shrine of Ise is the oldest sanctum of Shinto religion in Japan. The wooden temple buildings are renewed completely every twenty years, giving the ancient site a strange, timeless air of perfection. The minimal austerity of the gravel yards has a nobility that makes Western shrines seem tawdry by comparison. Walter Gropius, *Katsura.*

OPPOSITE
The garden of Katsura Imperial Villa, like that of a Shinto shrine, perfectly "fits into the landscape," as John Pilcher has written, "which remains unchanged" even though it manages to transport the visitor into another world. Photo: Derek Fell.

A Japanese six-fold painted screen of the seventeenth century called *Trees*. Freer Gallery of Art, Smithsonian Institution.

by a sea of raked white quartz. In contrast, most Western attempts to achieve such minimalism are reduced to caricature.

Nowhere has the configuration of the topography and composition of the natural landscape maintained its influence within the man-made garden more completely than in Japan. The gentle, green islands, disguising their violent volcanic origins, bounded by an immense, hostile sea, and dominated by an equally immense sky, serve as a topographical model, the epitome of the microcosmic garden. *Sakuteiki,* the classic Japanese treatise on garden-making dating from the eleventh century and attributed to the Fujiwara nobleman Tachibana-no Toshitsuna (1028–1084), recognizes that the essence of garden art is rooted in the deepest possible understanding of natural scenery. An accomplished gardener must travel, and it is essential to visit and study the famous scenic places throughout Japan before attempting to transmute their lesson into garden design, according to the treatise. Much of the book is given over to the practical tech-

niques to be used to express rivers, seas, waterfalls, and mountains in an aesthetically pleasing way. The vague formulas provided in *Sakuteiki* suggest the difficulties an artist has in attempting to come to terms with a seemingly modest but fundamental problem of creative expression.

The physical scale of Japan's natural landscape itself is small and varied. Soft, rounded mountains and river valleys take up seven-eighths of the land. Without native grass and open meadows to support animal husbandry, the small, intensively cultivated fields in the valleys and on the hillsides give the landscape a rich, compact appearance. Space for both agriculture and human habitation is limited, imposing an instinctively efficient and mathematically controlled perspective over the pockets of intense cultivation. No hint of level English lawns and pastures or of rational French views established by strict rules of perspective plays any part in or intrudes upon the indigenous environment. Those of us with a Western background think of gardens as little more than the cultivation of plants—trees and flowers. But in Japan, things are not so simple. "There, when men remembered nature they remembered it in its beauty," Loraine Kuck has written, "the hills and streams and rocks as well as the trees and blossoms." [36]

Considering the enormous influence of China on Japanese art, literature, and gardening at a critical juncture in Japan's cultural infancy, it is instructive to consider how much Japanese aesthetics had already absorbed from the physical environment, an environment so alien to mainland China, from which so much early inspiration was drawn. It is important to grasp the startling difference between these extremes of environment as the Japanese begin to assert their own unique interpretation of nature in a garden setting.

In contrast to Japan, China is "a land vast and pitiless" by any standards, in the words of historian Alexander Soper, and its overwhelming physical and cultural scale is only magnified in relationship to the miniature world of Japan. "The bleak, dusty plains [of China] are without end . . . and . . . the great wild river rolls from its unimaginable source into the world of men swift and irresistible; periodically it changes its course to the sea, and whole countries are obliterated. . . . A nature so immense and inhuman," Soper concludes, that it "must either crush its inhabitants into fatalism or rouse them to some sort of defiance." [37]

Yet despite the enormous physical differences between the two lands, producing profound emotional and psychological differences in their inhabitants' perception of the landscape and of nature, the Japanese did assimilate certain Chinese characteristics at an early stage of their own development that informed their own primitive beginnings of garden art. By the time there is any documentation of Chinese influence, Japanese gardens had already successfully encoded their unmistakable style—a style and quality that cannot be adequately captured in words or concepts.

When the first Japanese envoy from those underdeveloped islands arrived at the Chinese court in A.D. 607, Emperor Yang Di of the Sui dynasty was just completing his vast and fabled Western Park. With a garden imagination equal to his vision of empire, Yang Di decreed that his park should symbolize the riches of his domain while at the same time embellishing the natural landscape. Even discounting the legendary accounts of its scale, and the manpower it consumed, it was a startling imperial creation. One of the emperor's proclamations issued at the time of the park's construction directed that "all those in the vicinity [of the capital] possessing plants, trees, birds, and beasts should dispatch them to the park. From everywhere, then, were collected innumerable quantities of flowers, herbs, plants, trees, birds, beasts, fishes and frogs and even these were not sufficient." [38] Compared to the tiny, austere, graveled yards surrounding the primitive Shinto shrine, the Chinese extravagance must have overwhelmed the diffident Japanese envoys. Yet by the eighth century, when the city of Nara was laid out on the plans of the Chinese Tang capital of Ch'ang-an (present-day Xian), Chinese influences in garden design were already quite evident. The main feature of the royal garden in the capital of Nara was a lake with an island recalling the Chinese isles of the Immortals, although nothing whatever remains. Similar isles had been a major theme in Yang Di's great park.

In 794, a site some sixty kilometers from Nara was chosen for yet another new city, called Heian-kyo, the Capital of Peace and Tranquility, or as it is known today, Kyoto. The Heian period (794–1185) that followed the city's founding was in many ways the Golden Age of Japanese civilization. The cultivated refinement of Heian society in its intensity and elegance has probably never been surpassed in any other civilization. The court nobility concentrated most of its energy and imagination on perfecting the details of exquisite living, from writing poetry to making garden settings for their new Chinese-inspired pavilions. It is this long-vanished world that is superbly described by Lady Murasaki Shikibu (c.978–c.1026) in her *Tale of Genji*.

The pavilions that served as the background for Lady Murasaki's story were a symmetrical complex of buildings inspired by earlier Chinese Tang models. The main pavilion would have faced onto a lake large enough for pleasure boating, an important aristocratic pastime. The wings on either side, connected by covered passages and placed close to the lake, were known as "fishing pavilions." In front of the main pavilion, there would have been an open space covered with white sand where entertainments of dance and mime were performed. In summer the shuttered wall panels of the *shinden-zukuri*-style pavilions could be raised so that the interior space became a part of the surrounding gardens. Here Lady Murasaki describes such a garden.

> The eastern side of the *shinden* was opened and swept and an elevated mat hastily placed in it for the Prince. The garden streamlet had been designed unusually well [to suggest coolness]. The place was enclosed with a brushwood fence "in country style," and the plantings in the forecourt had been carefully arrayed. The murmurs of the insects were borne on the cool evening breeze, while the whirling of innumerable fireflies delighted the onlookers. The Prince and his attendants drank sake where they could see the pond rippling under the eastern pavilion. . . .[39]

Even at this earliest period of development in the new capital of Heian-kyo, that rarefied Japanese taste for combining the rustic with the elegant, "in country style," was already a part of the aesthetic. It also suggests something of the growing influence of Buddhism and the importance placed on simple, natural objects by Buddhist philosophers.

In another passage in the novel, Lady Murasaki describes the prince's own garden:

> He effected great improvement in the appearance of the grounds by a judicious handling of knoll and lake, for though such features were already in abundance, he found it necessary here to cut away a slope, there to dam a stream, that each occupant of the various quarters [his mistresses] might look out her windows upon a prospect as pleased her best. To the southeast he raised the level of the ground, and on this bank planted a profusion of early flowering trees. At the foot of this slope the

lake curved with special beauty and in the foreground, just beneath the windows, he planted borders of cinquefoil, of red plum, cherry, wisteria, kerria, rock azalea and other such plants as are at their best in springtime.[40]

These lake gardens were inspired by Chinese models and were no doubt introduced to complement the new hybrid architecture. But unlike the Chinese pavilions, the buildings were usually placed closer to the lake because of the greatly reduced scale of the Japanese garden. This siting at the edge of the lake may also have reflected the Japanese preference for the natural views out over open space. The lakes or ponds were usually fed by a stream, unlike the artificial Chinese garden lake that did not seem to take advantage of natural water courses. Quite aside from Chinese in-

Prince Genji in the Plum Blossom Gardens, c. 1849–50, a woodblock triptych by Hiroshige and Toyokuni III. Collection of Walton Rawls. Photo: Peter Siegel.

THE JAPANESE GARDEN 235

fluence, the development of the water garden in Kyoto was probably inevitable because the gentle slope of the city is on the ancient bed of the Kamo River, with a number of smaller streams feeding into it.

An invaluable source of information on early gardens is to be found in the *Sakuteiki,* which may well be the oldest treatise in the world on the practical art of garden construction. As it describes in detail the basic layout for a nobleman's estate the technical instructions on the building of ornamental waterfalls and a wide variety of naturalistic scenery are so thorough they have continued to be followed by Japanese gardeners for centuries. The treatise also deals with aspects of divination, or the religious significance of garden practices and taboos to be avoided, particularly the precise arrangement of stones and the prescribed direction for the flow of streams: "The fortunate stream should flow from the east of the building along the south and then away to the west. By flowing in this direction, the stream will cleanse the evil air which exists in the ill-omened quartet [the northeast] and carry it away to the west. In this way, the household may enjoy a peaceful, long and a healthy life never suffering from disease or unhappiness." [41]

At one point the treatise reminds the reader that the revered rules set out cannot be altered in any way without incurring the wrath of the gods. If a single precept is broken "the owner of the garden will sicken unto death, his residence shall also be laid waste, and shall become the dwelling place of demons." [42] No wonder Japanese garden traditions have survived so long and are so carefully maintained.

The Japanese arts of poetry and painting were at the same time highly developed and sophisticated, and their rules and aesthetic principles were interchangeable with the aesthetics of garden art. In painting and poetry as in garden art, Chinese influence was evident and served as a link to the shaping of the Japanese garden. Painters were often also garden designers. As early as the ninth century, for example, the all-important arrangement of the rocks in the imperial garden at Kyoto was entrusted to a court painter who had studied Chinese painting.

Almost contemporary with *The Tale of Genji* is a collection of essays by a Buddhist priest named Kenko (1283–1350?). *Essays in Idleness (Tzurezuregusa)* is one of the major classics of Japanese literature and should be read by any student of Japanese gardens trying to come to terms with Japanese aesthetics, even though the author is usually addressing issues of literature or the rules for gentlemanly behavior.

For Kenko the nature of beauty contains certain basic ingredients that are peculiarly Japanese. First is the pleasure and appreciation of age and seeming perishability. In the context of the garden, the fading blossoms, especially of the cherry tree, and the apparent impermanence of garden buildings made of wood and paper are good examples of this principle. The obsession with the changing seasons of the garden, as its yearly cycle moves from birth to death, is another example. An element of beauty, according to Kenko, is that of imperfection. "Are we to look at cherry blossoms only in full bloom, the moon only when it is cloudless? To long for the moon while looking at the rain, to lower the blinds and be unaware of the passing spring—these are even more deeply moving. Branches about to bloom or gardens strewn with faded flowers are worthier of admiration. . . . In all things it is the beginnings and ends that are interesting." [43] "Beginnings with promise," as Donald Keene has written, "and the end with its evocation of the past are classic metaphors of suggestion so important in all forms of Japanese art and they sum up Kenko's precepts of aesthetics." [44]

Irregularity and incompleteness, as well as simplicity, are elements that immediately strike every Western visitor who contemplates a Japanese garden path—the use of stones and the hint of vistas that disintegrate when we try to follow the obvious line of straight perspective.

The quality of understatement that so often

OPPOSITE
A Japanese two-fold painted screen of the sixteenth century called *Coxcombs, Maize, and Morning-Glories.* Even though the Zen tea ceremony during this period pushed garden art to the extremes of simplicity, this screen of flowers is reassuring, contradicting the prevailing fashion of austere rocks and greenery. Freer Gallery of Art, Smithsonian Institution.

OPPOSITE, TOP
The pond of the fourteenth-century Saiho-ji temple in Kyoto, in the shape of the Japanese character for "heart" or "spirit," has always been the central feature of this paradise garden. Photo: Gary Braasch.

OPPOSITE, BOTTOM
The garden of Saiho-ji is also known as Koke-dera, or moss garden, for the dozens of different mosses that have covered the grounds since the mid-nineteenth century. Photo: Gary Braasch.

eludes the most conscientious Western gardener, the simplicity that allows both the eye and the mind to freely roam and to fill in missing details, stands out in most Japanese gardens. The Zen gardens that surround the little monastery of Shinju-an within the precincts of Daitoku-ji, for example, in their shaded mystery are a supreme example of minimal refinement so appealing to the modern eye.

The Paradise Garden

Like all garden-makers, the Japanese believed that an earthly man-made garden could evoke idealized celestial landscapes. But when we use the word "paradise" to describe this type of Japanese garden we should not imagine ancient Persian or Islamic influence. The so-called paradise gardens of Japan have no connection with Western traditions, even though these Zen-inspired gardens of meditation were intended to conjure up a vision of eternity. The difference between the Japanese paradise garden and earlier garden forms is narrow and subtle, at least to the Western eye. Comparisons are difficult since only bare fragments survive from the earlier period. Where the water garden can be seen as a complete, straightforward, integrated pastoral

The right pavilion of the Phoenix Hall of the Byodo-in at Uji. For almost nine hundred years, this delicate structure, built on its own little island, has seemed poised to take wing, like the legendary phoenix that is said to transport souls to the Western Paradise. Photo: Elizabeth Scholtz.

composition, the paradise garden is itself more complex, introspective, visually discontinuous, and has to be experienced in discrete sections, as one might discover various parts of an imagined paradise. One of the earliest such gardens, the setting of the Phoenix Hall at Byodo-in, south of Kyoto, was built by the Fujiwara regent Yorimichi (922–1074) at the height of the Heian period. It is an idealized, serene metaphor of the Amida Buddha's Paradise in the West, a quality it shares with Saiho-ji, as we shall see below. Although reduced in space and changed by time, the reflected tranquility of Buddha's pool is the oldest surviving example of the paradise garden tradition. A twelfth-century description exists: "The water of the pond pure and clear, with all manner of lotus flowers growing in it . . . a bridge made of the seven precious things spanned this gold and jade pool. Vessels made of diverse precious things went to and fro among the reflections of the trees; while peacocks and parrots played on the central island."[45]

Later, with the establishment of the Muromachi period (1333–1573) by the Ashikaga shoguns, the imported aesthetics and tastes of the Chinese were to play an increasingly important role in Japanese culture.

The first important example of a paradise garden from this period is the Saiho-ji whose restoration (c.1339) by Muso Soseki (Muso Kokushi; 1275–1351), a Zen Buddhist priest, marked a turning point in the art of Japanese garden design. The origins of Saiho-ji are in the eighth century when the temple was first founded. By the late twelfth century major work on the garden had been carried out, providing the foundation for the restoration in the following century by Muso. In the meantime the fall of the Taira clan brought an end to the Heian period and Japan lapsed into almost continuous civil war. The chaotic condition of life that resulted gave broad encouragement to the introspective, meditative relief offered by Zen Buddhism. Amida Buddhism and its vision of a celestial garden—a Pure Land where believers would be

Kinkaku-ji, the Golden Pavilion, in Kyoto, was begun in 1397 and profoundly altered the course of Japanese architecture. The main parts of the small garden and lake were designed to be viewed from the balconies of the pavilion. Photo: Elizabeth Scholtz.

reborn—was also a powerful appeal in contrast to the tribulations of this sinful and miserable world of military conflict. Amida's heavenly abode was not a Golden City but rather a water garden not unlike those that had first been built in the new city of Heian-kyo.

Saijo-ji was an earthly model of Amida's celestial garden. Over the centuries, nature and periods of neglect have introduced other feelings into Saiho-ji. For example the soft gray-green velvet shroud of moss that now gives the garden such a special quality was not a part of the original scheme, and the original garden reached farther up the slope of Mount Arashi. But the lake, or "golden pond," has always been the organizing element of the design, and the negligently positioned pavilions scattered along its shore are a departure from the formal composition of the earlier Heian

architecture. The dry stream at Saiho-ji is composed of a number of meticulously selected rocks with flat tops and may well mark the beginning of a distinctively Japanese style of rock-work.

The image of a later Buddhist garden at Kyoto, the Kinkaku-ji, or Golden Pavilion (1397; rebuilt 1955), has become so ubiquitous as tourist-promotion art, it is difficult to reach back in our imagination six hundred years to its genesis at the end of the fourteenth century. Designed by the Ashikaga shogun Yoshimitsu (1358–1408) on the site of an earlier garden, it was originally named Rokuon-ji for the deer-park where Gautama Buddha first preached after attaining divine enlightenment. On the death of Yoshimitsu, an ardent student of Zen Buddhism, the estate was converted into a temple shrine, according to the builder's request. The original pavilion with its three verandas, may have once stood in the lake instead of to one side as it presently does. The middle porch projects over the water, but all three porches have a special "borrowed view" into the natural landscape beyond the garden boundaries.

When the pavilion was completed, the emperor was invited to a grand fete staged on the lake. The first evening was given over to an elaborate boating and poem-writing party. Fragrant pine-knot torches in iron baskets provided light along the shore. As the guests departed on their painted barges, they were given subjects for their poems to be composed during the boat ride. At the end of the evening, the party was delivered to a special pavilion where each of the poems was read.

It is important to recall this lavish garden party for the emperor, because the meditative mysticism of Zen Buddhism as expressed in such profoundly austere gardens as Ryoan-ji has all but obliterated the fact that Japanese gardens were not exclusively limited to religious contemplation and isolated introspection. Domestic Japanese gardens were first and foremost a center of upper-class family life, a place for entertainment and pleasure. Japanese paintings and wood cuts record the obvious delights of garden life on the faces of family and friends as they walk, play, chat on a veranda, or peer down from an elaborate treehouse.

Not far from the garden of Saiho-ji is Tenryu-ji, or Abbot's Garden, built beside a Zen temple about 1339 by the same talented priest, Muso Soseki, who designed Saiho-ji. Within its miniature rectangular space, only thirteen by forty-seven feet, some one hundred stones have been placed to poetically evoke an entire world. "Beginning with a suggested waterfall," Teiji Itoh has written, it "ends with an assumed ocean."[46] Tenryu-ji was once part of a larger garden. Fires and civil wars have caused major changes, but the rock arrangement carefully placed to link the view of the distant mountains Arashiyama and Kameyama with the small lake in the foreground is impressive and perhaps the old-

est example of the *shakkei,* or "borrowed scenery," concept.

The troubled times of the fifteenth century continued to reinforce the appeal that the contemplative life held out to the world-weary followers of Zen philosophy, and many scholars retreated into religious communities. This intuitive, meditative existence with its suspended introspection is nowhere more deeply communicated than in the gardens created by Zen priests. These austere spaces excelled in enhancing the inner life of the faithful, which further helped them in the selection and placing of garden stones such as those at Tenryu-ji. Many Zen Buddhist priests studied in China, and they avidly collected Song paintings. The influence of Song artists reaching Japan through the Zen clergy can be detected at the Abbot's Garden and particularly in the temple garden of Daisen-in (c. 1513), also in Kyoto. In two parts, Daisen-in runs in an L-shape around two sides of the temple veranda and is divided by a wall or partition. Both

A view of the dry landscape garden flanking the abbot's quarters at Daisen-in, part of the sixteenth-century Daitoku-ji temple complex in Kyoto. Photo: Gary Braasch.

by Westerners only after World War I, is less than four hundred square yards. On the south and west are low walls, while the other two boundaries are formed by the walls and long veranda of a temple. Within the severe rectangular space of raked quartz, fifteen rocks are set out in groups of five, two, three, two, and three, the mathematical relationships serving to combine these basic natural elements with the abstract, cerebral world of the imagination. From their spacing on the white plane, one is seduced into believing that the rocks might represent the notes for a sonata surviving from some mysterious civilization. In the moonlight the white bed of Ryoan-ji is illuminated like a still, glassy sea marked by dark islands where gods slumber.

The art of the use of natural stones seems to come instinctively to the Japanese from their primordial feeling for nature as embodied in the original Shinto cult. With their love of natural patterns and textures recalling the early Shinto shrine, it would have been surprising if this feeling had not developed into a major art form and particularly in a garden. But there is evidence that the earliest artistic skill displayed in the detailed selection and placement of garden stones was of Chinese origin. Surviving Chinese gardens and paintings of gardens are relatively late, and specific influences are difficult to trace. What is clear is that Japanese gardens and their elements developed quite differently at an early stage. A comparison of garden stones, for example, shows that the Japanese preferred smooth, quiet, flat forms while the Chinese garden stone typically was pocked with holes and deeply cut by erosion. An early poem written at Nara in Chinese, the fashionable court language, speaks ambiguously of "Garden stones glowing in the mellow light of Autumn." [48] Scholars agree, however, that the use of rocks as an aesthetic element in the garden is a skill that has not been fully mastered and acclimated to gardens outside of Japan. These most primitive, simplest of elements—stone, sand, quartz—were believed to hold the deepest spiritual meaning in Zen philosophy. Without a grasp of that

At Ginkaku-ji, the Silver Pavilion, in Kyoto, quartz gravel in the shrine's forecourt was shaped centuries ago into a symbolic mountain nearly two meters high. Photo: Elizabeth Scholtz.

OPPOSITE
The most famous Japanese dry landscape garden is at Ryoan-ji Temple in Kyoto, on a site that may have had an earlier garden in 1430. The present garden, seen here in three views, is believed to have been laid out in 1488. The diagram, upper left, shows the arrangement of Ryoan-ji's stones. Fifteen rocks are set in five groups of five, two, or three, each contributing to an esoteric and complex harmony of mathematical relationships.
Photos: Gary Braasch.

parts of the garden are dry landscape, one intended for meditation and the other an allegory of simulated mountains, a waterfall, and a stone representing a small boat set in a sea of white quartz.

With the use of stones, sand, or quartz and a few trimmed shrubs of small-leaf azalea, the dry garden in its profoundly abstract design perfectly complements the spiritual experience of Zen. The Zen priest who worked on the famous garden Ryoan-ji said that Zen garden art was summed up in the ability to reduce "thirty thousand miles to the distance of one foot." [47] No wonder that a universe could be distilled and packaged in little more than an acre of garden space. Difficult to fully comprehend by the Westerner, the refined, minimal form of the Zen garden was embraced by the newly discovered modern aesthetic in the early twentieth-century West. In the 1930s Christopher Tunnard (1910–1979) urged landscape artists to study the essential principles of Japanese garden art as a means of recovering for the modern garden a sense of direction that would be compatible with the work of Le Corbusier, Mies van der Rohe, and Frank Lloyd Wright.

The minimalist garden of Ryoan-ji (restored 1488–99), which was first discovered

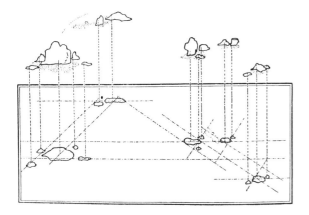

philosophy, one cannot convincingly manipulate these basic elements.

One of the stones at Ryoan-ji is signed with the name of someone identified as a gardener who might have played some part in the brilliant orchestration of this black and white composition that recalls Song and Yuan Chinese paintings. But the idea that one of the workers would covet immortality by his mark seems incompatible with the philosophy of

Zen Buddhism, a faith that is based on seeking selfless truth through contemplation. The fact that the work on the original garden extended over fifty or more years further diminishes the notion that a principle gardener-designer was in charge. Interestingly, the men who worked on Zen gardens were often recruited from the lowest class of laborers or outcasts who did socially unacceptable work such as slaughtering and skinning of animals and well-digging. It is a typical Zen paradox, with just a touch of Rousseau's romanticism, that such a primitive innocent, a "common man" without any background or comprehension of the rarified laws of Zen aesthetics, could well been chosen as being the best prepared to deal with the *tabula rasa*—the empty space of nature—in a naked, unconventional manner, uncorrupted by worldly, civilizing experience.

But extreme caution must be exercised in interpreting fugitive, undated characters on the bottom of a rock. "A visit to Japanese gardens can be a shattering experience," Brooks Wigginton warned, and not only because all of the sacred rules of Western design—symmetry, consistency, logic, emphasis—are violated.[49] Even functional considerations of directness and convenience are sacrificed. It is grasping at straws when we attempt to read folktales of dragons and tigers, or detect arcane symbolism or irrelevant Western analogies and esoteric messages concealed in the simplicity of gardens like Ryoan-ji.

Because its reductive abstraction is so appealing to our contemporary eye, Ryoan-ji has become one of the most celebrated gardens of the twentieth century. Here and in most of the gardens where quartz gravel spaces dominate the composition, the flat, raked spaces, with an occasional mound of molded sand a meter or so high, have an inexplicable yet overwhelming and universal appeal. The gravel itself is luminous, reflecting light that is impossible to capture on film. It is a little like seeing a celebrity in the flesh after knowing the image only in black-and-white newsprint.

The ineffable quietude that hangs over the dry Zen garden draws much of its power from the otherworldly restraint of the composition. But the latent power of the natural rock forms, quiescent in the sand, compels one toward the undertow of tranquility. The feeling of serenity is intensified by the horizontal position of the rocks.

The Tea Garden

Small and domestic in scale, infused with the simple, intimate ritual of taking tea with one or two friends in a rustic hut placed in its own ritual landscape, the tea garden is of the greatest importance in the history of the Japanese garden. It is astonishing that the older medieval religious or imperial concepts of garden art were so thoroughly conquered and transformed by the aesthetics of this ritual, with its intimate relationship to private life and the private residence and its refined distillation of domestic choreography. The evolution of the tea ceremony represents the discoveries of a new concept of sequence of spatial experiences created by the interplay between house and garden. Whereas in previous eras men had served as monks designing temple gardens of meditation they now became tea masters, finding in the ritual of the domestic ceremony a new avenue of spiritual escape from besetting perils of the time.

A solemn, formal rite, the tea ceremony is without any religious significance, but it is a deeply spiritual occasion nevertheless. It represents a break in the day's routine that provides a moment of repose, a time of quiet, pleasurable reflection, akin to but different from Zen meditation even though the followers of Zen quickly appropriated the ceremony as their own.

The teahouse, usually in a rustic style recalling the poet's traditional mountain hut, was not the focal point of the earliest tea ceremony, which dates from the late fifteenth century. The original tea-serving area was a room in the house, open on one side to a veranda and a small courtyard garden beyond. Since the courtyard was in full view of the guests during the ceremony, the tea masters demanded that nothing in their view should distract the guests' attention. The early tea-ceremony manual *Chasho Senrin* declared that "a garden of this type should preferably have no trees, no shrubs, no ornamental stones, and no ground cover of sand or pebbles, so that the guests will not be distracted by it, but can, instead concentrate on the spirit of tea and on the famous tea bowls and other prized objects that are to be used."[50]

The function of the veranda where guests could rest during the intermission of the ceremony and where the samurai could rack their swords was eliminated by the end of the sixteenth century, and a small, enclosed, separate teahouse in the garden took its place. The teahouse itself was a tiny hut or hermitage, an environment of the most concentrated aesthetics. Sen no Rikyu (1522–1591), a Zen Buddhist priest and the great tea master of the Momoyama period (1573–1603), introduced the enclosed structure, emphasizing its understated and contrived rusticity. At Rikyu's seaside tea garden, the only possible glimpse of the sea would be the moment when his guests stooped over washbasins during the ceremony—if they looked quickly out a window at floor level. Murata Soju, a famous tea master of Kyoto and son of the founder of the ceremony, further perfected the design of the classic teahouse. His own was described by a visiting nobleman: "The teahouse has the look of a small dwelling in the mountains. It expresses great feelings and must truly be called a quiet retreat in the city."[51]

The garden was no longer meant to be viewed from the tearoom and veranda, so its function changed into a long ceremonial alleyway for approaching the retreat. A path appeared with the addition of a few carefully constructed "still-lifes" of trees and shrubs along the way. These small, urban spaces took on an air of a solitary country retreat in a style of mannered rusticity even though they were in the heart of the city and the teahouse itself

Several elements of the typical Japanese garden were first introduced by tea masters in the sixteenth century: steppingstones, which preserved the delicate ground moss; stone lanterns, which lit the way to evening tea ceremonies; and stone water basins, which permitted cleansing of the hands before entering the rustic teahouse. Photos: Sam Abell.

The Toji-in/Autumn Tea House in Kyoto. Azaleas in the Zen gardens of the sixteenth century were ruthlessly pruned to look like green boulders—until they suddenly burst into bloom. Photo: Margaret Hensel, Positive Images.

was attached to a large, elaborate dwelling or temple. Such a garden was never intended to be viewed as other gardens. Rather it was designed to serve the psychological function of conditioning the visitor's mind and emotions to the right spiritual state as he approached the teahouse in anticipation of the ceremony. By chance, it seems that the tea garden was the first garden type in Japan that was conceived to be viewed sequentially, to be toured and enjoyed according to a certain predetermined order of visit. The extreme aesthetic of the rules governing the tea garden is summed up in the story of the gardener who carefully swept the garden of its fallen leaves, then deposited five or six along the path so that his garden would appear natural. Blooming

plants were not allowed in the most orthodox tea garden because they might compete with the few selected blossoms that were used in the teahouse itself. Even though Kenko wrote his classic essays on idleness long before the introduction of the tea ceremony, his special emphasis on the aesthetics of life embodied in suggestion, simplicity, and above all restraint is central to the taste reflected in the ceremony and its garden setting.

By the seventeenth century and the Edo period (1603–1867), tea gardens had become increasingly stylized and conventional. At the same time, the feudal urban household and the new domestic establishments of the merchant class demanded a good courtyard garden to serve the needs of a prosperous family.

Elements originating in the design of the tea garden were appropriated, but the new courtyard gardens never sought to be ideal, perfect creations of contrived nature. What they wanted and what they achieved was an urban space reflecting the good sense and traditions of the city garden, unburdened of the ritual, decorum, and intricate etiquette.

The influence of the tea garden aesthetic on the courtyard gardens of the Edo period suggests a few historical observations on this transition. Because the concept of the courtyard garden that developed out of this period extends into the urban gardens of modern Japan, it is important to keep this genealogy in mind.

Before the social and cultural stirrings of the seventeenth and eighteenth centuries, the great classic gardens were restricted to the imperial house, the nobility, and to temple or monastery bodies. This hermetic, feudal world was far more enclosed and narrowly defined than in any period of feudal Europe. The reasons for this restraint when it came to the creation of gardens are complex, but undoubtedly they have something to do with the small scale of the country and the unavailability of space for such a luxury as a substantial pleasure garden. The classic Kyoto garden of the Heian period rarely exceeded three acres.

This profound restraint in personal luxuries, such as private houses and villas, displays of paintings, sculpture, and furniture, traveling equipage, and all of the luxurious trappings that were considered essential to anyone in Western society claiming a position above the herd, has deep roots in Japanese history. Nyozekan Hasegawa has a perceptive discussion on the origins of this characteristic in his book *The Japanese Character*.[52] The same refined obsession with understatement pervades much of the art and craftwork of the early classical period. It is claimed that the Ashikagas were brought down in the fifteenth century because of their extravagance. Yet as Hasegawa points out, their most notable excess was their love of gold or silver foil on some of the paper walls of their tiny garden pavilions. Even the Momoyama period, which was marked by Japan's first major accumulations of wealth through the unification of the country, witnessed the perfection of the tea ceremony, and its complementary garden, with all of its exaggerated worship of the extravagantly simple utensils and settings. The most archaic, rustic, even misshapen bowls and pots became the most coveted. The upright timbers for a prince's teahouse would be selected for their twisted, gnarled form, and the gold smoking pipes of some Kyoto merchants were pretentiously plated with copper.

The teahouse and garden, for all of their rustic charm and self-conscious simplicity, are intensively artificial, even theatrical in their otherworldly ambience. The very impact of the ceremony is magnified by the concentration on the surface of things—the few utensils, the empty room, the single flower, the ritual movements and gestures, the silence.

This mannerism of the tea ceremony cult must be kept in mind in considering the great imperial gardens of the early Edo period in the seventeenth century. The villa retreat of Emperor Gomitsunoō (1596–1680) at Shugaku-in and the Katsura Imperial Villa or Detached Palace created by Prince Toshihito (1579–1629) reflect on a much larger scale the same pervasive sensibility of paring down, of rejection. While the scale and complexity of these two gardens are far removed from the miniature tea garden—Katsura originally had five teahouses within its landscaped boundaries—the all-consuming rigor in simplifying details of architecture and the seemingly natural design of the garden, with a hidden lavishness that was all the more unrestrained because it was masked in the guise of economy, heightens Katsura's illusion of unearthly fantasy.

The Stroll Garden

In the seventeenth-century Chinese gardening treatise *Yuan Ye,* the author describes the famous water garden of Ji Chang Yuan (Chi Ch'ang Yüan);

The Japanese garden was often designed for viewing rather than strolling. In this painted silk depiction of a party with Geisha, the outer panels of the building are slid back to present the garden in winter as a beautiful backdrop for the entertainment. Freer Gallery of Art, Smithsonian Institution.

OPPOSITE
A garden bridge at Katsura, the seventeenth-century imperial villa in Kyoto, the oldest surviving example of the Japanese stroll garden. Photo: Derek Fell.

. . . the garden contained a pond or lake of considerable dimensions, whose deep bays and confluent canals were spanned with bridges. In the farther part of the lake appears an island or promontory with fantastically formed rocks. The shores rise in gradual gradient towards the background; on one side, where the dwelling-houses are situated, the slope is terraced; on the other side the bank rises in the form of a medley of deeply creviced rocks with narrow paths winding up through the crevices; and with trees and pavilions on the highest terrace. The wooded part is extremely rich and varied, comprising tall pines, several kinds of deciduous trees and clumps of bamboo. . . . [53]

Edward Hyams suggests that this garden is in spirit and even in resemblance the prototype of the English eighteenth-century garden of Stourhead where the garden is laid out around the edge of an artificial lake in Wiltshire. But walking through Stourhead with a plan of Katsura at hand, one could easily think that

the English garden was modeled on this most celebrated example of the Japanese stroll or "tour" garden where a lake is also used as the garden's organizing element.

Designed so that visitors could walk around and along a prescribed route of views and settings, the Japanese stroll garden in its most refined form emerged in the Edo period. The oldest surviving example is that of Katsura, the imperial villa at Kyoto. It was begun in 1620 by Prince Toshihito, who seems to have directed much of the work with a copy of *The Tale of Genji* by his side so that he could introduce private literary allusions from the vanished society of Prince Genji into his green garden.

The building of the garden and villa complex at Katsura actually extended over a period much longer than the lifetime of the prince, and a substantial part of the work has been attributed by legend to the designer Kobori Enshu (1579–1649). In his study of Katsura, Akira Naito has suggested that Enshu was able to synthesize the aesthetic ideals of the Golden Age of the Heian court into the

secluded, even escapist atmosphere of the imperial court, reflecting its reduced power
under the Tokugawa shogunate when the emperor's political power had been effectively removed.[54]

The Heian period could easily supply an
emasculated court with an aesthetic model for
retirement, pastoral seclusion, and with-
drawal. Heian aristocrats, for all of their elegance and refinement, spoke in the diaries and
novels of the period about their desire to escape from the pettiness of court life, the exhausting love affairs, and the stultifying rituals
to a thatched-roof hut in the mountains or by
a secluded lake where they could write poetry.

Prince Toshihito was of course familiar
with the classic literature and was a student of
the poetry of the Heian period. With the usual
functions of a member of the imperial family
proscribed by the shogun, the prince and his
circle spent hours on scholarship, poetry, calligraphy, painting, the tea ceremony, and music. His son Noritada became even more
deeply preoccupied with the life of the mind
and actually ordered that a specific garden
scene described in *The Tale of Genji* be reproduced at Katsura.

The original site of Katsura was flat and
drained by the river Katsura-gawa where
clumps of thick wood grew along its bank.
The river was incorporated into lakes, and
elaborate molding of the ground was carried
out to create the complex, rolling hills scaled
perfectly to the 13.8 acres. The hills, mountains, fields, inlets, and beaches of Katsura are
entirely man-made. It is, as Geoffrey Jellicoe
has remarked, the natural landscape of Japan
brought into a very few acres and idealized.[55]
The lake is shaped like a flying crane while one
of the islands takes the form of a tortoise, a
symbol of longevity. The visitor follows a
path of steppingstones that leads clockwise
around the lake, reversing the direction of the
tour one follows at Stourhead. The stroll garden, and Katsura in particular, appropriated
certain traditional garden design elements
such as the steppingstone path of the tea garden and the even more ancient concept of

"borrowed scenery." As the visitor proceeds,
a series of scenes unfolds in the continuous
landscape drama: a maple-covered mountain,
a promontory on the lake shore, a bridge leading to a large teahouse while another leads to
the tortoise island, and in the lake a small Zen
temple. It is not surprising that, for Westerners grasping for a usable metaphor, Katsura
seems to follow the musical form of the sonata
with developments of themes, recapitula-
tions, passages of meditation all progressing
with a certain sonatalike rhythm and structure.

Unlike the earlier paradise garden where
only Buddha strolls while man quietly ob-
serves, at Katsura man is the hero recreating
and reconstructing the garden as he walks
through it for his own private enjoyment. His
enjoyment, and again Stourhead is recalled, is
increased if he has had a classical Japanese education. Katsura presumed a thorough knowledge of *The Tale of Genji* on the part of the
visitor, just as Henry Hoare at Stourhead expected his guests to discern the subtle references to Virgil's *Aeneid* he had woven into the
garden's composition.

The Japanese word for their concept of
"borrowed scenery" or "borrowed landscape"
is *shakkei*. In Japanese garden art it simply
means to incorporate into the garden setting
and its design distinctive and appealing distant
views, natural landscapes that are real and
have not been created merely for the effect.
The early Japanese gardeners referred to this
design conceit as "capturing alive." The concept was probably around as early as the
Heian period, but it was not until the Muromachi period several hundred years later that
recognizable *shakkei* gardens first appeared.
During the Ming dynasty in China, the garden treatise *Yuan Ye* used a similar expression,
jie jing, for the first time.

"There are no particular rules for constructing a garden, but for the borrowing of landscapes there are certain techniques and they
are of the greatest importance in designing a
garden with trees. The techniques are of four
different types: borrowing from a great dis-

tance, borrowing from nearby, borrowing from a high level, borrowing from a low level. Any one of these can be used according to the situation and the opportunities available."[56] The treatise provides only the guidelines, with no directions or techniques for carrying out the work, so that, as is common in Eastern garden manuals, much is left to intuition and native, traditional skills. The Chinese writer Li Yu (1611–1679) claimed he had penetrated the mystery of garden composition by employing a borrowed view but left his readers still mystified by refusing to divulge its precise role. Still, the concept of making a garden in such a way as to "capture alive" the larger natural landscape was an art that the East perfected, making a conscious aesthetic link between the garden and the countryside requiring a sophistication and a high degree of craftsmanship that the Japanese perfected. Shugaku-in, lying in the foothills of Mount Hiei, is approximately contemporary with Katsura, but its elevation of some 450 feet above sea level, the startling eastern dam shaped into four geometric tiers of stone walls concealed by trimmed hedges, and the panorama of "borrowed scenery" from Rin'un-tei, the "pavilion next to the clouds," is altogether different in design and spirit. It was built as a retirement retreat for Emperor Gomitsunoō after his abdication in 1629. The three separate villas on the estate are subtly placed in a natural environment of great variety—heavy woods on the hillsides, distant mountain views from the upper villa, and lakes placed to emphasize the dramatic difference in elevation. Cultivated and terraced rice fields occupy the agricultural spaces in between the grounds of the villas and teahouses, adding the illusion of bucolic bliss to the imperial retreat.

The ex-emperor has been credited with much of the design of Shugaku-in even though he was undoubtedly influenced by Kobori Enshu who had worked for his uncle at Katsura and at Sento Gosho, the imperial palace and his principal residence. Sento Gosho incorporated "the elegance of the court with the austerity demanded of the tea ceremony and Zen," as several students of these gardens have pointed out.[57] The architecture and landscape settings of the three gardens underline the nobility's utter alienation from the ornamented and polychromed palaces and houses of members of the shogunate who were the actual political and military rulers of the country. By separating themselves from the day-to-day turmoil and stimulation of administrating the state, the powerless ex-emperors and nobility were able to concentrate on the private aesthetics of perfecting nature into masterpieces of landscape design where the orchestrated movement of the viewer is primary.

The historical and literary allusion woven into the fabric of these gardens further deepens the visitor's experience. The path circulating through the stroll garden of the Edo period is like an unrolling horizontal scroll, forcing one to examine in detail the series of focal points that have been planned with consummate skill. Behind the theatrical illusion of constantly changing contrasts and surprises, the art creating the "illusion reality" is deftly concealed. Everything seems natural even though it is a completely make-believe world of landscape artifice. In this dynamic dreamworld, the sleight-of-hand element is even more remarkable because the scenes along the paths, over the bridges, from the terraces and moon-viewing platform are never spoiled by inept "behind the set" exposure. The trance, the willing suspension of disbelief, is never disrupted by an awkward prop or scrim even when the audience is moved over hills, around lakes, and across bridges—one moment in the foreground and next in the middle distance or on the other side of the stage looking back into the "audience." Even the words "theater," "audience," "stage," and "perspective" in the Western Baroque sense lose all meaning. Using them in the context of Katsura or Shugaku-in only adds to the confusion. The concentration on the irrationally placed steppingstones makes all thoughts of axial symmetry seem irrelevant and foolish. Unlike buildings sited in the Western fashion, which we are forced to face dead on, Japanese buildings in the stroll garden are approached obliquely, without confrontation. They are organically absorbed into the environment and never serve as some terminal reference or focal point. The reference between architecture and the landscape is invariably diagonal even though this oblique line is implied rather than explicitly stated by walks or paths.

The Modern Japanese Garden

The traumatic impact of the industrial West on the fragile, static, and essentially hermetic cultural values of Japan over the past hundred years, following the fall of the shogunate and the rise of modern Japanese society centered in the new capitol of Tokyo, has been difficult for the traditions of landscape art to absorb. Within fifty years of the beginning of the Meiji Restoration in 1868, Japan was able to engage in commercial and intellectual competition with the rest of the world, but at a price that took its toll on the environment and more importantly the values that had shaped both it and the cultivated garden fabric for which it was famed over the centuries.

Many of the gardens, villas, and places that are now so celebrated were allowed to deteriorate through neglect. Katsura was repeatedly vandalized by samurai operating in the area. Few people were interested in it or were aware of its vital international significance until the German architect Bruno Taut (1880–1938) fled to Japan from Nazi Germany in 1933, discovered Katsura, along with the old Imperial Palace in Kyoto and Shugaku-in, and brought attention to these masterpieces. He, like Walter Gropius, was drawn to the pure form of the architecture, which had such an appeal for the eyes of proponents of the international modern movement.

The history of this eclipse and resurrection in recent times is important to keep in mind when attempting to sort out a few of the

A view of the Japanese hill-and-pond garden at Brooklyn Botanic Garden in the early spring. Japanese gardens have been popular in the United States since the first one appeared in conjunction with Japan's exhibit at the Philadelphia Exposition of 1876. The Brooklyn creation, which opened to the public in 1915, is one of the more successful. Photo: Muriel Orans.

A wisteria-draped pergola at the Brooklyn Botanic Garden. Photo: Elvin McDonald.

Steppingstones cross an inlet to the pond at Brooklyn Botanic Garden. Photo: Elvin McDonald.

OPPOSITE
An azalea in bloom juxtaposed with a newly leafed-out Japanese maple is a rare touch of expert planning at Brooklyn Botanic Garden. Photo: Elvin McDonald.

A miniature waterfall in the Shozan garden in northern Kyoto, where an artists community was established about four hundred years ago. Photo: Elizabeth Scholtz.

to the fourteenth and fifteenth centuries, Kyoto garden designers and their clients continued to protest the alien influence by refining the basic qualities of traditional garden art, especially in the courtyard garden. Around their small gardens there developed a new set of aesthetic ideals that seemed to intensify the Japanese love of reductive scale and details of garden elements; shrubs, trees, and fences were deployed with a meticulousness and care that were remote from anything in the history of garden art in the West. Even the trimming and shaping of pine trees was changed in this period to distinguish Kyoto gardens from what locals called "Edo ideas of beauty." As Kento Shigemori points out in his study of the courtyard garden, these new refinements, including a new technique for thinning the needles of trees, were an expression of concern and rejection of the violent social changes brought about in the Meiji era. By adopting them, garden designers helped to safeguard traditional garden skills of pruning, laying steppingstones, spreading and protecting moss, arranging fountains and lanterns, constructing streams and ponds, and positioning intricate fences—small gardening tasks, to be sure, but absolutely essential to the quality and values that are so universally admired.[58]

themes that have distinguished landscape design in Japan in this century.

When the political center of the country shifted decisively to Tokyo in the last part of the nineteenth century, embracing Western values and adopting the eclecticism already rampant in the West, landscape design expressed the confusion and loss of deep-rooted convictions in the arts generally. More importantly, the era of the great garden estates supported by the nobility was finished.

Kyoto itself had been suffering a slow but steady erosion of its cultural power and leadership since the late eighteenth century, as more and more of the political power was drawn away from it. At the center of landscape design for the entire country and surrounded with major examples reaching back

In the 1930s and '40s a number of students of landscape design in the West fervently looked to Japanese garden tradition as a source of inspiration compatible with the values and aesthetics of modern architecture. The dry, raked sand of Ryoan-ji and Daisen-in or the perfectly selected and positioned steppingstones at Katsura are completely outside the comprehension of the rest of the world. Without pressing the analogy too far, the contemporary discovery of these design forms in garden design was not unlike the first impact of African and Oceanic primitive sculpture on Western artists at the beginning of this century.

Christopher Tunnard, in his *Gardens in the Modern Landscape,* sought to separate landscape as an art independent of the academic

The influence of Japanese aesthetics is very evident at the Isamu Noguchi Museum and Garden in Long Island City, New York. Photo: Sonja Bullaty/Angelo Lomeo.

traditions that had dominated garden design. In doing so he looked critically to the East and to Japan in particular for renewed inspiration. Like many others of the period, he believed that the strong threads of abstract design in the traditional Japanese garden composition had much to teach the West. For the modern movement, Katsura's purity of composition and line anticipated the ideals of the Bauhaus by four hundred years. Jellicoe remarked in his "Reflections from a Japanese Garden," "However much we may feel . . . that we in the west are remote from the principles of the Japanese garden, nevertheless underlying what the eye sees there is to be found something of the highest value to ourselves."[59]

VI. The New World

On August 1, 1498, Christopher Columbus saw in the distance a piece of green shoreline as he sailed along the southern edge of the island now called Trinidad. His failure to recognize a sliver of the American mainland on his third voyage is understandable, for he was the first European to have set eyes on it. To him the alluvial land in the Orinoco Delta, a scant ten miles away, looked like another island, so he called it *Ysla Saveta,* Holy Isle.

The next day, taking advantage of slack water, the admiral led his fleet of three small ships through the treacherous channels and reef he named Boca de la Sierpe, or Serpent's Mouth, into the Gulf of Paria bordered by what is now Venezuela. For two weeks the exhausted sailors enjoyed the mild breezes of the gulf and the hospitable, curious natives wearing gold ornaments. A full moon had appeared on the night of August 2, and the first night ashore on the unrecognized continent, bathed in the delicious light of a Caribbean moon, must have seemed like heaven itself. The water of the gulf was sweet and ran for forty miles into the sea, extending farther in fact than the waters of the Nile or the Ganges or any river Columbus had ever heard of. What was even more baffling to the admiral was that he had not observed lands extensive enough to produce such a quantity of fresh water.

The primary mission of the third voyage was to replenish the supplies of the little settlement he had left on the island of Hispaniola. For all of the tempting, unanswered questions raised by the lush jungle landscape, the gold-laden natives, and the mysterious freshwater currents running far out to sea, Columbus could not waste time exploring "an Other World," in the Gulf of Paria. As he prophetically wrote in his journal, "And your Highnesses will win these lands which are an Other World [*que son otro mundo*], and where Christianity will have so much enjoyment, and our faith in time so great an increase."[1]

After leaving the gulf and sailing north with fast currents and breezes moving the fleet along, Columbus continued to be puzzled by the sweet-water currents, the mild temperature so near the equator, the heavy vegetation, and particularly the unexplained compass deviation from true north as measured by the position of Polaris. Finally on August 17, as the fleet sped along making thirty-seven leagues on a smooth sea, he concluded that the land he had just skirted had to be the site of the Earthly Paradise, the biblical Garden of Eden. Again he confides in his journal, and Las Casas later reports, "that not finding any islands now assures him that the land whence he came is a great continent where is located the Terrestrial Paradise, 'because all men say that it's at the end of the Orient, and that's where we are' says he."[2]

The late Middle Ages had been full of speculation on the exact physical location of the First Garden. Maps and treatises described its position, its climate, and its botanical wonders still flourishing in the perpetual spring of a blessed landscape. Columbus was not the last to believe that man was finally nearing his ultimate goal in the quest for happiness and innocence in a great, unspoiled garden, which logically should be located in the natural paradise of the New World. The New World was the undoubted locus of the beautiful and enchanted Eden and would be the ultimate salvation for the worn-out civilization of Eu-

OPPOSITE
The Garden of Eden by Erastus Salisbury Field. Museum of Fine Arts, Boston; M. and M. Karolik Collection.

The flora of the New World was so exotic to European eyes that many explorers believed they were sure to come upon the site of the original Garden of Eden. Photo: Loren McIntyre.

enough to end his campaign for the New World gold when he came upon the royal Aztec gardens at Iztapaplan in 1519 during the Spanish conquest of Mexico. According to contemporary accounts these gardens were laid out in formal squares divided by trellis-bordered paths and served with aqueducts and canals—a description that might equally well apply to many Spanish and Italian gardens of the same period were it not for the special arrangement of the flora. Prescott's *History of the Conquest of Mexico* recounts from contemporary documents that the gardens "were stocked with fruit-trees imported from distant places, and with the gaudy family of flowers which belonged to the Mexican flora, scientifically arranged, and growing luxuriantly in the equable temperatures of the tableland."[3]

We also know something of the royal gardens at Tezcotinco, the residence of Nezahualcotl (c. 1403–c. 1470), whose alliance with the Aztecs had helped to form the wealthy empire that Cortés would wrest from Montezuma II. Tezcotinco's bird- and animal-filled gardens were described by Cortés's Aztec ally, Ixtilxochitl (fl. 1500–1550), as follows:

> The most pleasant of the gardens and of greatest curiosity was the Tezcotzinco wood, of enormous size. . . . To bring water for the fountains, *bassins,* and baths, it was necessary to build strong and very high walls of cement from one range of mountains to another, and these were enormous in size. . . . The wood was planted with great variety of trees and sweet smelling flowers, and there was a great variety of birds in them, in addition to those which the King kept in cages, which had been brought from many lands and which sang so sweetly and loudly that one could not hear the people. Beyond the flower gardens, which were enclosed by a wall, was a mountain, upon which could be found all kinds of deer, rabbits, and hares. . . . The basins of water were stocked with fish of various kinds and avi-

rope. It was the place where the sun first shone on the Day of Creation, and it would become the Land of Beginning Again.

But dreams of discovering the Earthly Paradise were not what Columbus's royal patrons had in mind. When the admiral wrote to Queen Isabella telling her that he had claimed the First Garden in the name of the Spanish sovereigns, there is nothing in the record to suggest that she was the slightest bit impressed by his astounding gift. It was the promise of gold and pearls to fill the royal coffers, to underwrite crusades, and to feed armies busy pushing the infidel out of Europe that fueled the admiral's risky enterprise in the eyes of her majesty. Fabled Eden would have to wait.

Nor was Hernando Cortés impressed

aries stocked with birds glowing in all the gaudy plumage of the tropics.[4]

In the Old World, royal gardens filled with wildlife—whether for hunting or for display—were a tradition reaching back to Assyrian times. The first European botanic gardens, however, were not founded until the 1540s, only a few decades after the conquest. Though there is no direct evidence that the "scientifically arranged" garden of the Aztecs served as a model for the European botanic garden, the effect of new flora arriving from the New World was certainly felt in Europe's botanical and scientific circles. The first development of scientific studies of natural history coincided with the Century of Discovery. As Hugh Honour has written, "During these years the medieval bestiary and herbal gave way, if only slowly, to manuals of ornithology, zoology, and botany based less on the authority of the ancients and hearsay than on direct observation."[5]

For the first English colonists venturing into the wilderness stretching along the Atlantic coast of North America a century later, their move from Europe to the New World held out the promise of a rebirth, of beginning again even though their particular vision of Eden was limited and austere compared to the Mediterranean imagination. But all had faith that nature's prodigality would produce a supply of all that was needed from a garden to exist, with little or no work on the part of the settlers. As late as the end of the eighteenth century, Thomas Jefferson (1743–1826) was

The cloister garden of the church of Acoma outside Mexico City may well be the oldest colonial garden in the Americas and dates from the second decade after the Conquest in 1519. Photo: Author.

adventurous settlers. The first explorers of Virginia claimed that the country was "so delightful and desirable; so pleasant and plentiful; the climate and air, so temperate, sweet, and wholesome; the woods and soil so charming, and fruitful, and all other things so agreeable, that Paradise itself seemed to be these in its first native luster."[6]

Compared to actual settlers, who were more realistic when it came to appraising their new environments, the imagination of early European explorers and travelers seemed to have been captivated by the beauty and physical qualities of the virgin country, no doubt conditioned by the Paradise myth. Captain Arthur Barlow, when he arrived near the coast of what is now North Carolina in 1584, was transfixed by the new sights, sounds, and especially smells. "We smelt so sweet, and so strong a smell as if we had been in the midst of some delicate garden abounding with all kinds of odeferous flowers by which we were assured that the land cannot be far distant."[7] And George Percy, youngest son of the earl of Northumberland, wrote in 1626 of the astonishing scenery: "We traced along foure miles . . . the ground all flowing over with faire flowers of sundry colors and kinds, as though it had been any garden or orchard in England. . . . We kept our way in this Paradise."[8] Twenty-five years later Edward Williams found that Virginia was "so delectable on aspect, that the melanchollyest eye in the World cannot look upon it without contentment."[9]

COLONIAL AMERICAN GARDENS

In their romantic response to nature in the New World, these literate travelers with their cultivated European sensibility were far different from those individuals who were prepared to settle down and scratch out a subsistence on the rocky coast of New England or in the remote cabin patch in the back-

claiming that a perfect English park in the latest picturesque style could be easily carved out of the Virginia woods simply by clearing away superfluous trees and undergrowth. He later had to admit that the equally rank crop of New World weeds, a side effect of too rich a soil and susceptible climate, did in fact require more work and attention than the casual editing of a few clumps in the middle distance.

Throughout the sixteenth and seventeenth centuries the land of the Americas was vividly painted as an ideal world to attract Europeans interested in colonization. A vision of the First Garden itself was frequently conjured up in promotional literature designed to entice

woods of the Carolinas. The hard-bitten, God-fearing European immigrants of the seventeenth and eighteenth centuries, especially in the northern colonies, rejected anything in nature that was not of immediate and practical use in their fight for survival. The indulgent aesthetics of pleasure gardening, demanding the luxury of time and leisure, were simply out of the question on both practical and moral grounds.

In New England, the villages of the first settlements integrated rudimentary town planning with transplanted English traditions of husbandry. While village settlements followed the basic form and outline derived from English experience, the physical arrangements of the landscape elements, sheds, barns, fences, meadows, and pastures for livestock, were placed according to local, pragmatic requirements.

The meetinghouse was at the center of all town plans. From it roads radiated out into the countryside. The graveyard was in front of the meetinghouse, or to one side, and a large open area of "green" was reserved for military exercises, religious gatherings, and livestock. Here the town herdsman took charge of the cows and horses owned by the townspeople, driving them each day to outlying pastures.

Each household was expected to maintain a small garden and orchard to serve the basic needs of the family. The man-made order of the townscape was rigid, predictable, and a visible barrier to the surrounding forest and wilderness that still harbored some of its medieval menace to the community's well-being. The New Englander's dread of the wilderness was due in part to his inherited recognition that the forest was "the chief symbol of infernal chaos latent in all men and restrained only by reason and society," as John Stilgoe has pointed out.[10] This dread was also fueled by the ominous threat from the wilderness to engulf the new settlements and reclaim its domain no matter how many trees were cut or how much brush was cleared. But in terms of a certain strain of American antipathy to the natural environment, the psychological roots may run much deeper into earlier Northern European beliefs and superstitions. Not only folktales but the half-remembered tenets of ancient pagan cults of the peasantry survived beneath a Christian veneer. Satan replaced Pan, and German fairy tales of Snow White, Hansel and Gretel, and Little Red Riding Hood lost in the forest perpetuated the belief that nature itself harbored all sorts of snares and evils for unsuspecting innocents who wandered into its preserve beyond human control and protection. "If a stranger traveled through a wood off the path," according to conventional wisdom of English countrymen, "and neither shout nor blow his horn, he may be assumed to be a thief, and as such either slain or put to ransom."[11]

Unlike Columbus, who confidently believed he had come close to discovering the remains of the First Eden hidden somewhere in the lush jungle behind the shores of Venezuela, the Puritans of Plymouth Plantation had a distinctly Protestant Paradise in mind. Even if colonization was held to reenact the first Creation in a new Promised Land, the inhospitable New England wilderness hardly matched the medieval vision of an earthly Paradise of eternal springtime, soft breezes, and perfect growing conditions. In the Puritan Eden, warmed by the Sun of Righteousness, a prolific nature of too much sensual beauty and abundance was recognized for what it was, the Devil's temptation. No doubt the idea of elevating gardens to a level of art was as alien to these settlers as any form of worldly extravagance. The humble backgrounds and standards of domestic life of most Puritans, conditioned by hard necessity, were reflected in relentlessly plain dress, manners, and houses. Following the Puritan ascendancy, those standards of unrelieved simplicity were raised to a central virtue.

Most settlers thought they would find the climate and growing condition comparable to the England they had left, if not quite as luxuriant as the first descriptions of Virginia where many of the colonists had expected to

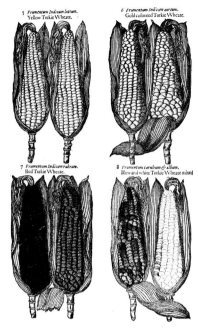

set ashore. The shock of the harsh, prolonged New England winters and the contrast between reality and expectations would have discouraged the most ardent gardeners among them. And it was obvious that the only way to survive was to exploit the environment, where the one thing they did have in abundance was timber. So the greatest and immediate change in the landscape was the exploitation of these timberland riches for survival. But though extraordinary labor was expended to cut wood, little was invested, beyond bare necessity, in turning the newly cleared ground into garden space—at least not until towns and a certain amount of private wealth made themselves evident.

Gardens "for meate and medicine" were essential, of course, for the first colonists in New England as soon as their ships' stores were exhausted. These gardens were primitive affairs, rectangular in shape and laid out next to the houses for protection and easy cultivation. The first surviving view or town plan that includes some garden plots is not English but a French engraving in Champlain's first edition of *Les Voyages,* published in 1619. The French village had been settled at the beginning of the century on an island in the St. Croix River now part of the State of Maine. Eight "parterres" of different sizes and with a distinctly medieval quality are shown.

Just as in medieval Europe and later, the gardens of the early American settlers were the chief source of medicines and "cures." Gardening and "physicking" were so interrelated that books such as George Baker's medicinal recipes, "wherein is contayned the most excellent secretes of Phisicke and Philosophy," were actually inventoried in Boston in 1660 as gardening books.

The primary published sources for the growing and use of herbs and herb remedies throughout New England were John Gerard's *Herball* as revised by Johnson in 1633, John Parkinson's *Paradisus in sole paradisus terrestris* published in 1629, and Nicholas Culpeper's *Herbal* that appeared in 1652. These seventeenth-century English herbals are repetitious and for the most part describe the same plants and recommend the same remedies. But precisely how the herb garden was laid out in the New World is undocumented. At their best, private gardens no doubt resembled the simple cottage gardens the immigrants had known in England dating from the late sixteenth century and earlier. This would have perpetuated the tradition of the raised planting bed, but precisely how it was laid out is a matter of conjecture. The practical garden books of the day advised that perennials of flowers, vegetables, and herbs be planted together, while another area was to be set aside exclusively for annuals. Annual seeds were often simply broadcast in a fine catholic mixture, as Sir Peyton Skipwith of Virginia reports, onions, lettuces, and radishes being mixed without any separation in his kitchen garden.

Still the ancient geometric patterns, usually with enclosing walls or fences—a formal, man-made organization reaching back to the Romans and beyond—seemed to prevail throughout the colonies. A late-seventeenth-century town plan of what is now lower Manhattan in New York City shows gardens laid out on a grid that the Dutch had efficiently imposed on their settlement at the foot of the island. John Parkinson was simply stating common and universal practice when he declared that a garden in "The four square forms is the most usually accepted with all, and doth best agree to any man's dwelling," even though he admitted, "To prescribe one forme for every man to follow would be folly, for every man will please his own fancie." [12]

Another garden book far more popular and accessible in the colonies than Parkinson's was Leonard Meager's *English Gardener,* which had appeared in six English editions by the end of the seventeenth century. Copies are recorded in private libraries in Pennsylvania, Virginia, and the Carolinas. The title page tells all, and its reassuring promise to answer every gardener's question would have had a special appeal for its colonial American audience who were in great need of published advice.

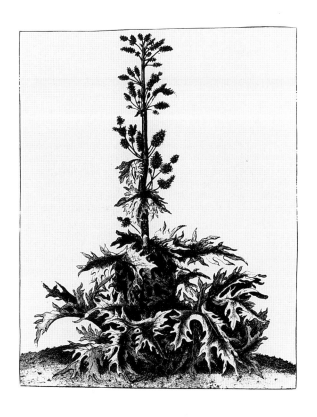

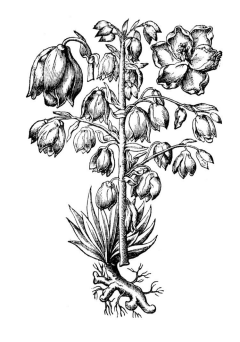

The English Gardener; or a Sure guide to young Planters and Gardeners in Three Parts. The first, Showing the way and order of Planting and Raising all sorts of Stocks, Fruit-trees and Shrubs with the divers ways and manners of Ingrafting and inoculating them in their several Seasons, Ordering and preservation. The second, How to order the Kitchin-garden for all sorts of Herbs, Roots, and Sallads. The third, The ordering of the Garden of Pleasure, with varietie of Knots, and Wildernesse-work after the best fashion, all cut in Copper Plates; also the choicest and most approved ways for the raising all sorts of flowers and their seasons, with directions concerning Arbors, and hedges in Gardens, likewise several other very useful things to be known of all that delight in Orchards and Gardens. Fitted for the Use of all such as delight in Gardening, whereby the meanest capacity need not doubt of success (observing the rules herein directed) in their undertakings. By Leonard Meager above thirty years a Practitioner in the Art of Gardening. London, Printed for T. Peirrepoint, and sold by the Booksellers of London, 1682.[13]

Meager was particularly keen on borders, knots, and edgings, giving in detail "easie and plain directions for their creation." In addition to his plant list for the kitchen garden, he also included an extensive flower list for "ordering" the "Garden of Pleasure."

Like most American gardeners of the seventeenth century, north and south, the Quakers in Pennsylvania combined the functional with the ornamental but gave special attention to flower cultivation. "There are very fine and delightful Gardens and Orchards, in most parts of this Country," as English traveler Gabriel Thomas wrote in 1698 from Philadelphia. "Edward Shippey (who lives near the Capitol City) has an Orchard and Gardens adjoining to his Great House that equalizes (if not exceeds) any I have ever seen, having a famous and pleasant Summer House erected in the middle of his extraordinary fine and large Garden abounding with Tulips, Pinks, Carnations, Roses (of several sorts), Lilies, not to mention those that grow wild in the Fields."[14]

Because of the Quaker interest in botany and horticulture, Philadelphia became without question the center of garden activities in the colonies. Many English plantsmen like Peter Collinson (1694–1768) and Dr. John Fothergill (1712–1780) were members of the Religious Society of Friends, as were their American correspondents John Bartram (1699–1777) and James Logan (1674–1751). This Quaker interest in gardening was not coincidental. Having excluded music, drama, most graphic art, and even color from their austere lives, along with the reading of plays, romances, novels, and other "pernicious" books, many sensually starved Quakers turned to natural science and gardening for an acceptable source of stimulation. Botany with its close links to medicine was given a tie to community service, assuring further satisfaction to the Quaker conscience.

John Bartram, who founded the first botanical garden in the colonies, became through his friendship with Collinson the principal conduit for indigenous American plants to reach Europe during the eighteenth century.

As an old man, Collinson recalled in his notebook his important ties to Bartram and the small circle of plant collectors in the American colonies.

My Public Station in Business brought Mee acquainted with Persons that were Natives of Carolinas, Virginia, Maryland, Pensilvania and New England. My Love for New & Rare Plants putt Mee often on Soliciting their assistance for Seeds and Plants from those Countries. . . . What was common with them (but Rare with us) they did not think worth sending. . . . At last some more artfull Man than the Rest contrived to get rid of my importunities By recommending a Person whose Business it should be to gather seeds & send over plants. Accordingly John Bartram was recommended as a very proper Person, being a native of Pensilvania. . . .[15]

With funds provided by his English friends and later with subscriptions obtained by Benjamin Franklin, Bartram extended his plant collecting travels into most of the important colonies, reaching as far as Florida in 1765 at the age of sixty-six. Being a more worldly Quaker in London, Collinson reminds his friend in Philadelphia that when he goes south to Virginia to meet William Byrd, John Custis, and other planters, he should dress properly in order "not to appear or disgrace thyself or me; for though I should not esteem thee less, to come to me in what dress thou will— yet the Virginians are a very gentle, well-dressed people—and look perhaps more at a man's outside than his inside. . . . pray go very clean, neat and handsomely dressed to Virginia."[16]

When Robert Beverly (c. 1673–1722) wrote his *History of the Present State of Virginia* in 1705, 120 years after the founding of Roanoke, he concluded that the "temperate, sweet and wholesome" climate of the colony had demoralized its settlers. Unlike the more rigorous, uplifting challenge nature had provided farther north along the New England coast, the easy, open country had also encouraged the exploitation of the new cash crop of tobacco. Not only Beverly but many travelers and observers thought the pernicious tobacco culture of Virginia bred indolence and decadence, producing even as early as 1640 a scruffy, worn-out landscape in the Tidewater. The inevitable exhaustion of land encouraged in turn a rootlessness and mobility among settlers who were forced to move in search of new fields for their voracious crop. This profligate use of the soil to produce a quick cash return to meet the demands of the insidious market nexus in London did nothing to encourage a serious garden tradition on a large and settled scale. There is little evidence that the "virtuous and independent citizen"

Thomas Jefferson eulogized in his *Notes on the State of Virginia* was any more advanced in his agricultural and gardening practices than he was in his architecture, which Jefferson found deplorable.

The cosmetic efforts of Colonial Williamsburg and the modern Southern romantic novel, not to mention twentieth-century films, have created a popular image of the South with its porticoed plantation houses, happy slaves, and stately gardens suffused with the heady smell of magnolias and boxwood growing in neat hedges. This is not to deny that some parts of this glamorous dream did exist, and a few restored plantations conform to our cinematic dreams. But such places were scattered in the remote stretches of the Tidewater South, stretching from the Chesapeake Bay of Maryland to the lowlands of South Carolina and Georgia. Most plantations were isolated in trackless, unbroken wilderness, shabby fields, and rutted roads.

A description by the Virginia planter-statesman George Mason (1725–1792) of his father's self-sufficient establishment on several thousand acres along the Potomac below the Port of Alexandria, Virginia, gives a sense of the scale and complexity of a far from typical plantation village.

My father had among his slaves carpenters, coopers, sawyers, blacksmiths, tanners,

The boxwood garden of Gunston Hall at Lorton, Virginia, is one of the most convincing recreations of the twentieth century, even though documentary evidence of its exact original design is missing. Photo: Everett Scott.

curriers, shoemakers, spinners, weavers, and knitters. . . . His woods furnished timber and planks for the carpenters and coopers and charcoal for the blacksmith; his cattle killed for his own consumption and for sale supplied skins for the tanners, curriers and shoemakers and his sheep gave wool and his fields produced cotton and flax for the weavers and spinners and his orchards fruit for the distiller. His carpenters and sawyers built and kept in repair all the dwelling houses, barns and stables, plows, barrows, gates, etc. on the plantations and the outhouses at the home house.[17]

The number of slaves required for such a complex economic operation was enormous, and all had to be housed and fed. The scale and organization of the extensive, self-sufficient plantation, which produced all the food needed by its large population, surely would have given it the appearance of a shabby, untidy village, quite unlike the civilized elegance suggested by the restorations we see at Carter's Grove, Brandon, Shirley, and Mason's own beautiful plantation Gunston Hall.

Jefferson himself spent his early years at Tuckahoe Plantation on the James River, and its surviving plantation street lined with whitewashed slave cottages and workrooms gives a hint of the kind of establishment Mason described.

In a chapter called "Of the Recreations, and Pastimes Used in Virginia," Robert Beverly not surprisingly succumbed to the sensual garden pleasures that had been developed by a few of the Virginian gardeners like Colonel Carter and William Byrd on their James River estates. His description does undermine any sour skepticism.

For their Recreation, the Plantations, Orchards, and Gardens constantly afford 'em fragrant and delightful Walks. In their Woods and fields, they have an unknown variety of Vegetables and other Rarities of Nature to discover and observe. . . .

Their Taste is regaled with the most delicious Fruits, which without Art, they have in great Variety and Perfection. And then their smell is refreshed with an eternal fragrancy for Flowers and Sweets with which Nature perfumes and adorns the Woods almost the whole year round.

Have you pleasure in a Garden? All things thrive in it, most surprisingly; you can't walk by a Bed of Flowers, but besides the entertainment of their Beauty, your Eyes will be saluted with the charming colours of the Humming Bird, which revels among the Flowers and licks off the dew and Honey from their tender Leaves on which it only feeds. Its size is not half so large as an English Wren, and its colour is a glorious shining mixture of Scarlet, Green and Gold. Colonel Byrd in his garden which is the finest in that Country has a Summer House set round with the Indian Honey-Suckle which all summer is continually full of sweet Flowers, in which these Birds delight exceedingly. Upon these Flowers I have seen ten or a dozen of these Beautiful Creatures together, which sported about me so familiarly, that with their little Wings they often fanned my Face.[18]

Because of the large number of people living on isolated Virginia plantations without the services of nearby villages or towns to supply them, the kitchen gardens and orchards were important. Beverly describes them and compares the great variety of English plants that did not miscarry in Virginia's temperate climate.

A Kitchin-Garden don't thrive better or faster in any part of the Universe than there. They have all the Culinary Plants that grow in England, and in far greater perfection, than in England: Besides these, they have several Roots, Herbs, Vine-fruits, and Salate-flowers peculiar to themselves, most of which will neither increase, nor grow to Perfection in England. These

they dish up various ways, and find them very delicious Sauce to their Meats, both Roast and Boild, Fresh and Salt; such are the Red-Buds, Sassafras-Flowers, Cymnels, Melons, and Potatoes. . . .

It is said of New England, that several Plants will not grow there, which thrive well in England, such as Rue, Southernwood, Rosemary, Bays and Lavender: And that others degenerate, and will not continue above a year or two at the most; such are July-Flowers, Fennel Enula, Campana, Clary, and Bloodwort: But I don't know any English Plant, Grain or Fruit, that miscarries in Virginia; but most of them better their kinds very much, by being sowed or planted there.[19]

Since Beverly is writing around 1705, his tantalizing observations no doubt reflect a far more advanced state of gardening among Virginia landowners than had existed in the first settlements. Garden practices in Virginia were labor intensive, and although slavery had been introduced in 1619 when twenty negroes were sold from a Dutch privateer, it had not grown much until the last decades of the seventeenth century. The monopolies of the great British companies engaged in slave trade were finally broken in 1697, and the lucrative privilege was extended to all British subjects. Further encouragement was given to the trade by concessions in the Treaty of Utrecht in 1714, bringing countless victims into the appalling commerce.

The first of the great eighteenth-century houses and gardens to be built in the Virginia colony was the Governor's Palace in Williamsburg. Its reputed elegance inside and out and in the elaborate formal gardens conceived by Governor Francis Nicholson (1655–1728) was due in part to a new tax on the importation of slaves. On June 10, 1700, Governor Nicholson wrote to the Council of Trade and Plantations in London: "I am in hopes that this year, please God: there will come in a good many Negroes. So that there may be money enough in a year or two to build a house for

his Majesty's Governor, as also the Capitol."[20] The commerce flourished and the slave tax built and furnished the palace. The slave-driven economy also made possible the expansion of plantations on the banks of the Virginia rivers over the next few decades. The large-scale introduction of slavery into the southern colonies began to show its effect by the second decade of the century, and it can be measured by the number of manor houses with extensive landscape settings that were built before the Revolution.

The perspective view of the Governor's Palace at Williamsburg in the well-known Bodleian Library plate (ca. 1740) indicates crude outlines of lozenge-shaped beds of flowers and topiary. It is conventional and sketchy, but from what we see in the plate the garden appears to reflect the Dutch-English tradition of parterres and geometric topiary. At the northwest and northeast corners of the walled garden can be seen two small garden buildings. The present reconstructed palace garden is based on the later extension of the original

The upper garden of the Governor's Palace in Williamsburg, following the original plan, consists of sixteen diamond-shaped parterres and twelve cylindrical topiaries. Photo: Pamela Harper.

plot when the ballroom wing was added to the rear in 1749–51. The north wall was moved back, and as it is now conjecturally restored, a wooden screen or *clairvoyée* on a low brick base gives a view or "visto" into the fields and woods beyond. Such framed perspectives were popular in English gardens in the early eighteenth century and even before the Picturesque landscape movement had gotten underway. The long avenues and axial drives in Charles Bridgeman's and Stephen Switzer's garden plans were often introduced for this purpose. On a much smaller scale, it was not an uncommon device in Virginia where views or perspectives were incorporated into the gardens and ground of Stratford, Mount Vernon, Carter's Grove, and Kingsmill.

The actual laying out of the palace garden was the work of Governor Alexander Spotswood (1676–1740) who arrived in Williamsburg in 1710. The original garden had been bounded on one side by deep, awkward gullies and ravines, so Spotswood organized them into an imaginative series of formal ter-

Many of the garden structures of Colonial Williamsburg are conjectural, but they add a great deal to the setting, dating from the 1930s and '40s. Photo: Steven Still.

OPPOSITE
The elaborate topiary in the recreated palace garden at Williamsburg suggests the Dutch garden fashion in England at the time of the construction of the original palace in the early decades of the eighteenth century. Photo: Pamela Harper.

The garden gates at Westover, Virginia, are probably the most elaborate imported garden ornaments to have survived from the colonial period. Photo: Everett Scott.

races and put a canal at the bottom of the slope to carry off the water.

Terracing was widely used in Virginia because the larger plantation houses were invariably placed facing and above rivers, the main "roads" to reach these remote establishments. The terraced slope reaching down to the river can be seen, for example, in the plan of Carter's Grove and at Kingsmill Plantation, which was built by Lewis Burwell between 1728 and 1736 not far from Carter's Grove. Excavations at Kingsmill have uncovered a series of large granite steps descending down broad terraces similar to those at its neighbor.

Ornaments and sculpture either in stone or lead were widely used to decorate gardens in England contemporary with the elegant formal gardens of the Governor's Palace and the

gardens of the larger plantations built before the middle of the century. Cut-stone wall caps and at least one ball finial were uncovered at Williamsburg during the restoration that began in 1926. The inventory of Governor Botetourt's estate lists six stone garden vases and twelve lead ones that were acquired during his 1768–70 tenure. By far the most sophisticated and traveled member of the early plantation gentry was William Byrd II (1674–1744), and it is not surprising that the great iron gates in the garden at his Westover estate are the most elegant pieces of garden ironwork to have survived. The carved stone finials of the gateposts are the finest group to have been brought from England to the colonies. John Bartram, the naturalist and friend of Byrd, was impressed when he saw the ensemble in 1740: "Colonel Byrd is very prodigalle with new Gates, gravel walks, hedges and cedars finely twined and a little green house with two or three orange trees . . . in short, he hath the finest seat in Virginia."[21]

Garden decorations were expensive to import, and although English garden books found in private Virginian libraries recommended embellishments, few planters could afford them. A contemporary of John Custis, a passionate Williamsburg gardener and friend of Peter Collinson, records that Custis's garden had statues of Venus, Apollo, and Bacchus. Philip Fithian, the tutor at Mount Airy, notes in his diary that the gardens of John Tayloe's new Palladian house, built in 1758, had both sculpture and other garden ornaments to complement Mount Airy's handsome orangery. It is important to underline, however, that these fugitive refinements were rare even in Virginia.

Except along the navigable rivers of the Tidewater of Virginia, Maryland, and the Carolinas, settlements of any kind were isolated and scattered. Beyond the coastal plantations, there extended what seemed to visitors from Europe an endless wilderness threaded by winding narrow trails. And these trails did not lead to Colonel Byrd's great gates or Colonel Tayloe's cool orangery.

Travelers in fact were appalled by the crude, desolate, unkempt rural southern households found in the occasional forest clearing. Nor was this scruffy domestic setting confined to Virginia or the South, but similar conditions seem to have prevailed even in the more settled sections all along the Eastern Seaboard. As J. B. Jackson has put it, there was "a kind of impatient insensitivity toward the environment" that seems to have been characteristic of colonial America.[22] William Byrd's account of a Virginia farmer chopping down a mature tree so his cattle could easily eat the moss growing on it is only one graphic vignette to support Jackson's indictment.

Robert Beverly claimed that too many Virginians "depend altogether upon the liberality of nature without endeavoring to improve its

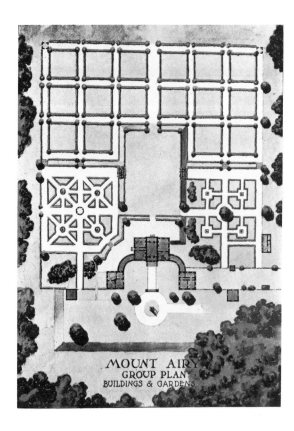

MOUNT AIRY
GROUP PLAN
BUILDINGS & GARDENS

Even though the conjectural Mount Airy Group Plan may not be archaeologically accurate, its geometry conforms to what we do know of James River gardens of the period. Journal of the American Institute of Architects.

This 1801 view by Benjamin Latrobe of a York County ferry house in Pennsylvania is much closer to the realities of house and garden on the first frontier in the decades following the Revolution than the familiar restored plantations. Maryland Historical Society.

The south wing of the ruined main house at Middleton Place, near Charleston, which was burned at the end of the Civil War. Its gardens were laid out in the eighteenth century. Photo: Pamela Harper.

A Low Country cypress swamp, embellished with azaleas, part of Magnolia Gardens, which were laid out near Charleston in the 1840s. Photo: Charles Marden Fitch.

OPPOSITE
The terraced gardens and butterfly lakes of the 1740s leading down to the Ashley River at Middleton Place Plantation are unique in American garden design and rank among the greatest creations of the colonial period. Photo: Derek Fell.

gifts by art and industry. They spunge upon the Blessings of a warm sun and fruitful soil. . . . I should be asham'd to publish this slothful indolence of my countrymen, but that I hope it will rouse them out of their lethargy and excite them to make the most of all those happy advantages, a garden is nowhere sooner made than made there, either for fruits or flowers. Tulips from seed flower the second year at farthest. All sorts of herbs have there a perfection in their flavor, beyond what I ever tasted in a more northern climate and yet," he concluded, "they haven't many gardens in the country, fit to bear that name." [23] Or as Byrd observed in his journal in 1733: "It is a common case in this part of the country that people live worse upon good land; and the more they are befriended by the soil and the climate, the less they will do for themselves." [24]

Even if the well-educated and established squires often pursued gardening with energy, importing from England all kinds of seeds and plants, the majority seemed to have neither the imagination nor inclination. Jefferson in his *Notes on Virginia* complained that while a few of his fellow Virginians had well-stocked vegetable gardens and orchards, "the poorest people attend to neither, living principally on milk and animal diet. This is the more inexcusable," he went on, "as the climate requires indispensably a full use of vegetable food, for health as well as comfort, and is very friendly to the raising of fruits." [25]

Even though South Carolina could boast of a number of outstanding gardens following the established patterns of formality of the eighteenth century, David Ramsey, writing his *History of South Carolina* in 1808, echoed the complaints in other former colonies that planters "have always too much neglected the culture of gardens." [26]

The Middletons, a rich planter family in South Carolina, did introduce original and sophisticated gardens at two of their Low Country plantations. Crowfield Plantation, developed in the 1730s, could boast of "a large fish pond with a mount rising out of the

middle of the top of which is level with the dwelling house and upon it a Roman temple."[27] Two other large pools on either side of the artificial plateau formed an elegant prospect of water on three sides of the house.

Nothing survives of Crowfield, but its builder's brother, Henry Middleton (1717–1784), created the celebrated gardens at Middleton Place, and they have been splendidly restored and maintained.

No clues to the name of the designer of Middleton Place have turned up in the records, but it is reasonable to suspect that Henry Middleton, who had been educated in England, availed himself of some professional advice to augment his own self-confident tastes. Garden designers were beginning to appear in the richer colonies. A few years before Henry Middleton began the grand, sculpted terraces running down to the Ashley River, Peter Chaffereau, "newly come from London," advertised his design services in a Charleston newspaper. The setting out of "grounds for gardens or parks in a grand or rural manner" were among Chaffereau's talents, which also included town planning, map making, and surveying.[28]

The plan of Middleton Place is firmly organized along a strong central axis in the old French tradition. But unlike the conventional French garden, which would have used cross axes to expand the scheme, Middleton's central line holds closely to its dominating intentions, running from the entrance along the open space approaching the house and then down the terraces to the river. An alley of camellias, perpendicular to the entrance drive in front of the house, leads to a 700-foot-long canal, forming one side of the elaborate garden parterres once "ornamented in a Serpentine manner with Flowers." Like Crowfield, this highly formal garden space also contains a mount that originally was capped by a classical temple pavilion.[29] Both Crowfield and Middleton Place show the influence of John James's *The Theory and Practice of Gardening,* a translation of the French treatise by Dezallier d'Argenville. At least one South Carolinian,

John Pringle, was a subscriber to the James translation.

Middleton Place's chief crop was rice, and the slaves who built the terraces and the ornamented pools next to the river and the canal would have learned the basic skills required from their work in the rice fields. The rice fields beyond the gardens themselves, with their ditches and terraces, can be glimpsed from the walks, providing a sensed unity between the garden and the working plantation itself.

The generous use of native magnolias and live oaks enhances the indigenous feeling and character while the *Camellia japonica* forming the *allée* to the canal introduce an exotic note and reflect the Middleton family's international connections and travels in the eighteenth century.

Tradition has it that the camellias were introduced by the French botanist and plant collector André Michaux (1746–1802) who visited Middleton Place a number of times. Charleston had developed a number of nurseries and private botanical gardens, distinguishing South Carolina for its comparatively advanced interests. After the Revolution Michaux purchased some one hundred acres outside Charleston and used it as a base for acquiring and sending trees, shrubs, and plants to the Jardin du Roi in Paris. Michaux's book on the American oak published in Paris was handsomely illustrated by the famous artist Pierre Joseph Redouté (1759–1841). The botanist's son François-André carried on his father's work, and his study of the trees of North America helped to introduce many of them into the European landscape.

John Bartram, the great Quaker plantsman who had settled outside of Philadelphia in 1729, traveled and collected plants in the Carolinas as well as Virginia, Maryland, Connecticut, Georgia, and Florida for European connoisseurs. His regular shipments of seeds and plants to Peter Collinson, Philip Miller, and other English plant and seed subscribers introduced a rich treasure of American species into English gardens and parks. His son Wil-

PRECEDING SPREAD
Middleton Bridge crosses one of the swampy inlets between banks of hundreds of azaleas. Photo: Pamela Harper.

liam followed his father's work and profited by the elder Bartram's network of connections, including Henry Laurens of Charleston. Lauren's garden, laid out in 1755, was exceptional in its range of ornamental and useful plants. Thomas Jefferson later at Monticello was one of the few eighteenth-century Americans who could match Laurens's knowledge and interest. "Among a variety of other productions," David Ramsey noted in his father-in-law's garden, were "olives, capers, limes, ginger, guinea grass, the alpine strawberry bearing nine months in the year, red raspberries, blue grapes . . . directly from the south of France . . . and vines which bore abundantly of the choice white eating grape called Chasselates blancs."[30]

From an early age, Thomas Jefferson had a deep and abiding interest in horticulture, botany, and garden design. Even before the foundation work was started at Monticello in 1769, he began to lay out an orchard on the south side of the hill he had selected for his house. Just as the house, which he built and rebuilt over the years, served as his architectural studio—a place where he could carry on his design experiments—so the gardens, orchards, and fields of the farm became a virtual horticultural laboratory. New plants were constantly introduced and matured in his experimental vegetable plots, orchards, and flower beds. If they were successful, the results were passed on to neighbors and to gardening friends throughout the country.

In 1766 Jefferson began a *Garden Book,* and although it was only sporadically kept in detail, the journal was continued until 1824, two years before he died, providing a remarkable document of the third president's devotion to gardening. As he wrote to Charles Willson Peale in a much quoted letter: "I have often thought that if heaven had given me a choice of my position and calling, it should have been on a rich spot of earth, well watered, and near a good market for the production of the garden. No occupation is so delightful to me as the culture of the earth, and no culture comparable to that of a gardener."[31]

John Bartram, one of the most productive of the early botanist-collectors of the colonial period, sent this sketch of his house and garden outside Philadelphia to his London correspondent Peter Collinson in 1758.

Classically educated in Latin and Greek, Jefferson was also well read in the English literature that had given rise to the English garden revolution in the early decades of the eighteenth century. Pope, Thomson, Addison, and Milton joined with Horace, Pliny, Virgil, and Ovid to provide the civilizing models and ideals to underpin the life Jefferson was set on creating at Monticello. The landscape as well as the house were intended to express the new myth of a reconstituted Roman life guided by Roman virtues on the edge of the wilderness in the New World.

The very siting of Monticello on top of a swelling foothill of the Blue Ridge Mountains was a bold, dramatic decision without precedent in the colonies. The view was breathtak-

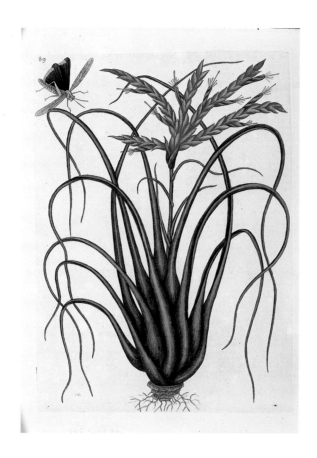

ing, allowing the young lawyer to visually soar above the plains stretching into the distance. The scale of the setting would ultimately fit the final scheme of the house although it was not to be completed for another forty years.

In his *Account Book* of 1771 Jefferson jotted down some of his more romantic notions for the grounds and surrounding park, which were to include cascades, a grotto, a Gothic temple, another temple decorated with a roof "Chinese, Grecian or in the taste of the Lantern of Demosthenes at Athens." Tame deer, peacocks, hares, pheasants, and a not-so-tame buck elk would be kept in the park in the spirit of the ancient menageries of the Persian paradise.

Except for the deer, few if any of the other decorative elements seemed to have materialized before Jefferson was caught up in public affairs and foreign service as minister to Paris. Always the garden student, Jefferson visited the latest *jardins anglais* in and around Paris before making a serious tour of English gardens when he went to London in 1786. Jefferson's guidebook to English gardens was Thomas Whately's *Observations on Modern Gardening,* a book he had owned before he came to France. The tour included Chiswick, Hampton Court, Pope's house at Twickenham, Esher Place, Claremont, Painshill, Woburn, Caversham, Wotton, Hagley, Blenheim, Enfield Chase, Moor Park, Kew, and the poet William Shenstone's The Leasowes.

The experience had an important effect on Jefferson's gardening ideas. He was to admire and envy the English landscape garden the rest of his life and worked to achieve an American version at his Virginia plantation. It was to England "without doubt we are to go for models in this art. . . . Their sunless climate has permitted them to adopt what is certainly a beauty of the very first order in landscape."[32] Later when he attempted to introduce the English style into the Virginia countryside, he discovered that it was more difficult to manage than it had appeared. William Hamilton of Philadelphia shared Jefferson's enthusiasm. He had also traveled and studied the new English gardens. His landscape park of Woodlands was, without question, the most successful English eighteenth-century landscape recreation in America. As Jefferson wrote to Hamilton, "Your pleasure grounds [are] the chastest model of gardening which I have ever seen out of England. . . . I should be very happy to see you and to take from you some of those lessons for the improvement of my grounds, which you have so happily practiced in your own."[33]

Aside from Whately's *Observations,* Jefferson purchased in 1765 William Shenstone's *Works* the year after it was published. The poet included an essay called "Unconnected Thoughts on Gardening." Under the heading "landskip or picturesque-gardening," Shenstone proclaimed that the purpose of this type of gardening was "in pleasing the imagination by scenes of grandeur, beauty and variety. Convenience merely has no share here; any further than as it please the imagination."[34]

Shenstone's ornamental farm The Leasowes was famous during his lifetime for its subtle integration of practical gardening with imaginative design and ornamental allusion expressed in lines of poetry scattered along the walks and in the woods. By the time Jefferson saw it, Shenstone had been dead several years and his *ferme ornée* had in Jefferson's opinion become an ordinary "grazing farm with a path round it." Nevertheless, the original concept appealed to the Virginian, and twenty-five years later he wrote out for his overseer a plan of a project inspired by Shenstone's landscape

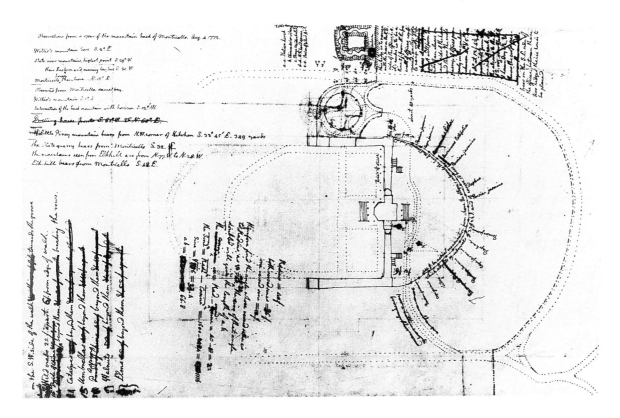

A plan drawn by Jefferson, about 1768, of the grounds at Monticello that shows elaborate planting directions. Massachusetts Historical Society.

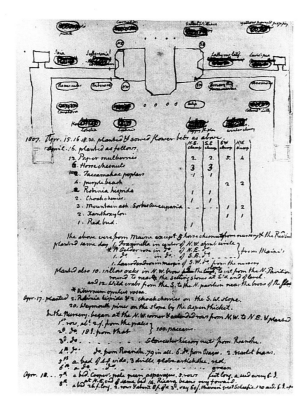

A plan drawn by Jefferson in 1807 shows his planting scheme for a series of round and oval flower beds at Monticello on either side of the raised terrace walks that flank the house. Massachusetts Historical Society.

ideas: "In all the open grounds on both sides of the 3rd & 4th. Roundabouts, lay off for the minor articles of husbandry, and for experimental culture, disposing them into a *ferme ornée* by interspersing occasionally the attributes of a garden." [35]

Jefferson's interest in scientific gardening and farming was, as Edwin Betts has pointed out, "tied up with the agricultural and horticultural needs of the United States." [36] As the foundation of Jefferson's philosophical and practical expression of agrarianism, the work at Monticello had deeper political meaning in a country that was yet to develop an educational system devoted to the training of gardeners and farmers.

Even though Jefferson was far more experimental in his pursuit of gardening in all of its dimensions, George Washington's (1732–1799) rather conservative example also impressed visitors to Mount Vernon, where kitchen and pleasure gardens were effectively incorporated into a plan made by the first president. Washington's garden library was limited to Batty Langley's *New Principles of Gardening*. A Polish guest at Mount Vernon, Julian Niemcewicz, was deeply impressed by the former president's personally guided tour. "The whole plantation, the garden, and the rest prove well that a man born with natural taste may guess a beauty without having seen the model. The General has never left America; but it seems as if he had copied the best samples of the grand old homesteads of England." [37] The Samuel Vaughan drawing of Mount Vernon's garden, made in 1787, shows no box-edged parterres in the large spaces divided by walks in front of the greenhouse. But ten years later the young English architect Benjamin Latrobe noted in his journal, with disdain, some fussy new beds at Mount Vernon that recalled layouts that were no longer fashionable in Europe. "For the first time again since I left Germany I saw here a parterre, clipped and trimmed with infinite care in the form of a richly flourished Fleur-de-lis: The expiring groans I hope of our Grandfather's pedantry." [38] In fact, Washington had in his employ two trained German gardeners during the years when the new parterres were made in 1787.

Like Jefferson, Washington dramatized in his domestic life the ancient republican virtues and myths described in classical literature. Far less self-conscious in appropriating the myth into new landscape ideals than his fellow Virginian did at Monticello, Washington saw to it that Mount Vernon evoked in its own way the pastoral ideals of agrarian life.

By the fortuitous preservation of Mount Vernon and Monticello, and particularly their garden settings, as national shrines to the remarkable men who built them, the pastoral, gardening ideal continues to be used to define the meaning of America. From the first discovery, the vision of the New World as a kind of garden Paradise has continued its hold upon our imagination. It is as if the old poetic and political fantasies of Europe have, at least in these private Elysiums created by two of the Founding Fathers, come alive and continue to flourish as a model of what the ideal life can or could be in the green, virgin environment of the New World.

THE CHANGING AMERICAN LANDSCAPE

Jefferson's abiding aversion to "cities as sores on the body politic" confirmed his basic political philosophy: a republic could only survive in the hands of the virtuous, small landowner free of the corruption of urban society. Simply put, "The country produces more virtuous citizens," Jefferson wrote as the key passage recording his agrarian faith.[39] With the opening up of the new Northwest Territory for settlement, Jefferson had the opportunity to translate into practical terms his agrarian ideology. The National Survey of 1785 inspired by Jefferson imposed a vast, geometric grid across the wilderness and permitted the formation of six-mile-square townships sub-

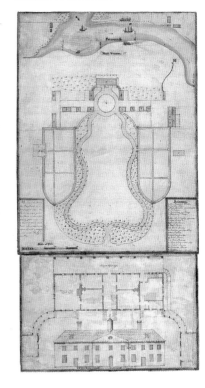

divided into three smaller grid sections of 640 acres on down to small farm holdings. The survey represented a clear, rational expression of Jefferson's dislike of large cities, centralized government, and his favoring of the small, self-sufficient farmer. Nowhere in the survey are there provisions anticipating cities in the utopian pattern of its ordered geometry. Rather, the new country would be settled by rural small landowners each on a piece of land and self-sufficient in their ideal world.

The rapid spread of settlement, the necessity for market centers since few of the pioneers even remotely approached a self-sufficient existence, and the unforeseen development of steam transportation brought villages, towns, and cities to spoil the Jeffersonian dream. With the extension of the regional grid into villages and eventually cities, the unvarying blocks and town lots that followed became the pattern for the urban environment. No one, and certainly not the third president, anticipated that the real legacy of the survey would be efficient urban speculation and development.

When roads and other improvements were laid out in the rural countryside they too followed the urban rectilinear pattern, imposing a "square deal" order on the national landscape. For new city dwellers settling on their freshly subdivided lots, garden patterns themselves—in walls, orchards, and fences—expressed the same grid geometry. Only in the more generous and luxuriant suburban estates that seemed almost like miniature English parks, with their large trees and rolling lawns, were private gardens able to escape the foreordained dictates of the surveyor's lines. In the new cities, the marginal, rough tracts of ground that defied the surveyor's straight lines became woodland cemeteries, often the only place in town where the grip of urban geometry was broken. In Cincinnati's Spring Grove, the landscape of death recaptured in its picturesque layout the pastoral ideal of nature that had been at the heart of the aesthetics of Capability Brown, Humphry Repton, and their followers a century earlier.

Aesthetic Reform

The deaths of two of the most conspicuous Founding Fathers, John Adams and Thomas Jefferson, on July 4, 1826, marked the end of the initial period of U.S. history during which much of the young country's attention had perforce been focused on the Old World cultures of Britain and France. In the decades that followed thoughtful Americans began to express a new concern and interest in the shape and appearance of their own landscape and in the achievements of native painters, sculptors, architects, and gardeners. Surprisingly, New England Transcendentalists articulated this new awareness and delight in nature and art. Men like Emerson and Thoreau, with their deep belief in divinely inspired individual self-fulfillment, also believed passionately in the spiritual significance embodied in material objects and in the idealization of nature. "Every Natural Fact is a symbol of some spiritual fact,"[40] Emerson declared. It was essential for man to understand his proper relationship with the natural world, a belief at the heart of the Transcendentalist philosophy of nature. The energy of the Supreme Being lay behind all material matter, and all of nature deserved reverence. "What we call wildness," Thoreau wrote, "is only another civilization other than our own. . . . It is monstrous when one cares but little about trees but much about Corinthian columns, and yet this is extremely common."[41]

As for the role of the artist in American society, Transcendentalist arguments suggested a functional basis for aesthetics serving as an indictment of mankind's shortcomings. Art should act as "a protest . . . on the deformity of our daily manners and our quotidian landscape," Emerson wrote to Margaret Fuller. "Fitness" according to Emerson, "is an inseparable accompaniment of beauty, that it has been taken for it."[42] Transcendentalist improvement and care of the landscape and gardening through art were in Neil Harris's words, "a means of individual fulfillment and as a symbol of a people living in harmony with nature, united with the Over-Soul." [43]

In marked contrast to the rarefied pronouncements coming out of Concord and Boston, the ordinary American landscape, with its few parks and private gardening efforts, seemed in the early nineteenth century to fall far below the exalted dreams and aspirations of the Transcendentalists. European travelers commented on the pervasive American indifference to natural scenery, to trees, and to the environment generally. William Blane was shocked by the stripped hillsides of the new town of Cincinnati, declaring that an American had no concept of the aesthetic pleasure of woodlands and forests. "To him a country well cleared . . . seems the only one that is beautiful." Mrs. Basil Hall, an English traveler, was dismayed to find no city parks and that most Americans viewed trees as enemies to be eradicated like the Indians. After visiting the Chesapeake countryside, another Englishman, Isaac Weld, sadly confirmed Mrs. Hall's indictment that most Americans had "an unconquerable aversion to trees." "To them the sight of a wheat field or a cabbage garden would convey pleasure far greater than that of the most romantic woodland views." [44]

In the 1830s and '40s the rapid, uncontrolled urban growth and expansion of the older cities of the Eastern Seaboard suddenly produced a revulsion against the spreading, man-made desolation of the landscape. Fed by the observations and philosophy of romantic poets like Wordsworth, a sudden nostalgia for the natural environment was heard in a number of quarters. Painters began to study and to appreciate trees, lakes, rivers, and mountains. And as Harris sums up the results, "The formal product of this era of reconciliation with nature was the school of landscape painters." [45] After they had so devasted nature by exploiting the land for farms and cities, roads, canals, and the new railroads, it was time for men to turn their back on the raw and ugly and attempt to rediscover the lost harmony with a once beautiful environment.

The short but brilliant career of Andrew Jackson Downing (1815–1852), whose books,

Edge of Walden Pond, near Concord, Massachusetts, where Henry David Thoreau spent his most productive period, next to nature. Photo: Owen Franken.

articles, and designs expounded the virtue of rural architecture and an improved landscape, symbolizes the aesthetic reform movement in the second quarter of the century. The son of a nurseryman, Downing grew up on the Hudson River above New York City where the valley had been divided into large estates originally settled by the Dutch in the seventeenth and eighteenth centuries. His gardening and architectural ideas were shaped first of all by his reading of Edmund Burke, William Gilpin, Uvedale Price, Humphry Repton, and John Claudius Loudon. In other words the genesis of the New Yorker's convictions regarding the ideal landscape was to be found in the solid English gardening philosophy and practice of the second half of the eighteenth century. Loudon's writings in particular had the greatest influence on Downing, and the Scotsman's gardening journalism became for the young American a model for his own publishing efforts.

A Treatise on the Theory and Practice of Landscape Gardening first appeared in 1841, followed the next year by *Cottage Residences.* In these books, Downing proposed a philosophy and program of improvement for the countryside that also drew inspiration from the

View from the Library Window at Wodenethe, looking south, an illustration from Andrew Jackson Downing's *Treatise on the Theory and Practice of Landscape Gardening.*

Transcendentalists, taking to heart Emerson's articulation of the moral need to "disgust men with cities," and to stimulate a new passion for country living. Downing and his followers were deeply conservative in their social values and believed that a national beautification campaign would correct the American "restlessness and disposition to change." It would also provide a check on "our passions for luxuries of all kinds."[46] As Downing wrote in *Cottage Residences,* beautiful homes and gardens would ultimately serve a moral purpose as "an unfailing barrier against vice, immorality and bad habits." Or as one impassioned supporter asked rhetorically, "can we conceive a voluptuary loving to put his hands to the real work of gardens."[47] Clearly Downing's message was that the house of correct design surrounded by a virtuous garden would save men from houses of ill-repute, and would shore up the most fragile American institution, the family.

Not only the family but the romantic pastoral environment that families had enjoyed and perfected during nearly two centuries of settled history along Downing's Hudson Valley would also be restored and preserved. This longing was partly a nostalgia for a way of life that was threatened, but it also reflected a reverence for the idyllic American landscape itself that reached back to the cherished era of the Revolution and before. An English traveler, Thomas Pownall, captured in his lyrical description, qualities of Downing's native New York countryside that were already firmly established forty years before Downing was born. "These successions of Valley appeared to me as I rode along them the most charming of Landscapes," Pownall wrote in his journal in 1776. "The Bottoms of the Vales are full of cultured Farms, with Houses such as Yeomanry, not Tenants, live in. These were bushed up with gardens, and with Peach and Apple Orchards all round them with every convenience and Enjoyment that Property and Plenty could give to Peace and Liberty.

My heart felt an over-flowing of Benevolence at the sight of so much and such real happiness."[48]

During his ten short professional years before he was killed in a steamboat accident in 1852, Downing searched for ways to harmonize architecture with the natural scenery, believing as Thoreau had written that "man's works must lie in the bosom of Nature, cottages be buried in trees, or under vines and moss, like rocks, that they may not outrage the landscape."[49]

In his admiration of the English school of landscape gardening, Downing understood the subtle relationship of the larger vernacular environment of fields, meadows, and woods to the man-made parkland and garden. He did not hesitate to preach his sermon to American farmers regarding their special aesthetic obligations. One optimistic convert thought

Downing's beautification campaign might turn into a mass movement and transform "the whole land" into a garden by dint of moral fervor. Echoing Alexander Pope's Augustan lines a century earlier. Emerson proclaimed that "we must regard the *land* as a commanding and increasing power of the American citizen."[50]

"Now, although we do not expect farmers to possess a gallery of pictures or statuary," Downing wrote, "yet they have a scarcely less instructive field open to them while tastefully disposing their gardens and grounds, in studying the various developments of beauty that occur." Downing's optimism was based in part on the Anglo-Saxon roots of the older American settlements. "As a people descended from English stock, we inherit much ardent love of rural life and its pursuits which belongs to that nation."[51] Still he realized that the great garden parks created by Capability Brown and his followers expressed an economic and political system utterly different from the one that had been established on the American continent by the Revolution. These fundamental, structural differences would make it impossible and undesirable to encourage the creation of American versions of a Stowe, Stourhead, or Blenheim. Since rural American farms and country estates were incomparably smaller and simpler than English models and the country itself was so enormous, the need to educate a larger public to the virtues of scenic embellishment was far more urgent and important, encouraging Downing in his publishing and popular propaganda to proclaim a message that was not without a political agenda. Suddenly, it seemed that Downing's sermons were paying off in the romantic new feeling for the natural environment. Houses were camouflaged in browns, buffs, and greens to blend in with the woods; factories and mills were seen as intrusions on nature; hiking was taken up with Christian energy; and improvement associations condemning imported Lombardy poplars, formal flower beds, and angular street patterns sprang up to accept Downing's challenge.

"In the United States, it is highly improbable that we shall ever witness such splendid examples of landscape gardens as those abroad, to which we have alluded," Downing wrote in his *Treatise*. "Here the rights of man are held to be equal; and if there are no enormous parks, and no class of men whose wealth is hereditary, there is, at least, what is more gratifying . . . a large class of independent landholders who are able to assemble around them, not only the useful and convenient, but the agreeable and beautiful, in country life."[52]

In his *Treatise*, Downing tried to suggest landscape ideas for the simplest rural cottage as well the large estate, ideas that were suited to the particular conditions of the American environment. Even the smallest house could have a perfect specimen tree on a lawn if the cottage were placed in a position to appropriate a glimpse of some nearby romantic woodland or attractive background.

Downing's principles of what he called "modern Landscape Gardening" distinguished between two "expressions," the beautiful and the picturesque: "The Beautiful is nature or art obeying the universal laws of perfect existence, easily, freely, harmoniously, and without the *display* of power. The Picturesque is nature or art obeying the same laws rudely, violently, irregularly and often displaying power only."[53] He concluded that given the prevailing American character formed by an ongoing battle with the wilderness, a law-abiding landscape reflecting the American interpretation of the English picturesque composed of native scenery seemed to be the approach best understood by most of his fellow citizens.

The impetus for a contemporary American style of gardening was of course not original with Downing. Jefferson, William Hamilton, and others had earlier spoken out for such a movement. In Downing's region of the Hudson River, a French immigrant, André Parmentier (1780–1830), who had professional training, also advocated a more relaxed form of landscape gardening. Between 1827 and 1828 Parmentier was engaged by the botanist Dr. David Hosack to work on his Hudson River estate. Parmentier referred to his informal, asymmetrical approach to design as the "modern style." "The modern style," he wrote, "presents to you a constant change of scene perfectly in accordance with the desires of a man who loves as he continues to walk, to have new objects laid open to his view."[54]

In Downing's brief survey of historic garden styles, the formal geometric garden design had, in his opinion, succumbed to unimaginative routine and repetition, and lacked the art and beauty called for in his *Treatise*. Still, he thought there might be a place for "the ancient style" in public squares and domestic gardens where "display, grandeur of effect and a highly artificial character are desirable." He also believed that a more formal organization was appropriate in small gardens where variety and irregularity were out of the question, or as a setting where "an old and quaint style of residence exists, the symmetrical and knotted garden would be a proper accomplishment." He also gave some sound advice regarding landscape preservation, a subject that would receive little further attention until well into the twentieth century, proposing that "pleached alleys, and sheared trees" should also be maintained and admired the same as "old armor or furniture, as curious specimens of antique taste and custom." He complained that Robert Morris's Lemon Hill in Philadelphia, "a brilliant and striking" old garden in the "geometric mode . . . with artificial plantations, formal gardens with trellises, grottoes, spring-houses, temples, statues, and vases with numerous ponds of water, jets-d'eau and other water-works," had been allowed to fall into decay.[55]

The editor of the ninth edition (1875) of the *Treatise on Landscape Gardening,* Henry Winthrop Sargent (1810–1882), a neighbor and friend of Downing, underscored Downing's comment by pointing out a growing revival of interest in historical garden styles in England. Sargent mentioned that Chatsworth, Woburn Abbey, Castle Howard, Bowood, and Eaton Hall had adopted "the Italian or architectural school on one or more sides of the house," as a sort of connection between art and nature. Sargent's own garden at his Hudson River estate, Wodnethe, across from Downing's home, incorporated a number of his neighbor's ideas, including an early use of Italian Revival elements in terraces, walks, and garden ornaments.[56]

Public Parks

Perhaps Downing's greatest contribution to the American landscape garden movement was his effort to stir up interest in the creation of public parks. In 1848 he had praised the rural cemetery movement in the pages of his magazine, *The Horticulturist,* "as one of the most remarkable illustrations of the popular taste in this country." "The great attraction of these cemeteries," he continued, "is not in the fact that they are burial places . . . all these might be realized in a burial ground planted with straight lines of willows and sombre avenues of evergreens . . . [but] in the natural beauty of the sites, and in the tasteful and harmonious embellishment of these sites of art."[57] Again Downing was following in the footsteps of J. C. Loudon who had earlier promoted the private garden cemetery and public park development.

It may well be that as the promise of a celestial Paradise became theologically less distinct in the nineteenth century, according to Neil Harris, "the living began to demand more certain means of communion with the dead."[58] Beginning with Mount Auburn in Cambridge (1831), Green-Wood in Brooklyn (1838), Green Mount in Baltimore (1839), and Laurel Hill in Philadelphia (1835), large tracts of unspoiled woodland were transformed into public parks for both the dead and the living. Mount Auburn was actually laid out on land specially selected by the newly founded Massachusetts Horticultural Society. Woodland Cemetery in Philadelphia itself had started out as William Hamilton's English park that Jefferson had admired so much. Significantly, these new earthly Elysiums were managed by professional gardeners and landscape specialists. The campaign of the rural cemetery movement was in fact an aesthetic crusade, a means of uniting art and nature, and the arguments advocating a marriage of the two were appropriated by advocates like Nehemiah Cleveland who declared in his promotional brochure, "Taste and Art join with nature herself in adorning the last home of the loved . . . here the man of business . . . would often reassure his hesitating virtue."[59]

Between the death of the last participants of the Revolution and the disorienting triumph

of an industrial capitalist society over the original agrarian, pastoral world of Washington, Jefferson, and Adams, Downing had played a key, pivotal role. A year after the steamboat carrying Downing south to work on his plans for the mall in Washington exploded, his friend and architect Alexander Jackson Davis (1803–1892) was commissioned to design Lewellyn Park in West Orange, New Jersey,

the first private developer's suburb in America. In layout the new suburb's plans captured the spirit of Downing's romantic, free-form designs in marked contrast to the rigid grid pattern of the city blocks that were firmly established in nearby New York City. Lewellyn Park itself was the idea of Lewellyn Haskell who as a member of the Swedenborgian movement saw the new development as a

A view of Mount Auburn Cemetery in Cambridge, Massachusetts, the first of the public parks set aside for both the living and the dead. Photo: Jerry Howard, Positive Images.

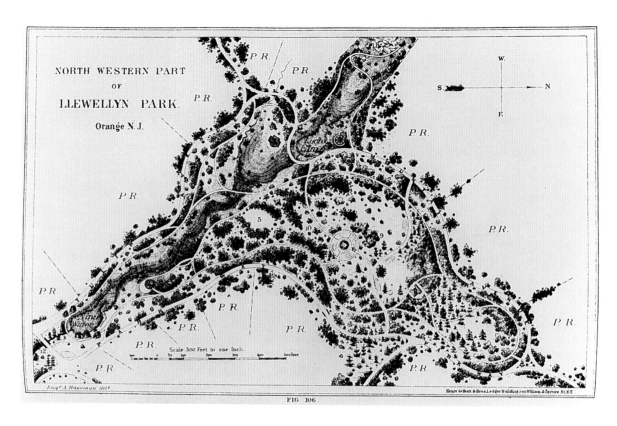

FIG. 106

The threat of the urban chaos of New York City, both physical and moral, stimulated dreams of suburban escape as early as the 1850s, when Llewellyn Park was first conceived and developed in Orange, New Jersey. The idea of living in a large, idealized park in the English style seemed to appeal to middle-class Americans, but it did nothing to encourage a seminal garden tradition. Andrew Jackson Downing, *A Treatise on the Theory and Practice of Landscape Gardening*.

model utopian community designed to preserve family life in a wholesome setting close to nature and at a safe distance from the corrupting city. In its curving drives and emphasis on the picturesque, the first suburb closely resembled the new fashionable cemeteries. But unlike Downing's rural retreats and estates where great natural, scenic views of rivers, mountains, and woods were a part of the setting, Davis's houses at Lewellyn Park looked isolated and abandoned in an ersatz English park. There was none of the picturesque unity that John Nash (1752–1835) and George Stanley Repton (1786–1858), Humphry Repton's son, achieved at Blaise Hamlet (1811) where ten pensioners' cottages were assembled in an informal, romantic group. The attempt to establish a harmonious balance of architecture and nature in a morally uplifting and sustaining environment in America's first planned suburb was a conspicuous failure, a failure that was to have far-reaching social,

aesthetic, and even political implications throughout the twentieth century.

In 1851, Downing had read an interesting description of the first new public park in England; called Birkenhead, it was in a suburb of Liverpool and designed by Sir Joseph Paxton in 1843. The account had been published in a travel book, *Walks and Talks of an American Farmer in England,* written by a young, unknown American named Frederick Law Olmsted (1822–1903) who had brashly sent Downing a copy. Downing, to the traveler's surprise, reprinted it in *The Horticulturist*. Downing had been among the first to realize the importance of the public park in America, and his trip to England and Europe in 1850 had convinced him that these public spaces had a special mission to play in an industrial democracy. There was, he said, "a social freedom" in the new European parks that somehow advanced "a fraternal spirit" among people. The function of these public spaces in the crowded, potentially stratified urban landscape was nothing less than to protect the body politic from the corrosion of an outdated class system. Parks would furthermore preserve democratic institutions from "the arid desert of business dissipation" that was spreading like a plague in urban centers.[60]

Downing's ideal was not so far from Jefferson's vision of a nation built on the self-sufficient farmer-protector of old republican virtues and educated to appreciate the more extended beauties of nature. But even in his idealism, Downing could see that industrialism, easy transportation, and a growing population were inexorably altering the American environment. The relentless pressure of these forces gave his public park crusade a moral urgency.

Frederick Olmsted had been attracted by Downing's advocacy of a program for the reform of the environment based on a set of social and ethical ideals. The older man's vision of a rural commonwealth of men of honor whose virtues were strengthened and supported by the beauty of nature had a potent appeal for Olmsted. Shortly after his description of Birkenhead had appeared, Olmsted decided to make a pilgrimage to Newburg, New York, to meet the celebrated garden-publicist. It was during this visit that Olmsted also first met the young English architect Calvert Vaux (1824–1895) whom Downing had personally recruited to come to the United States as his architectural partner. No doubt public parks were discussed even on that first meeting, since Downing and Vaux had just received the commission to design a park in the middle of Washington that would run from the White House to the Capitol.

Frederick Olmsted was thirty-six years old when he submitted his first landscape design in the competition for New York City's Central Park in 1858. Vaux, who had become his partner, collaborated closely on the project. As superintendent of works at the site already dedicated for a park in the large-scale town planning of upper Manhattan then underway, Olmsted knew the topography intimately and grasped its romantic potential. "The site is rugged, in parts excessively so," the younger planner noted, "and there is scarcely an acre of level or slope unbroken by ledges. With barely tolerable design, tolerably executed, the park will have a picturesque character entirely its own, and New Englandish in its association much more reflective of any European park."[61] The remarkable legacy of Central Park has been magnified by the urban pressure that now surrounds it, making the original visionary plan in the once empty midsection of Manhattan appear as nothing short of a miracle.

The great design innovations of Olmsted and Vaux's plan were in the engineering of the sunken transverse roads to quickly move the cross-town traffic through the park without interfering with the park's public services. By keeping the park clear of traffic the designers were able to achieve their goal of recreating a variety of rural, natural scenes, scenes they believed would contribute to democratic institutions and the moral health of the citizenry. There was a certain amount of double-talk in Olmsted's vision. Part of his plan was to encourage the rich to build their opulent villas around and overlooking the park. Olmsted himself saw the park as rolling English meadows with "clusters of level-armed sheltering trees" and "dainty cows and flocks of black-faced sheep."[62] Democracy and the new plutocracy would somehow be reconciled by the sylvan scenery. What Olmsted did not fully anticipate was the urban real estate speculation and density his idealism would attract.

In 1852, six years before Olmsted had begun to think about the new park in Manhattan, L. H. Burnell startled himself, and later the public, with the discovery of the Yosemite Valley high in a remote area of the Sierra Nevada Mountains. Only seven miles long and enclosed by high mountain ranges, this dramatic setting of monumental natural sculpture was a spectacle that quickly gained, after the Civil War, the reputation as the most beautiful natural spot in the United

The crab apple allée in New York's Central Park Conservatory Garden was designed in the 1930s, within the confines of Frederick Law Olmsted's 1858 plan. Photo: Karen Bussolini.

States. Artists, photographers, scientists, and preachers rushed to see it before entering the transcontinental dialog over its beauty, significance, and its importance to future generations.

As Thoreau and the New England Transcendentalists had earlier assumed, the Supreme Deity would be revealed to the persistent seeker in nature's wonders. The discovery of Yosemite offered new proof that the doctrine had survived the desolation and division caused by the national tragedy of the Civil War. With the arrival of the "Machine in the Garden," symbolized by the completion

of the transcontinental railroad in 1869, the surging postwar democracy would have access to this and other great national wonders of God's handiwork scattered across the unexplored Western territory.

Following Abraham Lincoln's signing of a bill transferring Yosemite Valley to the State of California in 1864, Olmsted was appointed by the governor to chair a commission to oversee and study the site. Olmsted, who had seen his man-made Central Park oasis threatened on all sides by the alarming political and commercial forces of New York City, was relieved and reassured when he first saw Yosemite protected by rugged, towering cliffs. Here in this last Earthly Paradise created by nature, the swelling anxieties and psychological bruises delivered to the heavily settled parts of the country could be fended off or at least greatly reduced. It could become a shrine people would repair to for spiritual and moral renewal. But Olmsted's vision of just how this was going to be accomplished was far more personal, subjective, romantic, and metaphysical than fellow members of the commission or the public could comprehend.

Olmsted rejected the notion of a carefully worked out, linear, point-to-point itinerary for this new God-given garden. There was to be no instructive path like Shenstone had created at The Leasowes, nor any authoritarian guidebook like Louis XIV had written for his park at Versailles. Furthermore, Olmsted was particularly critical of the vulgar, journalistic preoccupation with an exploitation of the valley's dramatic details such as waterfalls, giant trees, lake reflections, and theatrical mountain peaks. "By no statement of the elements of the scenery can any idea of that scenery be given," he declared, "anymore than a true impression can be conveyed of a human face by a measured account of the features."[63] To Olmsted, it was the mute, overall, luminous atmosphere, a kind of fusion of the unifying totality of nature's wonders and mysteries that carried a timeless message. It was this fragile language that had to be preserved from man's spoliation and corruption for future generations.

In his deep, personal search for the essence of Yosemite and its larger meaning, Olmsted resembles that other Victorian, John Ruskin (1819–1900), who had first pursued the aesthetic experience through the mind rather than the eye as a kind of physical and mental therapy. "If we analyze the operation of scenes of beauty upon the mind, and consider the nervous system and the whole physical economy," Ruskin declared, "the action and reaction which constantly occur between bodily and mental conditions, the reinvigoration from such scenes is readily comprehended."[64]

The Yosemite Valley in California was discovered in 1852, and quickly gained the reputation of most beautiful natural landscape in America, the ideal garden of the New World. Photo: Allen Rokach.

One of the spectacular waterfalls in what is now Yosemite National Park. Photo: Allen Rokach.

299

sented to the state commission in 1865. In it he outlined the basic principles of government policy for the protection and preservation of natural parkland. Later, with the establishment of the United States Park Service, the austere spirit of Olmsted's report was reflected in the management of the great national park system. If the United States has never been able to establish a truly native, indigenous gardening tradition, it is arguable that the vast national parks, created in the nineteenth and early twentieth centuries and proportioned to the grandeur of the American continent itself, express a garden ideal that recaptures the first explorers' image of the long sought Garden of Eden they believed was hidden somewhere just beyond the shore of the "New Found Land."

Olmsted's return to the East and his later career were almost exclusively directed to large urban schemes of public parks and parkways: Prospect Park in Brooklyn, the Capitol grounds in Washington, D.C., the Boston park system, and the Chicago World's Fair. But it is fair to say that concentration on these large canvases of romantic urban landscaping of boulevards, civic drives, parks, cemeteries, and monuments tends to distort or at least overwhelm some of the other issues of garden design in the second half of the nineteenth century. Olmsted was far more a pioneer in the field of large-scale urban design and landscape planning than as a garden designer.

VICTORIAN GARDEN DILEMMAS

By the middle of the nineteenth century, Victorian gardeners on both sides of the Atlantic were trying to figure out which of two garden paths to follow—the straight, classical, symmetrical, architectonic, and continental, or the more picturesque, self-consciously irregular, and "natural." Henry Winthrop Sargent had been impressed with the revival of Renaissance formality in the gardens of some of

In this small urban garden, photographed by a Dr. Barnum in 1865, Victorian taste for intricate details, color, and pattern in interior decoration was pursued outdoors. The role of the nurseryman in supplying flowers for carpet bed planting was important, unless the owner had a greenhouse or solarium. Madison County Historical Society, Oneida, New York.

The inherent power of the beauty of natural scenery, in other words, could, like a magic laser beam, confer health and well-being upon its beholder. To preserve the healing power of "the scene of beauty," Olmsted believed that all of the natural, original features of the landscape must be kept inviolate. Improvements at Yosemite were to be minimal, all roads hidden and structured as inconspicuously as possible. All service facilities and buildings were to be resisted no matter what the inconvenience might be for the eager public who was anxious to explore every corner of the new park.

Olmsted's management policy was prethe great estates he had recently visited in England. Well-traveled and well-heeled Englishmen had earlier been impressed with the old formal gardens of France and Italy, which seemed to them a more sympathetic type of setting for their classical country palaces such as Woburn Abbey, Chatsworth, and Blenheim than the old-fashioned Brownian parks they had inherited.

American architects, and particularly those who had trained in the tradition of the Beaux-Arts or spent a year at the new American Academy in Rome, agreed with the Formal Garden School. They admired the restored and reconstituted gardens of England with their strong architectural character at Montacute House, Cliveden, and at Athelhampton where the formal garden was congenial with the older architectural styles. The New Yorker Charles Platt (1861–1933) was so enthralled with the surviving Renaissance and Baroque gardens in Italy that he was moved to write a small book, *Italian Gardens,* on the subject in 1894. More sophisticated Americans were fed up with Victorian taste in both house and garden, so Platt's book found a small but eagerly sympathetic audience wanting to find acceptable alternatives to eclectic chaos.

The novelist Edith Wharton (1862–1937), with her architect friend Ogden Codman, Jr., had launched a movement to reform the cluttered American interior with their landmark publication *The Decoration of Houses* (1897). In 1904 Mrs. Wharton decided it was time to do something about the equally hopeless American garden. As a cultivated American expatriate and observer, Wharton believed that certain useful rules of good design could be drawn from the Renaissance gardens of Italian villas. "In the modern revival of gardening," she wrote in the introduction to *Italian Villas and Their Gardens,* "so little attention is paid to first principles of the art" of garden design. Americans should study closely old Italian gardens in order to understand the fundamentals. "The garden-lover should not content himself with a vague enjoyment" of these romantically overgrown and crumbling survivors of a remote, Golden Age of gardening and more importantly of living. "He should observe, for instance, that the old Italian garden was meant to be lived in—a use to which at least in America, the modern garden is seldom put." The grounds of the villa, she pointed out, were invariably placed within easy access of the house and with paths broad enough for two or more to walk abreast in conversation. In such a garden, plenty of shade is essential for summer. Terraces and alleys should be placed to effect a transition from the geometric lines of the architecture of the house into the surrounding woodlands—"each step away from architecture was a nearer approach to nature"—but it should be subtle and carefully worked out in stages of gradually relaxed composition.[65]

Mrs. Wharton was particularly distressed by the interior decorator's approach to garden design, believing that "a marble bench, gazebo or sun-dial was all that was necessary to give an Italian 'effect.'" She was almost as critical of the dominant role of the flower enthusiast and plantsman. Since flowers were "quite secondary in the Italian garden and are a late and infrequent adjunct to its beauties," she had a distaste for the Victorian obsession with flamboyant, exotic floral displays. In the first sentence of the Introduction she joins the issue head-on: ". . . to enjoy and appreciate the Italian garden-craft one must always bear in mind that it is independent of floriculture." The deeper, more permanent harmony of the design could be achieved only by eliminating flowers altogether or at least controlling them, "thinking" them away. Above all, "adventurous effects" in formal display must be banished as ruthlessly as the heavy velvet curtains, ornate furniture, and tables covered with tasteless bibelots were to be swept out of claustrophobic parlors and libraries.[66]

Wharton was not calling for Americans to mimic Italian garden design but rather urging them to grasp the underlying spirit: "a marble sarcophagus and a dozen twisted columns will not make an Italian garden; but a piece of

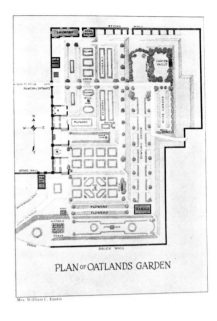

PLAN of OATLANDS GARDEN

Mrs. William C. Eustis.

In the late nineteenth century, Mrs. William C. Eustis, owner of the Virginia plantation Oatlands, expanded the original eighteenth-century garden into a full-blown estate garden with classic details. European ideas were translated into an American vocabulary that overwhelmed the older, simpler layout.

ground laid out and planted on the principles of the old garden craft will be, not indeed an Italian garden in the literal sense, but what is far better, a garden as well adapted, to its surroundings as were the models which inspired it."[67]

TWENTIETH-CENTURY SOLUTIONS

During the first decades of the twentieth century, American architects who designed elaborate houses for rich industrialists managed to hold on to the gardens of these estates as their preserves. But the cult of the Italian garden had reached the United States through secondhand English interpretations and, more often than not, with the same excesses and misunderstandings deplored by Mrs. Wharton. The results were often lifeless, dispiriting pastiches of misplaced fountains, stretches of Italianate balustrade along terraces, and vistas leading nowhere in particular. The lack of an indigenous, national gardening tradition, or even of a regional one except in neglected corners of the Old South, left America as open to eclectic influences in landscape design as it had been in architecture. The new fortunes were totally unprepared to do anything but to follow the most expensive garden solution.

The Landscape Architect

Charles Platt, who was instrumental in shaping the new profession of landscape architect, was not by training an architect but had studied painting and engraving in Paris in the 1890s. It was during his student travels in Italy that he became captivated by the Italian gardens, much as Mrs. Wharton had been, which helped him provide the new field of landscape architecture with the reassurance and validation that only European sources of garden design could bestow.

Platt's articles and his book on Italian gardens secured him his first design commission. His patrician family connections and his appreciation of European culture recommended him to well-traveled clients who were unsympathetic to the vulgarity of most American gardens.

Platt seemed to understand intuitively the internal logic of Italian design and how it could be adapted to the American setting. Much of his work was for large country estates where he discovered that the architects seemed unable to sympathetically adjust their houses to his garden design. It was through "the garden gate" that Platt entered architecture, influencing the direction of estate landscape planning during the critical years before and following World War I when endless money was being poured into new "country places," a label that has, in fact, been attached to the era.

One of the first women to achieve success as a landscape architect was Beatrix Farrand (1872–1959), who happened to be a niece of Edith Wharton. Like her novelist aunt, Farrand grew up in the rarefied world of old New York society—"a tight little world . . . old decencies, stratified codes, [and a] tradition of elegance," in the words of Henry James, who knew the scene intimately.[68]

Privately educated by tutors and with perhaps some introduction to drawing at the Académie des Beaux-Arts in Paris, Farrand followed the advice of family friend Charles Sprague Sargent, dean of American horticulture and professor at the Arnold Aboretum near Boston, to travel and study gardening.

Her trip to Europe in 1895 allowed her to concentrate on Italian gardens before going on to England. There she met Gertrude Jekyll and visited Penshurst Place in Kent whose restored garden was much praised by Jekyll in her *Some English Gardens* (1904). Farrand found the terraces and soft impressionistic lawns at Penshurst, with their picturesquely placed trees and perennial borders diffusing the formal outlines of the architecture, particularly appealing. It was a style of gardening that would soon find its way to America through the efforts of the fledgling American students.[69]

On her return to New York in 1896, Farrand received her first commission from William Garrison of Tuxedo, New York. Three years later she was the only woman to join the founding group of the professional association, the American Society of Landscape Architects. Farrand's reputation quickly grew, first among private clients and then with major universities. Her most important, large-scale projects were at Princeton (1913–1941) and Yale (1924–1947).

Farrand was, in her personal sympathies and cultivation, very much an Anglophile and like Gertrude Jekyll called herself a landscape designer or landscape architect. She was not only influenced by Jekyll's work and writing but she also understood William Robinson's use of native, wild plants in a naturalistic setting. The spirit of Jekyll and Robinson—that "simplicity of aim"—was translated onto the pastoral landscape of Farrand's slopes and woodland she created on the edge of the formal gardens of Dumbarton Oaks.

Her most celebrated work is the gardens of

Edith Wharton's call for a new type of garden "as well adapted to its surroundings as were the models which inspired it" in Europe is well summed up at Dumbarton Oaks in Washington, D.C., which was designed by Beatrice Farrand between 1921 and 1947 Photo: Derek Fell.

OVERLEAF
The pool, steps, and tulip border in the garden at Dumbarton Oaks, on the left, and the pebble garden, on the right. Photos: Derek Fell.

OPPOSITE AND LEFT
The gardens of Villa
Vizcaya, near Miami,
Florida, laid out be-
tween 1912 and 1916,
represent the finest in-
terpretation in America
of a sixteenth-century
Italian garden. Photos:
Charles Marden Fitch.

on his palette," was to be an important garden legacy.[71]

Unlike Jekyll's working methods of sending her planting schemes and plans through the mail and rarely visiting the site, Farrand's included the skillful management of a busy, professional office. She was prepared to give her rich clients everything they needed or could afford. It was an era of domestic American opulence, of aesthetic optimism, and of the innocence captured by Farrand's aunt in some of her novels, soon to disappear. A characteristic passage from Wharton's *Twilight Sleep* evokes the landscape gardens of a new American estate that could have been on the North Shore of Long Island, Boston, Philadelphia, or a dozen other affluent enclaves: "Seventy-five thousand bulbs this year, she thought as the motor swept by the sculptured gateway, just giving and withdrawing a flash of turf sheeted with amber and lilac, in a setting of twisted and scalloped evergreens."[72]

Historical Restorations and Regional Styles

The most influential force in American garden design during the second quarter of the twentieth century was not an individual or brilliant school of landscape designers. It was, rather, a group of archaeologists, architects, and historians assembled by John D. Rockefeller, Jr., to recreate the former seat of royal authority in Williamsburg, Virginia. Within a half-dozen years, following the first meeting between the philanthropist and Dr. W. A. R. Godwin, rector of Bruton Parish Church, formal gardens of the old provincial capital long gone except for a stray box or crepe myrtle were miraculously flourishing to the astonishment and pleasure of millions of Americans. It had never before occurred to most visitors who now walked in the palace gardens of Governor Spotswood or in the only slightly less opulent private gardens nearby that the American past had once har-

Views of the gardens at Old Westbury, on Long Island, New York, which were designed by George Crowley in 1906. Photos: Pamela Harper.

Restored terraces at the Governor's Palace in Colonial Williamsburg in Virginia. Photo: Everett Scott.

bored such pockets of unexpected splendor. The boldness and inventions of the archaeologists and the architects were breathtaking. "Even the winter holly, the yellow jasmine of spring, have to produce colonial credentials before they are allowed to come to berry or flower," the poet John Peale Bishop wrote in his essay on Mr. Rockefeller's Other City. "The pattern of the box in the Governor's knot garden can be vouched for by the Bodleian librarian. A hundred gardens of the period in Virginia, the Carolinas and Maryland have been searched, photographed and measured; as many more have given up their neglected box trees. . . . Over one of the Governor's gates now climbs a rose which was in the ground when Cornwallis marched unwarily into the Peninsula." [73]

With the flood of books and articles on the garden reconstructions at Williamsburg followed by other restorations throughout the East and Middle South, gardens in Texas, Illinois, Missouri, and California that suddenly claimed colonial credentials became a fashionable rage.

Even before Dr. Godwin met Mr. Rockefeller, interest in early Virginia houses and their gardens had been growing, paralleling the renewed appreciation of early American architecture, art, and furniture. George Washington's gardens and grounds at Mount Vernon had been gradually restored by the Mount Vernon Ladies Association with increasing accuracy in design and planting detail. The house and grounds of Monticello had been the subject of extensive reconstruction under the direction of Fiske Kimball (1924–1955), who as early as 1916 had written the first serious article on Thomas Jefferson's contributions to American landscape practices.

With the explosion of parvenu American

The original research
and planning of the re-
stored or often recreated
gardens of Williams-
burg, as here at the
Wythe House, was car-
ried on by Arthur
Shurcliff. Through his
work, Colonial Wil-
liamsburg became an
influential force in
American design.
Photo: Everett Scott.

Milburne, the James River villa and garden, was designed in 1934 by William Lawrence Bottomley, who did this site plan. The upper horseshoe drive leads down a slope to the house, where the river side presented a difficult site. Bottomley mastered this by working with Charles F. Gillette, a landscape architect of Richmond, Virginia.

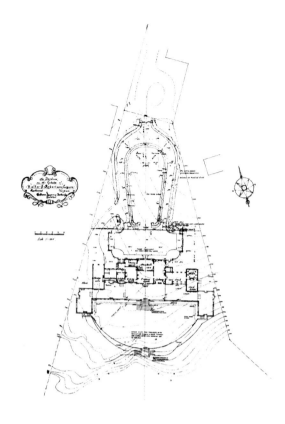

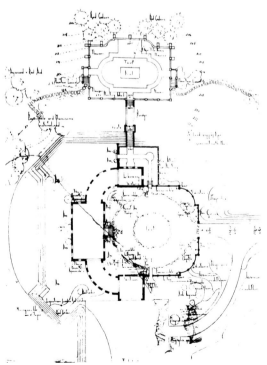

The mature results of many of the Bottomley houses in Virginia are the work of Charles Gillette, who prepared this planting and site plan in 1924 for Nordley and often carried on with the clients after the architect's work was finished. He is an important regional landscape architect who deserves wider attention. William O'Neal and Christopher Weeks, *The Work of William Lawrence Bottomley in Richmond.*

fortunes in the years following World War I, new country estates sprang up outside every American city. Kimball, who had been one of the leading advocates of "striving for a style which shall be specifically modern and American," argued that this building splurge should inspire a "conscious revival or perpetuation of local traditions of style, material and workmanship."[74] Through Kimball's energy and scholarship, studies of regional architecture began to spread in many of the former English colonies from Massachusetts to Georgia.

The translation of regional American architectural and landscape heritage into modern suburban estates by William Lawrence Bottomley (1883–1951) is a contribution to American design in the twentieth century that has been largely ignored. Soundly trained in the classic Beaux-Arts tradition, Bottomley gained his reputation as a residential architect during the building boom of the 1920s. His first commission, for the design of a villa in the suburbs of Richmond, Virginia, in what he called "James River Georgian" style, was in 1922. The success of "Nordley" was immediate and scores of local commissions followed.

Bottomley was of a generation that believed that the landscape setting for a house was as important as the architecture. The "right landscape treatment is essential," he wrote, "and the architect should design the lawns, terraces and roads immediately about the house."[75] Even though his Richmond villas had none of the historic constraints imposed by the archaeologists at Williamsburg, Bottomley admired the work of Arthur Shurcliff, the Boston landscape architect who directed the initial restorations of the gardens at the colonial capital. Like Shurcliff and others who had worked on the Williamsburg restoration, Bottomley was captivated by the beautiful yet unspoiled Virginia countryside and the tradition of civilized domestic arrangements in the old Virginian country house and grounds. "The Virginian families who maintained this tradition," he wrote in 1929, "were careful to nourish it and to enrich it as much as possible, by drawing on inspiration outside. . . . But the importations were so thoroughly absorbed into the Virginia Tradition that it remained absolutely American—American of the Old South."[76] For Bottomley and his circle of rich, successful Richmond admirers, it was a garden myth that still had creative vitality. Bottomley could and did allow his Richmond gardens to indulge in romantic inventions, but he was quick to browbeat hapless clients with ancient Virginian precedents if they attempted to assert their own untutored, wayward tastes or ideas. When Mrs. Benjamin Smith suggested that "two evergreens" might be nice by her Palladian front door at Nordley, the architect wasted no time in putting her in her place. "Where did the idea of flanking the front door with evergreens come from? I feel it is not yours. It would look like an attempt to imitate a California Bunglehouse or a neo-Italian Villa at Asbury Park."[77] He recommended that she drive down to Shirley, the eighteenth-century Carter plantation on the James River, where she for herself could see some ancient plantings and garden flowers firsthand. Mrs. Smith dutifully went and on her return made a list of flowers she admired at Shirley, a list that would have had Gertrude Jekyll's firm approval: cowslips, Persian lilac, lily of the valley, blue perennial dwarf phlox, pansies, japonica, iris, yellow jasmine, fig bushes, peonies, yellow forsythia, calycanthus, forget-me-nots, and roses. Bottomley and his landscape architect Charles Gillette then proceeded to incorporate these humble country cousins among the more exotic scented vines, anemones, and potted oleanders that Bottomley also had in mind for Nordley.

Bottomley's Richmond villas and grounds captured a growing feeling of nostalgia and appreciation for a vanished American past. They exuded, as did other neocolonial revivals in the fashion and taste of the period, an attempt to revive a setting for a vanishing way of life that was exceedingly pleasant for those who could afford to keep up the pretense well into the second quarter of the twentieth cen-

tury. Bottomley, like Edwin Lutyens whom he admired, believed that the revival and perpetuation of local traditions and style should be, in Kimball's words, the "dominant force" in country house design—but one, as Kimball ominously and correctly warned, that would not last forever. "If the choice of forms is retrospective and dependent, we may quiet our artistic conscience by reflecting that our civilization is still fundamentally that of a passing era, and that a truly creative art can triumph only with a new social order."[78]

It is hard to say just how much this poignant, nostalgic search for a past was fed by American literature of the period. The European expatriates of Henry James and Edith Wharton's era had complained that the American past lacked any visible, historic, picturesque texture—no ancient families, no ruins, no crumbling manor houses, no overgrown gardens like those scattered throughout the European countryside. But another generation of American writers was beginning to find more evidence of traditions than many had suspected, particularly in sections of the Old South where time had left surviving fragments of history largely undisturbed.

A New American Style

If gardeners as well as poets, writers, and architects searched for a usable past along the James River and countless other early settlements of the American continent, their midwestern counterparts were looking for other inspirations in the native fields, woods, and prairies of Illinois and Wisconsin. James River plantations were as remote from Frank Lloyd Wright's Racine, Wisconsin, as the châteaux of the Loire Valley. The folio edition of *Great Georgian Houses of America* edited by Bottomley, displaying obvious debts of inspiration to Old World traditions, was not what Wright and at least a few of his generation were looking for in American building traditions. In his article "The American Country House," Fiske Kimball had sympathetically confessed that

"the striving for a style which shall be specifically modern and American has had to face heavy odds since the overwhelming popular victory of the classical at Chicago in 1893 [i.e., at the World's Columbian Exposition]." But he admitted that a group of "progressives rallied by Mr. Sullivan and Mr. Wright have established a certain sovereignty in the vicinity of Chicago and have even secured recognition by foreign powers while still being regarded by our own ruling authorities as rebels beyond the pale of law."[79]

Frank Lloyd Wright (1867–1959), who did not go to Europe until he was forty and after he had already discovered Japan, was an artist in the American tradition of Emerson, Thoreau, and Andrew Jackson Downing. Like these creative predecessors, he held to the romantic notion that nature itself held the key to inspiration, a poetic preoccupation that would continue to inform his work into the modern movement. Wright never seemed to lose his boyhood vision of an ideal, pastoral garden reflected in his native Wisconsin farmland, a seemingly mystic terrain in which there was a direct, vital link between the landscape and the built forms it inspired.[80]

The paradise of Wright's childhood was his family farm in Spring Green in southern Wisconsin, a piece of topography known as the "Driftless Area." Like Columbus's Garden of Eden that he knew had somehow survived the Flood and would be found in the New World, the region of Spring Green, too, had been miraculously saved from destruction by the last glacier when it was diverted by the protective Baraboo hills that surrounded it.

Both in his architectural work and in his writings, Wright expressed his profound organic affinity with nature and his efforts to probe its inner meaning. "Man takes a positive hand in creation whenever he puts a building upon the earth beneath the sun," he wrote in *An American Architecture*. "If he has birthright at all, it must consist in this: that he, too, is no less a feature of the landscape than the rocks, trees, bears or bees of that nature to which he owes his being."[81]

Frank Lloyd Wright's Fallingwater was designed to fit seamlessly into the woods of western Pennsylvania. Photo: Everett Scott.

For all his ego, Wright turned Fallingwater over to nature's curatorship. Photo: Everett Scott.

Nowhere else in the idiom of modern architecture have building and nature achieved a closer unity than at Fallingwater (1936), Wright's house for Edgar J. Kaufmann at Bear Run, Pennsylvania. Here stream, waterfall, rocks, and trees were orchestrated into the mathematics of a concept so unified that architecture, engineering, and landscape design become inseparable. At Taliesin West (1938), his own house and studio near Scottsdale, Arizona, Wright married architecture to the tawny windswept desert in a setting that seemed to him as if imbued with consciousness: "The long, low lines of colorful, windswept terrain, the ineffable dotted line, the richly textured plain, great striated, stratified masses lying noble and quiet or rising with majesty above the vegetation of the desert floor: nature masonry is piled up into ranges upon ranges of mountains that seem to utter a form of language of their own."[82]

There is in Wright's faith in nature's power to inspire both through its immutable laws and through its beauty something of the spirit Jefferson tried to express in his *Notes on the State of Virginia*. Jefferson's appropriation into his domestic gardens of the ocean of landscape that could be viewed from Monticello's mountaintop anticipates Wright's majestic appreciation of his natural surroundings.

The landscape architect and contemporary of Wright whose philosophy and work most complemented the Prairie School of architecture was Jens Jensen (1860–1951). Born in Denmark, Jensen settled in Chicago in 1886 where he began his professional life as a gardener. Jensen's work on public parks around Chicago and in the planning of private estates relied heavily on the use of native midwestern trees and plants. Jensen believed that nature and ecology had a new and urgent message for man caught up in the accelerating congestion of urban life. Man, nature, and the garden had to redefine their relationship as the urban environment continued to undermine the ancient connections. The received principles governing those old connections could no longer function in the face of a new technology that was cutting all recognizable links between man and his natural environment. The garden was no longer, as Francis Bacon had defined it, a place for man to escape from the threats of nature; in the twentieth century it was becoming the last refuge from men and man-made depredation.

Jensen's Lincoln Memorial Garden and wilderness refuge in Springfield, Illinois, was based on a deceptively simple plan. Created on former farmland on the shores of Lake Illinois, the garden was planted with young native trees and shrubs massed together "for formal protection as in nature." Fifty years later it is impossible to detect the hand of a designer, so well did Jensen manage to return the once-cleared Illinois farm to an embowered natural woodland that would have satisfied Thoreau. As Alfred Caldwell wrote in his biography of Jensen, the designer's "sense of space repudiates the tyranny of closure. It repudiates the sterile masonry terrain of the cities today that are prisons, spaceless and visionless. It asserts the right to wide green earth."[83]

The Modern Movement

With the 1932 exhibition of the International Style at the Museum of Modern Art in New York, European and American modern masters of architecture—Wright, Sullivan, Gropius, Le Corbusier, Mies van der Rohe—were triumphant. Classicism in buildings and in the garden began a precipitous retreat. Its last stronghold remained in the field of domestic architecture and garden design, and in the public architecture of Washington where Lewis Mumford railed against the "birdcage of Peristyles" erected on the Tidal Basin as a memorial to Thomas Jefferson.

For Christopher Tunnard, it was obvious that the garden had been passed over by the modern movement: ". . . the garden of today cannot be called contemporary in spirit as can the modern movement in architecture, sculpture or painting," he wrote in 1938. "It is not

The garden of the Tremaine House in Santa Barbara, California, designed by Richard Neutra. Although born in Vienna and schooled in Europe, Neutra worked in New York and Chicago before joining Wright at Taliesin for several months. After touring Japan in 1930, Neutra saw his work in Southern California recognized as a bridge between the International Style in Europe and the oriental unification of architecture and environment. Photo: Julius Shulman.

of our time, but of a sentimental past; a body with no head and very little heart. Imagination is dead, romance a mere excuse for extravagance in decoration. . . . The great white bird of modern architecture has therefore not yet found a secure and decorative perch such as would be provided in a truly modern setting." [84]

Most of the leaders of the modern movement seemed indifferent or unconcerned about ornamental "perches." The classic principles of landscape design were not a part of their education nor did this represent an issue serious enough to draw much ideological fire. Most American architects working in the International Style thought they agreed with Henry-Russell Hitchcock's much-quoted but somewhat vague dictum, "The important principle is the preservation of all possible values previously in existence in the landscape setting." Le Corbusier (1887–1965) envisioned a kind of bucolic Poussinesque countryside for his suburban villa outside of Paris. "I shall place this house on columns in a beautiful corner of the countryside; we shall have twenty houses rising above the long grass of a meadow where cattle will continue to graze. . . . Grass will border the roads; nothing will be disturbed—neither the trees, the flowers, nor the flocks and herds. . . . The dwellers . . . domestic lives will be set within a Virgilian dream." [85] Richard Neutra (1892–1970) believed a house should function as kind of sanitarium with "generous opening[s] to health agents and a biologically minded appreciation of the soil in which all life is rooted." For others, the romantic, picturesque English park inherited from the eighteenth century would seem an ideal place to park the new "Machine for Living" and contemplate nature from a neutral position. Olmsted's mature Central Park had fortunately provided the picturesque setting for all of the skyscrapers crowding around the park's edges.

Modernists working in Latin America were not weighed down with the confusing eclecticism that history had bequeathed American architects and garden designers. Luis Barragán (1902–1989) the Mexican artist and Roberto Burle Marx (b. 1909) of Brazil were trained as artists in Europe where Barragán came under the spell of the writings of Ferdinand Bac, intellectual, painter, and landscape architect. Bac had written a book on Hispano-Moorish gardens called *Jardin enchantés* that made a deep impression on Barragán's thinking. The desire to create a garden, both men agreed, was an effort to unite, in Bac's words, "with the old solidarity which attracts all of us—that is the ambition to express through matter a common sentiment in many men and women in search for a contact with nature, through creating a place to rest, of pleasant serenity."[86]

As with Wright's Wisconsin farm, Barragán recalled in his architecture and in his garden designs the memory of the Edenic wonder of his own family's ranch near the Mexican village of Mazamitla.

It was a pueblo with hills, formed by houses with tile roofs and immense eaves to shield passersby from the heavy rains which fall in that area. Even the earth's color was interesting because it was red earth. In this village, the water distribution system consisted of great gutted logs, in the form of troughs, which ran on a support structure of tree forks. . . . This aqueduct crossed over the town, reaching patios, where there were great stone stables, with cows and chickens, all together. The channeled logs, covered with moss, dripped water all over town, of course. It gave this village the ambience of a fairy tale . . . there are no photographs. I have only its memory.[87]

Through poetic recollections and a nostalgic awareness of his personal past at Mazamitla, Barragán believed that architecture and the garden should exist as a continuum of space. The garden, simply put, was "architecture without ceiling." Barragán's architecture—solid, simple, logical, timeless—complemented and was subordinate to the surrounding somber mountains and wilderness. It is the sensitive juxtaposition of his buildings to their larger environment that gives, in the words of the architect Emilio Ambasz, "these creations the aura of inexorability which classical myths once possessed. It was as if Nature and Man's creations joined in an atavistic chant, monodic on first hearing, but which slowly began to reveal its richly intricate chromatic structure and subordinated differences of tone."[88]

Barragán visited the Moorish gardens of the Alhambra in 1924. The silence, magic, and solitude of the progressive spaces animated by the brilliant use of fountains and water channels was to have a profound effect on his work. The vision of Morocco and Moroccan gardens, which he knew only through photographs and books before 1951 when he finally traveled in North Africa, was another important influence. The Islamic courtyards, the high walls defining the connected spaces, the music of the water all play a part in his work. "Architecture [and gardens] besides being spatial is also musical. That music is played with water. The importance of walls is that they isolate one from the street . . . walls create silence. From that silence you can play with water as music."[89] Barragán saw the Islamic garden as "endowed with erotic and metaphysical properties," a place "for the pleasures of the senses and the mind," a bewitched region "leading to fantastic dreams

and fable making" and felt it represented an image of the garden as old as the art of garden-making itself.[90] Barragán's own gardens, with their extraordinary poetic compositions of materials, color, water, and light, are still among the most satisfying creations in the twentieth century. By reducing nature "to human proportion and in the service to man," the garden becomes in Barragán's words "the most efficient refuge against the modern world's aggression."[91]

Barragán's visionary attempt to reconcile man and nature at his house at El Pedregal seems to have evolved from his fascination with the wild, inhospitable lava terrain bordering the river La Magdalena near Mexico City. The topography of purplish gray lava rock forming ominous, convoluted crevices had come into being when Xitle volcano erupted twenty-five hundred years ago. Abandoned to exotic vegetation, it had become a haven for reptiles, scorpions, and wild plants. It was this sinister piece of volcanic ground that the artist proposed to transform into a garden refuge, a place to meditate and at the same time enjoy a mythical landscape violently created before the Tolmec and Aztec civilizations.

At Barragán's house at Tacubaya, begun in 1947, the architecture and garden are fused.

The vocabulary of design—rough, natural materials, lofty austerity, enclosing walls—recalls in a subtle visual drama both the art of Islam and its attenuated historical connections to the provincial architecture of Mexico. The garden itself was allowed to go wild within the walled enclosure, imposing its presence on the interior of the house through the large windows. A liquid, palpable silence seems to engulf the garden and overwhelms the adjoining, walled-in terrace. Like a medieval *giardino segreto* or an intimate Roman courtyard frozen in time by the volcano at Pompeii, its arresting, seductive animation comes only from "passing birds . . . winds and migrant clouds."

Barragán's equestrian school at San Cristóbal is his most complex creation, evoking in its elements of plaza, stable, house, and above all in the water his childhood *pueblo*. The artist's private memories of Mazamitla—the aqueduct bringing the water from great distances, the patios where fountain and basins receive the water, the dripping moss—have all been reformulated in his poetry of space of both architecture and garden.

In their ability to play with and to satisfy the human senses, gardens have always served through an intricate conceptual system, and Barragán's gardens are in the great tradition of garden art at its most sublime. As a visible source of moral instruction, "a program of metaphysical imperatives," Barragán's garden walls may well provide "one of the last defenses to preserve centuries of thought and emotion."[92]

A painter, sculptor, and designer of sets and landscapes, Roberto Burle Marx is considered the consummate artist-gardener of the twentieth century. In his lifetime he has been able to impose *O Stilo* Burle Marx on the dramatic and turbulent landscape of his native Brazil. Trained in the Beaux-Arts tradition, where little distinction was made between painting, architecture, and design, Burle Marx also studied at the Dahlem Botanical Gardens in Berlin. There his scientific curiosity was attracted to Brazil's extraordinary botanical riches which he determined to incorporate in his garden designs. By 1938 he was given the commission for a roof garden at the new Ministry of Health and Education in Rio de Janerio, a building conceived in design by Le Corbusier. While his plant hunting into the Amazon Valley and other remote spots in the country continued, he was overwhelmed with new commissions from the young architects in Brazil who were leading the modern movement in South America.

In his Brazilian gardens, Burle Marx has translated the abstract forms of modern painting into a contemporary landscape. Native plants and exotic flowers arranged into sculptural groups with a free-flowing framework of paths, pools, and ground cover characterize his work. His painting aesthetic in nature is playful, powerful, and knowing.

There is in the Burle Marx gardens a powerful sense of motion, of flowing energy, a combination of the Baroque and of Humphry Repton. As in Baroque gardens, there is an exhilarating feeling of movement in the organization of the space and in its sudden shifts and surprises, giving the composition a distinctly musical quality. It is this emotional element in the Brazilian's work that is so congenial to the modern sensibility.

Geoffrey Jellicoe has also pinpointed the ability of Burle Marx's gardens to respond to "a new set of emotions and reactions arising primarily from air travel. . . . His water curves with their crisp line of definition, are analogous to coast-line curves seen from the air, rather than land-locked lakes seen from the ground; the imposition of one pattern upon another is like the passage of cloud shadows over the landscape. . . . Certainly those gardens are designed for people themselves in motion . . . to movement in the beholder, a symptom of the restless energy of the age in which we live."[93]

Working in the spirit of twentieth-century art, Burle Marx, more than any other garden designer, has been able to lift the garden onto a plane equal to modern painting and architecture.

POSTSCRIPT

The garden as a work of art, an aesthetic composition beyond the pursuit of horticulture, therapy, or extravagance in support of power, has all but disappeared from the modern world. Yet few civilizations before this century have failed to establish a garden tradition. Whether the garden was meant to serve primarily some useful purpose or a deeper spiritual imperative, its creation and survival has been an integral part of the fabric of each society. No matter how diverse the geographical and chronological factors that shaped a particular garden tradition, utility and art could and often did intersect or coincide within it. The threat of wild beasts or of trespassing neighbors produced the garden wall and fence. The need to shelter tender plants from frost led to arbors and protective shade. Even such elaborate refinements as the water stairs at the Villa Lante and the shimmering basins at Versailles share an ancestry that is no less humble than it is ancient.

The basic elements of composition available to the modern garden-maker have scarcely changed from their commonplace origins, yet they do not seem to be able to produce the poetry and music they once did. While we sporadically struggle to remake nature in forms that are compatible with our own image, we seem no longer able to define our identity in the alien, fragmented, overcrowded environment we inhabit. Concocting a bogus image of a lost paradise only exposes our impoverishment.

Certainly the pressure of massive overpopulation in monstrous cities has raised critical questions about the form, function, and even the survival of gardens in any conventional sense. Dame Sylvia Crowe has attempted to be reassuring when she points out that "no space is too small to be developed into an oasis of peace, privacy and plants."[94] Yet this seems to put us back somewhere in the walled gardens of some barbarous medieval town or in the purlieus of Islam, but without any of the metaphysics to transform our isolation into a civilized, revitalizing environment.

The realities of restricted space have rarely been confronted in the major traditions of Western gardens dominated, and the expansive vista of the Beaux-Arts avenue was still the ideal composition for garden-makers like Farrand and Platt. Gertrude Jekyll's celebrated border at Munstead Wood ran to some three hundred feet, something that is overlooked by her later admirers. Even William Robinson whose garden philosophy was drawn from the modest tradition of the Arts and Crafts movement made it clear that his ideas were best suited for those who owned extensive "grounds." His drifts of naturalized daffodils alongside grassy drives could require thousands of bulbs and take years to develop. His meadows with a stream or lake bordered by bluebells were not something that could be easily translated into most suburban plots, no matter how enticing they sounded.

In an age that has been recklessly separating itself from the life of the soil and any stimulating proximity with nature, a concerned few have toyed with the possibility that the East might hold an answer for the crowded city. Christopher Tunnard, disillusioned with doctrinaire solutions, urged that Japan's mastery of nature in small spaces offered garden designers some alternative rules. "It is to the gardens of Kyoto that we must return, [where] all is restrained, calculated and under control," he wrote in 1938.[95] But a handful of humble, dedicated Zen priests working in a garden tradition that was old even by the fifteenth century produced, as Russell Page pointed out, something far more profound than mere aesthetic expression or technical virtuosity. Most attempts to translate the Japanese garden into a Western suburb, in London, Westchester, or even in California rarely come off as anything more than a superficial illusion.

Even in the distant past gardens often have

The sculpture garden as an outdoor gallery is a phenomenon of the twentieth century. The architectural setting of the Museum of Modern Art in New York is by Philip Johnson, and the landscape work has been carried out by Robert Zion. Photo: Scott Frances. Courtesy of the Museum of Modern Art.

Paley Park in New York City, designed by Robert Zion, is a triumph of simplicity. It remains one of the most successful urban gardens of this century. In this photograph, the white furniture detracts from the overall design. Photo: Sonja Bullaty/ Angelo Lomeo.

OPPOSITE, TOP
The Pavilion in Parc de la Villette, Paris, designed by Bernard Tschumi. Photo: Everett Scott.

OPPOSITE, BOTTOM
The J. Irwin Miller garden in Columbus, Indiana, designed by Dan Kiley. Photo: Everett Scott.

taken their forms in a reaction to urban tumult and pressure. The Islamic courtyard garden was a sane asylum in the middle of the surging chaos of Baghdad, Cairo, and Fez. The country villas and gardens of the Medicis served as a refuge from their plague-ridden city of Florence. These garden traditions were not so much nostalgic longing for a lost Eden as a practical response to the complexities of urban society, at least in the beginning.

In the twentieth century, an urge to recapture, preserve, or suggest the bucolic countryside that is now disappearing under the bulldozer of uncontrolled technological expansion and urban sprawl has led to the creation of "wild" and "natural" gardens in the middle of our steel, brick, glass, and concrete jungles. This desperate craving for contrast to urban life is understandable and has become a powerful force in urban landscape and garden design. The great public landscape parks of Birkenhead and Central Park were efforts to find both a moral and aesthetic alternate for masses of people who found themselves trapped in alien, unfamiliar cities.

Like the public parks, the romantic landscape cemetery was also a reaction to accelerated urbanization and the problems it was creating. In the United States, the new cemeteries were viewed as public pleasure-grounds on the order of a public park as well as a resting place for the dead. The awe and delight in the natural beauty of these burial parks derived in part from the belief that even if nature had been assisted by man, it was still closer to the spirit of its Creator.

The supreme example of a landscaped cemetery park in the twentieth century is Woodland Cemetery designed by Gunnar Asplund (1885–1940) outside of Stockholm. Because Sweden is a small country on the periphery of Europe, its historic fabric at the end of the nineteenth century had escaped the obvious damage sustained by countries where overpopulation and technology had caused major dislocations in the cities and in the countryside. Paralleling the search by William Morris in industrial England to find renewal in the

vernacular past and in native aesthetic traditions, Scandinavian artists began to discover inspirations in medieval arts and handicrafts. A romantic, naturalistic artist like Asplund could merge his identity with these older traditions and be profoundly inspired by the experience.

In the mid-1910s, reacting to an explosive growth of population that had occurred at the end of the nineteenth century, Stockholm's City Fathers decided the city's cemetery space required a major expansion. Asplund and his former classmate Sigurd Lewerentz entered and won the international design competition for a new graveyard.

Rather than turning to the English landscape tradition that had captivated the imagination of contemporary landscape architects in the United States, the two young architects were first drawn to Nordic traditions evident in some of the new parklike cemeteries of Germany. These new cemeteries had deliberately incorporated primeval native forests of pine trees into their compositions. Just as Brown had been inspired earlier by the vernacular English farmland and meadows, young architects of Northern Europe like Asplund were drawn to their own dark, brooding woodlands.

The late-nineteenth-century landscape painters had also begun to rediscover and admire romantic landscape painters like Caspar David Friedrich (1774–1840) whose paintings explored the meaning of nature in ways that were deeply sympathetic, recalling archetypal Nordic landscapes, as Stuart Wrede has written, of "deep evergreen forest, the endless sea, the dolmen on the heath surrounded by oaks and the wayfarer's cross." [96]

In Asplund's interpretation of the forest as a park yet somehow elevated by its transcendental function as a burial ground, nature's imagery is intensified. The architecture of the various chapels at Woodland is subordinated to nature and integrated, but on nature's own terms.

In 1935, Asplund began the design for a new chapel and crematorium. Placed at the

end of a long walk, the complex sits on top of a naturally sloping hill. The worn stone walk running along a low wall that leads up to the chapel recalls elements of the Mediterranean landscape tradition and particularly Pompeii's Via Sepulchra. Asplund had traveled in Italy during his student days, and the remains of the classical world he saw there made a lasting impression on him. It is a part of the poetry of his work that it recalls these romantic memories and incorporates them into the strong yet lyrical passages of Woodland Cemetery. Clearly Asplund drew an important lesson from what he had seen of the relationship of architecture to landscape during his long Mediterranean sojourn in the classical world.

Opposite the main chapel, there is a great, swelling knoll with a tree-lined meditation grove at its top. "It is both the simplest and profoundest of images," as Wrede describes it,

This long wall in Woodland Cemetery, Stockholm, recalls Gunnar Asplund's Italian travels and his interest in classical civilization. Photo: Everett Scott.

OPPOSITE
A view of Woodland Cemetery, Stockholm, Sweden, designed by Gunnar Asplund. Photo: Everett Scott.

The tree-lined meditation grove at the top of a swelling knoll at Woodland Cemetery, Stockholm. Photo: Author.

"one that in its archetypal nature brings us full circle to our beginnings."[97] Time and space in all their dimensions, that great preoccupation of the modern artist, seem to have been released on Asplund's Swedish hillside.

Sylvia Crowe (b. 1901) has concluded that most modern gardens satisfy neither the eye nor the soul. At least one of the causes for the trouble, Dame Sylvia believes, stems from the contemporary temptation of too many undigested garden traditions and aesthetics. We are victims of too many reductive images and too much information from books, museums, easy travel, and ready access to thousands of years of styles, fashions, and patterns of living. "The lack of peace in many gardens today is intensified because, although throughout history garden traditions have fertilized each other, never before have been so many cross currents and so little opportunity for the flood of ideas to evolve a tradition to local conditions."[98]

Few gardens of the twentieth century have been widely admired as works of art worthy of serious investigation and analysis. The psychological and metaphysical speculation that gardens once provoked is out of the question. Comfort, function, and an acceptable display of horticulture seem to be the only qualities most garden and landscape publications are capable of responding to, beyond rather tedious descriptions of the elements that make up the composition. Jory Johnson's observation that any critical discussion of the American garden must ultimately reach into the American landscape itself is a useful alternative strategy.[99] But reaching into the natural, vernacular landscape does not mean trying simply to capture or recreate a piece of "improved" nature to tantalize the starved city dweller. Nor does it mean the spontaneous regeneration of nature in vacant lots through benign neglect.

Beginning with William Robinson and Gertrude Jekyll, this century has a number of models to look to. It was in the neglected village gardens and vanishing yeoman farmsteads that the two found new and stimulating ways of thinking about gardens and gardening. From the commonplace impressions and designs piled up in their imagination—lumpy peony bushes softened by planting them in tall grass, a weeping willow transformed with the bronze drapery of Virginia creeper, a stone wall once seen in the Lake District—the two carried on a successful war against "the ugliest gardens ever made." Foolish old laws laid down by landscape gardeners perpetuate the notion that a garden is a "work of art," Robinson wrote in *The Wild Garden,* ". . . therefore we must not attempt to imitate nature!" "But," he concluded, "the true garden [differs] from all other arts in this that it gives us the living things themselves and not merely representations of themselves in paint, or stone or wood."[100]

Like Robinson, Jekyll kept faith with the complicated rules by which plants and flowers lived—their affinities, competitors, and patterns of reproduction—when she composed her painterly borders. Out of her imaginative study of forgotten corners of her region, she invented a whole new style of garden design. The strength of her response to the spiritual

values of the larger landscape around her enabled her gardens and her partner Edwin Lutyen's architecture to reconcile those divisions that had preoccupied architects and landscape designers for generations.

Roberto Burle Marx, like Jekyll, is both painter and plantsman, and currents from both worlds flow into his Brazilian gardens.

But his appreciation of the powerful Brazilian topography plays an equally strong role in his garden designs. On this he has been quite explicit. Looking from the top of a building in Rio where he was commissioned to design a roof garden, he saw the baroque forms of the distant mountains and introduced a metaphor of their silhouette in the composition.

Brion Cemetery, San Vito d'Altivole, Italy, designed by Carlos Scarpa. Photo: Everett Scott.

The John F. Kennedy Memorial at Runnymede, England, designed by Sir Geoffrey Jellicoe. Photo: Everett Scott.

production and uniformity, the spoiling of natural beauty, the destruction of cultural traditions."[101]

Jellicoe's memorial to John F. Kennedy on an acre of hillside overlooking the historic countryside of Runnymede is a good example of the way he makes us both feel and think our way through the artist's response to a difficult landscape commission. Jellicoe's account of his sensitive analysis of the site is moving and decisive. The idea that an assassinated president of the United States would be memorialized in Great Britain was in itself dramatic and unprecedented. So Jellicoe decided that "the essential visual monument to be was an 'acre' of land taken out of primitive meadowland on the slopes overlooking the flat fields of Runnymede."[102] Everything else was to be secondary. For all of Jellicoe's command and appreciation of other garden traditions, he felt the powerful, quintessential English countryside of Runnymede was the *genius loci*. The meadows of rough pasture, the mixed woodlands, the remnants of ancient hedgerows, and the flatlands below where the Magna Carta was signed not only must be respected but must be allowed to play a primary role in the memorial itself.

As with a good piece of abstract art, there is no visible figurative interest in the Kennedy Memorial nor any seductive, sentimental notes of landscape plantings or flowers. The approach is along an informal path through a wood paralleling the slope. The path is entered through a wicket gate, a subtle reference to the one described in Bunyan's *Pilgrim's Progress*. The path itself "gropes its way upward" along the edge of the remnants of an old forest with no open land to be seen before reaching the stone. At the end of the path made of discretely placed granite sets, the visitor reaches the horizontal, severe stone carved with its tragic message. The woods in their foreboding gloom do in fact recall Dante's "dark wood" as Jellicoe intended. But the skillful, sensitive introduction of a composition that also acknowledges Mondrian, Alexander Pope, Bunyan, Lancelot Brown,

As a scholar, artist, and writer, Sir Geoffrey Jellicoe carries more understanding of garden design traditions into his own work than any other living landscape architect. Yet the diversity of nature, the humane scale and space of older landscapes, and an artist's appreciation of natural beauty have all informed Jellicoe's designs. He too has eloquently expressed in his work and in his writing, his resistance to the modern world's determination "to produce an environment contrary to the condition of man and therefore against his ultimate happiness and welfare." Quoting Sir Julian Huxley's call to arms in an essay directed to the importance of that special divinity in the landscape man must respect, Jellicoe believes "We must combat everything that threatens the variety of interest needed for human fulfillment—the extermination of wildlife, overmechanization, the boredom of mass-

and the Magna Carta into a historic landscape to memorialize a twentieth-century hero requires a high order of intellectual and aesthetic ability. As an allegory in landscape, recalling the unfolding tour along the wooded path of a Japanese garden, where one is drawn by the universal power of a simple, classic Gréek slab, Jellicoe's memorial is a profoundly moving tribute. Fletcher Steele once remarked that the surest proof of the vitality of a design "is its power to provoke again and again question and answer 'Why and Why not. . . . We must be made to think and to feel"—as we surely do at the Kennedy Memorial—"whence must come understanding."[103]

Most gardeners dig no deeper for hidden meaning in their work than to get at some entangling bindweed or intruding thistle. Yet in the physical gestures of gardening with space, fork, trowel, and pruning shears we are linked in our urban disguises with the not-too-distant pastoral world of our common origins, participating in one of man's primal activities. Even as we reenact the simple gestures of survival, we are also engaging in a popular, universal art form that is part of a continuum of history, a language understood around the world. When art and nature collaborate and unite in leading us into a unique aesthetic adventure, we can participate in one of our richest, most satisfying experiences.

Because gardening uniquely engages man and his artifice with living materials to produce a composite creation, garden-making has long fascinated philosophers. Since the results, as John Dixon Hunt has pointed out, must ultimately transcend time as in any work of art, a successful garden must "actually invoke time . . . in which plants, shrubs and trees may grow, seasonal change which alters the whole appearance of a garden four times a year, and even the length of time during which the full extent of a garden's riches are discovered by its visitor."[104]

But beyond the unpredictable contributions of time and the traditions of a particular gardening culture with ties to the past, there is the garden-maker's distant projection of particular views, colors, scale, and even emotions that will probably not be fully realized for years or even generations. So the gardener's devotion that must infuse any garden if it is to survive and mature is in service of an ideal that only future and yet-unborn admirers will see realized. Thus the gardener's vision is in many ways far more conceptual and abstract than that of painters, architects, and poets who will more likely see their work brought to completion and received by the public. Only the gardener must accept on faith that long after his intervention with design, layout, and plantings, his efforts will ultimately form a living experience that approximates his visionary intentions.

But just as our larger environment is now mortally threatened, so is our ability to preserve and sustain a serious garden tradition that has any claim on future generations of admirers. Those forces and convulsions that Sir Julian Huxley identified in his essay as undermining the very foundation of human fulfillment have grown ominously. Even our human capacity to enjoy a garden's complex conceptual system has sadly deteriorated. Visual pollution has dulled our eyes. The level of our sensitivity to garden sounds has been eroded by an unspeakable cacophony. And as for garden scents, it would be unlikely that anyone could write to a friend, as Thomas Jefferson did in 1808 after visiting his friend's Philadelphia greenhouse, asking him to identify by a mutually recalled odor, a flower he had smelled a month earlier.

Aside from sensual pleasures, the garden's practical function down through the ages as a place for contemplation has been important in both East and West. Following Plato's example, the West, it is true, has thought of gardens as a place for intellectual meditation. The Zen garden, on the other hand, has concentrated on material objects—a tree, a rock, a bloom—within the garden as the means to reach a higher level of spiritual understanding. But as Geoffrey Jellicoe has noted, this age-old focus on concentration and introspection within the garden tradition of Japan has not saved the larger environment of that country from desolation in the twentieth century. "The floodtide of materialism . . . has overwhelmed Japan to make her cities unpleasurable, marring her incomparable landscape."[106] All this makes it difficult for any authentic influence of the traditional aesthetic of the Japanese garden to infiltrate the West except in a debased, watered down, meaningless pastiche.

Aside from feelings of serenity and beauty, there is an even more elusive quality that is all too often missing in modern gardens. What one might call magic, fantasy, enchantment, or charm is the most evanescent and subjective of all characteristics of the garden experience. Not all successful gardens, even those that are recognized for their grandeur and beauty, can claim this special transient aura.

Again, it is that equally enigmatic, ambiguous contribution of time that often produces the quality of enchantment that not even the maker could have anticipated or predicted. A particular massing of trees overlooking a terrace may alter the light and shadows in some magical way. The mist of color in a Jekyll flower border may transform a stone wall or nearby pool into an unforgettable memory. Even third-rate statues or urns can lend a note of grace to a vista, if time's cosmetics have muted their surface and missing appendages so they blend into nature's embrace.

It is the progressive, essentially unfinished quality of a garden at every stage of its development and growth that invokes the role of time in its deepest, metaphysical meaning. Time is also a distillation of the cycle of natural law to be enjoyed and contemplated as a metaphor of our own mortality. Yet as Francis Bacon assured even the most skeptical and discouraged gardener, garden-making does enjoy a universal reputation as "the greatest refreshment of the spirits of man."[105]

The problem is that what time requires for its work—stability, patience, and a willingness to postpone perfection—are characteristics that have all but disappeared from modern life, and gardens have suffered as a result.

It is in their understanding and acceptance of the role of time that the amateur gardener and the dedicated plantsman have been able to create some of the most memorable and enchanting gardens of the twentieth century. Ideal growing conditions and a national reputation for managing nostalgia on a grand scale have tended to overshadow this important component in the achievements of English gardeners. Except in the production of bourbon whiskey, time's unique contributions have never been highly valued by Americans. Andrew Jackson Downing foresaw the problems nearly 150 years ago when he began his one-man efforts in public education and reform. It was his melancholy recognition of the inevitable failure of Americans, with their rootless, restless character, to stay put in one place long enough to produce a mature garden that led him to advocate the public park as a practical alternative.

Amateur gardeners by a process of personal, intimate trial and error may have gradually discovered the mysterious laws that plants live by, enabling them to sustain a rich variety of horticulture. The harmony of colors and texture combined with the personal and idiosyncratic touch gives an amateur's garden its unique and pleasurable appeal. For amateur efforts to transcend, as they often do, personal pleasure in the growing of plants, becoming a special world to live in and to look at, some understanding of the laws of composition and unity is necessary. It is in this understanding that the amateur, if he succeeds, overlaps with the professional designer. On the other hand, many professionals could well deepen their grasp of the craft of horticulture, which is not simply spelling nature with a capital "N" as some architects insist on doing. Too many contemporary garden designers reflect an uneasiness and a lack of comprehension of the living and most critical ingredient of their art.

There is among some landscape architects and garden designers a lingering fantasy of a *tabula rasa* where nature can be reduced to an up-to-the-minute formula for the instant re-

demption of the modern environment. But the vagaries of nature forever elude the perfections of technology. The cycles of life and death, of renewal and decay in the garden, run counter to the rational, logical expectations modern science has led us to believe in. Garden poetry, rich with surprise, variety, contrast, a various entertainment of the senses, does not seem to have entered into design possibilities. We miss the "Grotto's thickets and pleasant Park of Deer with Fish Ponds and

other advantages" an English gentleman saw and admired in the seventeenth-century Italian garden during a Grand Tour.[107] Nor is mystery, romance, or charm to be found in minimalist austerity where a few boxed or potted trees have been sadly rushed in to relieve the measured boredom. "Such symmetry," Lord Byron wrote with the French order of things in mind, "is not for solitude."[108]

We take our gardens too seriously perhaps and at the same time not seriously enough, in

A modern variation on age-old Japanese themes in this private garden in Portland, Oregon. Photo: Elvin McDonald.

A restored perennial border designed by Gertrude Jekyll, Manor House, Upton Grey, Hampshire, England.

a responsive, critical way. Somehow we need to recapture that sense of romantic play between living plants and those everyday garden elements that have been around forever—paths, walks, ground covers, walls, water, and earth—and to renew our lost friendship with the garden's devoted, patient partner, time.

Whims, fashions, snap judgments, and "cost-effective" solutions must be resisted. It has always been true, as Francis Bacon pointed out, that men have found it easier "to build stately . . . than to garden finely," because, he concluded, gardening requires time if not a tradition to give it "the greater perfection." [109]

Notes

Introduction

1. Paglia, *Sexual Personae*, p. 105.
2. Jackson, *Necessity for Ruins*, p. 35.

Chapter 1

1. Quoted in Giamatti, *Earthly Paradise*, p. 40.
2. See Grimal, *Jardins romains*. Grimal's book is still the most comprehensive account of the subject, even though recent archaeological reports are not included.
3. Quoted in Gothein, *History of Garden Art*, vol. 1, p. 29.
4. Quoted ibid., p. 30.
5. Quoted ibid., p. 40.
6. Quoted ibid., p. 40.
7. See Battisti, "Natura Artificiosa," pp. 5–6.
8. Thacker, *History of Gardens*, p. 18.
9. Quoted in Giamatti, *Earthly Paradise*, p. 35.
10. Quoted in Chase, *Horace Walpole*, p. 5.
11. Gothein, *History of Garden Art*, vol. 1, p. 53.
12. Quoted in Thompson, "Ancient Gardens," pp. 41–47.
13. These sensual lines of Aristophanes suggest that the Greek garden had moved beyond the utilitarian medical collection of herbs.
14. Quoted in Chase, *Horace Walpole*, p. 48, n. 6.
15. Scully, *Earth, Temple, Gods*, p. 1.
16. Jellicoe and Jellicoe, *Landscape of Man*, p. 117.
17. Quoted in Gothein, *History of Garden Art*, vol. 1, p. 20.
18. Homer, *Odyssey*, p. 467. I am indebted to Christopher Thacker's analysis of the garden of Alcinous. Although, like the Garden of Paradise, Alcinous's garden serves as a major garden image from remote antiquity, it seems already far removed from what we would realistically expect to find in the period of transition from basic agriculture to garden cultivation.
19. The Land of Punt has been located on the coast of Somaliland, now art of Somalia.
20. Quoted in Gothein, *History of Garden Art*, vol. 1, p. 18.
21. Ibid.
22. Brown, *Roman Architecture*, p. 4. Brown's book is a good introduction to its subject.
23. Ibid., p. 19.
24. Pliny, *Letters*, p. 57.
25. Ibid., pp. 75–79, provides the most detailed description of the villa at Laurentum.
26. Ibid., pp. 139, 140.
27. Ibid., pp. 139–44, provides a vivid picture of the Tuscan villa.
28. Brown, *Roman Architecture*, p. 21.
29. Pliny, *Letters*, p. 141.
30. Ibid., p. 139.
31. Varro, *De re rustica*, p. 330.
32. Pliny, *Letters*, p. 77.
33. Jashemski, "Campagnia Peristyle Garden," p. 34.
34. Clark, *Rome and a Villa*, pp. 141–94. Clark's essay "Hadrian's Villa" is a brilliant evocation of the personality of Hadrian as expressed in the villa and the garden.
35. Ibid., pp. 148–49.
36. Ibid., p. 144.

Chapter 2

1. Fairbrother, *Men and Gardens*, p. 66. Although based primarily on English sources, Fairbrother's essay is particularly good on the thinly documented Dark Ages and Middle Ages.
2. Quoted in Gothein, *History of Garden Art*, vol. 1, p. 171.
3. Stannard, "Alimentary and Medieval Uses," p. 74.
4. Harvey, *Medieval Gardens*, p. 364.
5. Quoted in Calkins, "Piero de' Crescenzi," p. 157.
6. Pliny, *Letters*, p. 140.
7. Burrell, *Garden*, p. 113.
8. See Fairbrother, *Men and Gardens*, pp. 63–66. See also Battisti, "Natura Artificiosa," p. 13.
9. Moynihan, *Paradise as a Garden*, p. 39.
10. Stronach, *Pasargadae*, quoted ibid., p. 16.
11. Quoted in MacDougall and Ettinghausen, *Islamic Garden*, p. 72.
12. Koran, pp. 18–19.
13. Pirenna, *Mohammed and Charlemagne*, p. 151.
14. Quoted in Gothein, *History of Garden Art*, vol. 1, p. 152.
15. Dickie, "Islamic Garden in Spain," p. 89.
16. Ibid.
17. Ibid., p. 99.
18. Harvey, *Medieval Gardens*, p. 43. I have relied extensively on Harvey's chapter on "Gardens of Southern Europe," pp. 37–51.
19. Quoted in Gothein, *History of Garden Art*, vol. 1, p. 160.
20. See Van Buren, "Hesdin."
21. Harvey, *Medieval Gardens*, p. 43.
22. Boccaccio, *Decameron*, p. 225.
23. Quoted in Moynihan, *Paradise*, p. 49.
24. Ibid., p. 50.
25. Wescoat, "Mughal Garden," p. 157. Wescoat's perceptive essay explores the relationship between the visual documents of Mughal gardens recorded in miniatures and the actual sites. It is a paper that should be read by all garden historians.
26. Koran, p. 50.
27. Quoted in Moynihan, *Paradise*, p. 83.
28. Ibid., pp. 82–83.
29. Ibid., p. 83.
30. This and the following Bābur quotations are taken from Villars-Stuart, *Gardens of the Great Mughals*, pp. 38–40.
31. Lehrman, *Earthly Paradise*, p. 41.
32. Ibid., p. 139.
33. Susan Jellicoe, "Mughal Garden," p. 140.
34. Begley and Desai, *Taj Mahal*, p. 10.
35. Ibid.
36. Ibid.
37. Quoted in Lehrman, *Earthly Paradise*, p. 140.
38. Irving, *Indian Summer*, p. 226.

Chapter 3

1. Quoted in Foster, *Lorenzo de' Medici's Villa*, p. 23.
2. Masson, *Italian Gardens*, p. 56.
3. Quoted in Masson, "Palladian Villas," p. 18.
4. *Claudian*, vol. 1, p. 247.
5. Petrarch was a passionate gardener and established a garden wherever he lived.
6. Boccaccio, *Decameron*. In book 3 of his tales, Boccaccio provides a narrative description of a Florentine garden of the early Renaissance.
7. Battisti, "Natura Artificiosa," pp. 5–6.
8. Vasari, *Lives*, vol. 1, p. 207.
9. Cataneo was one of many early Renaissance poets and writers whose celebration of country life set the image of cultivated rural retreats for the next four hundred years.
10. Alberti, *Ten Books of Architecture*, book 5, chap. 17, p. 104.
11. Quoted in Foster, *Lorenzo de' Medici's Villa*, p. 19.
12. Haskell and Penny, *Taste and the Antique*, p. 7.
13. Goethe, *Italian Journey*, p. 347.
14. Clark, *Hadrian's Villa*, pp. 148–49.
15. Quoted in "Villa d'Este," in Jellicoe et al., *Oxford Companion*, p. 141.
16. Coffin, *Villa d'Este*, chap. 5.
17. Vasari, *Lives*, p. 207.
18. Filarete, *Trattato*, p. 196.

19. Jellicoe and Jellicoe, *Landscape of Man*, p. 165. This work contains a succinct account of the Baroque and its relationship to the environment.
20. Ibid.
21. Quoted in Miller, "Domain of Illusion," p. 177. See also Miller's excellent work on the grotto in *Heavenly Caves*.
22. Quoted in Haskell and Penny, *Taste and the Antique*, p. 37.
23. Le Corbusier, *Precisions*, quoted in Tunnard, *Gardens in the Modern Landscape*, p. 78.
24. Zerner, *School of Fontainebleau*, p. 11.
25. Proust, *Pleasures and Days*, p. 100.
26. Quoted in "Marly," in Jellicoe et al., *Oxford Companion*, p. 356.
27. In his *Memoirs*, Saint-Simon speaks well of Le Nôtre's achievement, so his comment may not have been as censorious as it is usually considered to be.

Chapter 4

1. Walpole, *Modern Taste in Gardening*, pp. 9–15.
2. Hoskins, *English Landscape*, chap. 6, has provided most of the background for this discussion. Too often garden historians have concentrated narrowly on specific gardens and periods without considering the larger setting and traditions of interventions into the natural landscape.
3. Quoted ibid., p. 139.
4. Quoted ibid., p. 140.
5. Hadfield, *British Gardening*, pp. 29, 30.
6. Quoted in Amherst, *Gardening in England*, pp. 17–18.
7. Strong, *Renaissance Garden*, p. 22.
8. Rackham, *History of the Countryside*, p. 125.
9. Strong, *Renaissance Garden*, p. 164.
10. Woolridge, *Systema Horti-Cultura*, quoted ibid., p. 165.
11. Parkinson, *Paradisi in sole*, p. 489.
12. Quoted in Willis and Hunt, *Genius of the Place*, p. 98.
13. Quoted ibid., p. 99.
14. Quoted in Chase, *Horace Walpole*, p. 14.
15. Quoted in Spence, *Anecdotes of Pope*, vol. 1, p. 249.
16. For a comprehensive study of all the essential literature on the English landscape school, see Willis and Hunt, *Genius of the Place*.
17. Hunt, *Garden and Grove*, p. 184.
18. Quoted in Willis and Hunt, *Genius of the Place*, pp. 48–50.
19. Quoted ibid., p. 79.
20. Hussey, *English Gardens and Landscapes*, still contains the best discussion on the aesthetic roots of English landscapes.
21. Ibid., p. 16.
22. Ibid.
23. Quoted in "Castle Howard," in Jellicoe et al., *Oxford Companion*, p. 99.
24. Quoted in Hussey, *English Gardens and Landscapes*, p. 115.
25. Ibid., p. 117.
26. Quoted in Willis and Hunt, *Genius of the Place*, pp. 211–14.
27. Quoted in Chase, *Horace Walpole*, p. 25.

28. Whately, *Observations*, p. 165. Whately's *Observations*, which provides descriptions of a number of celebrated English gardens as they looked in his day, was used as a travel guide by visitors from the Continent and helped promoted the idea that gardening deserved to be counted among the liberal arts.
29. Quoted in Chase, *Horace Walpole*, pp. 25–26.
30. See, for example, Hussey, *Picturesque*, p. 30, which qualifies Pope's reputation as a champion of the picturesque movement.
31. Veryard, *Divers Choice Remarks*, p. 28.
32. Quoted in Willis and Hunt, *Genius of the Place*, p. 206.
33. Quoted in Hyams, *Capability Brown*, p. 21.
34. Hogarth, *Analysis of Beauty*, p. 200; Quoted in Willis and Hunt, *Genius of the Place*, p. 75.
35. Quoted in Chase, *Horace Walpole*, pp. 37–38.
36. Quoted in Willis and Hunt, *Genius of the Place*, p. 347.
37. Quoted in Turner, *Capability Brown*, pp. 78–79.
38. Quoted in Hoskins, *English Landscape*, p. 176.
39. The source of the quoted phrase is now lost to the author, but it might well have come from Wordsworth et al., *William Wordsworth and the Age of English Romanticism*, which provides important background on the Romantic Revolution.
40. See Hunt, *William Kent*, p. 163. See pp. 79–82 for a comprehensive discussion of Rousham.
41. Quoted in Strored, *Capability Brown*, p. 79.
42. Warton, an early enthusiast of "real" nature, would have preferred Stourhead in its infancy before the trees and shrubs covered the hillsides.
43. See Woodbridge, *Landscape and Antiquity*, pp. 130–49, for a comprehensive study of Stourhead.
44. Quoted in Chase, *Horace Walpole*, p. 32.
45. Girardin's *Essay on Landscape* is an important treatise on the *"jardin anglais."*
46. Gothein, *History of Garden Art*, p. 294.
47. Stern's calendar is reproduced in Crowell, *Garden as Fine Art*, p. 194.
48. See the excellent note on "Linnaeus and His Students" by W. T. Stern in Jellicoe et al., *Oxford Companion*, pp. 338–40.
49. Quoted in Harris, "Loudonesque Garden," p. 51.
50. Quoted in Desmond, "Horticultural Journalism," p. 81.
51. Quoted in "Loudon," in Jellicoe et al., *Oxford Companion*, p. 344.
52. Robinson, *Wild Garden*, p. 264.
53. Ibid.
54. Quoted in Willis and Hunt, *Genius of the Place*, p. 57.
55. Quoted in Pliny, *Letters*, p. 141.
56. Addison, Pope, and others complained loudly about gardeners who had turned into "green sculptors."
57. Pliny, *Epistles*, vol. 4, pp. 339, 383.
58. Robinson, *Wild Garden*, p. xxv.
59. Quoted in Chase, *Horace Walpole*, p. 213.
60. Steele, *Gardens and People*, p. 127.
61. Young, *Travels in France*, pp. 101–2.
62. Girardin, *Essay on Landscape*, p. 115.
63. Chambers, *Oriental Gardening*, p. 63.
64. Quoted in Harris, "Loudonesque Garden," p. 51.
65. Repton, *Art of Landscape*, p. 144.

66. Sirén, *Gardens of China*, p. 45. The chapter on "Gardens in Literature and Painting," pp. 70–84, discusses the parallel lines of garden art and landscape painting.

Chapter 5

1. See Chase, *Horace Walpole*, p. 189. The definition comes from Lovejoy, "Chinese Origin of Romanticism," pp. 8–11.
2. Sirén, *Gardens of China*, p. 3. Chapter 1, "A Work of Art in Forms of Nature," is an excellent introduction to Chinese gardens.
3. Ibid.
4. Jellicoe et al., *Oxford Companion*, p. 111.
5. Chuang Tzu, in Legge, *Texts of Taoism*, vol. 2., p. 59.
6. Keswick, *Chinese Garden*, p. 76. Her chapter "The Gardens of the Literati" is very useful background.
7. Steele, *Gardens and People*, p. 191.
8. Quoted ibid.
9. Quoted in Sirén, *Gardens of China*, p. 53.
10. For a brief summary of the early period, see "China" in Jellicoe et al., *Oxford Companion*, p. 111.
11. Quoted in Schafer, *Golden Peaches of Samarkand*, p. 92.
12. Quoted in Sirén, *Gardens of China*, p. 72.
13. Steele, *Gardens and People*, p. 192.
14. Quoted in Sirén, *Gardens of China*, p. 75.
15. Quoted in Keswick, *Chinese Garden*, p. 155.
16. Sirén, *Gardens of China*, p. 17.
17. Waley, *The Way and Its Power*, p. 238.
18. Kuo Hsi, *Landscape Painting*, p. 42.
19. See "China" in Jellicoe et al., *Oxford Companion*, p. 115.
20. Quoted in Sirén, *Gardens of China*, p. 10.
21. Ibid., pp. 12–16.
22. Polo, *Travels*, pp. 132–35.
23. Quoted in Keswick, *Chinese Garden*, p. 87.
24. Quoted in Sirén, *Gardens of China*, p. 75.
25. Ibid., p. 136.
26. Quoted ibid., pp. 15–16.
27. Steele, *Gardens and People*, p. 201.
28. Ibid.
29. Quoted ibid., p. 199.
30. Quoted in Plaks, *Archetype and Allegory*, p. 152.
31. Quoted in Sirén, *Gardens of China*, p. 29.
32. Quoted ibid., p. 31.
33. Quoted ibid., p. 35.
34. Gropius and Tonge, *Tradition and Creation*, p. 10.
35. From the entry on "Japan" by Pilcher and Patrick Goode in Jellicoe et al., *Oxford Companion*, p. 293.
36. Kuck, *Japanese Gardens*, p. 3.
37. Soper, *Buddhist Architecture*, p. 14.
38. Quoted in Kuck, *Japanese Gardens*, p. 9.
39. Quoted ibid., p. 59.
40. Murasaki, *Tale of Genji*, pp. 430–31.
41. Quoted in Itoh, *Japanese Garden*, p. 117. See also the translation of *Sakuteika* by Shimoyama.
42. Quoted in Itoh, *Japanese Garden*, p. 157.
43. Kenko, *Essays in Idleness*, p. 115.
44. Ibid., p. xix.
45. Translated from a twelfth-century document in

Soper, *Buddhist Architecture*, pp. 132–33.

46. Itoh, *Space and Illusion,* p. 120.
47. Quoted in Itoh, *Japanese Garden,* p. 140.
48. Quoted in Gropius and Tonge, *Tradition and Creation,* p. 11.
49. Wigginton, *Japanese Gardens,* p. 22.
50. Quoted in Itoh, *Space and Illusion,* p. 60.
51. Quoted ibid., p. 67.
52. Hasegawa, *Japanese Character*, pp. 27–58.
53. Quoted in Hyams, *English Garden*, pp. 31–32.
54. Naito, *Katsura*, p. 109. See pp. 119–34 for a discussion of the underlying cultural and political forces that helped to shape the aesthetics at Katsura.
55. See "Reflections from a Japanese Garden" in Jellicoe, *Studies in Landscape Design.*
56. Quoted in Sirén, *Gardens of China*, p. 11.
57. Treib and Herman, *Gardens of Kyoto*, p. 74.
58. This period of change is well discussed in Shigemori, *Japanese Courtyard Garden.*
59. Jellicoe, *Studies in Landscape Design*, p. 91.

Chapter 6

1. Quoted in Morison, *Admiral of the Ocean Sea*, p. 547.
2. Quoted ibid., p. 556.
3. Quoted in Patrick Goode's note on pre-Spanish Mexican gardens in Jellicoe et al., *Oxford Companion*, p. 371.
4. Quoted ibid.
5. Honour, *New Golden Land*, p. 34.
6. Beverly, *State of Virginia*, pp. 15–16.
7. Quoted in Huth, *Nature and the American,* p. 4.
8. Quoted ibid.
9. Quoted ibid.
10. See Stilgoe, *Common Landscape*, pp. 7–12, for a discussion of the place of the wilderness in European attitudes toward nature.
11. Ibid.
12. Quoted in Leighton, *Early American Gardens*, p. 172.
13. Quoted ibid., pp. 174–75.
14. Quoted in Myers, *Early Pennsylvania*, p. 92.
15. Quoted in Stearn, *Botanical Gardens*, p. lxxx.
16. Ibid., p. lxxxiii.
17. Quoted in Stilgoe, *Common Landscape*, p. 17.
18. Beverly, *State of Virginia*, pp. 183–86.
19. Quoted in Leighton, *American Gardens in the Eighteenth Century*, pp. 32–33.
20. Quoted in Waterman, *Mansions of Virginia*, p. 29.
21. Bartram, *Observations*, p. 107. Bartram's work provides an early account of gardening and agriculture in the middle colonies.
22. Jackson, *Necessity for Ruins*, p. 55. See the chapter titled "Nearer to Eden," pp. 19–35, for an account of pragmatic horticultural origins of gardening.
23. Beverly, *State of Virginia*, p. 45. Leighton, *American Gardens*, pp. 20–35, contains a good selection of

excerpts from Beverly.
24. Byrd, *Prose Works*, p. 222.
25. Jefferson, *Notes on Virginia*, p. 152.
26. Quoted in Rogers, "Gardens and Landscapes," p. 149.
27. Lockwood, *Gardens of Colony and State*, pp. 380–81.
28. Ibid., p. 244.
29. I am indebted to Edward K. A. Wendt for sharing with me his research paper on Middleton Place.
30. Quoted in Rogers, "Gardens and Landscapes," p. 149.
31. Betts, *Jefferson's Garden Book*, p. 461.
32. Ibid., p. 323–24.
33. Ibid., p. 320–21.
34. Shenstone, *Works*, pp. 112–13.
35. Betts, *Jefferson's Garden Book*, p. 461.
36. Ibid., p. vi.
37. Quoted in de Forest, *Mount Vernon*, p. 21.
38. Carter, *Journals of Latrobe*, p. 111.
39. Jefferson, *Notes on Virginia*, pp. 164–65.
40. Quoted in Harris, *Artist in American Society*, p. 173.
41. Quoted ibid.
42. Quoted ibid., p. 118.
43. Ibid., p. 179.
44. Quoted ibid., p. 199.
45. Ibid., p. 200.
46. Quoted ibid., p. 209.
47. Quoted ibid.
48. Pownall, *Topographical Description*, p. 213.
49. Shepard, *Thoreau's Journals*, p. 169.
50. Quoted in Harris, *Artist in American Society,* p. 209.
51. Ibid., p. 23.
52. Ibid.
53. Ibid., p. 54.
54. Downing claimed that Parmentier, despite his brief career, influenced landscape gardening more than any other individual.
55. Downing, *Landscape Gardening*, p. 27.
56. Ibid., pp. 427–36.
57. Quoted in Jellicoe et al., *Oxford Companion*, p. 145.
58. Harris, *Artist in American Society*, p. 200.
59. I am particularly indebted to Schuyler, "Anglo-American Rural Cemetery," for this section.
60. Beginning in 1849, Downing had begun a series of editorials in *The Horticulturalist* advocating public parks. His forceful essays were instrumental in convincing New York City to create its Central Park.
61. Quoted in Fein, *Landscape into Cityscape*, p. 65. Fein's work contains a number of documents on Central Park.
62. Ibid., pp. 385–89. "The Spoils of the Park" records Olmsted's disillusionment with the park by 1882.
63. See Fein, *Frederick Law Olmsted*, p. 167.
64. Ruskin's aesthetics and philosophy influenced the Arts and Crafts movement, leading to a general rejection of the Victorian values that had produced the era's overwrought garden designs.
65. Wharton, *Italian Villas*, pp. 11–13.

66. Ibid., pp. 5–8.
67. Wharton, *Twilight Sleep*, pp. 252–53.
68. Quoted in Balmori, McGuire, and McPeck, *Farrand's American Landscapes*, p. 14.
69. Ibid., pp. 19–20.
70. Quoted in Brown, *Gardens of a Golden Afternoon*, p. 103.
71. Ibid., pp. 41–43.
72. Wharton, *Twilight Sleep*, p. 253.
73. Bishop, *Collected Essays*, p. 415.
74. Kimball, "American Country House," p. 87. Kimball was a critic, historian, and occasional practitioner of landscape architecture whose contributions have not yet been adequately documented.
75. Quoted in O'Neal and Weeks, *Bottomley*, pp. 13–14.
76. Quoted ibid., p. 130.
77. Quoted ibid.
78. Kimball, "American Country House," p. 92.
79. Ibid., p. 90.
80. Wright, *Writings and Buildings*, p. 107.
81. Wright, *An American Architecture*, p. 73.
82. Wright, *Writings and Buildings*, p. 115.
83. Caldwell, *Prairie Spirit*, quoted in Allan Ruff's note on "Ecology and gardens" in Jellicoe et al., *Oxford Companion*, p. 153. See also Jensen, *Siftings*.
84. Tunnard, *Gardens in the Modern Landscape*, p. 126.
85. Quoted ibid., p. 78.
86. Quoted in Racine, Boursier-Mougenot, and Binet, *Gardens of Provence*, pp. 112–13.
87. Barragán, interview in *Landscape Architecture*, which provides a rare personal glimpse of the reticent architect.
88. Ambasz, *Barragán*, p. 12.
89. Barragán, interview in *Landscape Architecture*.
90. Ibid.
91. Ibid.
92. Ibid.
93. Jellicoe, *Studies in Landscape Design*, p. 106.
94. Crowe, *Garden Design*, p. 69.
95. Tunnard, *Gardens in the Modern Landscape*, p. 86.
96. Wrede, *Asplund*, p. 32.
97. Ibid., p. 204.
98. Crowe, *Garden Design*, p. 11.
99. Johnson, "Preface," pp. 7–8.
100. Robinson, *Wild Garden*, p. 269.
101. Jellicoe, *Guelph Lectures*, p. 72.
102. Jellicoe, *Studies in Landscape Design*, vol. 3, p. 25.
103. See ibid., pp. 23–33, where Jellicoe addresses Steele's comments with a detailed explication of the evolution of the Kennedy Memorial.
104. Hunt, *Garden and Grove*, p. 90.
105. Quoted in Jellicoe et al., *Oxford Companion*, p. 113.
106. Quoted in Willis and Hunt, *Genius of the Place*, p. 51.
107. Quoted in Hunt, *Garden and Grove*, p. 93.
108. Ibid., p. 101.
109. Quoted in Willis and Hunt, *Genius of the Place*, p. 51.

Selected Bibliography

Alberti, Leon Battista. *Ten Books of Architecture.* Translated by J. Leoni, edited by J. Rykwert. London, 1955.

Ambasz, Emilio. *The Architecture of Luis Barragán.* New York: Museum of Modern Art, 1976.

Amherst, Alicia. *The History of Gardening in England.* London: Bernard Quaritch, 1896.

Balmori, Diana, Diane Kostial McGuire, and Eleanor M. McPeck, eds. *Beatrix Farrand's American Landscapes: Her Gardens & Campuses.* Sagaponack, N.Y.: Sagapress, 1985.

Barragán, Luis. Interview. *Landscape Architecture*, January 1982, pp. 68–73.

Bartram, John. *Observations on the Inhabitants, Climate, Soil, etc. . . . Made by John Bartram in His Travels from Pensilvania to Lake Ontario.* London, 1751.

Battisti, Eugenio. "Natura Artificiosa to Natura Artificialis." In *The Italian Garden*, edited by David Coffin, pp. 3–36. Washington, D.C.: Dumbarton Oaks, 1972.

Begley, W. E., and Z. A. Desai, eds. *Taj Mahal: An Anthology of Seventeenth-Century Mughal and European Documentary Sources.* Cambridge: Harvard University Press and M.I.T. Press, 1989.

Betts, Edwin Morris, ed. *Thomas Jefferson's Garden Book, 1766–1824, with Relevant Extracts from His Other Writings.* Philadelphia: American Philosophical Society, 1944.

Beverly, Robert. *The History and Present State of Virginia.* 1705. Reprint edition. Charlottesville: University of Virginia, 1968.

Bishop, John Peale. *The Collected Essays of John Peale Bishop.* Edited by Edmund Wilson. New York: Charles Scribner's Sons, 1948.

Boccaccio, Giovanni. *The Decameron.* Translated by Francis Winivor. New York: Modern Library, 1955.

Brown, Frank E. *Roman Architecture.* New York: George Braziller, 1961.

Brown, Jane. *Gardens of a Golden Afternoon.* London: Penguin, 1985.

Burrell, Julia. *The Garden.* New York: Viking Press, 1966.

Byrd, William. *Prose Works.* Edited by Marion Tinling. Charlottesville: University of Virginia, 1966.

Calkins, Robert L. "Piero de'Crescenzi and the Medieval Gardens." In *Medieval Gardens*, edited by M. Stokstad, pp. 157–73. Washington, D.C.: Dumbarton Oaks, 1986.

Chambers, William. *Dissertation on Oriental Gardening.* London, 1772.

Chase, I. *Horace Walpole: Gardenist.* Princeton, N.J.: Princeton University Press, 1943.

Clark, Eleanor. *Rome and a Villa.* New York: Macmillan, 1952.

Claudian. Translated by M. Platnauer. New York: Loeb Classical Library, 1922.

Coffin, David. *The Villa d'Este at Tivoli.* Princeton, N.J.: Princeton University Press, 1960.

Coffin, David, ed. *The Italian Garden.* Washington, D.C.: Dumbarton Oaks, 1972.

Crowe, Sylvia. *Garden Design.* London, 1981.

Crowell, F. R. *The Garden as a Fine Art.* London: Weidenfeld and Nicolson, n.d.

de Forest, Elizabeth Kellam. *The Gardens and Grounds of Mount Vernon.* Mount Vernon, Va.: Mount Vernon Ladies Association, 1982.

Desmond, Ray. "19th Century Horticultural Journalism." In *John Claudius Loudon and the Early Nineteenth Century in Great Britain*, edited by Elisabeth MacDougall, pp. 79–103. Washington, D.C.: Dumbarton Oaks, 1980.

Dickie, James. "The Islamic Garden in Spain." In *The Islamic Garden*, edited by Elisabeth MacDougall and Richard Ettinghausen, pp. 89–105. Washington, D.C.: Dumbarton Oaks, 1976.

Downing, A. J. *A Treatise on the Theory and Practice of Landscape Gardening Adapted to North America.* Reprint of the 9th edition. New York: Orange Judd, 1976.

Fairbrother, Nan. *Men and Gardens.* New York, 1956.

Fein, Albert. *Frederick Law Olmsted and the American Environmental Tradition.* New York: George Braziller, 1972.

Fein, Albert, ed. *Landscape into Cityscape.* New York: Van Nostrand Reinhold, 1981.

Filarete, S. Forina. *Trattato di architettura.* Bk. 9, fol. 68. Translated by J. Spencer. New Haven: Yale University Press, 1965.

Foster, Philip Ellis. *A Study of Lorenzo de' Medici's Villa at Poggio a Ciano.* New York: Garland Publishing, 1978.

Giamatti, A. B. *The Earthly Paradise and the Renaissance Epic.* Princeton, N.J.: Princeton University Press, 1966.

Girardin, Louis-René. *An Essay on Landscape. . . .* Translated by Daniel Malthus. London, 1783.

Goethe, Johann Wolfgang von. *Italian Journey, 1786–1788.* Translated by W. H. Auden and Elizabeth Mayer. New York: Schocken Books, 1968.

Gothein, Marie-Louise. *A History of Garden Art.* 1928. Reprint edition. Translated by Laura Archer Hind. New York: Hacker Books, 1966.

Grimal, Pierre. *Les jardins romains.* Paris, 1969.

Gropius, Walter, and Ishimoto Tonge. *Tradition and Creation in Japanese Architecture.* New Haven: Yale University Press, 1960.

Hadfield, Miles. *A History of British Gardening.* London: John Murray, 1960.

Harris, John. "Genesis of the Loudonesque Garden." In *John Claudius Loudon and the Early Nineteenth Century in Great Britain*, edited by Elisabeth MacDougall, pp. 47–57. Washington, D.C.: Dumbarton Oaks, 1980.

Harris, Neil. *The Artist in American Society.* New York: George Braziller, 1966.

Harvey, John. *Medieval Gardens.* London: Batsford, 1981.

Hasegawa, Nyozekan. *The Japanese Character: A Cultural Profile.* Translated by John Bester. New York: Kodansha International, 1982.

Haskell, Francis, and Nicholas Penny. *Taste and the Antique*. New Haven: Yale University Press, 1981.

Hogarth, William. *The Analysis of Beauty*. London: J. Reeves, 1753. Reprint edition. Edited by Joseph Burke. Oxford: Clarendon Press, 1955.

Homer. *Odyssey*. Translated by Robert Fitzgerald. New York: Doubleday, 1961.

Honour, Hugh. *The New Golden Land*. New York: Pantheon Books, 1975.

Hoskins, W. G. *The Making of the English Landscape*. London: Hodder and Stoughton, 1977.

Hunt, John Dixon. *Garden and Grove*. Princeton, N.J.: Princeton University Press, 1986.

————. *William Kent*. London, 1987.

Hussey, Christopher. *English Gardens and Landscapes, 1700–1750*. London: Country Life Books, 1967.

————. *The Picturesque*. London: G. P. Putnam's Sons, 1927.

Huth, Hans. *Nature and the American*. Lincoln: University of Nebraska Press, 1972.

Hyams, Edward. *Capability Brown and Humphry Repton*. New York: Charles Scribner's Sons, 1971.

————. *The English Garden*. London: Thames and Hudson, 1964.

Irving, Robert Grant. *Indian Summer, Lutyens, Baker and Imperial Delhi*. New Haven: Yale University Press, 1981.

Itoh, Teiji. *The Japanese Garden*. New Haven: Yale University Press, 1972.

————. *Space and Illusion in the Japanese Garden*. Tokyo: Tankosha, and New York: Weatherhill, 1973.

Jackson, John Brinckerhoff. *The Necessity for Ruins*. Amherst: University of Massachusetts Press, 1980.

Jashemski, Wilhelmina F. "The Campagnia Peristyle Garden." In *Ancient Roman Gardens*, edited by Elisabeth MacDougall and Wilhelmina Jashemski, pp. 31–48. Washington, D.C.: Dumbarton Oaks, 1981.

Jefferson, Thomas. *Notes on the State of Virginia*. Edited by William Peden. Chapel Hill: University of North Carolina Press and Institute of Early American History and Culture, 1955.

Jellicoe, Geoffrey. *The Guelph Lectures on Landscape Design*. Guelph, Ont.: University of Guelph, 1983.

————. *Studies in Landscape Design*. London, 1970.

Jellicoe, Geoffrey, and Susan Jellicoe. *The Landscape of Man*. New York: Viking Press, 1975.

Jellicoe, Geoffrey, Susan Jellicoe, Patrick Goode, and Michael Lancaster, eds. *The Oxford Companion to Gardens*. Oxford and New York: Oxford University Press, 1986.

Jellicoe, Susan. "The Development of the Mughal Garden." In *The Islamic Garden*, edited by Elisabeth MacDougall and Richard Ettinghausen, pp. 109–24. Washington, D.C.: Dumbarton Oaks, 1976.

Jensen, Jens. *Siftings*. Chicago: Ralph Fletcher Seymour, 1930.

Johnson, Jory. Preface. In *Transforming the American Garden*, edited by Michael R. Von Valkenberg, Margaret B. Reeve, and Jory Johnson, pp. 7–8. Cambridge: Harvard University Graduate School of Design, 1986.

Kenko. *Essays in Idleness*. Translated by Donald Keene. New York: Columbia University Press, 1967.

Keswick, Maggie. *The Chinese Garden: History, Art and Architecture*. New York: Rizzoli, 1978. Revised edition. New York: St. Martins, and London: Academy Editions, 1986.

Kimball, Fiske. "American Country House." *Architectural Record* 46 (October 1919).

Koran, The. Translated by N. J. Dawood. London: Penguin Books, 1956.

Kuck, Loraine. *The World of the Japanese Garden*. New York: Weatherhill, 1968.

Kuo Hsi. *An Essay on Landscape Painting*. Translated by S. Sakanishi. London: John Murray, 1935.

Latrobe, Benjamin. *The Virginia Journals of Benjamin Henry Latrobe, 1795–1798*. Edited by Edward C. Carter. New Haven: Yale University Press, 1977.

Legge, James. *The Texts of Taoism*. Oxford, 1891.

Lehrman, Jonas. *Earthly Paradise: Garden and Courtyard in Islam*. Berkeley: University of California Press, 1980.

Leighton, Ann. *American Gardens in the Eighteenth Century: "For Use or for Delight."* Boston: University of Massachusetts Press, 1976.

————. *Early American Gardens. "For Meate or Medicine."* Boston: University of Massachusetts Press, 1970.

Lockwood, Alice E. B. *Gardens of Colony and State*. New York: Charles Scribner's Sons, 1931.

Lovejoy, A. O. *Essays in the History of Ideas*. 1948. Reprint edition, pp. 99–135. New York: Greenwood, 1978.

MacDougall, Elisabeth, ed. *"Fons Sapientiae": Renaissance Garden Fountains*. Washington, D.C.: Dumbarton Oaks, 1978.

————. *John Claudius Loudon and the Early Nineteenth Century in Great Britain*. Washington, D.C.: Dumbarton Oaks, 1980.

————. *Medieval Gardens*. Washington, D.C.: Dumbarton Oaks, 1986.

MacDougall, Elisabeth, and Richard Ettinghausen, eds. *The Islamic Garden*. Washington, D.C.: Dumbarton Oaks, 1976.

MacDougall, Elisabeth, and Wilhelmina Jashemski, eds. *Ancient Roman Gardens*. Washington, D.C.: Dumbarton Oaks, 1981.

Macoubbin, Robert P., and Peter Martin, eds. *British and American Gardens in the Eighteenth Century*. Williamsburg, Va.: The Colonial Williamsburg Foundation, 1984.

Masson, Georgina. *Italian Gardens*. London: Thames and Hudson, 1961.

Myers, Albert Cook. *Narratives of Early Pennsylvania, West New Jersey, and Delaware, 1630–1707*. New York: Charles Scribner's Sons, 1912.

Miller, Naomi. "Domain of Illusion: The Grotto in France." In *"Fons Sapientiae": Renaissance Garden Fountains*, edited by Elisabeth MacDougall, pp. 177–205. Washington, D.C.: Dumbarton Oaks, 1978.

————. *Heavenly Caves*. New York: George Braziller, 1982.

Morison, Samuel E. *Admiral of the Ocean Sea*. Boston: Little, Brown, 1942.

Moynihan, Elizabeth. *Paradise as a Garden in Persia and Mughal India*. New York: George Braziller, 1979.

Murasaki, Shikibu. *The Tale of Genji*. Translated by Arthur Waley. New York: Modern Library, 1977.

Naito, Akira. *Katsura, a Princely Retreat*. Tokyo, New York, and San Francisco: Kodansha International, 1977.

O'Neal, William B., and Christopher Weeks. *William Lawrence Bottomley*. Charlottesville: University of Virginia, 1985.

Paglia, Camille. *Sexual Personae*. New Haven: Yale University Press, 1990.

Paine, James. *Plans of Noblemen's and Gentlemen's Houses*. London: Privately printed, 1783.

Parkinson, John. *Paradisi in sole paradisus terrestris*. London, 1629.

Pirenna, Henri. *Mohammed and Charlemagne*. New York: Meridian Books, 1957.

Plaks, Andrew H. *Archetype and Allegory in the "Dream of the Red Chamber."* Princeton, N.J.: Princeton University Press, 1976.

Pliny. *Epistles*. Vol. 6. Translated by Betty Redice. New York: Loeb Classical Library, 1915.

———. *The Letters of the Younger Pliny*. London: Penguin Classics, 1963.

Polo, Marco. *Travels of Marco Polo*. New York: Orion Press, n.d.

Pownall, T. A. *Topographical Description of . . . North America*. London, 1776.

Proust, Marcel. *Pleasures and Days*. Translated by Louise Varese. New York: Doubleday, 1957.

Racine, Michael, Ernest J.-P. Boursier-Mougenot, and Françoise Binet. *The Gardens of Provence and the French Riviera*. Cambridge: M.I.T. Press, 1987.

Rackham, Oliver. *The History of the Countryside*. London: J. M. Dent, 1986.

Repton, Humphry. *Art of Landscape*. 1795. Reprint edition. Boston: Houghton Mifflin, 1907.

Robinson, William. *The Wild Garden*. 1894. Reprint of the 4th edition. Introduction by Robin Lane Fox. London: Scolar Press, 1977.

Rogers, George C., Jr. "Gardens and Landscapes in Eighteenth Century South Carolina." In *British and American Gardens in the Eighteenth Century*, edited by Robert P. Macoubbin and Peter Martin, pp. 148–58. Williamsburg, Va.: Colonial Williamsburg Foundation, 1984.

Sakuteika: The Book of Gardens. Translated by Shigemaru Shimoyama. Tokyo: Town and City Planners, 1976.

Schafer, Edward. *The Golden Peaches of Samarkand*. Berkeley and Los Angeles: University of California Press, 1963.

Schuyler, David. "The Evolution of the Anglo-American Rural Cemetery." *Journal of Garden History* 4, no. 3, pp. 291–304.

Scully, Vincent. *The Earth, the Temple and the Gods*. New Haven: Yale University Press, 1962.

Shenstone, William. *Shenstone's Works*. London, 1773.

Shepard, Odell, ed. *The Heart of Thoreau's Journals*. New

York: Dover Publications, 1961.

Shigemori, Kento. *The Japanese Courtyard Garden*. New York: Weatherhill, 1981.

Sirén, Osvald. *Gardens of China*. New York: Ronald Press, 1949.

Soper, Alexander. *Evolution of Buddhist Architecture in Japan*. Princeton, N.J.: Princeton University Press, 1942.

Spence, Joseph. *Observations, Anecdotes and Characters of Books and Names*. New York: Oxford University Press, 1966.

Stannard, Jerry. "Alimentary and Medieval Uses." In *Medieval Gardens*, edited by Elisabeth MacDougall, pp. 71–91. Washington, D.C.: Dumbarton Oaks, 1986.

Stearn, William Thomas. *Botanical Gardens and Botanical Literature*. Pittsburgh, 1961.

Steele, Fletcher. *Gardens and People*. Boston: Houghton Mifflin Company, 1964.

Stilgoe, John R. *Common Landscape of America, 1580 to 1845*. New Haven: Yale University Press, 1982.

Stronach, David. *Pasargadae: A Report on the Excavations Conducted by the British Institute of Persian Studies from 1961–1963*. Oxford, 1978.

Strong, Roy. *The Renaissance Garden in England*. London: Thames and Hudson, 1979.

Thacker, Christopher. *The History of Gardens*. Berkeley and Los Angeles: University of California Press, 1979.

Thompson, Dorothy Burr. "Ancient Gardens in Greece and Italy." *Archaeology* 4 (1951): 41–47.

Treib, Marc, and Ron Herman. *A Guide to the Gardens of Kyoto*. Tokyo: Shufunotomo, 1980.

Tunnard, Christopher. *Gardens in the Modern Landscape*. Revised edition. New York: Charles Scribner's Sons, 1948.

Turner, Roger. *Capability Brown*. New York: Rizzoli, 1985.

Van Buren, Ann Hagopian. "The Park of Hesdin." In *Medieval Gardens*, edited by Elisabeth MacDougall, pp. 117–34. Washington, D.C.: Dumbarton Oaks, 1986.

Varro. *De re rustica*. Translated by W. D. Hooper and H. B. Ash. London: Loeb Classical Library, 1934.

Vasari, Georgio. *The Lives of the Painters, Sculptors, and Architects*. 1550. Reprint edition. Edited by William

Gaunt. New York: E. P. Dutton, 1963.

Veryard, Ellis. *An Account of Divers Choice Remarks. . . .* London, 1701.

Villars-Stuart, C. *Gardens of the Great Mughals*. London: Adam and Charles Black, 1913.

Waley, Arthur. *The Way and Its Power: Translations from Tao Te Ching*. London: Roger Houghton, 1934.

Walpole, Horace. *The History of Modern Taste in Gardening*. 1771. Reprint edition. Edited by I.W.U. Chase. Princeton, N.J.: Princeton University Press, 1943.

Waterman, Thomas. *The Mansions of Virginia, 1706–1776*. Chapel Hill: University of North Carolina Press, 1945.

Wescoat, James L., Jr. "Picturing an Early Mughal Garden." *Asia Art*, Fall 1989, n.p.

Wharton, Edith. *Italian Villas and Their Gardens*. New York: The Century Company, 1904.

———. *Twilight Sleep*. New York: Appleton Press, 1927.

Whately, Thomas. *Observations on Modern Gardening*. London, 1788.

Wigginton, Brooks. *Japanese Gardens*. Marietta, Oh.: Marietta College, 1963.

Willis, Peter, and John Dixon Hunt. *The Genius of the Place: The English Landscape Garden, 1620–1820*. 1975. Revised edition. New York: M.I.T. Press, 1988.

Woodbridge, Kenneth. *Landscape and Antiquity: Aspects of English Culture at Stourhead*. Oxford: Oxford University Press, 1970.

Wordsworth, Jonathan, Michael C. Jaye, and Robert Woot, eds. *William Wordsworth and the Age of English Romanticism*. New Brunswick, N.J.: Rutgers University Press, 1987.

Wrede, Stuart. *The Architecture of Erik Gunnar Asplund*. Cambridge: M.I.T. Press, 1983.

Wright, Frank Lloyd. *An American Architecture*. Edited by Edgar J. Kaufmann, Jr. New York: Horizon Press, 1955.

———. *Frank Lloyd Wright: Writings and Buildings*. Edited by Edgar Kaufmann, Jr., and Ben Raeburn. New York: Meridian Books, 1960.

Young, Arthur. *Travels in France*. London: Bell, 1890.

Zerner, Henri. *The School of Fontainebleau*. New York: Harry N. Abrams, 1969.

Index

Italic page numbers refer to captions and illustrations.

Abbot's Garden (Tenryu-ji), Kyoto, Japan, 241
Abd ar-Rahman I, Umayyad ruler of Spain, 62
Abode of Love gardens. *See* Shalamar Bagh
abreuvoir, at Marly, 128
academic gardens, 27–28
Académie des Beaux-Arts. *See* Beaux-Arts influences
Academy, Athens, 27, 89
Account Book (book; Jefferson), 284
Acer pseudoplatanus, 33
Achabal, Anantnag, Kashmir, pool, *80*
Acoma, Mexico, cloister garden, *264*
Adams, John, 288, 295
Addison, Joseph, 139, 156, 158, 159, 167, 190–91, 283
Adonis, Garden of, 29
Adriana, Villa. *See* Hadrian's Villa
Aeneid (book; Virgil), 252
aesthetic reform movement, 287–94
Afghanistan, 75
Agedal gardens, Marrakesh, Morocco, 24
Agora, Athens, 27
Agra, India, 77, 79. *See also* Taj Mahal
agriculture: in England, 141–42, 159; and gardening,
  17–18, 25–26
Agriculture et maison rustique, L' (book; Estienne), 131
aguedal gardens, 61
Ailanthus, 203
Akbar, Mughal emperor of India, *78*, 78–79, 80
Alberti, Leon Battista, 71–73, 93–95, 100, 119
Alcázar, Seville, Spain, 65
Alcinous, king of the Phoenicians, garden of, 25–26, 27,
  31–33, 34, 169
Aldobrandini. *See* Villa Aldobrandini
Alexander VI, pope, 46
Alexander the Great, king of Macedonia, 19, 23, 24,
  75–76, 210
Alfonso II, king of Naples, *95*, 95–96, 114
Alfred the Great, king of Wessex, 144
Alhambra, Granada, Spain, *58*, *61*, 65, *66*, 66–67, *67*,
  70, *72*, *73*, 321
Al Himyari, 67
allées: Central Park, *298*; pleached, 51, *51*; Pliny's, 37
Amalienburg, Nymphenburg, Munich, 96
amateur gardeners, 338
Ambasz, Emilio, 321
Amber, Jaipur, India, 80
Amboise, Georges, Cardinal d', *116*, 145
Amboise, Indre-et-Loire, France, 96, 114, 117, 119, 122
Amenhotep III, king of Egypt, 33; garden plan of his
  high official, *32*, 33
American Academy, Rome, 301
American Architecture, An (book; Wright), 317
"American Country House, The" (article; Kimball),
  315–17
American Society of Landscape Architects, 303

Amherst, Alicia, 143
Amida Buddhism, 239–40
Amorosa Visione, L' (Boccaccio), 71
Analects (book; Confucius), 218
Analysis of Beauty, The (book; Hogarth), 173
"ancient style," 203
Andalusia, Spain, Islamic gardens, 62, 65
anemone, 29
Anet. *See* Château d'Anet
animals, 38, 210–11, 262–63
Anne of Denmark, queen of James I of England, 147
Apollo, Basin of, Versailles, *112*
Apollo Belvedere (sculpture), 97
Arabs, 59, 60, 67, 71, 73, 74. *See also* Islamic gardens
archaeology, 21, 27, 39–40, 42
architecture: and gardens, 158, 159, 321; and landscape,
  29–30, 122, 176, 220, 319–20
Aristophanes, 27
Arnold Arboretum, Jamaica Plains, Massachusetts, 302
Arts and Crafts movement, 190, 306, 329
Ashikaga shoguns, 239, 240, 249
Ashridge, Hertfordshire, England, *184*
Asplund, Gunnar, 331–34, *332*, *333*, *334*
Astrée, L' (book; d'Urfé), 150
Athelhampton, Dorset, England, 301
Athens, Greece, 27, 29, 30
Augusta, Princess, 200
Augustine, Saint, 50
Australia, plants from, 185
Autumn Tea House (Toji-in), Kyoto, Japan, *248*
aviaries, 38
azaleas, *248*, *257*, *278*, *280–81*
Aztec gardens, 262–63

Bābur, Mughal emperor of India, *26*, *60*, 77–78, *78*, 79,
  83
Babylonian parks, 23, 77
Bac, Ferdinand, 321
Bacon, Francis, 158, 190, 319, 338, 339
Badminton House, Gloucestershire, England, 157, *157*
Badminton House (painting; Canaletto), 157
Bagatelle, Bois de Boulogne, Paris, 183, 195, 200
Baghdad, Iraq, 104
Bagh-i-Wafa (Garden of Fidelity), Kabul, Afghanistan,
  60, 78, *78*, 79
Bagnaia, Italy. *See* Villa Lante
Bagshot Heath, Surrey, England, 141
Baker, George, 266
bamboo, *225*, 229
Banks, Joseph, 185
Barlow, Capt. Arthur, 264
Barnum, Dr., *300*

Baroque gardens: French, 125–37; Italian, 105–10. *See
  also* Villa Garzoni
Barragán, Luis, 321–25, *322*, *323*; house at Tacuyaba,
  Mexico, 323–24
Bartram, John, 268, 276–77, 282–83, *283*
Bartram, William, 282–83
Basin of Apollo, Versailles, *112*
basins. *See* water basins
Batey, Mavis, 167
Bathhurst, Allen, Lord, 157, 158, 159
Baths of Titus, 101
Battisti, Eugenio, 92
Bauhaus, 259
bay tree, 47
Beaudesert, Staffordshire, England, 188
Beaufort, Henry Somerset, duke of, 157
Beaux-Arts influences, 301, 302, 314, 325, 329
"bedding out," 189
Bedford, countess of, 154
Bee-balm (painting; Curtis), *188*
Begley, W. E., *85*
Beijing, China. *See* Chang Chun Yuan; Imperial Palace
  Garden; Summer Palace
Bélanger, François-Joseph, 197
Belvedere Court, Vatican, Rome, *96*, 96–97, 100, 120,
  122
Bembo, Pietro, Cardinal, 46
Benedictines, 51–52
Betts, William, 286
Beverly, Robert, 268, 271–72, 277–78
Bhagavad Gita (poem), 17
Bible, 67
Birkenhead Park, Liverpool, England, 296, 297, 331
Bishop, John Peale, 312
Blaikie, Thomas, 183, 187
Blaise Hamlet, Gloucestershire, England, 296
Blane, William, 289
Blenheim Palace, Oxfordshire, England, 144, *170*, 171,
  175, 176, *177*, 284, 293, 300
Blois, Loir-et-Cher, France, 96, 117, 119, 131, 145, 147
Blondel, Jacques-François, 195
Boboli Gardens, Florence, 46, *104*, 105, 119
Boccaccio, Giovanni, 67–71, 74, 91, 92
Bodin, Soulange, 187
Bodleian Library, 273, 312
Bodnant Garden, Gwynedd, Wales, 201
Bois de Boulogne. *See* Bagatelle
Bokhara, 104
Bomarzo, Italy. *See* Villa Orsini
Book of Mechanical Devices (book; Ibn al-Razzaz al-Jazari),
  73, 74
Borghese *Gladiator* (sculpture; Le Sueur), 150
"borrowed views" (*jie jing*; *shakkei*), 218, 241, 252–54
bosquets: de Marais, Versailles, 104; Villa Garzoni, *90*

Boston, Massachusetts, park system, 300
botanical illustration: in China, 229; Ligozzi's, *263*
Botanical Magazine, illustrations from, *188*, *284*
botanical studies: in England, 154, 185; in Italy, 92; of
    Linneaus, 185–86; in Muslim world, 65, 67, 73–74;
    of New World species, 263; Quaker interest, 268
botanic gardens: Aztec, 262, 263, *263*; in colonial
    America, 268; earliest European, 74, 154, 185, 263,
    263; of Linnaeus, 186, *186*, *187*. *See also* Brooklyn;
    Jardin Royal des Plantes Médicinales; Kew Gardens;
    physic gardens
Botetourt, Norborne Berkeley, baron de, 276
Bottomley, William Lawrence, 314–15, *314*
boulders, in Chinese gardens, 214. *See also* stones and
    rocks
Boullée, Étienne-Louis, 197
Bourbon, Pierre II, duc de, 114
Boursault, M., 187
Boutin, M., 194
Bouts, Dirk, 49
bowling-green, plan for, *183*
Bowood Gardens, Wiltshire, England, 294
box, boxwood, 134; at Gunston Hall, *269*; Hatfield
    House maze, *153*; in Roman gardens, 23, 37, 42, 53;
    at Villandry, *136*. *See also* topiary
Boyceau, Jacques de la Barauderie, 116, 134–37
Bramante, Donato, 46, *96*, 96–97, 122
Brandon, Prince George County, Virginia, 271
Brazil, 325
Bridgeman, Charles, 159, 162, 163, 166, 275
bridges: Blenheim Palace, *177*; Katsura Imperial Villa,
    251; Middleton Place, *280-81*; Stowe, *164*
Brion Cemetery, San Vito d'Altivole, Italy, *335*
Britannia illustrata (book; Kip), 173
Brooklyn, New York: Botanic Garden, *256*, *257*;
    Green-Wood Cemetery, 294; Prospect Park, 300
Brosse, Salomon de, 119
Brown, Lancelot (Capability), 144, *146*, 157, *170*, 170–
    79, *171*, *174*, 182, 184, 185, 191, 194, 195, 200,
    201, 217, 287, 293, 300, 333, 336
Brunelleschi, Filippo, 92
Buddhism, 17, 229, 234, 239–40, 241, 242, 243, 254
Bunyan, John, 336
Burghley House, Stamford, Northamptonshire, England,
    144, 174
Burke, Edmund, 197, 289
Burle Marx, Roberto, 41, 321, 325, *325*, 335
Burlington, Richard Boyle, earl of, 166
Burnell, L. H., 297
Burwell, Lewis, 276
Byodo-in, Uji, Japan, *238*, 239
Byrd, William, 268, 271, 276–77, 278
Byron, George Gordon, Lord, 339
Byzantine gardens, 67, 74; influence on Italian
    Renaissance, 104

cabbage, 23, *134*
Caesar, Julius, 38
Caldwell, Alfred, 319
California, 298, 312
Camellia japonica, 282
Canada, plants from, 185
Canaletto, Antonio: *Badminton House*, 157
canals: in French gardens, 123; at Nishat Bagh, 77; at
    Peterhof, 131; at Shalamar Bagh, Kashmir, 80

Cang Lang Ting (Ts'ang Lang T'ing), Suzhou, China,
    220, *224*, *225*
Canopus, Hadrian's Villa, 44
Cape of Good Hope, plants from, 185
Capitol grounds, Washington, D.C., 300
Capitulare de villis vel curtis emperii (decree; Charlemagne), 51
Capraecola, Italy. *See* Palazzo Farnese
"capturing alive," 252–54. *See also* "borrowed views"
Carafa, Cardinal, 46
Careggi, Italy, Medici Villa, 89
Carlisle, 3rd earl of, 159, 162, 163; daughter of, 159–62
Carolinas, 266, 268, 282, 312; North, 264; South, 269,
    278–82
Caroline gardens, England, 147–57
Carter, Colonel, 271
Carter plantation, 315
Carter's Grove, Williamsburg, Virginia, 271, 275, 276
Carvallo, Joachim, *134*
cascades: Blenheim, 176; La Granja, 129; Marly, 128;
    Peterhof, *130*; Shalamar Bagh, Kashmir, 81; Vaux-le-
    Viscount, *125*; Villa d'Este, *98*; Villa Garzoni,
    90; Villa Lante, *103*
Caserta (La Reggia), Naples, Italy, 129
Casino Villino, Palazzo Farnese, *106-7*
Castiglione, Baldassare, 46
Castle Howard, North Yorkshire, England, *138*, 159–62,
    160-61, *162*, 163, 179, 294
Cataneo, 93
Catesby, Mark, *284*
Catherine de' Médicis, queen of France, *104*, 122, 137
Cato, Marcus Porcius, 23, 36, 52, 89
Caus, Isaac de, 148
Caus, Salomon de, 147–48, 149–52
Caversham, England, 284
Cecil, Robert, 152, 154
Celaenae, Persia, royal park, 23
Cels, M., 187
cemeteries, 288, 294, 331–34, *335*
Central Park, New York City, 297, 298, *298*, 321, 331
Cerceau. *See* Du Cerceau
Chaffereau, Peter, 282
chahar bagh (fourfold garden), 62, 75, 83; Taj Mahal, *86*
Chambers, Sir William, 195, 200–201, 202
Champlain, Samuel de, 266
Champs-Elysées, Paris, *127*
Chamula Indians, *19*
Ch'ang-an (now Xian), China, 233
Chang Chun Yuan, Beijing, China, *214*
Chang-lun, 214
Chanteloup. *See* Pagoda of Chanteloup
Chantilly, Oise, France, 118, 123, 127, 131, 194
chapel gardens, England, 143
Charageat, Marguerite, 73
Charlemagne, Holy Roman emperor, 51, 52
Charles I, king of England, 149, 150
Charles II, king of England, *144*, 150, 157
Charles II, king of Naples, 92
Charles III, king of Naples, 129
Charles IV, Holy Roman emperor, 74
Charles VIII, king of France, 96, 114, 115, 117
Charleston, South Carolina, 282
Charleval, France, design for, 122
Chartres, duc de, 199
Chasho Senrin (manual), 245
Château d'Anet, Eure-et-Loir, France, 119, 121–22, 131
Château de Richelieu, Richelieu, France, *122*, 122–23

Château de Vallery, France, *118*, 119, 131
Château de Villandry, Indre-et-Loire, France, 131–34,
    132-33, *134*, *135*, *136*
Château Montceaux, France, 119, 122
Château of Amboise. *See* Amboise
Château of Dampierre, Yvelines, France, 118–19
Chatsworth, Derbyshire, England, 166, 171, 173, 176,
    294, 300
Chaundler (fountain designer), 152
Chelsea Physic Garden, London, 203
Ch'en Hung-shou: woodcut after, *229*
Chenonceaux, Indre-et-Loire, France, *118*, 119, *119*
cherry trees, 65, 237
Chevaux de Marly (sculpture), *127*
Chiang Jiang (Yangtze) River, 211
Chiang Shen: painting of Lu-shan mountains, *209*
Chiapas, Mexico, corn harvesting in, *19*
Chicago, 317, 319; World's Fair (1893), 300, 317
Chiericat. *See* Villa Chiericat
China: plants from, 185, 189, 203, 226–27; topography,
    209–10, 233
Chinese gardens, 17, *55*, 205–30, 249–50; European
    notions of, 200–202, 205; influence on: English gar-
    dens, 156, 200–202, 206–8; Japanese gardens, 231,
    233, 237, 239, 241, 242
Chiswick House, London, 166, 284
Christianity, 17, 46, 54, 67, 90. *See also* monastery gardens
chrysanthemum, 229
Chuin Tung, 217
Cibot, Frère, 221–24
Cicero, 38, 95
Cimon of Athens, 27
Cincinnati, Ohio, 289
circle, 62
Cirencester Park, Gloucestershire, England, 157–58, 170
Civil War, 298
clairvoyées, 275
Claremont, Surrey, England, 284
Clark, Eleanor, 42, 44, 46, 99
Claude Lorrain, 109, 159, 162, 176, 195
Claudian, 91
Clement VII, pope, 100
Cleopatra (sculpture), 97
Cleveland, Nehemiah, 294
Cliveden, Buckinghamshire, England, 301
Cobham, Richard Temple, viscount, 159, 162, 163, 166,
    170
Codman, Ogden, Jr., 301
Coffin, David, 100
Colbert, Jean-Baptiste, 117, 125
Collinson, Peter, 268, 277, 282, *283*
colonial American gardens, 264–87
Colonial Williamsburg. *See* Williamsburg
Colonna, Francis, 91, 143
color, 306–9
Columbus, Christopher, 261–62, 265
Columella, Lucius Junius Moderatus, 52
Column House, Désert de Retz, *199*, 199–200
Commodus as Hercules (sculpture), 97
Compleat Gentleman, The (book; Peacham), 182
Confucianism, 229
Confucius, 218
Connecticut, 282
Constantinople, 104
Córdoba, Spain, gardens, 62, 63, 65; Court of Orange
    Trees, *64*

corn (*Zea mays*), *266*; cultivation by Mayans, 18–19
cornflower, 29
Cornwallis, Charles, 312
Corsignano (Pienza), Italy, 95
Cortés, Hernando, 262, *263*
Cortona, Domenico da, 114
Cottage Residences (book; Downing), 289, 290
Cours d'architecture (book; Blondel), 195
Court of Orange Trees (Patio de los Naranjos), Córdoba, Spain, *64*
Court of the Lions (Patio de los Leones), Alhambra, 66–67, *67*
Court of the Long Pond (Patio de la Acequia), Generalife, 66, *72*
Court of the Myrtles (Patio de los Arrayanes), Alhambra, 66, *72*
courtyard gardens: Greek, 29; Islamic, *58*, 61–62, 331; Japanese, 248–49, 258; Roman, 29, 37–38
Coxcombs, Maize, and Morning-Glories (Japanese screen), *236*
Crescenzi, Pietro de', *49*, 52, *53*, *91*, 92
Crete, island of, Greece, 29
Crooked House, Villa Orsini, *105*
Crowe, Dame Sylvia, 104, 329, 333
Crowfield Plantation, South Carolina, 278–82
Crowley, George, *311*
Cröye, Prince of, *194*
Crusades, 56, 73, 74, 89
Culpeper, Nicholas, 266, *267*
Curtis, William, *284*
Custis, John, 268, 277
Cyrus the Great, king of Persia, park of, 23, 59
Cyrus the Younger, satrap of Asia Minor, garden of, 23–24, 25

Dafoe, Daniel, 141
Dahlem Botanical Gardens, Berlin, 325
Daisen-in, Kyoto, Japan, *241*, 241–42, 258
Daitoku-ji temple complex, Kyoto, Japan, 238, *241*. *See also* Daisen-in
Dampierre. *See* Château of Dampierre
Dante, 336
Daoism, 208–9, 212, 214, 215, 218, 220, 229
Dartington Hall, Devon, England, 201
date palms, *32*
Davidson, John, 87
Davis, Alexander Jackson: paintings of Montgomery Place, *291*, *292*
Dayr al-Baḥrī, temple of, Egypt, 33, 34, *34*
Decameron (book; Boccaccio), 74, 91
Decoration of Houses, The (book; Wharton and Codman), 301
Delhi, India, 77; palace, *79*; Shalamar Bagh, 80
De l'Orme, Philibert, 119, 121
Delphi, Greece, 30
"Deluge" fountain, Villa Lante, 102
De materia medica (book; Dioscorides), 73
Deprez, Louis, *201*
De re aedificatoria (book; Alberti), 95
De re rustica (manuscript; Palladius), 50
De re rustica (treatise; Cato), 23, 36
Désert de Retz, Chambourcy, Yvelines, France, 194–95, *197*, *198*, *199*, 199–200, *220*
Designs of Chinese Buildings (book; Chambers), 200
D'Este. *See* Este, Ippolito; Villa d'Este

Détails de nouveaux jardins à la mode (book; Le Rouge), 202–3; engravings from, *194*, *200*
Dezallier d'Argenville, Antoine-Joseph, 131, 183, 282
Dickie, James, 65
Diderot, Denis, 127–28
Dioscorides, 73
Dissertation on Oriental Gardening (book; Chambers), 200–201, 202
domestic gardens: Greek, 29; Japanese, 241; Roman, 36
Domitius, 42–43
Dormer, Gen. James, 167
dovecote, Rousham, *169*
Downing, Andrew Jackson, 187, 203, 289–94, *290*, *293*, *295*, *296*, 296–97, 317, 338
Dream of Aeneas (painting; Rosa), 176
Drottningholm, Stockholm, 129, 131
Dryden, John, 156
dry landscape gardens, *241*, 242–44, *243*
Du Cerceau, Jacques Androuet, 114, *116*, 117, *119*, *121*, 131, *131*, 145
Duchene, Henri, *123*
Dumbarton Oaks, Washington, D.C., 303–6, *303*, *304*, *305*, *306*
Durham, England, 140
Dutch gardens: in colonial America, 266, 273, *274–75*; at Hampton Court, *141*
Du Verdier, Saulnier, 150

Early Spring in a Palace Garden (painting), 213
Eaton Hall, England, 294
Eclogues (book; Virgil), 22
Eden. *See* Garden of Eden
Edo period, Japan, 248–49, 250, 254, 258
Egypt, 26, 77, 202; gardens, *18*, 30–35, 76
Elements of Architecture (book; Wotton), 158
Elements of Criticism (book; Kames), 27
Elizabeth I, queen of England, 139, *140*, 144
Elizabeth, daughter of James I of England, 147, 150
Elizabethan gardens, 139, *140*, 143, *146*, 147, *156*, 188
El Pedregal, near Mexico City, 323
Elysian Fields, Stowe, Pennsylvania, 166
Emerson, Ralph Waldo, 21, 288, 290, 317
Enclosure Acts, 141
Encyclopedia of Gardening (book; Loudon), 187–88
Enfield Chase, England, 284
England: agriculture, 141–42, 159; gardening books, 92, 143, 174, 187; plant imports, 186, 189, 203. *See also* English gardens
English Flower Garden, The (book; Robinson), 306
English Garden, The (book; Mason), 202
English Gardener (book; Meager), 266–67
English gardens, 139–203; Chinese influence on, 156, 200–202, 206–8; Elizabethan and Tudor periods, 139, *140*, 143, 144–47, *146*; formal style, 157–58; French influence on, 131, 145–47, 150, 157, 166; influence on American gardens, 203, 275, 276, 284–85, 286, 306; influence on French gardens, 194–95, 200 (see also *jardins anglais*); Jacobean and Caroline periods, 147–57; landscape revolution, 139, 142, l58–85, 203; medieval period, 142–43; Renaissance (Italianate) style, 144, 147, 152–55, *155*, 173; Robinson's reforms, 189–91; stroll gardens, 250; Victorian period, 188–89
English Physician (book; Culpeper), *267*
Enlightenment, the, 77, 141, 203

Enshu, Kobori, 250, 254
Epicurus, 50
Epidaurus, Greece, 30
Epigrams (book; Martial), 191
Erechtheum, Athens, 44
Ermenonville, Oise, France, 183, 195–197, *195*, *196*, *197*
Esher Place, Surrey, England, 284
Essai sur les jardins (book; Watelet), *194*
Essay on Criticism (book; Pope), 156
Essay on Landscape (book; Girardin), 183
Essays in Idleness (*Tzurezuregusa*) (book; Kenko), 237, 248
Este, Ippolito, Cardinal d', 46, 98, 100. *See also* Villa d'Este
Esterhazy estate (Süttör), Hungary, *194*
Estienne, Charles, 131
Eton College, chapel garden, 143
Eustis, Mrs. William C., *301*
Evelyn, John, *155*, 157, 159

Fairbrother, Nan, 50
Fallingwater, Bear Run, Pennsylvania, *316*, *317*, *318*, 319
false plane tree, 33
Fan K'uan: painting after, *209*
farm gardens: Egyptian, 34; Greek, 25–26; Roman, 36
Farnese, Alexander, Cardinal, 46
Farnese family, 102
Farnese Palace, Caprarola, Italy, 101, *106*–7, 122
Farnese Palace, Rome, 159
Farrand, Beatrix, 302–6, *303*, 309, 329
Fatehpur Sikri, India, garden palace of, *79*
Feate of Gardening, The (treatise; "Mayster Ion Gardener"), 143
feng shui, 217, 218
ferme ornée, *194*, 285, 286
Ficino, Marsilio, 89
Ficus sycomoros, 33
Fidelity, Garden of. *See* Bagh-i-Wafa
Field, Erastus Salisbury: *Garden of Eden*, *260*
Filarete (Antonio di Pietro Averlino), 104
Fithian, Peter, 277
Florence, Florentines, 53, 89, 92, 93, 102, 110, 219, 331; botanic gardens, 185
Florida, 268, 282
Florimen (masque; Molière), 125
flower cultivation: Chinese attitudes, 226–29; in colonial America, 267–68; in Egypt, 34; in England, *142*, 143, 185, 186–87, 189, 201, 202; in France, 137; in Greece, 28–29; in Roman world, 41, 42, 46, 47; Wharton's views, 301
Fontainebleau, Seine-et-Marne, France, 98, 116, 118, 119–20, *121*, 144, 147
formal gardens: Downing's view, 293–94; English, 157–58
Formal Garden School, 301
Fortune, Robert, 227
Fothergill, Dr. John, 268
Fountain of the Dragons, Villa d'Este, 99
fountains: Dumbarton Oaks, *306*; Het Loo, *128*; Islamic, *61*, 67; Italian Renaissance, 98, *98*, 99, *99*, 100, 104; Mughal, 74, *80*, *81*, 86, *87*; Roman, 22, 40, *40*, *41*; Versailles, *126*, 127
Fouquet, Nicolas, 123–25
four-square gardens, 54, 62, 78, 266. *See also* *chahar bagh*
Fragonard, Jean-Honoré, 98, 109

France: gardening books, 92, 131; hunting forests, 123; land holdings, 142; topography, 113
François I, king of France, 98, 116, 119, 120, *121*, 144
Franklin, Benjamin, 268
Frederick V, elector Palatine, 147–48
Freemasons, 199
French gardens, 113–37, 205; influence on English, 131, 145–47, 150, 157, 166; international variations, 129–31; Italian influence on, 96, 119, 122; *jardins anglais*, *194*, 194–95; medieval period, 73, 113; parterre plantings, 131–37; scent in, 137
Friedrich, David Caspar, 333
Fujiwara era, Japan, 239
Fuller, Margaret, 288

Gaillon, Eure, France, *116*, 131, 145, 147
Galileo, 105
Galvez, Antonio: house and garden of, near Mexico City, *323*
Gambara, Cardinal, 38, 102
Gamberaia. *See* Villa Gamberaia
Garden, The (magazine), 190
Garden Book (book; Jefferson), 283
garden buildings, Japanese attitudes on, 237
garden cities, Chinese, 219–20
Gardener's Magazine, 187
Gardenesque movement, 202
gardening: and agriculture, 18–19, 25–26; as an art form, 185; Jefferson's view, 283; and landscape painting, 168, 208, 212, 215, 217, 229, 289; meaning of, 337; as a royal activity, 24–25, 35, 115
gardening books: in colonial America, 266: English, 92, 143, 174, 187; French, 92, 131; medieval, 50
gardening tools and implements: medieval, 50–51; Roman, 36
garden journalism, 187
Garden of Adonis, 29
Garden of Couples' Retreat. *See* Ou Yuan
Garden of Ease. *See* Yi Yuan
Garden of Eden, in New World, 261–62, 264, 265, 300, 317
Garden of Eden (painting; Field), *260*
Garden of Eternity, 17
Garden of Fidelity. *See* Bagh-i-Wafa
Garden of Paradise, *16*
Garden of the Golden Horde, Iran, 75
"Garden of the Humble Politician." *See* Zhuo Zheng Yuan
garden ornaments, in colonial America, *276*, 276–77
garden scents, 137, 337
Gardens in the Modern Landscape (book; Tunnard), 258–59
Gardens of China, The (book; Sirén), 202, 208
garden theater, 120–21
garden walls. *See* walled gardens
Garrison, William, 303
Garzoni. *See* Villa Garzoni
Gautama Buddha, 240
Generalife gardens, Granada, Spain, *61*, 65, *71*; Court of the Long Pond, 66, *72*
Genghis Khan, 75, 77
genius loci, 29
geometric gardens: disappearance of, 139; Downing's view, 293–94; Loudon's view, 187–88; Mughal, 79
George III, king of England, 185
Georgia, 269, 282

Georgics (book; Virgil), 22
Gerard, John, 154, 266, *266*
Germany: gardens, 150, 194, 202–3; gardening books, 92
giardini segreti, 101, *101*
Gibbs, James, *145*
Gillette, Charles F., *314*, 315
Gilpin, William, 289
Ginkaku-ji (Silver Pavilion), Kyoto, Japan, *242*
Giocondo, Fra, 114
Girardin, Louis-René, marquis de, 183, 195, 197, *197*, 199
Giulia, Villa, Rome, 100–101, *101*, 102
Glorious Revolution (1660), 141
Godwin, Dr. W.A.R., 309, 312
Goethe, Johann Wolfgang von, 98, 174
Golden Cupids, House of, Pompeii, 40
Golden Horde, Garden of, Iran, 75
Golden Pavilion. *See* Kinkaku-ji
Gomez, Olivo, estate, San José dos Campos, Brazil, *324*, *326–27*
Gomitsunoō, emperor of Japan, 249, 254
Gothein, Marie-Louise, 26, 183–84
Governor's Palace, Williamsburg, Virginia, *272*, 272–76, *273*, *274–75*, 309, *312*
grafting, 52–53
Granada, Spain, Islamic gardens, 65–67, *68–69*. *See also* Alhambra; Generalife gardens
Grand Cascade, Vaux-le-Vicomte, *125*
Grand Parc, Versailles, 127
Grand Trianon, Versailles, 96, 137
Granja, La, near Madrid, 129
Gravetye Manor, West Sussex, England, 191
Great Georgian Houses of America (book; Bottomley), 315
Greece, 23, 26–27, 202; gardens, 27–29, 36; grafting, 52; response to Persian gardens, 23–24, 75–76; temple landscapes, *28*, 29–30
Green Mount Cemetery, Baltimore, Maryland, 294
Greenwich, England, palace of, 147
Green-Wood Cemetery, Brooklyn, New York, 294
Gropius, Walter, 231, 255, 319
Grotta Grande, Boboli Gardens, *104*
grottoes, 105–9; at Désert de Retz, *200*; Jones's design, 149; Pope's, *170*; at Stourhead, 176; at Stowe, 170; at Wilton House, *149*, 149–50
Groves of Eden, 21
Guillaume de Lorris, 55, 91
Gunston Hall, Lorton, Virginia, *269*, *270*, 271
Gustaf III, king of Sweden, 200, *201*

Hadfield, Miles, 142–43
Hadrian, Roman emperor, 30, 42, 43, 44, 46, 47
Hadrian's Villa (Villa Adriana), Tivoli, Italy, *40*, 42–47, 95, 97, *97*, 99, *99*, 100
Haga, Stockholm, Sweden, 200, *201*
Hagley Park, 158, 284
ha-has, 119; Claremont, *166*; Stowe, 163–66
Hall, Mrs. Basil, 289
Hall of Private Audience, Taj Mahal, 82
Hall of Public Audience, Shalamar Bagh, Kashmir, 80
Hamilton, William, 285, 293, 294
Hampton Court Palace, London, 131, *140*, *141*, *142*, *144*, 145, 147, 157, 173, 284
Handel, Georg Friedrich, 22
Han dynasty, China, 210, 229
Hangzhou, China, 219–20
Harcourt, 2nd earl of, 202

Hardouin-Mansart, Jules, 128
Hardwick, England, 144
Harris, John, *155*
Harris, Neil, 288–89, 294
Hartwell House, Buckinghamshire, England, *145*
Hārūn ar-Rashīd, 51, 73
Harvey, John, 52, 67, 74, 143
Hasegawa, Nyozekan, 249
Haskell, Francis, 96–97
Haskell, Lewellyn, 295
Hatfield House, Hertfordshire, England, 152–54, *153*, 173
Hatshepsut, queen of Egypt, 33, 34, 35, 47
Hawksmoor, Nicholas, 162
Hedvig Eleonora, dowager queen of Sweden, 129
Heian-kyo (later Kyoto), Japan, 233, 234, 240
Heian period, Japan, 233, 239, 249, 250–52
Heidelberg, Germany, 148, 150, 154
Heliopolis, Egypt, 35
Hellenistic gardens, 28, 36
Henri II, king of France, 121, 122, 157
Henri IV, king of France, 116
Henrietta Maria, queen of Charles I of England, 150
Henry VI, king of England, 143
Henry VIII, king of England, *141*, 144, 147, 154
Henry, Prince of Wales, 147, 150
Hephaistos, temple of, Athens, 27
Herbal (book; Culpeper), 266
Herball (book; Gerard), 154, 266, *266*
herbals, 266
herb gardens, 74, 266
herbs, 50, 52, 266
Herculaneum, Italy, 21, 38–39, 47
Hercules and Antaeus (sculpture), 97
Hesdin, Pas-de-Calais, France, 73
Hestercombe, Somerset, England, *190*, *307*
Het Loo, Apeldoorn, Netherlands, *128*, 129, *129*, 131
Himera, Sicily, 29
Hindus, 55, 78, 79, 83
Hindustan, 78, 83
Hindu temple, Sezincote, *180*
Hippocrates, 28
Hiroshige: *Prince Genji in the Plum Blossom Garden*, *235*
Hispano-Arab gardens, 62–65
Historia naturalis (book; Pliny the Elder), 89
historical restorations, United States, 309–15
History of Modern Taste in Gardening (book; Walpole), 139, 194
History of South Carolina (book; Ramsey), 278
History of the Conquest of Mexico (book; Prescott), 262
History of the Countryside, The (book; Rackham), 139
History of the Present State of Virginia (book; Beverly), 268, 271
Hitchcock, Henry-Russell, 320
Hoare, Henry, 176, 252
Hogarth, William, 173
Holkham Hall, Norfolk, England, 174
Holland, plant imports, 154
Homer, 25–26, 27, 28, 31–32, 169–70
Honour, Hugh, 263
Horace, 21–22, 35, 41, 89, 170, 283; garden of, 21–22
Horticulturalist, The (journal), *293*, 294, 296
Horticultural Society of London (later Royal Horticultural Society), 185, 227
hortus, 35, 36
hortus conclusus, 49, 101, 148

Hortus Palatinus, Heidelberg, Germany, 150
Hosack, Dr. David, 293
Hoskins, W. G., 142
House of Julia Felix, Pompeii, *44–45*
House of Loreius Tiburtinus, Pompeii, *22*
House of M. Lucretius Fronto, Pompeii, *39*
House of the Golden Cupids, Pompeii, 40
House of the Vettii, Pompeii, 40
House of the Water Jets (Maison aux jets d'eau), Coním-
    briga, Portugal, *40, 41, 41*
House of Venus Marina, Pompeii, *43*
Howard, Castle. *See* Castle Howard
Hsieh Ling-yin, 212
Hua-kuang, 229
Hudson Valley, New York, 187, 289, 290–91, 293
Humayun, Mughal emperor, tomb and garden of, 75, *87*
Humble Politician, Garden of. *See* Zhuo Zheng Yuan
Hungary, 194
Hunt, John Dixon, 158, 337
hunting parks, 26; Chinese, 210; English, 144; French,
    116, 127
Hussey, Christopher, 159
Huxley, Sir Julian, 336, 337
hyacinths, 185
Hyams, Edward, 201, 250
hydraulic engineering: Caus's treatise, 148; Egyptian, 31,
    33; Hatfield House, 154; Versailles, 127
hydraulic societies, 33, 77
Hypnerotomachia poliphili (*Love's Struggle in a Dream*)
    (book; Colonna), 91–92, 143

Ibn al-Baytar, 74
Ibn al-Razzaz al-Jazari, 73, *74*
Ichnographia rustica (book; Switzer), 157
Ile Adam, L', near Paris, *201*
Ile de France, 113, 122
Ile de Peupliers, Ermenonville (illustration), *197*
Iliad (book; Homer), 91
Illinois, 312, 315
Immortals, 211, 212, 214, 233
Imperial Palace, Kyoto. *See* Katsura Imperial Villa
Imperial Palace Garden (Yu Hua Yuan), Beijing, China,
    215, 217, 219
Incarville, Fr. Pierre d', 203
Indian influences, *179, 180,* 202. *See also* Mughal gardens
Industrial Revolution, 184, 306
Instruction pour les jardins fruitiers et potagers (book; La
    Quintinie), 137
International Style, 319–20, *320*
Iran, 75. *See also* Persia
Irish National Botanical Garden, 189
Irving, Robert, 87
Isabella, queen of Castile, 262
Ise, Shrine of, Japan, 231, *231*
Islam, 17, 54, 59, 60, 62, 67
Islamic gardens, 59–74, 331; Barragán's response,
    321–23; influence on Italian Renaissance, 89, 104; in
    Mughal India, 74–87
Isle of Poplars, Ermenonville, *196, 197, 197*
Italian gardens: Baroque style, 105–10, 301; influence of:
    in America, 301–2, *309*; in England, 148, 149, 159,
    166; in France, 115, *115,* 119, 127; Renaissance
    style, 89–105, 122, 147, 148, 149, 301. *See also*
    Roman gardens
Italian Gardens (book; Platt), 301

Italian Villas and Their Gardens (book; Wharton), 301–2
Italy, 52, 59, 76, 154; topiary, 53
Itoh, Teiji, 241
Ixtilxochitl, 262
Iztapaplan, Mexico, royal Aztec gardens, 262

Jackson, Alexander David, 295
Jackson, Andrew, 187
Jackson, J. B., 19, 277
Jacobean gardens, 147–57
Jacopo di Carlo: woodcut, *52*
Jahangir, 79, 80, 83
James, Henry, 302, 315
James, John, 131, 183, 282
James I, king of England, 147
James River plantations, 271, 278, 315
Janiculum Hill, Rome, 22
Janury, Olivier Choppin de, *201*
Japan: topography, 232; plants from, 185; rice culture, 19
Japanese Character, The (book; Hasegawa), 249
Japanese gardens, 17, *55,* 208, 231–59, 329, 337–38;
    Chinese influences on, 231, 233, 237, 239, 241, 242;
    influence on American gardens, *256, 259,* 329, *339;*
    types: courtyard, 248–49, 258; dry landscape, 241–44;
    imperial, 249; modern, 255–59; paradise, 238–41,
    252; stroll, 249–55; tea, 244–49
jardin de l'intelligence, 123
Jardin de plaisir, Le (book; A. Mollet), 150, 157
Jardin de Wilton, Le (book; S. de Caus), 150
Jardin Potager, Château de Villandry, *131, 132–33, 135*
Jardin Royal des Plantes Médicinales (Jardin du Roi),
    Paris, 185, 203, 282
jardins anglais, 183, *194,* 194–95, 284
jardins de plaisir, 119
Jardins enchantés (book; Bac), 321
Jashemski, Wilhelmina, 39–40, 41, 42
Jefferson, Thomas, 27–28, 37, 131, 185, 199, 263–64,
    269, 271, 278, 283–88, 293, 294, 295, 297, 312, 319,
    337
Jekyll, Gertrude, 143, *156,* 190, 191, *191,* 302, 303,
    306–9, *307,* 315, 329, 334–35, 338, *340*
Jellicoe, Geoffrey, 30, 105, 252, 259, 325, *336,* 336–38
Jellicoe, Susan, 81–82, 105
Jensen, Jens, 319
"Jentyl Gardener," Lincoln Cathedral, 143
Jerome, Saint, 54
Jesuits, 203, 205
Ji Chang Yuan (Chi Ch'ang Yüan), 249–50
Ji Cheng, 205
jie jing, 252
Johnson, George, 185
Johnson, Jory, 334
Johnson, Philip, *330*
Johnson, Samuel, 173
Johnson, Thomas, 266, *266*
Jones, Inigo, 148–49, *149*
Jonson, Ben, 22
Julia Felix, House of, Pompeii, *44–45*
Julius II, pope, 96, 120
Julius III, pope, 100, 101

Kames, Lord, 27
Kamo River, Japan, 237
Kashmir, India: Mughal gardens, 79, 80

Katsura-gawa River, Japan, 252
Katsura Imperial Villa (Detached Palace), Kyoto, Japan,
    230, 231, 249, 250–52, *251, 253,* 254, 255, 258,
    259
Kaufmann, Edgar J., 319
Keene, Donald, 237
Kendall, Donald M., Sculpture Garden, Purchase, New
    York, *328*
Kenilwirth Castle, Warwickshire, England, 147
Kenko, 237, 248
Kennedy, John F., Memorial, Runnymede, England,
    336, 336–37
Kensington Palace, London, 157
Kent, William, 159, 162, 166–68, 169, 170, *173,*
    174–76, 179
Kepler, Johannes, 105
Keswick, Maggie, 209, 217
Kew Gardens (Royal Botanic Gardens), London, *17,*
    185, 200, 202, 284
Kiley, Dan, *330*
Kimball, Fiske, 312–14, 315–17
Kingsmill Plantation, Virginia, 275, 276
King's Peace, 149
Kinkaku-ji (Golden Pavilion), Kyoto, Japan, *240,*
    240–41
Kin-sai (now Hangzhou), China, 219–20
Kip, Johannes, 139, 173
kitchen gardens: at Château de Villandry, *132–33, 135;*
    in colonial America, 266, 267, 271–72, *272, 287*
Knight, Richard Payne, 174, 184, 191
Knossos, Crete, 30
knot gardens, 139, *140, 153*
Knyff, Leonard: painting of Hampton Court, *144*
Kokedera (moss garden), Saiho-ji, *239,* 240
Kokushi. *See* Soseki
Koran, *26,* 60, 61, 67, 77, 83, 92
Kuck, Loraine, 233
Kuo Hsi, 209
Kyoto, Japan, 233–37, 249, 258, 329. *See also* Daisen-in;
    Katsura Imperial Villa; Ryoan-ji Temple; Sanzen-in;
    Sento Goshu; Shinju-an; Shozan garden;
    Shugaku-in; Tenryu-ji

Laborde, J.-J., 197, 199
La Fontaine, Jean de, 125
La Granja, near Madrid, 129
Lahore, Pakistan, 77; Shalamar Bagh, *79,* 80, *81, 82,*
    82–83
Lake Tai rocks, *214, 228*
Lambert, George: drawing of ha-ha, Claremont, *166*
Landscape, The (book; Knight), 174
landscape architects, 302–9
landscape design: and architecture, 122, 176, 220,
    319–20; vs. garden arts, 258–59
landscape gardens: in colonial America, 285; Downing's
    views, 289–94; in England, 139, 142, 158–85, 203; in
    France, 194–97
landscape painting, and gardening, 168, 208, 212, 215,
    217, 229, 289
Langley, Batty, 174, 286
Lante. *See* Villa Lante
Laocoön (sculpture), 97
La Quintinie, Jean-Baptiste, 137
La Reggia, Caserta, Naples, Italy, 129
Las Casas, Bartolomé de, 261

Latrobe, Benjamin, 286; sketch of ferry house, *277*
Laurel Hill Cemetery, Philadelphia, 294
Laurens, Henry, 283
Laurentian Villa (of Pliny), Ostia, Italy, 37, 38, 95, 143
La Ziza Palace, Palermo, Sicily, 71
Leasowes, The, Warwickshire, England, 284, 285, 299
Le Blond, Alexander-Jean-Baptiste, 131, *131*
Le Brun, Charles, 125
Le Comus, Denis, *128*
Le Corbusier, 110, 242, 319, 320, 325
Lecore, Italy, Verino's villa, 95
Ledoux, Claude-Nicolas, 197
Leiden, Netherlands, 154
Leipzig, Germany, 154
Lemercier, Jacques, 122–23
Lemon Hill, Philadelphia, 294
lemon trees, 42, 71
L'Enfant, Pierre, 131
Le Nôtre, André, 65, 116, *121*, 122, 123, *123*, 125, *125*, 128, *128*, 129, 131, *131*, 137, 156, 157, 158, 176, 197, 205
Le Nôtre, Jean, 137
Le Nôtre, Pierre, 137
Leonardo da Vinci, 105–9, 119
Leonora (Addison), 158
Le Pautre, Jean, 137
Le Rouge, Georges-Louis, *194*, *200*, 202–3
Le Sueur, Hubert, 150
Le Vau, Louis, 125, *125*, 127, 205
Levens Hall, Westmorland, England, *151*, *152*, 166
Levi, Reno, *325*
Lewellyn Park, West Orange, New Jersey, 295–96, *296*
Lewerentz, Sigurd, 333
Liber ruralium commodorum (book; Crescenzi), 52, 92
Ligne, prince de, 200
Ligorio, Pirro, 46, 100, 122
Ligozzi, Jacopo: botanical drawings, *263*
Lincoln, Abraham, 298
Lincoln Cathedral, England, 143
Lincoln Memorial Garden, Springfield, Illinois, 319
Lindisfarne Castle, Ireland, *190*
Lingering Garden, Suzhou, China, *228*
Linnaeus, Carl, 185–86; botanic garden, 186, *186*, *187*
Li River, China, *210*
Liverpool, England. *See* Birkenhead Park
Livia, villa of, Pompeii, 41
Livingston Papers, *290*
Li Yu, 254
Logan, James, 268
London, George, 157
Longleat House, Wiltshire, England, 144, 157, 173
Loreius Tiburtinus, House of, Pompeii, *22*
Loudon, John Claudius, 187–88, 202, 289, 294
Louis XII, king of France, 117, 145
Louis XIII, king of France, 116, 123, 185, 205
Louis XIV, king of France, 42, 79, 116, 117, 121, 123, 125, 127, 128, 129, 131, 137, 199, 205, 299
Louis XV, king of France, 115
Louvre, Paris, 113
Lucca, Italy, 93
Lucullus, 38
Lu Kuang: *Spring Dawn over the Elixir Terrace*, *211*
Lully, Jean-Baptiste, 125
Lu-shan Mountains, China, *209*
Lutyens, Edwin, 86–87, *191*, 306, *307*, 315, 335
Luxembourg Palace, Paris, *104*, 119, 157

Lyceum, Athens, 27
Lysander, 23

Machine de Marly (waterwheel), 127
"Machine in the Garden," 298
Madama. *See* Villa Madama
Madīnat al-Zahra gardens, Córdoba, Spain, *63*
Madīnat-Habu, temple of, Egypt, 35
Madonna lily, 47
Magic Flute (opera; Mozart), 101
Magna Carta, 336, 337
Magnolia Gardens, near Charleston, South Carolina, *278*
Maison aux jets d'eau (House of the Water Jets), Conímbriga, Portugal, *40*, 41, *41*
Maison Chinoise, Désert de Retz, 200
maize (*Zea mays*), *266*
Malmaison, Hauts-de-Seine, France, 194
Manakata Shrine, Fukuoka Prefecture, Japan, 231
Marie Antoinette, queen of France, 195, *203*
Marie de' Médicis, queen of France, *104*, 119
Maries, Charles, 227
Maritime Theater, Hadrian's Villa, 46
Marly, Yvelines, France, *127*, 127–28, 199, *200*
Marot, Daniel, *122*, 129, *129*, *141*, 144
Marrakesh, Morocco, Royal Park, 61, 71, *73*
Martin, Jean, 120
Mary II, queen of England, 129, 131, *141*
Maryland, 268, 269, 282
Mason, George, 269–71
Mason, William, 182, 202
Massachusetts Horticultural Society, 294
Masson, Francis, 185
Masson, Georgina, 89
Master of the Fishing Nets Garden (Wang Shi Yuan), Suzhou, China, *221*, *224*
mausoleum, Stowe, 162, *162*
Mayan agriculture, 18–19
Mazzoni, Guido, 114
Meager, Leonard, 266–67
Medici, Giulio, Cardinal de' (later Pope Clement VII), 100
Medici, Cosimo de', 89, 92
Medici, Lorenzo de', 37, 93, 95
Medici family, 102; Florence palace, 122; villas, 101, *104*, 110, 219, 331
Medicis, Catherine de , *104*, 122, 137
Medicis, Marie de , *104*, 119
medieval gardens, 49–56; in England, 142–43; in France, 113; in Italy, 91
Meiji era, Japan, 255, 258
Meket-Re, Tomb of. *See* Thebes
Mercogliano, Pacello da, 114, 145
Mercure galant (newspaper), 205
Méréville, Essonne, France, 195, *195*, 197
Metamorphoses (book; Ovid), 120
Mexico, Mayan agriculture, 18–19
Mexico City, *263*, *264*
Michaux, André, 282
Michaux, François-André, 282
Michetti, Niccolo, *131*
Middle Ages, 49–56, 110. *See also* medieval gardens
Middleton, Henry, 282
Middleton family, 278–82
Middleton Place, near Charleston, South Carolina, *278*, *279*, *280*–81, 282

Mies van der Rohe, Ludwig, 242, 319
Milburne, Virginia, *314*
Miller, J. Irwin, Garden, Columbus, Indiana, *331*
Miller, Philip, 203, 282
Milton, John, 158–59, 283
Ming dynasty, China, 217, 227, 252
Ministry of Health and Education, Rio de Janeiro, Brazil, 325
Ministry of State, Brasilia, 41
Minmakht, Tomb of. *See* Thebes
modern gardens, Japan, 255–59
modern movement, 319–25
modern style, 293
Mohammed, the Prophet, 59, 60, 61, 77
Mohammad I ben Al-Ahmar, sultan of Granada, 66
Mohammed V, sultan of Granada, 66
Mollet, André, 137, *144*, 150, 157
Mollet, Claude, 125, 134, 137, 150
Mollet family, 134, 137
Momoyama period, Japan, 245, 249
monastery gardens, 49–50, 51–52, *52*, 143
Mondrian, Piet, 336
Mongols, 74–75, 83
Montacute House, Somerset, England, 144, *156*, 301
Montague, Elizabeth, 171–73
Montceaux. *See* Château Montceaux
Montespan, Mme. de, *104*, 205
Montezuma II, Aztec emperor of Mexico, 262, *263*
Montgomery Place, New York, *291*, *292*
Monticello, Charlottesville, Virginia, 283–84, *285*, 285–87, *286*, 312, 319
Monville, François Racine, baron de, *198*, 199, 200
moon gates: Wang Shi Yuan, *221*; Yi He Yuan, *204*; Yi Yuan, *226*
Moor Park, Hertfordshire, England, 149, 154–56, 284
Moroccan gardens, 24, 61, 62, 321
Morris, Robert, 294
Morris, William, 190, 331–33
moss garden, Saiho-ji, *239*, 240
mountain-rocks, 214
mountains: in Chinese gardens, 209, 213–14, 217; at Ginkaku-ji, *242*
Mount Airy, Richmond County, Virginia, 277, *277*
Mount Auburn Cemetery, Cambridge, Massachusetts; 294, *295*
Mount Usher, England, 201
Mount Vernon, Fairfax County, Virginia, 275, 286–87, *287*, 312
Mount Vernon Ladies Association, 312
Mt. Vesuvius, 21, 38, 96
Moynihan, Elizabeth, 59
Mozart, Wolfgang Amadeus, 22, 101
Mughal gardens, *26*, 60, 62, 74–87
Mughal-Rajput style, 78
Mumford, Lewis, 319
Mumtaz Mahal, 83
Munstead Wood, Surrey, England, *191*, 329
Murasaki, Shikibu, Lady, 233–35
Muromachi period, Japan, 239, 252
Museum of Modern Art, New York City: International Style exhibition, 319; sculpture garden, *330*
Mycenae, Greece, 30

Naito, Akira, 250–52
Nakht, Tomb of. *See* Thebes

Names of Herbs in Greek, Latin, English, Dutch and French with the Common Names that Herbaries and Apothecaries Use (book), 154
Nanjing, China, 205; Treaty of, 203, 227
Naples, Italy, 114; Bay of, *36*, 38, *95*, *96*
Nara, Japan, 233
narcissus, 28
Nash, John, 296
National Survey of 1785, United States, 287–88
Natural History (book; Pliny the Elder), 22
Natural History of Carolina, Florida, and the Bahama Islands (book; Catesby), *284*
nature, 17, 18; English view, 156; French view, 194; Oriental attitudes, 208, 231
Near East, plants from, 51, 185
Nebot, Bathasar: painting of Stowe, *145*
Nero, Roman emperor, 38
Netherlands, plant imports, 154. *See also* Dutch gardens; Het Loo
Neutra, Richard, *320*, 320–21
New Delhi, India, Viceregal Palace, 86–87
New England: colonial gardens, 265–66, 268, 272; Transcendentalists, 288–89, 290, 298
New Principles of Gardening (book; Langley), 174, 286
Newton, Isaac, 105
New York City, 295, *296*. *See also* Central Park; Paley Park
New York State, 289, 290
Nezahualcoyotl, Aztec king of Tezcuco, 262
Nicholson, Francis, 272–73
Niemcewicz, Julian, 286
Nile (sculpture), 97
Nishat Bagh, Srinagar, Kashmir, *76*, 77
niwa, 231
Noguchi, Isamu, Museum and Garden, Long Island City, New York, *259*
Nolhac, Pierre, 109
Nonsuch Palace, London, 147
Nordley, Richmond, Virginia, 314, *314*, 315
Noritada, Prince, 252
North Africa, Islamic gardens, 61, 62, 104
North America, plant materials from, 154, 185, 282
Notes on the State of Virginia (book; Jefferson), 269, 278, 319
Nouvelle Héloïse, La (book; Rousseau), 195–97
"Novelties in Description of the Spring" (horticultural list; Al Himyari), 67
Nuneham Park, Oxfordshire, England, 202
Nymphaea (painting; Young), *17*
Nymphaeum, Villa Giulia, 101, *101*
Nymphenburg, Munich, 96

Oatlands, Loudoun County, Virginia, *301*
Observations on Modern Gardening (book; Whately), 167, 284, 285
Observations on the Theory and Practice of Landscape Gardening (book; Repton), 186, 202
Odyssey (book; Homer), 25, 33
Oedipus at Colonus (play; Sophocles), 28
Of Gardens (book; Bacon), 158, 190
Old Westbury Gardens, Long Island, New York, *51*, *310*, *311*
Olmsted, Frederick Law, 296, 297, *298*, 298–300, 321
orange trees, *64*, 65, 71, 127
Orford, Lady, 139

Orsini, Vincent, 105; Villa, 105, *105*
Otto I, Holy Roman emperor, 49
Ou Yuan (Garden of Couples' Retreat), Suzhou, China, *224*
Ovid, 113, 120, 283
Oxford Botanic Garden, England, 154
Oxford Companion to Gardens, The (book; Jellicoe et al.), 217

Padua, Italy, botanic gardens, 74, 154, 185, *263*
Page, Russell, 329, *329*
Pagello, Bartolomeo, 90
Pagoda of Chanteloup, Indre-et-Loire, France, *128*
Paine, James, 176
Painshill, Surrey, England, 284
painting, and garden arts, 197, 208, 212, 215, 217, 237
pairidaëza, 76
Palazzo Farnese, Caprarola, Italy, 101, *106*–7, 122, 159
Palazzo La Zisa, Palermo, Sicily, 71
Palazzo Piccolomini, Pienza, Italy, *94*, 95
Palermo, Sicily, Islamic garden, 71
Paley Park, New York City, *330*
Palladian Bridge, Stowe, *164*, 170
Palladian villas, 102
Palladius, Rutilius Taurus Aemilianus, 50, 52
Palmieri, Matteo, 25
paradise gardens, Japanese, 238–41, 252
"Paradise Gardens," Persian, 23, 24
Paradise Lost (book; Milton), 158
Paradisi in sole paradisus terrestris (book; Parkinson), 154, 266
Parc de la Villette, Paris, *331*
Paris, 110, 113. *See also* Bagatelle; Jardin Royal des Plantes Médicinales; Luxembourg Palace; Parc de la Villette; Tuileries
Parkinson, John, 154, 185, 266, *267*
parks: American, 294–300; Babylonian, 23; Chinese, 210; English, 144–45; Persian, 23, 24, 52, 75
Parmentier, André, 293
parterres: in France, *115*, 131–37; at Hampton Court, *144*; at Williamsburg, *273*
parterres de broderie, 131, 134; at Chenonceaux, *118*; Dezallier d'Argenville's pattern, *149*; at Fontainebleau, *121*; at Wilton House, *149*
Pasargadae, Iran, 59
Patel, Pierre: painting of Versailles, *126*
paths: Chinese, 217–18; Islamic, 66; Japanese, 237, 245, *245*, 246; Kennedy Memorial, 336; stroll gardens, 254–55
Patio de la Acequia (Court of the Long Pond), Generalife, 66, *72*
Patio de los Arrayanes (Court of the Myrtles), Alhambra, 66, *72*
Patio de los Leones (Court of the Lions), Alhambra, 66–67, *67*
Patio de los Naranjos (Court of Orange Trees), Córdoba, Spain, *64*
Patrician Garden, The (book; Crescenzi), *48*, 91
patte d'oie, 123, 131
Paul, Saint, 52–53
Pavilion of the Dark Blue Waves, Cang Lang Ting, *224*
pavilions: Japanese, 234, 235, *240*; medieval, 56; Mughal, 80; Persian, 59–60
Paxton, Sir John, 296

Peacham, Henry, *182*
Peacock Water Fountain, Islamic, *74*
Peale, Charles Willson, 283
Pembroke, Philip Herbert, 4th earl of, 148, 149, 150
Pennsylvania, 266, 267, 268
Penny, Nicholas, 96–97
Penshurst Place, Kent, England, 302
Percy, George, 264
pergola, *256*
peristyle gardens, 36, 37–38, 41, 46
Persia, 26, 59, 77; gardens, 23–24, 26, 59–60, 75, 83; parks, 52, 75, 210
persimmon, Oriental, *61*
perspective, 120
Peter the Cruel, king of Castile and León, 65
Peter the Great, czar of Russia, 131, *131*
Peterhof, near Leningrad, Soviet Union, *130*, 131
Petit Trianon, Versailles, 96, 195, 200
Petrarch, 74, 91
Pharmacopoeia (book; Ibn al-Baytar), 74
Philadelphia, 268, 285, 294; Centennial Exposition (1876), *256*
Philip V, king of Spain, 129
Phoenix Hall, Byodo-in, *238*, 239
physic gardens, 52, 74, 203, 266
Piccolomini, Aeneas Silvius (later Pope Pius II), 95
Piccolomini Palace, Pienza, Italy, *94*, 95
Picturesque, 156, 184, 191, 293
Piddletown, England, Orford estate, 139
Pièce des Nappes, Marly, 127
Pienza, Italy, 95
Pierre de Bourbon, 114
Pilcher, Sir John, 231, *231*
Pilgrim's Progress (book; Bunyan), 336
Pinder-Wilson, Ralph, 75
pine trees, 229, 258
Piper, F. M., *201*
Piranesi, Giambattista, 197
Pisa, Italy, botanic gardens, 154, 185, *263*
Pius II, pope, 46, 95, *95*
Plaisirs de l'Ile Enchantée (fete; Louis XIV), 121
Plaks, Andrew, 213
Plan of Mount Vernon (book; Vaughan), 287
plantations, colonial American, 269–73, 276, 286
Plato, 27, 50, 89, 337
Platt, Charles, 301, 302, 329
pleasances: Poggio Reale, 95–96; Versailles, 96, 205; Villa Lante, 102
pleasure gardens, England, 147, 148–50, 154
Pliny the Elder, 22, 38, 89
Pliny the Younger, 21, 36–38, 39, 41, 42–43, 47, 50, 53, 89, 90, 95, 100, 102, 109, 143, 191, 283
Plus excellents bâtiments de France, Les (book; Du Cerceau), 114, *116*, *119*, *121*
Plutarch, 27
Plymouth Plantation, Massachusetts, 265
Po Chü-i, 213, 221
poetry, and garden arts, 159, 237
Poggio a Caiano, Tuscany, Italy, *93*, 93–95
Poggio Reale, near Naples, Italy, *95*, 95–96, 114
Poitiers, Diane de, *119*, 121–22
Poland, 194
Polo, Marco, 219–20
Pompeii, Italy, *20*, 21, 22, *22*, *24*, 25, 29, 36, 38–41, *39*, *40*, *41*, 42, *42,43*, 44–45, 51, 62, 333
Pompey, 38

Pope, Alexander, 21, *28*, 139, 156, 158, 163, 166, 167, 168–70, *170*, 189, 190–91, 283, 292, 336; garden of, Twickenham, London, 170, *170*
Poppeae, Villa, Oplontis, Italy, *36*
Portland, Oregon, private garden, *339*
Poussin, Nicolas, 109
Pownall, Thomas, 290–91
Praeneste, Rousham, *168*
Prairie School, 319
Prescott, William, 262
Price, Uvedale, 174, 184, 191, 289
Primaticcio, Francesco, 120
Prince Genji in the Plum Blossom Garden (triptych; Hiroshige and Toyokuni III), *235*
Pringle, John, 282
private gardens, 26; American, 287, *339*; Chinese, 212–17, 221; Greek view, 26; medieval, 56. *See also* domestic gardens
Prospect Park, Brooklyn, New York, 300
public gardens, Greek, 27
public parks, American, 294–300, 331
Punt, Land of, 33, 35, 47
Pure Land Buddhism, 239–40
Pyramid, Désert de Retz, *198*, 199

Qin (Ch'in) dynasty, China, 210
Quakers, 267–68, 282
Quintus Curtius, 24
Quintilian, 95

Rackham, Oliver, 139, 144
Raisons des forces mouvantes, Les (book; S. de Caus), 148
Rajpath, Viceregal Palace, New Delhi, 86
Rambouillet, Yvelines, France, 194
Rameses III, king of Egypt, 35
Ramsey, David, 278, 283
Raphael, 46, *100*, 100, 119
Red Books (book series; H. Repton), 179, 182, 184
Redouté, Pierre Joseph, 282
regional styles, United States, 309–15
Renaissance gardens: England, 144, 147, 152–54, 173; France, 114, 120, 131; Germany, 150; Italy, 24–25, 36, 46, 89–104
Repton, George Stanley, 296
Repton, Humphry, *171*, 173, 174, *179*, 179–85, *182*, *184*, 186, 188, 191, 194, 201–2, 224, 287, 289, 296, 325
Restoration period, England, 154, 157
Rheum palmatum (turkey rhubarb), *267*
Richelieu, Cardinal, 122, 123; Château de, *122*, 122–23; gardens at Rueil, 157
Richmond Lodge, London, 185
Richmond Palace, London, 147, 150–52
Richmond, Virginia, 314–15
Rikyu, 245
Rin'un-tei, 254
Robert, Hubert, 98, 109, 197
Robert II, count of Artois, 73
Robinson, Thomas, 166
Robinson, William, 189–90, 191, 201, 303, 306–9, 329, 334
Rockefeller, John D., Jr., 309, 312
rocks. *See* stones and rocks
Rodary, Ashridge, *184*

Rokuon-ji. *See* Kinkaku-ji
Romance of the Rose, The (book; Guillaume de Lorris), 55, 91, 113, 142
Roman de Renaud de Montauban (book), 51
Roman Empire, 50, 59
Roman gardens, ancient, 21–23, 29, 35–47; grafting, 52; in Spain, 62; topiary, 53
Romano, Giulio, *100*, 100
Romant des Romans (book; Du Verdier), 150
romantic love, 55–56
Rome, Renaissance gardens, 93, 100, 102, 110, 122, 159. *See also* Villa Giulia; Villa Madama
Rosa, Salvator, 176
rose garden, Sissinghurst, *193*
Rousham, Oxfordshire, England, 167, *167*, *168*, *169*, *173*, 174–76
Rousseau, Jean-Jacques, 174, 195–97, *196*, *197*, 199, 244
royal gardens, 19, 76–77; in Ancient Near East, 23–24; Aztec, 262–63, *263*; Chinese, 210, 217; Crescenzi's recommendation, 52; Egyptian, 35; English, 145; French, 117, 121, 123; Moroccan, 61, 71, *73*; Mughal, 75, 77–86; in Renaissance Italy, 24
Royal Horticultural Society, 185, 227
Rueil, Hauts-de-Seine, France, 159
Ruskin, John, 190, 299
Russian gardens, *130*, 131
Rydal Mount, Cumbria, England, 190
Ryoan-ji Temple, Kyoto, Japan, 231, 241, 242, *243*, 243–44, 258

Sabine farm of Horace, 21–22
Saiho-ji, Kyoto, Japan, *239*, 239–40, 241
Saint-Cloud, Hauts-de-Seine, France, 157
St. Gall, Switzerland, monastery plan, 51–52
Saint-Germain-en-Laye, Yvelines, France, 116, 122
St. James's Palace, London, 150, 157
Saint-Simon, Louis de Rouvroy, duc de, 137
Sakuteika (book; Toshitsuna), 232, 237
Samarkand, Uzbekistan, Soviet Union, 75, 104
San Cristobal estate, near Mexico City, *322*, 325
Sangallo, Antonio the Younger, *100*, 100
Sangallo, Giuliano da, 46, 93, 95
Sanzen-in, Kyoto, Japan, *255*
Sargent, Charles Sprague, 302
Sargent, Henry Winthrop, 294, 300
Scarpa, Carlos, *335*
Schiller, Johann Christophe Friedrich von, 174
Schwetzingen, Baden-Württemberg, Germany, 202
Scully, Vincent, 29
sculpture: in colonial American gardens, 276–77; in English gardens, *167*; in French gardens, 120; in Greek gardens, 29; in Renaissance gardens, 96, 97–98; in Roman gardens, *22*, 43, 44, 46
sculpture gardens, *328*, *330*
Seeley, B., *163*
Segesta, Sicily, ruins of, *28*
Senmut, consort of Hatshepsut, *34*
Sen no Rikyu, 245
Sento Goshu, Kyoto, Japan, 254
Sercy, Charles de, 123–27
Serlio, Sebastiano, 119, 120
Serres, Olivier de, 120, 134
Seville, Spain, Islamic gardens, 65, 74
Sezincote, Gloucestershire, England, *179*, *180*, *181*

Shaftesbury, Anthony Ashley Cooper, 3rd earl of, 139, 156
Shāh Jahān, Mughal emperor of India, *76*, 78, 79, 80, 83
Shāh Rokh, 75
shakkei (borrowed view), 241, 252
Shalamar Bagh (Abode of Love) gardens, 80; Kashmir, 80–82; Lahore, *79*, 80, *81*, *82*, 82–83
"sharawadgi," 156, 206
Sheffield Park, Sussex, England, *171*, 171–73, *172*
Shen Fu, 220
Shenstone, William, 284, 285, 299
Shepherd's Paradise, The (court play), 149, *149*
Shigemori, Kento, 258
Shi Huang Di, emperor of China, 210
shinden-zukuri-style pavilions, 234
Shinju-an, Kyoto, Japan, 238
Shinto, 231, *231*, 242
Shippey, Edward, 267–68
Shirley, James River plantation, Virginia, 271, 315
Shozan garden, Kyoto, Japan, *258*
Shrewsbury, countess of, 144
Shrine of Ise, Japan, 231, *231*
Shugaku-in, Kyoto, Japan, 249, 254, 255
Shurcliff, Arthur, *313*, 314
Sicily, 52, 67; Greek gardens, *28*, 29; Islamic gardens, 67–71, 71
Siena, Italy, 93
Silver Pavilion. *See* Ginkaku-ji
Silvestre, Israel, 137
Sirén, Osvald, 202, 208, 215
Sissinghurst, Kent, England, 44, *192*, *193*
Six Chapters of a Floating Life (book; Shen Fu), 220
Skipworth, Sir Payton, 266
"slash and burn" agriculture, 17
slavery, 271, 272, 273
Smith, Mrs. Benjamin, 315
Soju, Murata, 245
Some English Gardens (book; Jekyll), 302
Somerset House, London, 147
Song dynasty, China, 215, 229, 241, 243
Song of Solomon, 91
Soper, Alexander, 233
Sorbière, M. de, 152–53
Soseki, Muso (Muso Kokushi), 239, 241
South Carolina, 269, 278–82
Southcote, Mr., 170
Spain: Islamic gardens, *61*, 62–67, *63*, *64*, 74, 104; Roman gardens, 62
Spectator, The (periodical), 158
Spence, Joseph, 159
Spenser, Edmund, 22
Spotswood, Alexander, 275–76, 309
Spring Dawn over the Elixir Terrace (painted scroll; Lu Kuang), *211*
square gardens, 62. *See also* four-square gardens
statues. *See* sculpture
Steele, Fletcher, 194, 209, 212, 226, 227, 337
steppingstone paths, in Japanese gardens, *246*, 252, *256*
Stern, W. T., 185
Stilgoe, John, 265
Stockholm, Sweden, 331. *See also* Drottningholm; Haga; Woodland Cemetery
stone benches, Pompeian, *24*
stone lanterns, Japanese, *247*
stones and rocks: in Chinese gardens, 211, *214*, 213–15, 217, 242; in Japanese gardens, 240, 241, 242–43, *243*, *246*, *253*

"Story of the the Western Pavilion, The": woodcut from, *229*
Stourhead, Wiltshire, England, 158, 176–79, *178*, 250, 252, 293
Stowe, Buckinghamshire, England, *145*, 159, 162, *163*, 163–66,*164*, *165*, 167, 170, 179, 293
Strabo, 24, *36*
Stratford, Westmoreland County, Virginia, 275
stroll gardens, 249–55
Stronbach, David, 59
Strong, Sir Roy, 143–44, *146*
suburbs, planned, 295–96
subsistence gardening, 50
Sui dynasty, China, 217, 233
Sulla, Roman dictator, 38
Sullivan, Louis, 317, 319
Sumer, 54
Summer Palace (Yi He Yuan), Beijing, China, *204*, *216*
Süttör (Esterhazy estate), Hungary, 194
Suzhou (Suchow), China, 220. *See also* Cang Lang Ting; Lingering Garden; Ou Yuan; Wang Shi Yuan; Yi Yuan; Zhuo Zheng Yuan
Swedenborgians, 295–96
Switzerland, botanical studies, 154
Switzer, Stephen, 157–59, 275
symmetry, 62, *96*, 102, 116
Syracuse, Greece, 27
Syria, 62, 77, 127
Systema Horti-Cultura (book; Woolridge), 150

Tabriz, Iran, 75
Taj Mahal, Agra, India, 79, 82, 83, *84–85*, 86, *86*
Taj Mahal, The Illumined Tomb (book; Begley), *85*
Tale of Genji (book; Murasaki), 234–35, 237, 250, 252
Taliesin West, Scottsdale, Arizona, 319
Tang dynasty, China, 211, 221, 229, 233, 234
Tao Te Ching (book), 215
Taste and the Antique (book; Haskell and Penny), 96–97
Tatler, The (periodical), 158
Taut, Bruno, 255
Tayloe, John, 277
tea ceremony, *237*, 244–48, *246*, 249, 254
tea gardens, 244–49
teahouse, 244, *245*, 245–48, 249
Tell el-Amarna, Egypt, 34
Temple, Sir Richard. *See* Cobham
Temple, Sir William, 149, 154–57, 169–70, 205–7
Temple de la Philosophie, Ermenonville, *195*
temple garden, Egyptian, *18*
Temple of Ancient Virtue, Stowe, *165*
Temple of the Four Winds, Castle Howard, *138*, *162*
Temple of Venus, Stowe, 170
temples: Egyptian, *18*, 34–35; Greek, 27, *28*, 29–30
Tenryu-ji (Abbot's Garden), Kyoto, Japan, 241
terracing: in colonial America, 276, *279*, 282; in Egypt, 35; in England, 152–53
Tessin, Nicodemus the Younger, 129
Tezcotinco, Mexico, 262
Thacker, Christopher, 25
Théâtre d'agriculture et mesnage des champs (book; Serres), 120, 134
Théâtre des plans et jardinages (book; C. Mollet), 125, 134
Theatrum botanicum (book; Parkinson), *267*
Thebes, Egypt, 33–34; agricultural wall painting from Tomb of Nakht, *30*, 33–34; model garden from

Tomb of Meket-Re, *31*; temple garden from Tomb of Minmakht, *18*
Theobalds Park, Hertfordshire, England, 147
Theophrastus, 50
Théorie et la pratique du jardinage, La (book; Dezallier d'Argenville), 131, *149*, *183*; James translation (*The Theory and Practice of Gardening*), 131, 183, 282
Thomas, Gabriel, 267
Thomson, James, 283
Thoreau, Henry David, 288, *289*, 291, 298, 317, 319
Thouin, André, 185
Tiber (sculpture), 97
Timoleon the Liberator, tomb of, 27
Timur (Tamerlane), 75, 77
Titus, Baths of, 101
Tivoli, Italy. *See* Hadrian's Villa; Villa d'Este
Toji-in (Autumn Tea House), Kyoto, Japan, *248*
Tokyo, Japan, 255, 258
Toledo, Spain, Islamic gardens, 74
tomb gardens, Mughal, 83, *87*
Tomb of Meket-Re. *See* Thebes
Tomb of Minmakht. *See* Thebes
Tomb of Nakht. *See* Thebes
topiary, 42, 53; Governor's Palace, Williamsburg, 273, *273*, *274–75*; Hampton Court, 145; Levens Hall, *151*, *152*
Toshihito, Prince, 249, 250, 252
Toshitsuna, Tachibana-no, 232
town planning: of Le Nôtre, 131; suburban, 295–96
Toyokuni III: *Prince Genji in the Plum Blossom Garden*, *235*
Tradescant, John, 154
Traité du jardinage selon les raisons de la nature et de l'art (book; Boyceau), 116
Transcendentalists, 288–89, 290, 298
Tratatto d'architettura (book; Filarete), 104
Treatise on the Theory and Practice of Landscape Gardening, A (book; Downing), 289, *290*, 293, *296*
trees: in Ancient Near East, 23–24; in Chinese gardens, 226; in Egypt, 31, 33, 35, 76; in England, 140; grafting on, 52; in Mughal gardens, 86; North American, 282, 289; in Pompeii, 42; as prerogative of victor, 24 127; symbolism of, 23
Trees (Japanese screen), 232
Tremaine House, Santa Barbara, California, *320*
Trianons, Versailles, France, 96; Grand, 137; Petit, 195, 200; de Porcelaine à la Chinoise, 205
troubadours, 91, 113
Ts'ang Lang T'ing. *See* Cang Lang Ting
Tschumi, Bernard: Parc de la Villette, *331*
Tuckahoe Plantation, Goochland County, Virginia, 271
Tudor gardens, 139, *140*, 143, 144, 145
Tuileries, Paris, *104*, 116, 123, 137, 157
Tunis, Tunisia, 61
Tunnard, Christopher, 242, 258–59, 319–20, 329
Turkey, 51, 202
turkey rhubarb (*Rheum palmatum*), 267
Turk's cap lily, *284*
Turner, William, 154
Tuscan Villa (of Pliny), Italy, 37, 38, 41, 47, 143, 191
Tuscany, Italy, 37, 89, 93
Twickenham, London, Pope's garden, 170, *170*, 284
Twilight Sleep (book; Wharton), 309

unicorn, 56, *57*
United States: aesthetic reform movement, 287–94; colo-

nial-era gardens, 264–87; English garden influences, 203, 275, 276, 284–85, 286, 306; historical restorations and regional styles, 309–15; Japanese garden influences, *256*, *259*, 329, *339*; modern movement, 319–21; national parks system, 300; public parks, 294–300
United States Park Service, 300
University of Virginia, 27–28
Upon the Gardens of Epicurus (essay; Temple), 149, 205–6
Upper Rhenish Master: painting of the Virgin in the garden, *54*
Upton Grey, Hampshire, England, *340*
urban gardens: Chinese, 219, 221; Japanese, 244–49
Urfé, Honoré d', 150

Vale of Venus pool, Rousham, *173*, 176
Vallery. *See* Château de Vallery
Vanbrugh, Sir John, 162, 163, *170*, 176, *176*
Vanvitelli, Luigi, 129
Varro, 38, 52
Vasari, Giorgio, 92, 100, 101
Vatican, 46, 101, 120; Belvedere Court, *96*, 96–97, 100, 120, 122
Vaughan, Samuel, 286, *287*
Vaux, Calvin, 297
Vaux-le-Vicomte, Seine-et-Marne, France, *121*, *123*, 123–27,*124*, *125*, 131, 197
vegetable gardens: Château de Villandry, *134*, *135*; Mount Vernon, 287. *See also* kitchen gardens
Veneto, Italy, 92, 102, 144
Venice, Italy, 74, 93, 104, 110
Verdier, Saulnier du, 150
Verino, Michele, 95
Verneuil-sur-Oise, France, design for, 122
Versailles, Yvelines, France: compared to other gardens, 42, 44, 46, 79, 122, 123, 125, 163, 299; construction of, 47, 127; English influences, 194–95; flower displays, 137, 205; fountains, basins, and water system, 47, 55, 104,*112*, *126*, 127, 131, 329; geometry and plan, 17, 46, 102, *114*, 116, 122, 131; as a hunting lodge, 116, 123, 205; influence of, 65, 131, 157, 163; Marie-Antoinette's village, *203*; palm trees and orangerie, *115*; political significance, 117, 123; terraces, *115*, *117*, 137; theater and fetes at, 76, 121; Trianons, 96, 137, 195, 200, 205
Vettii, House of, Pompeii, 40
Viceregal Palace, New Delhi, India, 86–87
Victorian gardens, 188–90, *300*, 300–302
Vignola, Giacomo da, 101, 102, 119, 122
Villa Adriana. *See* Hadrian's Villa
Villa Aldobrandini, Frascati, Italy, 105, 109, *110–11*, 127, 166
Villa Belvedere, Vatican, Rome, 96. *See also* Belvedere Court
Villa Chiericat, Pozzoserrato, Italy, *96*
Villa d'Este, Tivoli, Italy, 44, 47, *98*, 98–100, *99*, 109, 119, 122, 159
Villa d'Este at Tivoli (book; Coffin), 100
villae maritimae, 38
Villa Gamberaià, Settignano, Italy, 101
Villa Garzoni, Collodi, Italy, *88*, *90*, 105, *108*, *109*
Villa Giulia, Rome, 100–101, *101*, 102
Villa Lante, Bagnaia, Italy, 38, 46, 101–2, *102*, *103*, 109, 119, 122, 127, 329

villa gardens: Italian Renaissance, 93–108; Roman, 36–39

Villa Madama, Rome, 46, 100, *100*, 102, 119
Villa Medici, Fiesole, Italy, 101
Villandry. *See* Château de Villandry
Villa Orsini, Bomarzo, Italy, 105, *105*
Villa Poppeae, Oplontis, Italy, *36*
Villa Vizcaya, Miami, Florida, *308*, *309*
Virgil, 22, 89, 109, 252, 283
Virginia, 185, 264, 265, 268, 269–78, 282, 284–85, 312, 314–15
"visto," 275
Vitruvius, 100, 119
Vizcaya. *See* Villa Vizcaya
Voyages, Les (book; Champlain), 266

Walks and Talks of an American Farmer in England (Olmsted), 296
walled gardens: Islamic, 61; medieval, *48*, 49, 55
Walpole, Horace, 21, 25, 139, *139*, 142, 157, 158, 159, *163*, 166–68, 170, 173, 176, 194
Wang Shi Yuan (Master of the Fishing Nets Garden), Suzhou, China, *221*, *224*
Warburg Hours (book), page from, *16*
Ward, Nathaniel Bagshaw, 189
Wardian case, 189
Warton, Joseph, 176
Warwick Castle, Warwickshire, England, 170
Washington, George, 37, 286–87, *287*, 295, 312
Washington, D.C., 131, 295, 297, 319. *See also* Dumbarton Oaks
Watelet, Claude-Henri, 194
water: in Chinese gardens, 209, 215–17; in Egyptian gardens, 31; in English gardens, 148, 149–50, 174–76; in French gardens, 73, 117–19, 131; in Islamic gardens, 61, 62, 65, 67; in Italian gardens, 38, 98, *98*, 99, *103*, 104, 109; meaning of, 54–55, 77; in Mughal and post-Mughal gardens, 78, 80, *80*, 81, 84–86, 87; in Persian gardens, 59; in Roman gardens, 38, 40–41, 46. *See also* canals; cascades; fountains; grottoes; hydraulic engineering; water basins; water falls
water basins: at Fontainebleau, *121*; Islamic, 61; Japanese, *247*, *255*; at Marly, 127, 128; Mughal, *81*, 82, 83–86; patterns, *126*; Pompeian, *41*, *42*; at Villa d'Este, *99*

waterfalls: Fallingwater, *318*; Shozan garden, *258*. *See also* cascades
Waterworks (book; S. de Caus), 150
Weld, Isaac, 289
Wescoat, James, 77
Western Park, China, 233
Westover, Charles City County, Virginia, *276*, 276–77
Wharton, Edith, 301–2, *303*, 309, 315
Whately, Thomas, 167, 182, 194, 284, 285
Whig estates, 158, 159–66
Whitehall Palace, London, 147
White/purplish red primroses (painting; Curtis), *188*
Wigginton, Brooks, 244
wild garden, 189–90
Wild Garden, The (book; Robinson), 189, 191, 306, 334
wild pine, *284*
William III of Orange, stadholder of the Netherlands and king of England, 129, *129*, 131, *141*, 157
Williams, Edward, 264
Williamsburg, Virginia, 269, *272*, 272–76, *273*, *274–75*, *275*, 309–12, *312*, *313*, 314
Wilson, Ernest, 226–27
Wilson, Richard, 173
Wilton House, Wiltshire, England, 148–50, 173
Wimbledon House, London, 150
Wisconsin, 315, 317
Wise, Henry, *141*, 157
wisteria, *256*
Woburn Abbey, Bedfordshire, England, 173, 284, 294, 300
Wodenethe, New York, *290*, 294
Wollaton Hall, Nottinghamshire, England, *146*
Wolsey, Cardinal, 144
Woodland Cemetery, Philadelphia, 294
Woodland Cemetery, Stockholm, 331–34, *332*, *333*, *334*
Woodlands, Philadelphia, 285
Woodstock Park, Blenheim Palace, 144, 157
Woolridge, John, 150
Wordsworth, William, 189–90, 289
World's Columbian Exposition (Chicago World's Fair; 1893), 300, 317
Wotton, Sir Henry, 158
Wotton House, Surrey, England, *155*, 284
Wrede, Stuart, 333

Wren, Christopher, *141*, *144*
Wright, Frank Lloyd, 242, 315, *317*, 317–19, *318*, *320*, 321
Wythe House, Williamsburg, Virginia, *313*

Xenophon, 24
Xian, China, 233
Xüan Zung (Hsüan Tsung), emperor of China, 211, 214

Yale University, 303
Yang Di, emperor of China, 217, 233
Yellow Mountains, China, *206*, *207*
Yi He Yuan (Summer Palace), Beijing, China, *204*, *216*
yin-yang forces, 209, 217
Yi Yuan (Garden of Ease), Suzhou, China, *226*
Yong-lo, emperor of China, 217
Yorimichi, Fujiwara regent, 239
York County, Pennsylvania, ferry house, 277
Yosemite National Park, California, 297–300, *299*
Yoshimitsu, Ashikaga shogun, 240
Young, Arthur, 195
Young, William: *Nymphaea*, *17*
Yüan Chung-lang, 227
Yüan dynasty, China, 217, 243; scroll, *211*
Yuan Ye (*Garden Tempering*) (Ji Cheng), 205, 208, 209, 218–19, 220, 224, 229, 249–50, 252–54
yucca (*Yucca glorioso*), *267*
Yu Hua Yuan (Imperial Palace Garden), Beijing, China, *215*, *217*, *219*
Yu Kung, 229
Yusuf I, 66

Zea mays (sweet corn), *266*
Zen Buddhism, 239, 240, 241, 242, 243, 254
Zen gardens, 238, 241–44, 248, *248*, 337
Zen tea ceremony. *See* tea ceremony
Zerner, Henry, 120
Zhou (Chou) dynasty, China, 210
Zhuo Zheng Yuan (Cho-cheng Tüan; "Garden of the Humble Politician"), Suzhou, China, 221, *222*, *223*
Zion, Robert, *330*